Dante's *Convivio*

Leeds Studies on Dante

Series Editors

Claire E. Honess, University of Leeds
Matthew Treherne, University of Leeds

PETER LANG
Oxford · Bern · Berlin · Bruxelles · New York · Wien

Dante's *Convivio*

Or How to Restart a Career in Exile

Edited by Franziska Meier

PETER LANG
Oxford · Bern · Berlin · Bruxelles · New York · Wien

Bibliographic information published by Die Deutsche Nationalbibliothek.
Die Deutsche Nationalbibliothek lists this publication in the Deutsche National-
bibliografie; detailed bibliographic data is available on the Internet at http://dnb.d-nb.de.

A catalogue record for this book is available from the British Library.

Library of Congress Control Number: 2017945171

Published with the help of funding from the Italienische Kulturinstitut Berlin.

Cover image: Portrait of Dante in Florence's Palazzo dell'Arte dei Guidici e Notai.
Photograph by Sailko (source: Wikimedia Commons).

ISSN 2235-1825
ISBN 978-3-0343-1835-8 (print) • ISBN 978-1-78874-315-0 (ePDF)
ISBN 978-1-78874-316-7 (Epub) • ISBN 978-1-78874-317-4 (mobi)

© Peter Lang AG, International Academic Publishers, Bern 2018
Hochfeldstrasse 32, CH-3012 Bern, Switzerland
info@peterlang.com, www.peterlang.com, www.peterlang.net

All rights reserved.
All parts of this publication are protected by copyright.
Any utilisation outside the strict limits of the copyright law, without the permission of
the publisher, is forbidden and liable to prosecution.
This applies in particular to reproductions, translations, microfilming, and storage and
processing in electronic retrieval systems.

This publication has been peer reviewed.

Printed in Germany

Contents

Abbreviations and Note on Translations   vii

Notes on Contributors   ix

FRANZISKA MEIER
Introduction   1

ZYGMUNT G. BARAŃSKI
1 'Oh come è grande la mia impresa': Notes towards Defining Dante's *Convivio*   9

ENRICO FENZI
2 'Per suo desiderio sua perfezione non perde': Knowledge and Happiness in the Third and Fourth Books of the *Convivio*   27

THEODORE J. CACHEY JR
3 'Alcuna cosa di tanto nodo disnodare': Cosmological Questions between the *Convivio* and the *Commedia*   55

ANNA PEGORETTI
4 'Da questa nobilissima perfezione molti sono privati': Impediments to Knowledge and the Tradition of Commentaries on Boethius' *Consolatio Philosophiae*   77

FRANZISKA MEIER
5 'Questa sarà luce nuova, sole nuovo': Dante and the Vernacular in *Convivio* I   99

ALBERT RUSSELL ASCOLI
6 'Ponete mente almeno come io son bella': Prose and Poetry, 'pane' and 'vivanda', Goodness and Beauty, in *Convivio* I   115

MARIA LUISA ARDIZZONE
7 'Ne la selva erronea': Dante's *Quaestio* on Nobility and the Criticism of Materialism   145

ANDREA ALDO ROBIGLIO
8 'Poi che purgato è questo pane': Vindication and Recognition in Dante's *Convivio*   173

LORENZO VALTERZA
9 'Però si mosse la Ragione a comandare che ...': Roman Law and Ethics in the *Convivio*   191

ENRICA ZANIN
10 'Miseri, 'mpediti, affamati': Dante's Implied Reader in the *Convivio*   207

DONATELLA STOCCHI-PERUCCHIO
11 'Tu l'hai fatto di poco minore che li angeli': Nobility, Imperial Majesty, and the *Optimus Finis* in *Convivio* IV and *Monarchia*   223

LUCA AZZETTA
12 'Di questo parla l'autore in una chiosa d'una sua *canzone*': The *Convivio* through the Eyes of Its First Readers   247

Index   283

Abbreviations and Note on Translations

The following editions are used throughout, unless otherwise stated:

Commedia	*La Commedia secondo l'antica vulgata*, ed. by Giorgio Petrocchi, 2nd edn, 4 vols (Florence: Le Lettere, 1994)
Conv.	*Convivio*, ed. by Franca Brambilla Ageno, 2 vols (Florence: Le Lettere, 1995)
	Dante's 'Il Convivio' (The Banquet), trans. by Richard Lansing (New York and London: Garland, 1990) <https://digitaldante.columbia.edu/text/dantes-works/the-convivio/>
DVE	*De vulgari eloquentia*, ed. by Mirko Tavoni, in Dante Alighieri, *Opere*, dir. by Marco Santagata, vol. I (Milan: Mondadori, 2011)
Ep.	*Epistole*, ed. by Arsenio Frugoni and Giorgio Brugnoli, in *Opere minori*, II (Milan: Ricciardi, 1979–88), 505–643
Inf.	*Inferno*, in *La Commedia secondo l'antica vulgata*
Mon.	*Monarchia*, ed. by Diego Quaglioni, in Dante Alighieri, *Opere*, vol. II (Milan: Mondadori, 2014)
	Monarchy, ed. by Prue Shaw (Cambridge: Cambridge University Press, 1996)
Par.	*Paradiso*, in *La Commedia secondo l'antica vulgata*
Purg.	*Purgatorio*, in *La Commedia secondo l'antica vulgata*
VN	*Vita nuova*, ed. by Domenico De Robertis, in *Opere minori*, I. i, 1–247

Notes on Contributors

ALBERT RUSSEL ASCOLI is Gladyce Arata Terrill Distinguished Professor of Italian Literature at the University of Berkeley.

MARIA LUISA ARDIZZONE is Professor of Italian Literature at New York University.

LUCA AZZETTA is a lecturer in Italian Studies at the University of Florence.

ZYGMUNT BARAŃSKI is Notre Dame Professor of Dante and Italian Studies at the University of Notre Dame and Emeritus Serena Professor of Italian at the University of Cambridge.

THEODORE J. CACHEY JR is Professor of Italian and the Albert J. and Helen M. Ravarino Family Director of Dante and Italian Studies at the University of Notre Dame.

ENRICO FENZI is an expert in Italian Medieval Studies.

FRANZISKA MEIER is Professor of French and Italian Literature at the Georgia Augusta University, Göttingen.

ANNA PEGORETTI is Assistant Professor of Italian Literature at the University Roma Tre.

ANDREA ALDO ROBIGLIO is Associate Professor of Medieval and Renaissance Philosophy at the Katholieke Universiteit Leuven.

DONATELLA STOCCHI-PERUCCHIO is Associate Professor of Italian and head of the Italian programme at the University of Rochester.

LORENZO VALTERZA is Visiting Assistant Professor of Italian Studies at the University of Notre Dame.

ENRICA ZANIN is a senior lecturer in Comparative Literature at the University of Strasbourg.

FRANZISKA MEIER

Introduction

Dante's *Convivio*, or how to restart a career in exile: the title of the volume is a contentious statement indeed. It has been chosen to emphasize the admittedly provocative purpose underlying this project. Instead of repeating the idea of a more or less continuous evolution in Dante's thinking and writing across his career, and instead of following a slow and occasionally tortuous dilatation punctuated by bouts of growth in his thought and expression, this volume isolates the years from 1304 to 1308, the very time Dante started to live by himself, having left the *universitas* of his political fellows, the *bianchi*. It is based on the proceedings of several conferences over recent years on the *Convivio*, which draw attention to Dante as the author of the *Convivio*. In these conferences, discussions were consistently faced with the question of whether, and to what extent, the poet wanted to make a new start in his career in a quite different socio-political and linguistic context. Could a new start even have been forced upon him?

As Dante's first undertaking in exile, the *Convivio* had been long neglected by scholarship which in any case had remained spellbound by Bruno Nardi's narrative in *Dal 'Convivio' alla 'Commedia'*. Nardi, in fact, accurately placed the *Convivio* in the middle of the poet's gradual evolution passing from the lyrical youth full of love songs which were collected in the *prosimetrum Vita nova* to the poetry of maturity, the *Commedia*. In this picture the *Convivio* belongs to the so-called philosophical period which embraces both the moral *canzoni* of the 1290s and their unfinished prose commentary dating from 1304 to 1308, which would be superseded by a new and sacred understanding of the poet's first love and of the role of poetry itself.[1] As a result, the *Convivio* was, and continues to be, largely studied for the sake of exploring Dante's philosophical reading and its impact on the *Commedia*.

Besides Maria Corti's groundbreaking as well as controversial work on Dante's possible adherence to radical Aristotelianism,[2] it has been up to historians of medieval philosophy to reveal the revolutionary aspects of the voluminous text. Subsequent to Cesare Vasoli and Domenico De Robertis' 1988 edition highlighting the *Convivio*'s encyclopaedic dimension, a bilingual edition supervised by Ruedi Imbach and Francis Cheneval was carried out by Thomas Ricklin.[3] Apart from the extensive documentation concerning Dante's likely reading and the source of specific formulas, this Fribourg research team were the first to credit Dante with being a philosopher in his own right. Ruedi Imbach went so far as to claim that Dante, by explicitly addressing the Latin-illiterate members of the courts, gave birth to a new understanding of philosophy. For Imbach, Dante was the first to take the definition of man as 'animale rationale' (rational animal) seriously and aimed at educating people, most of all lay people.[4]

Yet the *Convivio* took some time to arouse the interest of Dante scholars and philologists. Under the pressure of burgeoning philosophical studies which consider the unfinished book to be a theoretical treatise, scholars of Italian Literature finally began to pay attention to the text.[5] In 2004, Zygmunt Barański asked crucial questions about the genre to which the *Convivio* ought to be assigned,[6] while in 2010 Paolo Falzone dedicated a

---

1   *Dal 'Convivio' alla 'Commedia' (Sei saggi danteschi)* (Rome: Istituto storico italiano per il medio evo, 1992).
2   See Maria Corti, 'La felicità mentale', in *Scritti su Dante e Cavalcanti* (Turin: Einaudi, 2003), pp. 95–175.
3   *Das Gastmahl*, 4 vols (Hamburg: Felix Meiner, 2004).
4   *Dante, la philosophie et les laïcs. Initiation à la philosophie médiévale* (Paris and Fribourg: Éditions du Cerf and Éditions universitaires de Fribourg, 1996).
5   Peter Dronke's *Dante's Second Love: The Originality and the Contexts of the 'Convivio'* (Leeds: Maney, 1997), did not quite leave the shadow of the philosophical interpretation.
6   *Il 'Convivio' e la poesia: problemi di definizione*, in *Contesti della 'Commedia': Lectura Dantis Fridericiana 2002–2003*, ed. by F. Tateo and D. M. Pegorari (Bari: Palomar, 2004), pp. 9–64.

book to the central issue of *Desiderio della scienza e desiderio di Dio*. These two publications represent a budding interest in the text from a literary perspective. In May 2012 Johannes Bartuschat and Andrea Robiglio organized a conference in Zurich in which Dante scholars along with historians of philosophy discussed the *Convivio*.[7] During the previous summer in 2011, while the Zurich conference was being planned, an *Oberseminar* on Dante's *Convivio* was held at the University of Göttingen and was attended by students and scholars from different disciplines, such as Italian Literature, Philosophy and History. A project which was initially supposed to serve as an enlightening foray into Dante's broad range of philosophical knowledge, in order to better understand the *Commedia*, surprisingly turned into an outright engagement with the *Convivio* for its own sake.

This volume gives an idea of the academic steps which led us to organize the workshops, culminating in an international conference. We started in November 2011 with a tiny, rather casual workshop on 'Dante's *Convivio* between Commentary and Hermeneutics' which was generously funded by the Alexander von Humboldt Foundation. We did not invite philosophical specialists in the *Convivio*, as we were more interested in elucidating the broader context on which Dante in exile probably leaned: such as the tradition of medieval commentaries (Alastair Minnis), medieval philosophy as seen in the longue durée (Wilhelm Schmidt-Biggemann), the fashion of vernacularization in Duecento-Italy in general (Alison Cornish) and the construction of authority (Albert Russel Ascoli). In the aftermath of this first intellectual exchange we increasingly got the sense that neither an exclusively philosophical nor an exclusively textual or philological approach really fitted, nor could either of these approaches offer a convincing explanation of why Dante in exile set about writing the *Convivio*.

Dante's *self-fashioning* in the first treatise, above all, struck us as rather novel. Was the *Convivio* to be read as a serious attempt to launch a new kind of author who tried to promote himself as a courtly educator and entertainer? Did it bear testimony to his ambition to match or even overshadow the emerging universities and their new, increasingly self-confident

---

7 *Il Convivio di Dante* (Ravenna: Longo, 2015).

and socially acknowledged academic personnel? To put it in a nutshell: we were considering the specific reasons and motivations for Dante's composition, or what Wilhelm Dilthey called: its *Sitz im Leben* [its setting in life].

It has become a common assumption that the *Convivio* was conceived mainly out of apologetic reasons. It is certainly true that the exiled Dante was suffering from an 'infamia' which must have stuck hard on his heels wherever he went, due partly to his political banishment in 1302, but also to the taint of being declared a 'barattiere', that is of being found guilty of corruption while in office. It is astonishing though that in the *Convivio* the apology is primarily concerned with the gossip regarding the poet's presumed infidelity as a lover of Beatrice and, furthermore, that this apology fades from view as the text progresses. It has completely disappeared by the fourth treatise, when Dante amazingly reinvents himself as a moral guide and as a model of the four ages of life. So, if we understand apology as the initial spur for the project, it must have soon been replaced by other motivations. And here further, the old issue arises as to the consistency of the text. Did the *Convivio* derive from a movement that was driving and determining Dante's writing? To what extent was it formed by interior, or exterior, circumstances? And how do we reconcile such a movement with a composition that was from the outset, at least sketchily, laid out in fifteen books by its author?

In the footsteps of Maria Corti, who emphasized the cleft between the third and fourth treatise, which was presumably caused by a profound philosophical change of mind in Dante's thinking,[8] scholars have become interested in retracing the chronological order of the poet's first post-exile writings and the respective circumstances to which he may have at least partially responded. However, as far as the *Convivio*'s relation with the contemporaneous *De vulgari eloquentia* is concerned, which Dante hints at in the first treatise, the painstaking attempts of reconstruction remain controversial and are not likely to be resolved.[9]

---

8   On this point see in particular her chapter 'Distanza testuale e cronologica del trattato IV?', in *Scritti su Dante e Cavalcanti*, pp. 145–66.
9   See the different positions held by Enrico Fenzi, 'Dal *Convivio* al *De vulgari eloquentia*', in *Il 'Convivio' di Dante*, pp. 83–104, and by Tavoni in his introduction to *De vulgari*

In Göttingen we opted for another path and sought clues in the historical context in which and impacted by which the composition took shape. In criticism the *Convivio* is often connected to Dante's sojourns in Verona or the Lunigiana, and therefore to Tuscan and North Italian courts. However, we increasingly realized just how hard it is to understand what the courts at that time looked like and what role an exiled poet could have figured out to play in them. Taking Petrarch's much-quoted anecdote in *Rerum memorandum libri* into account, Dante's *self-fashioning* in the *Convivio* as a solemn educator of courtiers could only have amounted to a totally inappropriate attempt, a self-conceit or even an involuntary joke.

In December 2012 we organized a second workshop focusing on the historical circumstances, having received generous funding from the Deutschen Akademischen Austauschdienst. We invited Gianfranco Fioravanti and Mirko Tavoni, editors of the *Convivio* and *De vulgari eloquentia* respectively in the new Meridiani edition of Dante's *Opere*. We also invited Marco Grimaldi, editor of Dante's poetry for the publishing house Salerno, Stefano Rezzoni and experts in the field of social and political change from the first Trecento on, such as Gianmaria Varanini and Andrea Zorzi, in order to learn more about the burgeoning Italian courts Dante may have moved in and about the troubadours he might have met and their role in courtly life. Nonetheless, the picture remained rather confusing. The standard distinction between *comuni* and *signorie* or feudal remnants was far from clear cut. Historians, it seems, no longer speak about the decay of popular communities and the gradual rise of the *Signorie*, the rule of individual usurpers or mighty families. Instead, they nowadays stress a manifold bundle of political, social and cultural dynamics which unfolded in both a sporadic and interwoven manner. The assumption here is of an ultimately unsuccessful attempt to bring about the much-cherished goal of stability, peace and order. Only by 1320 can we sensibly suppose that the forms of popular and *signorile* government and their respective social orders are neatly separated. In short, the *Convivio* was written in a highly transitional and experimental period.

eloquentia as well as Fioravanti's carefully balanced assessment in his introduction to the *Convivio*. In *Opere*, vol. 2 (Milan: Mondadori, 2014), pp. 8–10.

Therefore, when Dante speaks about courts, it should be put in inverted commas. And if, according to Ruedi Imbach, the *Convivio* is eagerly adopting the need of the courts in Northern Italy, the background, or in Imbach's words the *Erwartungshorizont*, must have been nothing less than plain, to say the least. Yet the *Erwartungshorizont* was itself in the making, however seductive it may be to imagine Dante having his say in this development. The truth is, we simply do not know the extent to which the outstanding and dynamic circumstances in Italy may have contributed to the shaping of Dante's first undertaking in exile nor how alluring it may have been to him. What we can be sure of is that the historical circumstances, the very dynamics in play in 1304, while provoking a profound sensation of uneasiness and troubling anxieties, offered Dante extraordinary opportunities and a margin he badly needed after leaving this political fellows. The continuous flux of social settings, especially those of the so-called courts, might have appealed to the forty-year-old man both as a field which was crying out to be cultivated and as a kind of springboard for restarting his writing and career outside of the former municipal habitat. I have a suspicion that, from a social and political point of view, Dante in 1304 was more revolutionary or, we might say, more open-minded than some years later in the *Commedia*. Yet, all this, actually, remains open for discussion.

Finally, in May 2013 a major interdisciplinary conference on Dante's *Convivio* took place. At the Göttinger Lichtenberg-Kolleg, thanks to the sponsorship of the Deutsche Forschungsgemeinschaft and the Niedersächsische Ministerium für Kultur und Wissenschaft, historians of philosophy and Dante scholars from Italy, Great Britain, Belgium, the US and Germany spent two full and exciting days giving papers and challenging positions. This volume bears witness to this inspiring interdisciplinary and scholarly event which simultaneously served as the inauguration of the Göttinger Dante Forum, a platform which is dedicated to organizing interdisciplinary and international conferences on cultural issues from the turn of the Trecento.

The onus is now on the reader to ascertain whether, and the extent to which, the heuristic decision to isolate the *Convivio* from what came before – the *Vita nova* – and after – the *Commedia* – proves to be helpful and enlightening. While it may be difficult and somewhat artificial to study the *Convivio* in isolation, the treatise in form of a commentary does deserve to be analysed as a full-blown and equally ambitious project which may have taken its author a long way and which might have introduced us to a markedly different Dante had the *Commedia* not interrupted its completion at such an early stage. The essays in this volume tackle extremely variegated issues, ranging from philological to more philosophical and cosmological questions, yet at the same time share a common thread, which is central to our undertaking: through the contributions of this eclectic group of scholars Dante comes into focus, snared by ambiguities, and sometimes by outright paradoxes of the *Convivio*. This entanglement is particularly rife in statements relating to very specific and important aspects of what he is about to do and to write. These ambiguities may well mirror the difficult situation which had been foisted on the exiled Dante and the degree to which he became disorientated. They may also bear testimony to the scope of his ambition, that is to give his writing in both prose and poetry a new direction that was able to keep pace with an astonishing range of new knowledge, as well as with the new circumstances of his life.

I would like to close this introduction by expressing my deep gratitude to the *Istituto italiano di cultura* in Wolfsburg and Berlin, which never wavered in their support of my endeavours to promote Italian culture in Göttingen and which gave a substantial contribution to the conferences and workshops, and to the publication of this volume. It is a great pleasure and honour for me that Claire Honess and Matthew Treherne kindly welcomed the proceedings into their Leeds Dante series and their patience is much appreciated. I am very grateful to Tristan Downs for assistance in editing the articles and to Maria Ximena Ordóñez as well as to Petra Löb-Kompart who in different ways took care of formatting the manuscript.

ZYGMUNT G. BARAŃSKI

1 'Oh come è grande la mia impresa': Notes towards Defining Dante's *Convivio*[1]

The *Convivio* is changing – or rather, more accurately though less dramatically, I should have said that scholarly attitudes to it are changing, which necessarily entails a shift in perceptions of the work's status and concerns, and hence of the text itself. Thus, according to several of those who have seriously engaged with the *Convivio* in recent years, the long-held and widely disseminated idea that the work can be straightforwardly defined as a philosophical treatise, a 'trattat*o* teoric*o*' [theoretical treatise],[2] and specifically a 'trattato di filosofia morale' [a treatise on moral philosophy],[3] is no longer really sustainable.[4] At the most basic level, and if I may put

1   The problem of the *Convivio*'s formal and ideological character deserves a much fuller analysis than I am able to undertake here. I intend to publish a substantial study on the matter in the none-too-distant future. I should thus like to apologize for the brevity, the effect of the understandable constraints governing a collection of conference papers, with which I discuss matters of some sophistication and complexity. Despite its concision, I hope the chapter can give an idea of the general directions of my thinking on Dante's 'quasi comento' (I. iii. 2).
2   Cesare Vasoli, 'Introduzione', in Dante Alighieri, *Convivio*, ed. by Cesare Vasoli and Domenico De Robertis, Dante Alighieri, *Opere minori* (Milan and Naples: Ricciardi, 1979–88), II, part 1 (1988), pp. xi–lxxxix (p. xi). All translations are my own.
3   Roberto Mercuri, 'Genesi della tradizione letteraria italiana in Dante, Petrarca e Boccaccio', in *Letteratura italiana. Storia e geografia.* I. *L'età medievale*, ed. by Alberto Asor Rosa (Turin: Einaudi, 1987), pp. 229–455 (p. 248).
4   See in particular Peter Dronke, *Dante's Second Love: The Originality and the Contexts of the 'Convivio'* (Leeds: Maney, 1997); Paola Nasti, *Favole d'amore e 'saver profondo'. La tradizione salomonica in Dante* (Ravenna: Longo, 2007), pp. 93–130, and '"Vocabuli d'autori e di scienze e di libri" (*Conv.*, II. xii. 5): percorsi sapienzali di Dante', in *La Bibbia di Dante. Esperienza mistica, profezia e teologia biblica in Dante*, ed. by

it so crudely, the *Convivio* does not look like a medieval philosophical treatise: its content is too dispersive and its argumentative structures are frequently not those of a standard written *tractatus, disputatio* or *quaestio*.⁵ It is enough to recall the determining function of metaphor in book I. Even when scholastic procedures are in the foreground – most notably in book IV – other approaches vigorously intrude. Thus, in chapters xxv to xxviii of the 'quarto trattato' (I. i. 17) [fourth tractate], commentary, specifically the exegesis of the classical *auctores*, becomes the dominant manner of presentation. Furthermore, as Ambrogio Camozzi Pistoja's groundbreaking study suggestively reveals, the same 'treatise' constitutes both a theoretical assessment of satire and a practical application of the genre's various modes.⁶ In light of the present argument – the definition, however preliminary, of the *prosimetrum* – the obvious question immediately arises: What might be the implications for the status of the *Convivio* of Dante's decision to bring together the *quaestio*, the *commentum ad auctores* and

Giuseppe Ledda (Ravenna: Centro Dantesco dei Frati Minori Conventuali, 2011), pp. 121–78. See also Paolo Falzone, *Desiderio della scienza e desiderio di Dio nel 'Convivio'* (Naples: Società editrice Il Mulino, 2010); Laurence E. Hooper, 'Dante's *Convivio*, Book 1: Metaphor, Exile, *Epochē*, *MLN*, 127 Supplement (2012), 86–104; Andrea Mazzucchi, 'Per una nuova edizione commentata del *Convivio*', in *Leggere Dante oggi*, ed. by Enrico Malato and Andrea Mazzucchi (Rome: Salerno, 2012), 81–107 (100–5). In this regard it is highly suggestive that Mario Marti should hint at the 'contradditorietà anche ideologica dell'opera': '*L'incipit* del *Convivio*', in his *Il trilinguismo delle lettere 'italiane'* (Galatina: Congedo, 2012), pp. 37–43 (p. 43).

5   See Bernard C. Bazàn et al., *Les Questions disputées et les questions quodlibétiques dans les facultés de théologie, de droit et de médecine* (Turnhout: Brepols, 1985); Palémon Glorieux, *La littérature quodlibétique de 1260 à 1320*, 2 vols (Le Saulchoir, Kain: Revue des sciences philosophiques et théologiques, 1925 and Paris: Vrin, 1935); Olga Weijers, *La 'disputatio' dans les Facultés des arts au moyen âge* (Turnhout: Brepols, 2002); *Disputatio 1200–1800. Form, Funktion und Wirkung eines Leitmediums universitärer Wissenskultur*, ed. by Marion Gindhart and Ursula Kundert (Berlin-New York: de Gruyter, 2010); *Theological Quodlibeta in the Middle Ages. The Thirteenth Century*, ed. by Christopher Schabel (Leiden-Boston: Brill, 2006); *Theological Quodlibeta in the Middle Ages. The Fourteenth Century*, ed. by Christopher Schabel (Leiden-Boston: Brill, 2007).

6   Ambrogio Camozzi Pistoja, 'Il quarto trattato del *Convivio*. O della satira', *Le tre corone*, 1 (2014), 27–53.

the *stylus satiricus*? And, by extension, what might have been his purpose in effecting such a rapprochement? And how does he succeed, if indeed he actually does succeed, in integrating the three forms? I do not have the space here to address the last two questions. On the other hand, I should like to say something about at least some of the implications of the strange coming together of three *modi* that, in the Middle Ages, were not normally deemed to be complementary. To be precise, my focus will not be on book IV as such, but on what the 'mixed' character of the *trattato* can reveal about the overall textual identity of the *Convivio*.

Essentially, the generic eclecticism of the fourth book implies that the *Convivio*, like so much of Dante's œuvre, is a textual hybrid – a fact which, of course, is immediately obvious from its prosimetrical structure. Even if most recent studies of the work may not have stated as much explicitly, at the same time, given that several of these have established the *Convivio*'s dependence on a variety of medieval textual forms, their conclusions, when taken together, have inescapably pointed to its hybridity, namely to what, in the wake of Contini,[7] is more normally termed 'plurilingualism'. The *Convivio* thus reveals the clear influence of an extraordinarily wide range of medieval genres, from the *artes poetriae* to autobiographical writing, from satire to the literature of exile, from philosophical commentary and treatises to the erotic broadly understood, from the *volgarizzamenti* to the Bible and hence Scriptural commentary, from the works of the theologians to the compendia on the virtues and vices, from cosmological literature to texts on the *scala Naturae*, and from the 'encyclopaedias' to literary exegesis. And I am certain that we shall continue to discover in its pages the presence of yet other traditions, for instance, that of the chronicles. As with any paradigm shift, there are dangers associated with this new research and with the definition of the *Convivio* as a textual hybrid. Thus, on the one hand, the temptation exists to substitute a new single overarching structure, for instance the cosmological or the satirical, for the old philosophical one, and thereby once again deflect attention away from the *Convivio*'s broad engagement with the texts and intellectual traditions of its world. On the

---

[7] Gianfranco Contini, 'Preliminari sulla lingua del Petrarca', in *Varianti e altra linguistica* (Turin: Einaudi, 1970), pp. 169–92 (p. 171).

other hand, by overstating or banalizing its eclecticism, the *prosimetrum* becomes a sort of textual and ideological free-for-all, and therefore not the sort of work that an author of Dante's sophistication would have composed to fulfil pedagogical and self-authorizing ends. In any case, as we well know, *ordo* and *ordinatio*, and hence hierarchy, are fundamental in Dante, as evidenced, in the *Convivio*, by his recourse to cosmology to systematize different 'sciences', and by his discussion of the differing status of Latin and the vernacular and of poetry and commentary. More specifically, even if it is no longer appropriate to deem the *Convivio* an essentially philosophical work, this does not mean that philosophy, and specifically Aristotelian philosophy, does not play a substantial role in it, so that, consequently, this dimension needs to be given an appropriately foregrounded position in any discussion of its formal and intellectual structures – a question to which I shall return. Equally, if the *Convivio* should not still be judged the product of a strictly 'rationalist' phase in Dante's career – indeed as several scholars have shown, beginning with Nardi,[8] its notion of *Filosofia* is at least fourfold, a combination, yet more hybridity, of Aristotelian natural and ethical philosophy, Boethian *Philosophia*, Solomonic *Sapientia* and the New Testament idea of Christ as Logos – there is nonetheless a strong and determining rationalizing imperative within it. Yet, such rationalism is tempered and circumscribed by the *Convivio*'s evident engagement with Christian notions of Wisdom, revelation, salvation and affective understanding, as well as with the idea of the unity of knowledge in God, a position which explicitly challenged Aristotelian proposals regarding the independence of philosophy,[9] and which aligned Dante, as Paola Nasti has definitively

---

8   Bruno Nardi, *Nel mondo di Dante* (Rome: Edizioni di Storia e Letteratura, 1944), pp. 215–18 and 228.
9   See Gyula Klima, '*Ancilla Theologiae* vs. *Domina philosophorum*: St Thomas Aquinas, Latin Averroism and the Autonomy of Philosophy', in *What Is Philosophy in the Middle Ages? Proceedings of the Tenth International Congress of Medieval Philosophy*, ed. by Jan A. Aertsen and Andreas Speer (Erfurt: Akademie Gemeinnütziger Wissenschaft zu Erfurt, 1997), pp. 393–402. See also Luca Bianchi, *Il vescovo e i filosofi. La condanna parigina del 1277 e l'evoluzione dell'aristotelismo scolastico* (Bergamo: Lubrina, 1990); Alessandro Ghisalberti, *Medioevo teologico* (Bari: Laterza, 1990), pp. 85–145; Etienne Gilson, *History of Christian Philosophy in the Middle Ages* (London: Sheed and Ward,

demonstrated, with a 'sensibilità mistico-agostiniana' [mystical-Augustinian sensitivity] and with a great Franciscan thinker such as Bonaventure.[10] At the same time, by associating Solomon and Aristotle, Dante was also aligning himself with those exegetes of the Sapiential books and those encyclopaedists, such as Peraldus and Brunetto, who were attempting a similar rapprochement between the two great *savi*.[11]

It is such complications – the different ideological and textual layers which not only make up the *Convivio*, but also record Dante's attempts to come to terms with and negotiate between the competing epistemologies and intellectual activities of the early fourteenth century – that make mapping and explicating the *Convivio*'s 'pluristylistic' identity so demanding, though also so alluring. This task entails, *come minimo*, both establishing and defining the different traditions that constitute the *Convivio*, and evaluating the mechanisms of their inter-relationships and, more importantly, the relative standing of each of these in the text's make-up, namely, their rank in the *Convivio*'s structural and ideological hierarchy. Indeed, translating Solomon, Dante underlined the proliferation and hierarchical nature of the 'sciences', as well as their perfect integration in the divine:[12]

> Di costei (theology, which the poet here equates with Christ's word) dice Salomone: 'Sessanta sono le regine, e ottanta l'amiche concubine; e delle ancille adolescenti non è numero: una è la colomba mia' (Song of Songs 6. 7–8). Tutte scienze chiama regine e drude e ancille; e questa chiama colomba, perché è sanza macula di lite, e questa

---

1980), pp. 325–485; Martin Grabmann, 'Il concetto di scienza secondo S. Tommaso d'Aquino e le relazioni della fede e della teologia con la filosofia e le scienze profane', *Rivista di filosofia neo-scolastica*, 26 (1934), 127–55; J. M. M. H. Thijssen, *Censure and Heresy at the University of Paris: 1200–1400* (Philadelphia: University of Pennsylvania Press, 1998); Fernand van Steenberghen, *La Philosophie au xiiie siècle* (Louvain and Paris: Publications universitaires, 1966).

10   Nasti, *Favole*, pp. 105–6.
11   Nasti, *Favole*, pp. 96, 105–6, 108, 110–11 and 120–22. See also Nasti, '"Vocabuli"', pp. 159–72.
12   See Zygmunt G. Barański, 'Dante and Doctrine (and Theology)', in *Reviewing Dante's Theology*, ed. by Claire E. Honess and Matthew Treherne, 2 vols (Bern: Peter Lang, 2013), I, 9–63 (pp. 28–45).

chiama perfetta perché perfettamente ne fa il vero vedere nel quale si cheta l'anima nostra. (*Conv.*, II. xiv. 20)

[Solomon says about it: 'There are sixty queens, and eighty concubines; and as for the young handmaids, they are without number: yet my dove is unique'. He calls all the sciences queens and lovers and handmaids; but this one he calls dove, because it is unblemished by strife, and this he calls perfect because it perfectly reveals the truth in which our souls find rest.]

The type of critical undertaking that I am all too rapidly sketching requires no little delicacy, especially given the challenging textual condition of the *Convivio*: not so much the fact that it is unfinished, but the unusual aura of provisionality and partiality that surrounds the editions that we read today, a bit too often, given the precariousness of the manuscript transmission,[13] the product of editorial conjecture and dispute rather than of philological discrimination. Indeed, one cannot but wonder whether a more precise appreciation of the *Convivio*'s *forma*, *materia* and genealogies will not also help to establish a somewhat less problematic text than the ones on which we currently rely.

What is intriguing about Dante's recourse to the quotation from the Canticle is that, in general terms, it offers an accurate insight into the make-up of the *Convivio*. By underscoring that human knowledge, its ostensible subject-matter, is fragmented into 'sixty queens, eighty concubines and countless handmaidens', the poet highlights and legitimates his work's necessary hybridity. Once again, Dante serves as the most reliable guide to his own writings. Thus, as far as the *Convivio* is concerned, it is of some import that the poet never openly labelled his *prosimetrum* in light

---

13   See Luca Azzetta, 'La tradizione del *Convivio* negli antichi commenti alla *Commedia*: Andrea Lancia, l'"Ottimo commento" e Pietro Alighieri', *Rivista di studi danteschi*, 5 (2005), 3–34, and 'Il *Convivio* e i suoi più antichi lettori', *Testo*, 61-2 (2011), 225–38; Saverio Bellomo, *Filologia e critica dantesca* (Brescia: La scuola, 2012), pp. 110–18; Claudio Ciociola, 'Dante', in *Storia della letteratura italiana*. X. *La tradizione dei testi*, ed. by Enrico Malato (Rome: Salerno, 2001), pp. 137–99 (pp. 157–61); Guglielmo Gorni, 'Appunti sulla tradizione del *Convivio*. A proposito dell'archetipo e dell'originale dell'opera', *Studi di filologia italiana*, 55 (1997), 239–51; Mazzucchi, 'Per una nuova edizione', pp. 82–100.

of established philosophical textual forms. Nor is this at all surprising. Contemporary philosophical genres could not highlight and substantiate its plurilingualism, and also provide an insight into its intricately composite understanding of *Filosofia*. Instead, Dante defined the *Convivio* as a 'quasi comento' (I. iii. 2) [almost commentary] – a designation which not only accurately described its basic status, but also had the potential to draw attention to its hybridity, and even, as we shall soon see, to its totalizing notion of Wisdom. As a genre, the *comentum* was among the very few medieval forms that granted an author the freedom, within a single work, to deal with a wide array of subjects, and hence, hypothetically at least, to engage with a plurality of distinct genres. While in practice I know of no literary and scholastic commentary that actually did the latter – however varied the subject-matter explicated, this was always constrained within standard interpretive structures –[14] the *Convivio*, especially on account of its reliance on *digressio*, ably shifts between generic discourses.[15] Indeed, among the *Convivio*'s aims is that of indicating the limitations of conventional literary

14   See Rita Copeland. 'Gloss and Commentary', in *The Oxford Handbook of Medieval Latin Literature*, ed. by Ralph Hexter and David Townsend (Oxford and New York: Oxford University Press, 2012), pp. 171–91.
15   On the *Convivio*'s 'digressive' character, see Bruno Nardi, *Dal 'Convivio' alla 'Commedia'. Sei saggi danteschi* (Rome: Nella sede dell'Istituto, 1960), pp. 31–2; Alessandra Stazzone, '"Movemi timore d'infamia"': Digresser pour se défendre de l'infamie, du *Convivio* à la *Comédie*', in *La Digression dans la littérature et l'art du Moyen Âge*, ed. by Chantal Connochie-Bourgne (Aix-en-Provence: Centre universitaire d'études et de recherches médiévales, 2005), pp. 363–75. In the prologue to his commentary to Aristotle's *Physics*, Albertus Magnus states that he will introduce *digressiones* into his work to clarify *dubia* and discuss matters which the Philosopher had left 'obscure'. Albert also affirms that such digressions are clearly marked in the text: *Physica* ed. by Paul Hossfeld (Monasterii Westfalorum in aedibus Aschendorff, 1987–93), I. i. 1 (p. 1); see also Thomas Ricklin, 'Albert le Grand, commentateur: L'exemple de *De somno et viglia III, 1*', *Freiburger Zeitschrift für Philosophie und Theologie* 45 (1998), 31–55. Although digression is not uncommon in commentaries, such *digressiones*, as occurs in Albert the Great, are closely connected to and controlled by the text being glossed. Conversely, in the *Convivio*, the digressions are rarely highlighted and they regularly and quite radically depart from the ostensible subject-matter of the *canzoni* under analysis.

commentary. Thus, by concentrating on the allegoresis of the *auctores* in book IV, Dante highlighted the restrictively ethical character of this brand of criticism, which, as a result, compared poorly to his new wide-ranging 'convivial' *esposizione*. I have examined elsewhere, and at some length, the ways in which Dante constructed the *Convivio* as a radically new type of totalizing commentary.[16] Among the points I discussed was the fact that, although Dante's *disposizione* displays the same type of large-scale exegetical commitment that marks *commentaria* on philosophical and theological texts, its range of interests is much more eclectic and diffuse than theirs. Rather its critical approach, its digressiveness and the broad remit of its interests recalls the eclectic commentary tradition to the Song of Songs in particular, and, by extension, that to the Bible in general.[17] Consequently, one of the key ways in which Dante established the profoundly religious character of his new beloved, the 'bellissima e onestissima figlia de lo imperadore de lo universo' (II. xv. 12) [most beautiful and most honest daughter of the emperor of the universe], was thanks to the *Convivio*'s *imitatio* of Scriptural hermeneutic forms.

Still, as is well known, the *Convivio* opens with that peremptory 'Si come dice lo Filosofo' (I. i. 1) [As the Philosopher says], whom later, in the ninth chapter of the same book, Dante acknowledges as 'il mio maestro' (9) [my teacher]. What is the position therefore of Aristotle and his 'science' in our new plurilingual and Scripturally inflected *Convivio*? As I have already acknowledged, and as Dante makes clear throughout his *prosimetrum*, the philosopher's role is important, vital even; nevertheless, it is in no way absolute, as some have liked to maintain, or even, I would suggest, is it of primary significance. It is in fact circumscribed by and defined in terms of an idea of Wisdom which finds its origin and fulfilment in God

---

16 Zygmunt G. Barański, 'Il *Convivio* e la poesia: problemi di definizione', in *Contesti della 'Commedia'. Lectura Dantis Fridericiana 2002–2003*, ed. by Francesco Tateo and Daniele Maria Pegorari (Bari: Palomar, 2004), pp. 9–64. It is gratifying to note that scholars are beginning to accept my proposal that the *Convivio* be deemed a commentary; see, for instance, Mazzucchi, 'Per una nuova edizione', pp. 102–3.

17 Barański, 'Il *Convivio*', pp. 27–34; Dronke, *Dante's Second Love*; Nasti, *Favole* and '"Vocabuli"', p. 160.

and Dante's own overarching religious orthodoxy.[18] Indeed, already in the opening chapter, the poet makes clear the limits of Aristotle's philosophy. However, before I come to this, and following my 'maestro' Dante, I should like to introduce a digression.

Before establishing the *Convivio*'s status as a commentary in chapters 3 and 4 of the first book, the poet had in fact taken a stab at defining his *prosimetrum* in chapter 1. The problem, however, is that in this instance he had not presented the work as a *comentum*, but as belonging to a different genre: 'E io adunque, che non seggio alla beata mensa, ma, fuggito della pastura del vulgo, a' piedi di coloro che seggiono ricolgo di quello che da loro cade' (10) [And therefore I, who do not sit at the blessed table, but, having fled the pasture of the common people, at the feet of those who do sit there I gather up a part of what falls from them]. The reference is allusive; nevertheless the allusion would have been fairly obvious to a medieval reader. Dante explains that, if in the past he had provided others with a small part of what he had gathered – 'alcuna cosa' (10) [some thing] – he now intends to give them much more: a 'generale convivio' (11) [general banquet] to be precise, where 'generale', in contrast to 'alcuna', stands for 'wide-ranging'.[19] The substance of the *Convivio*, its 'bread', is composed by what its author has collected while sitting at the feet of the wise during their feast. The image fittingly describes the *Convivio*. It emphasizes its variety,[20] while also recognizing that the work is far from systematic, since its development is controlled by the form and

18 See Zygmunt G. Barański, '(Un)orthodox Dante', in *Reviewing Dante's Theology*, II, 252–330.

19 Fioravanti glosses 'generale convivio' as 'cioè pubblico, aperto a tutti' [namely public, open to all], a meaning which the epithet can certainly also bear: Dante Alighieri, *Convivio*, in Dante Alighieri, *Opere*, ed. by Gianfranco Fioravanti (Milan: Mondadori, 2011), II, 3–805 (p. 103).

20 See Cesare Vasoli, 'La Bibbia nel *Convivio* e nella *Monarchia*', in *Dante e la Bibbia*, ed. by Giovanni Barblan (Florence: Olschki, 1986), pp. 19–39 (pp. 21–2). At the same time, Vasoli does not recognize the religious, specifically Scriptural, emphasis of the metaphor, which I examine below. Both Imbach and Fioravanti note the Scriptural character of Dante's imagery, but do not effectively develop its implications: Ruedi Imbach, *Laien in der Philosophie des Mittelalters* (Amsterdam: Gruner, 1989), p. 133; Fioravanti, *Convivio*, p. 101.

content of fourteen discrete canzoni: 'La vivanda di questo convivio saràe di quattordici maniere ordinata, cioè [di] quattordici canzoni sì d'amor come di vertù materiate' (14) [The food of this banquet will be ordered in fourteen ways, that is in fourteen canzoni whose subject-matter is both love and virtue]. By the early fourteenth century, collecting isolated elements drawn from the works of authoritative figures and integrating these into a new structure represented an important intellectual and writerly pursuit. I am naturally thinking of the *compilatio*.[21] Indeed, like Dante, some compilators described their activity as 'collecting' fragments, leftovers and droppings.[22] The verb they frequently employed was *colligere* [to gather or to collect together into a whole], which Dante translated as *ricogliere* (I. i. 10). Equally, like the poet, authors of *compilationes* brought together pagan and Christian sources, though, once more like him, they were careful to maintain the superiority of Scripture.[23] As is typical of Dante, when establishing the parameters of one of his works, he gets his cultural co-ordinates just right. However, as with the association of the *Convivio* with the commentary tradition, what becomes quickly and increasingly apparent are the substantial differences between Dante's 'banquet' and other compilations. Although *compilationes* could take on different forms, they essentially shared a number of defining features. In particular, compilators refrained from passing judgement on the validity

21   See in particular Bernard Guenée, 'Lo storico e la compilazione nel XIII secolo', in *Aspetti della letteratura latina nel secolo XIII*, ed. by Claudio Leonardi and Guido Orlandi (Perugia: Regione dell'Umbria and Florence: La Nuova Italia, 1986), pp. 57–76; Alastair J. Minnis, 'Late-medieval Discussions of *Compilatio* and the Role of the *Compilator*', *Beiträge zur Geschichte der deutschen Sprache und Literatur*, 101 (1979), 385–421, and '*Nolens auctor sed compilator reputari*: The Late-medieval Discourse of Compilation', in *La Méthode critique au Moyen Âge*, ed. by Mireille Chazan and Gilbert Dahan (Turnhout: Brepols, 2008), pp. 47–63; Malcolm B. Parkes, 'The Influence of the Concepts of *Ordinatio* and *Compilatio* on the Development of the Book', in *Medieval Learning and Literature: Essays Presented to R. W. Hunt*, ed. by Jonathan James Graham Alexander and Margaret T. Gibson (Oxford: Clarendon Press, 1975), pp. 115–41. But see also Neil Hathaway, '*Compilatio*: From Plagiarism to Compiling', *Viator* 20 (1989), 19–44.
22   Minnis, 'Late-medieval Discussions', pp. 410 and 415–16. As far as I am aware the technical force of *ricogliere* has not been recognized by Dante scholarship.
23   *Ivi*, pp. 389, 391–2 and 409.

of the views they were 'repeating'. The opinions they reproduced remained squarely the responsibility of their original authors. Instead, the *compilatores* deemed their duty to be in presenting the excerpts relating to a specific topic in a comprehensive, brief, clear, highly ordered and hierarchized manner which would make consultation easy.[24] In fact, they did not even consider themselves accountable for how their readers might react to the competing views they were recording. They thus saw themselves as distinct from and subordinate to the *auctores* whom they were anthologizing.[25] Dante's attitude in the *Convivio* could not have been more different from that of other compilators. Indeed, his approach was diametrically opposed to theirs. He evaluated different opinions; he limited the *Convivio*'s organizational logic to being in 'quattordici maniere ordinata' [ordered in fourteen ways] – *ordinare* here is of course technical[26] – thereby making it clear that he did not give high priority to presenting information according to a rigorously ordered and explicitly signposted hierarchical sequence (which does not mean that such matters were not important to him; they were: he simply chose to deal with them in less mechanistic and more intellectually demanding ways); and he took his obligations for educating his readers extremely seriously. Most of all, as Albert Ascoli has conclusively established, he did not place himself in a position of subservience with regard to the *auctoritates* he was introducing and expounding.[27] Rather he used these to establish his own 'authoritativeness', concrete evidence of which was the *novitas* of his 'convivial' *compilatio*. Finally, there is no contradiction between Dante's two definitions of the *prosimetrum*. Both genres effectively stress the wide-ranging and eclectic nature of the *Convivio*. Together they also offer further proof of its generic hybridity. As Laurence Hooper has intelligently suggested, it is the adverb *quasi*, in the tag 'quasi comento' [almost commentary], that is of special significance, since it rightly indicates that the *Convivio* is not exclusively a commentary.[28]

24 Minnis, '*Nolens*', pp. 47–9 and 59–60.
25 Minnis, 'Late-medieval Discussions', pp. 387 and 389–91.
26 See Minnis, '*Nolens*', pp. 59–60; Parkes.
27 Albert Russel Ascoli, *Dante and the Making of a Modern Author* (Cambridge: Cambridge University Press, 2008).
28 Hooper, p. S93.

Yet, is Dante's authorizing experimentation in the *prosimetrum* not at odds with his self-description as someone who 'a' piedi di coloro che seggiono [alla beata mensa] ricolgo di quello che da loro cade' [at the feet of those who do sit there I gather up a part of what falls from them]? The answer to this question, I believe, fundamentally depends on what it is that the poet claims to be collecting, as well as the purpose to which he intends to put his unusual harvest – issues which conveniently return my argument to Aristotle.

Sonia Gentili has clearly and correctly illuminated the profound Aristotelianism of the *Convivio*'s opening paragraphs and the ways in which elements from the *Ad Herennium* and from the Augustinian inspired 'trattatistica *De elemosyna*' [treatises *On alms*] are subsumed into it.[29] This has allowed her to locate the work within a vernacular 'spinta etica all'atto divulgativo' [ethical drive to reach a wider audience][30] – she mentions Brunetto and Taddeo Alderotti – from which, typically, Dante was distinguishing himself. There is, however, rather more in the opening paragraphs than just the weighty presence of Aristotle. Thus, the ties of these to the prologue of Hugh of St Victor's *Didscalicon* have been known for nearly twenty years.[31] Furthermore, the undoubted Aristotelian tenor of especially the first five paragraphs is tempered by Christianizing formulations such as 'acciò che la scienza è ultima perfezione della nostra anima, nella quale sta la nostra ultima felicitate' (I. 1) [since knowledge is the ultimate perfection of our soul, in which resides our ultimate happiness], which hint at the *Convivio*'s religious interests. Aristotle thus shares the stage with other thinkers and intellectual traditions; and this is, of course, confirmed by the fact that Dante admits that his feast is based on the offerings of a small elite group and not just a single individual or 'setta' (II. iv. 9) [sect]: 'Oh

---

29 Sonia Gentili, *L'uomo aristotelico alle origini della letteratura italiana* (Rome: Carocci, 2005), pp. 127–49.
30 Gentili, *L'uomo aristotelico*, p. 142.
31 See Zygmunt G. Barański, 'La vocazione enciclopedica', in *Dante e i segni* (Naples: Liguori, 2000), pp. 77–101 (pp. 96–7); originally published as 'Dante fra "sperimentalismo" e "enciclopedismo"', in *L'enciclopedismo medievale*, ed. by Michelangelo Picone (Ravenna: Longo, 1994), pp. 383–404.

beati quelli pochi che seggiono a quella mensa dove lo pane delli angeli si manuca!' (7) [Oh blessed are those few who sit at that table where the bread of angels is eaten!] – and it is the 'bread of angels' that significantly undercuts the *Convivio*'s Aristotelianism. Thus, I am not aware that hitherto it has been noted that Dante did not actually define the *materia* of his *prosimetrum* – just as he did not define its form – with regard to Aristotle. Although the poet conventionally opens with the philosopher's dictum that 'tutti li uomini naturalmente desiderano di sapere' (I. i. 1) [all men by nature desire to know], follows him by referring to '*l'*abito di scienza' (2) [the habit of knowledge], and replicates the *impedimenta* to study that Aristotle had elaborated (3–6), he does not, as might have been expected, qualify the stuff of his work as Aristotelian. In discussing the 'desire to know', Dante had recourse to the pagan philosopher on matters relating to ethics, to human psychology and physiology, and to politics broadly understood. It was only after he had dealt with these problems that the poet went on to delimit what he meant by 'sapere' and 'scienza'; and what he understood by 'knowledge' and 'science' he pithily and aptly encapsulated in the Scriptural phrase 'lo pane delli angeli' [the bread of angels]. The sudden shift in focus is dramatic – unnerving even. In the Middle Ages, the popular image of the 'bread of angels', which has its source in the seventy-seventh Psalm – 'panem angelorum manducavit homo; cibaria misit eis in abundantia' (25) [man ate of the bread of angels; and He sent them food in abundance] – and in the sixteenth chapter of the Book of Wisdom – 'Pro quibus angelorum esca nutristi populum tuum; et paratum panem e caelo praestitisti illis sine labore. Omne delectamentum in se habentem, et omnis saporis suavitatem' (20) [Instead of which things, You fed Your people with the food of angels; and gave them bread from heaven, prepared without labour. It had in it everything that is delicious, and the sweetness of every taste] – was normally interpreted as Christ and, by extension, the Wisdom that comes from Christ, namely, divine knowledge.[32] Yet most

---

32 See, for instance, Augustine, *Enarr. in Ps.* LXXVII. 17; CXXXIV. 5; *Sermones*, CXXVI. 5, in PL XXXVIII, col. 701; Thomas Aquinas, *Super Sent.* IV. 9. q. 1. a. 2. qc. 5. arg. 1; *Summa Theol.* II-II. q. 189. a. 1 ad 4; III. q. 80. a. 2 arg. 1; *Contra retrahentes*, 7. See also Nasti, *Favole*, pp. 94–5; William J. O'Brien, '"The Bread of Angels" in

Dantists have been unwilling to accept this simple fact, insisting mistakenly that the metaphor refers either exclusively to secular knowledge or to 'teologia e filosofia e, dunque, alla sapienza in generale' [theology and philosophy, and hence to wisdom in general],[33] values *panis angelorum* simply did not have in the Middle Ages. Dante thus made it abundantly and unambiguously clear that the origin of his own 'impure bread' (I. ii. 1), as well as his appreciation of *Filosofia* more generally, was inextricably tied to that Wisdom which reaches us through Christ and the Bible, and which is a *signum* of God's Truth. These are, and they most certainly were in the Trecento, hugely significant matters; and it behooves us to listen to Dante and to draw the necessary inferences when treating the *Convivio*, not least because the extended metaphor of 'collecting' the 'scraps' of 'angelic bread' that 'fall from the blessed table' reiterates insistently the same key point as that adumbrated in the 'pane delli angeli'.

Dante's image specifically recalls a series of key and interconnected Scriptural texts in which scraps – significantly, for the *Convivio*, crumbs, pieces of bread and bread-making grains – and the gathering of such scraps play a central role. Three of these passages were especially popular in the Middle Ages: Ruth, who 'colli*git* spicas quae metentium fugerint manus' (Ruth 2. 2) [gathers the ears of corn that will have escaped the hands of the reapers]; the feeding of the five thousand and the twelve baskets of *fragmenta* that were collected by the apostles (Matthew 14. 13–21; 16. 5–12; Mark 6. 31–44; Luke 9. 10–17; John 6. 5–15), and which Dante would evoke explicitly in connection with the 'pane orzato del quale si satolleranno migliaia, e a me ne soperchieranno le sporte piene' (xiii. 12) [barley bread

---

Paradiso II: A Liturgical Note', *Dante Studies*, 97 (1979), 97–106; Daniel J. Ransom, '*Panis Angelorum*: A Palinode in *Paradiso*', *Dante Studies*, 95 (1977), 81–94 (pp. 81–5), but who arrives at very different conclusions from mine as regards the function of the phrase in the *Convivio*; Mary Alexandra Watt, 'Take This Bread: Dante's Eucharistic Banquet', *Quaderni d'italianistica*, 22 (2001), 17–35. For a 'materialist' reading of the banquet metaphor, see Diane R. Marks, 'Food and Thought: The Banquet of Poetry in Dante and Charles of Orléans', *Acta*, 21 (1994), 85–98.

33   Vasoli, *Convivio*, p. 9, where Vasoli provides an excellent summary of the principal interpretations of the phrase in Dante scholarship. See also Fioravanti, *Convivio*, p. 99.

with which thousands will be satisfied, and for me my full baskets will overflow with it] in the *explicit* of book I; and the parable of Lazarus 'cupiens saturari de micis quae cadebant de mensa divitis' (Luke 16. 21) [desiring to be filled with the crumbs that fell from the rich man's table]. In addition, exegetes associated Ruth with the Canaan woman who,[34] humbly asking Jesus for a miracle to cure her sick daughter, replied to His chiding that 'et catelli edunt de micis quae cadunt de mensa dominorum suorum' (Matthew 15. 27) [the whelps too eat of the crumbs that fall from the table of their masters].[35] Indeed, commentators drew equations between the four events and, unsurprisingly, in broad terms at least, tended to interpret them in the same way.[36] Thus, the leftovers, like the 'bread of angels', were elucidated as Christ's Wisdom, divine knowledge and the Scriptures.[37] Then again, those who do the gathering are presented as *humiles* who, like Dante, perform

34 See for instance Albertus Magnus, *Super Matthaeum*, ed. by Bernhardt Schmidt (Monasterii Westfalorum in aedibus Aschendorff, 1987), XV. 27, ll. 57–9 (p. 446); Hugh of St Cher, *Opera omnia in Vniversvm Vetus et Novvm Testamentvm* (Lugduni: Sumptibus Societatis Bibliopolarum, 1645), I, 216r, col. 1C k; *Glossa ordinaria*, II, p. 294E [all references to the *Glossa* are taken from *Biblia sacra, cum glossa ordinaria ... ab infinitis mentis purgatis: in commodioremque ordinem digestis* (Lugduni: n.p., 1589)], II, 294E.
35 Fioravanti, *Convivio*, p. 101, refers to Luke 16. 21 and Matthew 15. 27; however, he does not examine their status in medieval culture.
36 See Judges 1. 7, Psalms 147. 17 and Ezechiel 13.19 for further Scriptural passages that deal with fragments of food. See also Vittorio Bartoli, 'Similitudini e metafore digestive e nutrizionali nel *Convivio* e nella *Commedia*', *La cultura* 50 (2012), 65–94 (especially p. 67).
37 See for instance Albertus Magnus, *Super Matthaeum*, XIV. 17 (pp. 429–30); XV. 26, ll. 31–2 (p. 446); Hugh of St Cher, I, 215v, cols 1–2B b; 216r, col. 1C t and D i; Thomas Aquinas, *Super Evangelium Matthaei*, XIV. 2; XV. 2; XVI. 1; *Super Ioannem*, VI. 3 (where Thomas alludes to 'cibus quo Angeli vivunt'); *Catena aurea in Matthaeum*, XV. 5 (the sources are the *Glossa*, Remigius of Auxerre and Rabanus Maurus); *Glossa ordinaria*, II, 291C, 293B, 294G, 295A. See also Henri de Lubac, *Exégèse médiévale*, 4 vols (Paris: Aubier, 1959–64), English translation from which I cite: *Medieval Exegesis: The Four Senses of Scripture*, 3 vols (Grand Rapids, MI: Eerdmans, 1998–2009), I, 29. Scriptural exegesis also associated scraps of food with the theme of 'broken bread', whose relevance for the *Convivio* ought to be self-evident: Albertus Magnus, *Super Matthaeum*, XIV. 19, ll. 74–86 and 1 (pp. 430–1).

acts of charity;[38] in particular, they were deemed to be 'instructing the minds' – the phrase is John Chrysostom's – of those less fortunate, because more ignorant, than them.[39] Furthermore, and of particular significance for the *Convivio*, exegetes used these stories in order to examine the nature of and the inter-relationship between divine and human wisdom, as well as the limitations of the latter.[40] Equally, in the *prosimetrum*, though as ever in his own inimitable manner, Dante explored and documented exactly these same epistemological issues; and, from this perspective, the 'pane delli angeli' can be extended to embrace secular 'science', and hence, first and foremost, Aristotle. However, as the poet's carefully chosen Scriptural intertexts unambiguously confirm – and let us not forget that the entire metaphorical system of the first chapter, with its emphasis on bread, food, sheep, banqueting, thirst, fountains, water, sweetness, darkness and light is quintessentially biblical – his primary idea of 'sapere' is not Aristotelian but Christ-centred.[41] This is why, in chapter 1, as occurs in the remainder

38   See also Albertus Magnus, *Super Matthaeum*, XIV. 19, ll. 2–16 (p. 431); *Catena aurea in Matthaeum*, XV. 5 (the source is Remigius of Auxerre).
39   See for instance Hugh of St Cher, I, 216r, col. 2C t; Thomas Aquinas, *Super Ioannem*, VI. 1; *Catena aurea in Matthaeum*, XIV. 4 (the sources are Jerome and John Chrysostom); *Glossa ordinaria*, II, 291C, 293A-B.
40   See for instance Hugh of St Cher, I, 215v, col. 2B o; Thomas Aquinas, *Super Evangelium Matthaei*, XVI. 1; *Super Ioannem*, VI. 1; *Glossa ordinaria*, II, 293B.
41   The fundamental Scriptural character of the opening chapter of the *Convivio* casts serious doubt on earlier suggestions regarding the relative insignificance of the Bible in the work in general and in the first three books in particular; see especially Vasoli, 'La Bibbia', pp. 19–22. The chapter in fact illustrates, as Paola Nasti has argued, 'la perizia di Dante che, già all'altezza del *Convivio*, si atteggiava a esperto *biblicus*, aggiornato sugli ultimi sviluppi dell'esegesi biblica, o sugli usi di quest'ultima nella sfera del dibattito scientifico e filosofico' ('"Vocabuli"', p. 161). On the very rare use in scholastic circles of the metaphor of bread – though without reference to the 'bread of angels' – to denote '*profane* wisdom, and especially [...] philosophy', see Luca Bianchi, '"Noli comedere panem philosophorum inutiliter". Dante Alighieri and John of Jandun on Philosophical Bread', *Tijdschrift voor Filosofie*, 75 (2013), 335–55 (p. 347, italics in original; but see also p. 339 and 346). In his important study, Bianchi also argues that two Pauline *sententiae* – 1 Corinthians 3. 2 ('lac vobis potum dedit non escam') and Hebrews 5. 14 ('perfectorum autem est solidus cibus') – are significant for an appreciation of the opening chapter of the *Convivio*. In the Middle Ages, the passages

of the *Convivio*, Aristotle is restricted to ethics and to what Maierù acutely described as 'l'esperienza del sensibile' [the experience of the perceptible].[42] For the Dante of the *Convivio*, as for the poet of the *Vita nova* and the *Commedia*, true Wisdom resides exclusively in God. Like Ruth or the apostles, to be selected to gather the *reliquiae* of the supernatural feast is a rare privilege that needs to be undertaken with the utmost humility. However, such a calling is also a mark of great personal merit – the kind of merit that goes hand in hand with *auctoritas*. In the *Convivio*, too, Dante presented himself as one of God's chosen.

The *Convivio*'s 'virility' (I. i. 16) in comparison to the *Vita nova* can in part be recognized in its attempt to go beyond the latter's essentially 'literary'[43] appreciation of divine Wisdom. It engages instead with as broad an array as possible of intellectual traditions in order to arrive at a more sophisticated understanding of that Wisdom. This is why Dante insisted

---

were employed 'to emphasize that there are different kinds of food [*viz.* knowledge], not always suitable for all' (p. 345), and thus can help illuminate Dante's thinking about the audience of the *Convivio*. This suggestion deserves further investigation. In particular, it would be desirable to establish whether or not the verses from Paul were associated with the Scriptural *auctoritates* discussed above, since, unlike these, they do not seem to be intertextually present in *Convivio* I. i, where Dante neither mentions 'milk' nor 'solid food'. In my limited researches, I have not found such a connection. This may be because the different sets of biblical passages do not refer to the same things. Thus, the *panis angelorum* and the *fragmenta* were associated with a knowledge that potentially is accessible to all, while the Pauline verses were used to distinguish between different forms of knowledge and their respective audiences. Given that Dante does not discriminate between those whom he deems worthy to enjoy his 'banquet', it is not surprising that he should not have wished to allude to Paul's epistles. On the other hand, even if 1 Corinthians 3. 2 and Hebrews 5. 14 are not directly pertinent to *Conv.*, I. i, indirectly they do help us appreciate more clearly the 'charitable' didactic intent of the 'almost commentary' – an intent which, as Bianchi demonstrates, separated Dante both from some Scriptural exegetes and from the philosophers (pp. 345–54).

42 Alfonso Maierù, 'Tecniche d'insegnamento', in *Le scuole degli ordini mendicanti, secoli XIII–XIV* (Todi: Accademia Tudertina, 1978), pp. 305–52 (p. 351).

43 By 'literary' I mean that the *Vita nova*'s intellectual and artistic parameters are essentially established, on the one hand, by religious literature with the Bible at its head and, on the other, by the Romance vernacular literary tradition.

that 'non intendo [...] a quella [the *Vita nova*] in parte alcuna derogare, ma maggiormente giovare per questa quella' (16) [I do not intend to disparage that book in any way, but rather more greatly to benefit that one with this one], since, in the last analysis, both works are directed towards achieving a perception of the divine. The task that Dante had set himself in the *Convivio* was hugely ambitious, though he was not alone in the late Middle Ages in trying to systematize in religiously orthodox terms the competing ideas of knowledge that were in circulation. As Paola Nasti has also recalled, the writers of the *quodlibeta*, yet another genre to add to the mix of forms that affect the *Convivio*, were attempting something very similar.[44] However, despite Dante's recourse – admittedly highly idiosyncratic – to two great medieval 'encyclopaedic' standbys, the *comentum* and the *compilatio*, his attempt to comprehend the 'gentle lady', is uniquely his own. It is difficult to think of a medieval text quite like the *Convivio*. Its formal originality and extreme hybridity are obvious markers of the seriousness of Dante's intent, as well as of his sense of the complexity of human knowledge and the means of its transmission, never mind of the ineffability of divine wisdom. To what extent the poet's operation in the *Convivio* actually functions, not least on account of the *prosimetrum*'s provisionality – it is not just unfinished but also much of what has reached us is still decidedly *in fieri* – lies beyond the remit of these brief notes, whose modest aim, as my title announces, is to offer some suggestions 'towards defining' the 'almost commentary'. And yet, whatever conclusions we might reach about the *Convivio*'s effectiveness, or even about its status, there is no doubt that Dante could have assuredly said the same of his *prosimetrum*, as he did of *Le dolci rime d'amor* [The sweet verses of love]: 'Oh come è grande la mia impresa' [Oh how great is my undertaking].[45]

44 Nasti, '"Vocabuli"', pp. 162–71.
45 I completed and submitted this chapter several years ago. In the meantime, several studies have appeared that in fact depend on the present contribution; see in particular Nicolò Maldina, 'Raccogliendo briciole. Una metafora della formazione dantesca tra *Convivio* e *Commedia*', *Studi danteschi*, 81 (2016), 131–64.

ENRICO FENZI

2 'Per suo desiderio sua perfezione non perde': Knowledge and Happiness in the Third and Fourth Books of the *Convivio*

Let us start from afar, from the Bible, and – in particular – from Ecclesiastes 1. 16–18: 'my heart had great experience of wisdom and knowledge. And I gave my heart to know wisdom, and to know madness and folly: I perceived that this also is vexation of spirit. For in much wisdom *is* much grief: and he that increaseth knowledge increaseth sorrow.'[1] Let us immediately highlight the interpretation of this sentence given by Hilary of Poitiers. Commenting on Psalm 127: 'you who eat the bread of sorrows', Hilary annotates 'whoever is aware of being a man born and living in sin eats the

---

1   'Cor meum ut scirem prudentiam / atque doctrinam erroresque et stultitiam / et agnovi quod in his quoque esset labor et adflictio spiritus; / eo quod in multa sapientia multa sit indignatio, / et qui addit scientiam addat et laborem'. This is the base text of the *Biblia sacra iuxta vulgatam versionem* ed. by R. Weber *et al.* (Stuttgart: Württembergische Bibelanstalt, 1975) which often does not correspond to the authors taken into examination when they resort to the *Vetus latina*, which states, besides other divergences (e.g. 'multitudo furoris' instead of Jerome's 'multa indignatio'): 'qui apponit scientiam apponit (et) dolorem'. We comply with the text as it is progressively quoted, without going into the detail of the translation variants, and exhaustive framework which is provided by Dahan, together with an analysis of the lexicon and of the modern translations. (G. Dahan, 'L'Ecclésiaste contre Aristote? Les commentaires de Eccl. 1, 13 et 17–18 aux XIIe et XIIIe siècles', in *Itinéraires de la raison: Études de philosophie médiévale offertes à Maria Cândida Pacheco*, ed. by J. F. Meirinhos (Louvain-La-Neuve: Féderation Internationale des Instituts d'Études Médiévales, 2005), pp. 205–33: see in particular, as related to variants, pp. 209–11. From the Bible, we might add more, starting from the very conclusion of Ecclesiastes 12. 12: 'Faciendi plures libros nullus est finis, / frequensque meditatio carnis adflictio est'.

bread of sorrows'[2] and appends, as a confirmation of this quote, the reference to *Qohélet* (*Sup. Psalm*, in *PL* IX, 698–9). Later, Jerome endorses such an interpretation, according to which knowledge corresponds to the awareness of the fragility and sinfulness of the human condition, in his *Comm. in Ecclesiasten* (*PL* XXIII, 1023): 'The more one has achieved wisdom, the more he will be indignant to be subject to vice and far from the virtues he would like to have.'[3]

The discourse of Saint Augustine continues along this pathway, albeit far richer, more complex and therefore bound to be reiterated several times. He goes back to the words of *Qohélet* and he completes them, in *De trinitate* IV. i. 1. At the very beginning of the *Soliloquia*, in a quickfire exchange between the protagonist and *Ratio*, Augustine focuses on the core of the matter, which is never retracted in any of his reflections or teaching: beyond all the most complex discourses that can still be made on the theme of knowledge, 'I would understand God and know mine own soul. Wouldst thou know any thing more? There is nothing I wish more to know than this' (*Sol.*, I. ii. 7).[4]

These three statements provide a solid basis, from which it is sufficiently easy to follow the intertwining of such themes through the subsequent centuries, passing through further comments to the biblical text.[5] However,

2   'Qui manducatis panem doloris'; 'Panem doloris manducat quisque se hominem in vitiis natum ac vivere meminit'. Hilary mentions the biblical text in form: *apponit ... apponit*, for *addit ... addit*, which will then be usual (see n. 1).
3   'Quanto magis quis sapientiam fuerit consecutus, tanto plus indignatur subjacere vitiis, et procul esse a virtutibus quas requirit'.
4   'A. Deum et animam scire cupio. R. Nihilne plus? A. Nihil omnino'. Obviously, many other quotations from Augustine could be reported, starting from *De spiritu et littera*, where the pertinent words of Romans 8. 6 are mentioned: 'sapere autem secundum carnem mors est'.
5   See, for example, Gregory the Great, especially *Moralia in Job* I. xxv. 34 and XVIII. xli. 66, and then again in the *Homiliae* in Hiezechihelem X. 43, and, amongst others, we find subsequent confirmation of the widely consolidated exegesis of the *Moralia in Job* by Odone of Cluny (PL CXXXIII, 110), in the *Liber meditationum et orationum* by Anselm of Canterbury (PL CLVIII, 741), in the *Sermones in cant. Canticorum* by Bernard of Clairvaux who – following Augustine and together with

the simple linearity of this exegetical tradition is complicated by a partial, though significant, change of course in 1195 – *De miseria humanae conditionis* by Lotario di Segni. The whole of chapter XII, *De diverso studio sapientum* – including its very title – shows for the first time – even if somewhat polemically – an external interlocutor, who at least tends towards the autonomous: the man of science. The future Pope Innocent II would no longer take it for granted that knowledge corresponds *ipso facto* to the knowledge of oneself and of one's own imperfect nature, nor indeed to the progressive adhesion to the truths of faith, but he has to somehow account for the field of science which goes beyond confession and embraces the physical nature of the world as well as metaphysics, meaning to speculate on a divine *ratio* that presided at creation, and ends up investing the universe with the whole variegated complex of human activity. For the first time the tone of such traditional statements, whose orthodoxy is nevertheless failsafe, is no longer the one of an undisputed and undisputable truth, but instead it betrays the urgency of a real juxtaposition, of a conflict in progress and finally – I would say – a proof which rests upon the accumulation of biblical quotations.

Some sixty years later we face a new situation. Bonaventure, in his comment on the passage from Ecclesiastes above, seems to assimilate the traditional reading: 'the better Man knows good and evil, the more he afflicts himself when he errs';[6] but – a few lines later, when mentioning Solomon's *multa indignatio* (and this also applies to the *furor* of the *Vetus*) – the discourse takes a more intricate turn: the *indignatio* deriving from acquiring knowledge can consist of condemning the evil you have become aware of, and the *dolor* deriving from knowledge can then be intended as 'penitence', but can also be intended as 'puffing up' (I Corinthians 8. 1) or further still, and more specifically, as the violent frustration you feel when measuring the distance between what you know and what you can know. With some amazement we hit on something new: 'the great clerics

---

many others – goes back to relating Solomon's adage to I Corinthians 8. 1: 'Scientia inflat, caritas vero aedificat' (*Serm.* XXXVI, in PL CLXXXIII, 967–8).

6   *Comm. in Ecclesiasten*, I, in *Opera omnia*, VI, 19: 'quando homo melius cognoscit bona et mala, tanto magis affligitur quando errat'.

are easily indignant when they do not obtain what they want [...]. And then he adds: "Qui addit scientiam addit et dolorem" [He that addeth knowledge addeth also sorrow] as the impatient man greatly suffers, since nobody manages to fulfill all his wishes'.[7]

However, the interest in Bonaventure's position does not lie in this subtle game which in any case has the effect of weakening solid, traditional annotation when faced with the unsolvable tangle of the man of science's frustrations, but – rather – in what follows, which – to say the least – subverts it under the pressure of a new set of questions. Here is the first *Quaestio* that interrupts chapter II and shows how tangled the matter is in comparison with the times of Hilary of Poitiers:

> This statement is being discussed: *Qui addit scientiam addit et dolorem*. Contrary to this, indeed: 1) all men desire to know by their own nature: but the desire, when satisfied, lightens the spirit up, etc.; 2) more, if it is a matter of real knowledge, then that statement is false, as written in *Sap*. 8 [16]: 'the attendance of knowledge does not know bitterness'. But even when treating of *curious* science, this is equally false, since those who manage to know something have great pleasure of it. I reply saying that the opposite positions are both comprehensible. About *curious* science it is true because, as greed grows together with wealth and the desire to possess, the curious increases his own desire to know. If we speak instead of *true knowledge*, since it means to have a *taste* of it, it is a source of delight; if it is meant as *cognition*, it is instead an indirect cause of sorrow as related to both the dirtiness of your own consciousness and the vision of others' viciousness.[8]

7   *Comm. in Ecclesiasten*, p. 19: 'magni clerici, cum non habent quod volunt, facillime indignantur [...] Et ideo sequitur: Qui addit scientiam addit et dolorem, quia homo impatiens multos sustinet dolores, quia nemo est cui cuncta ad votum perveniant'.
8   *Comm. in Ecclesiasten*, p. 21: 'Quaeritur de hoc, quod dicit: 'Qui addit scientiam addit et dolorem'. Contra: 1. Omnes homines natura scire desiderant; sed desiderium, si compleatur, delectat animam: ergo etc. 2. Item, aut loquitur de vera sapientia, et hoc falsum quia Sapientia octavo: 'Non habet amaritudinem conversatio illius'. Si de curiosa, hoc falsum, quia magna est delectatio quando possunt aliquid scire. – Respondeo dicendum quod de utraque potest intelligi. De curiosa verum est quia, sicut cum divitiis crescit avaritia et appetitus habendi, sic curioso appetito addiscendi. Si vero de scientia veritatis: secundum quod dicit saporem, delectat; secundum quod cognitionem, occasionaliter contristat vel propter immunditiam conscentiae propriae, vel propter aspectum perversitatis alienae'. A few pages forward, the sense of this 'savour'

Before having a closer look at this statement, I would like to draw from Dahan's essay a commentary by Jean de Varzy which dates back to the second half of the thirteenth century (the author is a Dominican friar, *maître* in Paris about 1270 and who died in 1277), which is not a mere *reportatio* of Bonaventure's, as has been said, because it changes and adds something: it is remarkable, for instance, that he explicitly refers to Aristotle, and that he mentions Proverbs 13. 19 as a countercheck:

> *Addit et dolorem*. On the contrary, in the principle of metaphysics. 'All men, by their own nature, desire to know'. And 'The desire accomplished is sweet to the soul' (*Prov.* XIII [19]) Therefore, [...] the same applies either you mean the *true* knowledge or the *curious* one. In case of the true one, it is contradicted by Wisdom. VIII [16] 'the attendance of knowledge does not know bitterness'. If, instead, in case of the curious one, this is contradicted by the fact that learning new things is a source of great pleasure for the curious.[9]

---

of 'knowledge' (with a pun on *sapere* and *sapore* that cannot be translated into English) and the cognitio it procures: 'sapientia non modo importat cognitionem solum, et sic dicitur sapientia rerum divinarum humanarumque cognition' (Cicero, *Tusc.* V. 7, and *De officiis* I. 153 and II. 5); 'alio modo importat gustum et affectus saporem et ordinem, et sic dicitur sapientia a sapere. Primo modo sapere est in bonis et malis, qui habent intellectum illuminatum ad videndum multa vera de Deo et creaturis; secundo modo, tantum est in bonis. Vid. Isidoro, *Etym.*, X. 240: "Sapiens dictus a sapore, quia sicut gustus aptus est ad discretionem saporis ciborum, sic sapiens ad dinoscentiam rerum atque causarum"'. And William of Auvergne, in his comment on the passage of the *Qohélet*: 'sapientia est virtus saporandi spiritualiter, quemadmodum fides virtus credenda'. I obtain the quote from Dahan, 'L'Ecclésiaste contre Aristote?', p. 232. The scholar publishes the comment in his Appendix, pp. 230–3, obtaining it from the manuscript, Tours, Municipal Library 77, ff. 10–11 e 12–14. But for this notion of a 'savour' that makes science into an emotional experience and therefore transforms it into a participatory knowledge, which is organic to the subject and that cannot therefore be given up once the subject has 'savoured its taste' and because of the centrality of the *affectus* in all this, see in particular the beautiful pages of Jean-Luc Solère, *La philosophie dans ses rapports avec la théologie au Moyen Âge*, ed. by J. L. Solère and Z. Kaluza (Paris: Vrin, 2002), pp. 1–44: Other indications are also in *Sapientia sapida* in Paola Nasti, *Favole d'amore e 'saver profondo': la tradizione salomonica in Dante* (Ravenna: Longo, 2007), pp. 93–8.

9   Ms. BNF Lat. 14259 f. 129v: 'Addit et dolorem. Contra in principio Methaphisice: 'Omnes homines natura scire desiderant'. Sed 'desiderium si compleatur delectat

Obviously, we are at the other end of the arc which was inaugurated by Hilary of Poitiers. Then, knowledge wholly corresponded to the consciousness of sin, to the pain of earthly exile and to the frustrated longing for the heavenly homeland. Now, knowledge has – so to say – retracted and made itself autonomous with regard to its contents: in this case, from those which involved unrest and unhappiness. They will certainly continue to trouble the consciousness of Man, but only as a partial, inevitable consequence of an act of the intellect which, *per se*, in its natural ability to fulfill the desire of knowing, is not subject to any limit or negative connotation.

***

The latter statements relating to Ecclesiastes, which can be located in or around the 1270s, offer us the precious key of the famous sentence in Aristotle, *Metaph.*, I. 1. 980a. 21, which by convention is translated into Latin as: 'omnes homines natura scire desirant' [All men by nature, desire to learn] and is consecrated by Dante in the now well-known beginning of the *Convivio*: 'Sì come dice lo Filosofo nel principio de la Prima Filosofia, tutti li uomini naturalmente desiderano di sapere' [As the Philosopher says at the beginning of the First Philosophy, all men by nature desire to know].[10] It has recently been insisted upon that the famous quotation is 'conventional and established', and mainly attended to in the different

---

animam': Prov. XIII. Ergo etc. Item aut intelligitur de vera sapientia aut de curiosa. Si de vera, contra Sap. VIII: 'Non habet amaritudinem conversatio illius'. Si de curiosa, contra: multum delectat curiosos nova scire'. See Dahan, 'L'Ecclésiaste contre Aristote?', p. 224, yet – curiously enough – the scholar does not quote anything from Bonaventure (nor from Augustine or Gregory the Great, who are at the origin of many of the passages he quotes from the commentaries of the thirteenth century).

10 As related to the replacement of the ablative *natura* by the adverb *naturaliter* (naturally), see the *incipit* of the *Metaphysics* in the so-called *Auctoritates Aristotelis*: 'Omnes homines naturaliter scire desiderant': see J. Hamesse, *Les Auctoritates Aristotelis. Un florilège médiéval* (Louvain-Paris: Publ. Univ.-Beatrice-Nauwelaerts, 1974), p. 115. See also Thomas, *Sent. Metaph.* I lect. 1 n. 3: 'naturaliter desiderium hominis inclinatur ad intelligendum, et per consequens ad sciendum'. On this, see Paolo Falzone, *Desiderio della scienza e desiderio di Dio nel 'Convivio' di Dante* (Bologna: Il Mulino, 2010), p. 1, n. 1 and the valuable comment that follows.

sermons which praise Philosophy, while as a starting rhetorical topos it would be present in 'several works of anthropology, psychology and morals'.[11] It may well be so, but what really counts is that the examples which are available so far, if we exclude some addenda in the fourteenth century, date back to a precise arc of time, namely the second half of the thirteenth century, and give a hint that at that time it was not a harmless *topos* but, rather, a *senhal*, which even contained profuse polemic meanings. We have seen that the texts which we have considered so far indeed attain something we could define, reversing the title of Dahan's essay as: Aristote contre l'Ecclésiaste. Along this way, we are also led to widen the horizon of

11   Sonia Gentili, *L'uomo aristotelico alle origini della letteratura italiana* (Rome: Carocci, 2005), p. 134, In particular, see Gianfranco Fioravanti, 'Sermones in lode della filosofia e delle logica a Bologna nella prima metà del XIV secolo', in *L'insegnamento della logica a Bologna nel XIV secolo*, ed. by D. Buzzetti, M. Ferriani and A. Tabarroni (Bologna: Istituto per la Storia dell'Università, 1992), pp. 165–85. The earliest citations of Aristotle's passage date back to 1246–7 with the anonymous commentary on Isagoge 'sicut dicit Ysaac'(Monaco, ms, Clm 14460), where it is stated that the natural disposition is not sufficient to make a philosopher out of a man (see R. Imbach, 'Einführung in die Philosophie aus dem XIII. Jahrhundert', in *Quodlibeta: ausgewählte Artikel*, ed. by F. Cheneval *et al.* (Freiburg: Universitätsverlag, 1996), pp. 63–91 (p. 80); R. Imbach, *Dante, la philosophie et les laïcs. Initiation à la philosophie médiévale* (Paris and Fribourg: Editions Universitaires-Editions du Cerf, 1996), p. 29. Even before 1250, a *Scriptum super Metaphysicam magistri Ricardi* related the statement that all men naturally desire to know to the 'bonum quod omniua optant' of the beginning of the Nichomachean Ethics (the work is preserved in codex Vat. Lat. 4538: I draw the quote from Gentili, *L'uomo aristotelico*, p. 136, n. 13, where she quotes in her turn A. D. Callus, 'The Subject-Matter of Metaphysics According to Some Thirteenth-Century Oxford Masters', in *Die Metaphysik im Mittelalter. Ihr Ursprung und ihre Bedeutung*, ed. by Paul Wilpert and W. P. Eckert (Berlin: De Gruyter, 1963), pp. 394–5. Worthy of special attention, as related to the praise of Frederick II and Manfred in *De vulgari eloquentia* I. xii. 4, and to the imperial ideology in *Monarchia*, is the quote from *Metaphysics* in a famous letter addressed by Manfred to the Faculty of Arts of Paris in 1263 approx.: the passage is quoted by Falzone, *Desiderio della scienza*, p. 2, n. 2, who in turn mentions R. A. Gauthier, 'Notes sur les débuts (1225–1240) du premier "averroïsme"', *Revue des sciences philosophiques et théologiques*, 66 (1982), 321–73 (p. 323). See also Imbach, *Dante, la philosophie*, pp. 112–14.

the conflict that – on the basis of Aristotle's texts, at last made accessible through the Latin translations – was caused by those who had started, in a more or less direct form, to assert the autonomy of philosophical and scientific research over theology. The discourse immediately becomes complex. It should be noticed that, in our case, both a Franciscan – no less a figure than Bonaventure – and a Dominican, Jean de Varzy, resort to Aristotle to limit the weight of the biblical *auctoritas*. On the other hand, it cannot be denied that the background theme which is dealt with in Ecclesiastes – namely the relationship between knowledge and happiness – has ended up by actualizing and multiplying its valences within the particular philosophical 'season', which some scholars have restricted to the sixties and eighties of that century. Later on, a series of philosophers and intellectuals which had been previously defined *tout court* as 'disciples of Averroes' and then – most likely more accurately – as 'radical Aristotelians', traditionally identified in the magistri artium of Paris University, developed a series of positions on this matter which were resoundingly condemned by the Bishop of Paris, Etienne Tempier, in 1277.

The bishop had condemned a series of propositions, generally derived from the Aristotelian comments, namely from the tenth book of Aristotle's *Ethics* (in particular, chapter 7, 1177a 12 and following), which – since they maintained that the *ultima perfectio hominis* laid in speculation – were univocally oriented to affirm that only philosophical contemplation was really worthwhile for Man and that only the philosopher, as 'master' of rationality, would be able to attain truth and happiness in this life, reaching by his sole undertaking an understanding of the separate substances and of the First Cause. The others, the uneducated ones, moving down the scale of knowledge, would be nothing more than brutes who could be defined as 'men' only because of a sort of linguistic convention, *equivoce*. This notion of transcendental happiness, according to the brilliant and inspired formula found by Maria Corti (1981 and 1983),[12] which culminates

---

12   In these two essays, in order to characterize the late thirteenth-century mode and – in particular – the influence of radical Aristotelianism on Cavalcanti and Dante, Corti focuses on the fortunate notion of 'mental happiness', referring mainly to *De summo bono* by Boetius of Dacia and on the *Quaestio de felicitate* by Giacomo

in a mysticism of the intellect and in some sort of natural beatitude that can be humanly attained, *naturaliter adepta*, and presents 'un authentique contre-modèle à la théorie chrétienne des vertus',[13] could not help attracting the attentions of the Church.[14] As has frequently been noted, Bishop Tempier's initiative was particularly ineffective. Several reasons for this ineffectiveness have been proposed. One such reason lies in the fact that those propositions expressed the claim for a higher social *status* by the corporations of the *magistri artium*. Another reason was due to the deeply felt need to better define the field that was open to scientific rationality and to its logic instruments, thus freeing it from the binds of theology and from the direct subjection to the ecclesiastical authorities. The case of the debate on the eternity of the world, which was developed at that same time, fits well into this discourse, as does the accusation raised at the philosophers regarding their 'double truth' approach: the truth of

---

da Pistoia (dedicated to Cavalcanti after 1290). See, now, mainly I. Zavattero, 'La *Quaestio de felicitate* di Giacomo da Pistoia. Un tentativo di interpretazione alla luce di una edizione critica del testo', in *Le felicità nel Medioevo*, pp. 355–409, which is also important for the comparison between the two texts and which confirms that Giacomo actually lacks such pathos that characterized the extolling of the speculative activity in Boethius, as well as the rarefied elitist dimension which separates the life of the philosopher from that of mere mortals.

13   Alain De Libera, 'Averroïsme éthique et philosophie mystique. De la félicité intellectuelle à la vie bienheureuse', in *Filosofia e Teologia nel Trecento. Studi in ricordo di Eugenio Randi*, ed. by Luca Bianchi (Louvain-La Neuve: FIDEM, 1994), pp. 33–56.

14   See Roland Hissette, *Enquête sur les 219 articles condamnés à Paris le 7 mars 1277* (Louvain-Paris: Publications Universitaires-Vander-Oyez, 1977), where the different articles are commented on. In order: art. 8, 27–30: 'Quod intellectus noster per sua naturalia potest pertingere ad cognitionem Primae Causae'; art. 9, 30–2: 'Quod Deum in hac vita mortali possumus intelligere per essentiam'; art. 1, 15–18: 'Quod non est excellentior status quam vacare philosophiae'; art. 2, 18–20: 'Quod sapientes mundi sunt philosophi tantum'; art. 166, 257–60: 'Quod si ratio recta, et voluntas recta'; art. 171, 265–6: 'Quod homo ordinatus quantum ad intellectum et affectum, sicut potest sufficienter esse per virtutes intellectuales et alias morales, [...] est sufficienter dispositus ad felicitatem aeternam'. See also David Piché, *La condamnation parisienne de 1277* (Paris: Vrin, 1999).

their particular science and the other of faith.[15] Another reason was that the intellectual eudemonism of Aristotle and of all those who had made of the exercise of reason the maximum ethical imperative, and who – on that imperative – had founded the very opportunity of human happiness, had by then become the official ideology and the established flag-bearers of all those who had elected knowledge as their profession and passion.

This would already allow an insight into how indispensable it was to recall – even though in short – the terms of this conflict so as to grasp the sense and importance of the positions Dante takes in the *Convivio*. Before we get there, however, we need to consider a further issue. Together with Tempier's action of censorship and the call to orthodoxy, we also need to define what the 'orthodox' version of this new, challenging knowledge-happiness knot was: this means, in other words, paying special attention to the solution given by Thomas Aquinas. Thomas accepts Aristotle's notion that all the good and happiness of Man lays in exerting his most noble part,

---

15   It is worth reminding ourselves that the condemnation of 1277 represents a decisive moment within the framework of a progressive legitimation of the scientific research as released from the perspective of otherworldly salvation: a framework which involves setting aside an idea of nature conceived only as an expression of divine omnipotence (see Hans Blumenberg, *La legittimità*, in particular chapter III., pp. 151–90, and chapter VIII, pp. 371–89). I can only mention the most significant bibliography on the topic: Kurt Flasch, *Aufklärung im Mittelalter? Die Verurteilung von 1277 – das Dokument des Bischofs von Paris* (Mainz: Dieterich, 1989); Luca Bianchi, *Il vescovo e i filosofi. La condanna parigina del 1277 e l'evoluzione dell'aristotelismo scolastico* (Bergamo: Lubrina, 1990); Luca Bianchi, 'Filosofi, uomini e bruti. Note per la storia di un'antropologia averroista', *Rinascimento*, XXXII (1992), 185–201; Luca Bianchi, *Pour une histoire de la 'double verité'* (Paris: Vrin, 2008); Alain De Libera, *Albert le Grand et la philosophie* (Paris: Vrin, 1990), with particular reference to pages 242 and following on 'intellect theology'); Alain De Libera, *Penser au Moyen Âge* (Paris: Seuil, 1991): see, for instance, the pages dedicated to the 'myth' of double truth, 'invented' by Bishop Tempier, pages 122 and following, and the leading role ascribed to Dante throughout the volume, and Alain De Libera, *La philosophie médiévale* (Paris: PUF, 1989), in particular the final pages. See also – in *Le felicità nel Medioevo* – the two updates by Fioravanti and Luca Bianchi, '"Felicità intellettuale", "ascetismo" e "arabismo": nota sul *De summo bono* di Boezio di Dacia', pp. 13–34. Very useful is the small volume *Thomas d'Aquin, Boèce de Dacie. Sur le bonheur*, trans. and ed. by Ruedi Imbach and Ide Fouche (Paris: Vrin, 2005).

that is, the intellect, and through a solid speculative progression (which is mainly pursued in questions *1–5* of the *Prima Secundae* of the *Summa*, from which the passages mentioned hereinafter derive: but we should also read question 12 of the first book, *Quomodo Deus a nobis cognoscatur*), where he maintains that: 'all agree in desiring the last end: since all desire the fulfillment of their perfection, and it is precisely this fulfillment in which the last end consists'.[16]

At this point, after saying and reiterating many times that happiness is the *ultima hominis perfectio* and that it is an operation of the non-sensitive, intellective function : 'the operation whereby man's mind is united to God will not depend on the senses',[17] but from the intellective act, and especially from the speculative intellect rather than from the practical one, Thomas specifies that the speculative sciences do not go beyond the sensitive knowledge, in which ultimate happiness cannot lie:

> Therefore man's final perfection must be through knowledge of something above the human intellect. But it has been shown, that man cannot acquire through sensibles, the

16 *Prima Secundae* q. 1 art. 7: 'omnes conveniunt in appetitu finis ultimi, quia omnes appetunt suam perfectionem adimpleri, quae est ratio ultimi finis'; *Prima Secundae* q. 2 art. 7–8: 'Res ergo ipsa, quae appetitur ut finis, est id in quo beatitudo consistit et quod beatum facit [...]'; 'impossibile est beatitudinem hominis esse in aliquo bono creato. Beatitudo enim est bonum perfectum quod totaliter quietat appetitum [...]. Obiectum autem voluntatis, quae est appetitus humanus, est universale bonum; [...] nihil potest quietare voluntatem hominis, nisi bonum universale. Quod non invenitur in aliquo creato, sed solum in Deo [...]. Unde solus Deus voluntatem hominis implere potest [...] In solo igitur Deo beatitudo hominis consistit'.

17 *Prima Secundae* q. 3 art. 3: 'Non autem tunc operatio qua mens humana Deo coniungetur a sensu dependebit; essentia beatitudinis in actu intellectus consistit'; *Summa* I 12 art. 1: '[...] quidam posuerunt quod nullus intellectus creatus essentiam Dei videre potest. Sed hoc inconvenienter dicitur. Cum enim ultima hominis beatitudo in altissima eius operatione consistat, quae est operatio intellectus, si nunquam essentiam Dei videre potest intellectus creatus, vel nunquam beatitudinem obtinebit, vel in alio eius beatitudo consistet quam in Deo. Quod est alienum a fide. [...] Inest enim homini naturale desiderium cognoscendi causam, cum intuetur effectum, et ex hoc admiratio in hominibus consurgit. Si igitur intellectus rationalis creaturae pertingere non possit ad primam causam rerum, remanebit inane desiderium naturae. Unde simpliciter concedendum est quod beati Dei essentiam videant'.

knowledge of separate substances, which are above the human intellect. Consequently it follows that man's happiness cannot consist in the consideration of speculative sciences. However, just as in sensible forms there is a participation of the higher substances, so the consideration of speculative sciences is a certain participation of true and perfect happiness.[18]

The scheme becomes increasingly clearer, and the discussion becomes denser. Does happiness, then, consist of contemplation (which we should remember is greater than action, since the action tends to something whilst contemplation is a goal *per se*), of what is higher than human intellect, that is, the separate substances, and – finally – the angels? The answer is parallel to the one which was already given as related to speculative sciences: the angels have a participated being, and – consequently – only God is in essence the truth, and only his contemplation can provide perfect happiness:

> Final and perfect happiness can consist in nothing else than the vision of the Divine Essence [...]. Wherefore the intellect attains perfection, in so far as it knows the essence of a thing. If therefore an intellect knows the essence of some effect, whereby it is not possible to know the essence of the cause, *i. e.* to know of the cause 'what it is'; although it may be able to gather from the effect the knowledge of what cause is. Consequently, when man knows an effect, and knows that it has a cause, there he naturally desires to know of the cause 'what it is'. And this desire is one of wonder, and causes inquiry, as is stated in the beginning of the *Metaphysics* (I 2). For instance, if a man, knowing the eclipse of the sun, considers that it must be due to some cause, and knows not what that cause is, he wonders about it, and from wondering proceeds

---

18   *Prima Secundae* q. 3 art. 6: 'Non enim aliquid perficitur ab aliquo inferiori, nisi secundum quod in inferiori est aliqua participatio superioris. Manifestum est autem, quod forma lapidis vel cuiuslibet rei sensibilis est inferior homine. Unde per formam lapidis non perficitur intellectus inquantum est talis forma, sed inquantum in ea participatur aliqua similitudo alicuius quod est supra intellectum humanum, scilicet lumen intelligibile vel aliquid huismodi. Omne autem quod est per aliud, reducitur ad id quod est per se. Unde oportet quod ultima perfectio hominis sit per cognitionem alicuius rei quae sit supra intellectum humanum. Ostensum est autem quod per sensibilia non potest deveniri in cognitionem substantiarum separatarum, quae sunt supra intellectum humanum. Unde relinquitur quod ultima hominis beatitudo non possit esse in consideratione speculativarum scientiarum. Sed sicut in formis sensibilibus partecipatur aliqua similitudo superiorum substantiarum, ita consideratio scientiarum speculativarum est quaedam participatio verae et perfectae beatitudinis'.

to inquire. Nor does this inquiry cease until he arrives at a knowledge of the essence of the cause. If therefore the human intellect, knowing the essence of some created effect, knows no more of God than 'that He is'; the perfection of that intellect does not yet reach simply the First Cause, but there remains in it the natural desire to seek the cause. Wherefore it is not yet perfectly happy. Consequently, for perfect happiness the intellect needs to reach the very Essence of the First Cause. And thus it will have its perfection through union with God as with that object, in which alone man's happiness consists.[19]

There is one last passage which requires our close attention. Thomas has already explained that humanity has the potential to attain perfect bliss, on the grounds of an argument that Dante, as we will see, shall resume and bend to different meanings in the *Convivio*: 'if the intellect of the rational creature could not reach so far as to the first cause of things, the natural desire would remain void. Hence it must be absolutely granted that the blessed see the essence of God' (*Summa*, I. 12. 1; mentioned above in note 28). But here there is already the answer to the question which is now decisive: can such 'union with God', which is the sole perfect happiness, be achieved in this life? For many reasons the answer is no, it cannot. On

19 *Prima Secundae* q. 3 art. 8: 'ultima et perfecta beatitudo non potest esse nisi in visione divinae essentiae [...] intantum procedit perfectio intellectus, inquantum cognoscit essentiam alicuius rei. Si ergo intellectus aliquis cognoscat essentiam alicuius effectus, per quam non possit cognosci essentia causae, ut scilicet sciatur de causa quid est, non dicitur intellectus attingere ad causam simpliciter, quamvis per effectum cognoscere possit de causa an sit. Et ideo remanet naturaliter homini desiderium, cum cognoscit effectum, et scit eum habere causam, ut etiam sciat de causa quid est. Et illud desiderium est admirationis, et causat inquisitionem, ut dicitur in principio *Metaphysicae* (*Met*. I 2, 982b 12; 983a 12). Puta si aliquis cognoscens eclipsim solis, considerat quod ex aliqua causa procedit, de qua, quia nescit quid sit, admiratur, et admirando inquirit. Nec ista inquisitio quiescit quousque perveniat ad cognoscendum essentiam causae. Si igitur intellectus humanus, cognoscens essentiam alicuius effectus creati, non cognoscat de Deo nisi an est, nondum perfectio eius attingit simpliciter ad causam primam, sed remanet ei adhuc naturale desiderium inquirendi causam. Unde nondum est perfecte beatus. Ad perfectam igitur beatitudinem requiritur quod intellectus pertingat ad ipsam essentiam primae causae. Et sic perfectionem suam habebit per unionem ad Deum sicut ad obiectum in quo solo beatitudo hominis consistit'.

Earth, humanity can enjoy but a little imperfect happiness, as any science he can have is by its very nature imperfect. He must wait to obtain perfect happiness in the afterlife, when, and only when, union with God can be attained.[20] According to Thomas (and this also has a very important bearing on what Dante will say in the *Convivio*), the imperfection of knowledge and of all happiness does not stand out in the exceptional case of humanity which has progressed so far in the earthly 'speculative' knowledge to have – as it were – exhausted it, to the point of wanting to transcend it through a final 'impossible' intellectual tension. Instead, knowledge and happiness are imperfect every time, from the beginning, because the experience of knowledge is inevitably also the experience of its own limits, in a world of 'effects' of which we ignore the *quid est* of the first cause event, even though it is well known that such cause does exist. From this point of view, it can be maintained that Thomas made the transfer of meaning of Solomon's adage: *qui addit scientiam addit et dolorem* from an old environment that was related to the awareness of one's own sins and the evil of the world to an intellectual environment, which is strictly philosophical and relevant to the relationship between knowledge and happiness.[21] In the *Summa contra Gentiles* III. 48. n. 16, Thomas remarks how much

20   *Prima secundae* q. 5 art. 3 '[…] perfecta […] et vera beatitudo non potest haberi in hac vita. […] Nam beatitudo, cum sit perfectum et sufficiens bonum, omne malum excludit, et omne desiderium implet. In hac autem vita non potest omne malum excludi. Multis enim malis praesens vita subiacet, quae vitari non possunt […]. Similiter etiam desiderium boni in hac vita satiari non potest. Naturaliter enim homo desiderat permanentiam eius boni quod habet. Bona autem praesentis vitae transitoria sunt, cum et ipsa vita transeat, quam naturaliter desideramus, et eam perpetuo permanere vellemus […]. […] si consideretur id, in quo specialiter beatitudo consistit, scilicet visio divinae essentiae, quae non potest homini provenire in hac vita […]. […] manifeste apparet quod non potest aliquis in hac vita veram et perfectam beatitudinem adipisci'.
21   Imbach was right to observe in the introduction to his precious booklet: 'Comment ne pas voir l'incroyable tension entre le désir de connaître et d'être heureux et l'impossibilité d'y parvenir? Cette tension est, selon Thomas, cause d'angoisse' (*Thomas d'Aquin, Boèce de Dacie. Sur le bonheur*, p. 30).

anguish the thinkers of ancient times – in particular Alexander of Afrodisia, Averroes and Aristotle[22] – must have endured, anguish from which devout Christians are liberated as they know with certainty that – after death – their immortal souls shall enjoy perfect happiness, because their knowledge will be the same as that of the angels.

***

The passages of the *Convivio* which are being discussed here analyse in depth the relationship between knowledge and happiness (*Conv.*, III. xv. 6, 10 and IV. xiii. 1–9), where the latter resumes and completes the former. An essential contribution to the matter at hand is the volume by Paolo Falzone; I will be content, here, to add some considerations. The first point I would like to make is that the things I have said so far are essential to help us perceive the novelties and the even polemic substance of Dante's positions. The second is that it seems to be important to try to understand the reasons that have led Dante to take those positions, beyond the thick network of correspondence and the 'status' of the debate which, *per se*, could hide their novelty. To clarify, I would like to mention an example drawn from *De vulgari eloquentia*, which was written more or less at the same time. As is known, in the first chapters Dante deals with the issue of the angelic *locutio*, a theme which is neither new nor simple, as Irène Rosier-Catach has shown very well.[23] The crux of the matter, for us, is not

---

22   'In quo satis apparet quantam angustiam patiebantur hinc inde eorum praeclara ingenia'. Obviously, from the *Summa contra Gentiles* many other statements could be taken, with particular reference to book III chapters 25–63. Chapters 47 and 48 again broadly state that God cannot be contemplated in his essence and that the ultimate happiness of Man cannot be attained, whilst the further chapters attempt to explain the difficult issue of the contemplation of divine essence by the blessed and the angels. In chapter 54 he completes his explanation of how such contemplation by the blessed is possible and how – instead – the opinion of those who deny it is false and heretical (remember the passage of *Summa* I. 12. art. 1, mentioned above, n. 17: 'quidam posuerunt quod nullus intellectus creatus essentiam Dei videre potest').

23   Irène Rosier-Catach, '"Solo all'uomo fu dato di parlare". Dante, gli angeli e gli animali', *Rivista di filosofia neoscolastica*, 3 (2006), 435–65; see also her 'Une forme

to place Dante's thesis within the thick grid of the *auctoritates*, but to grasp the unprejudiced freedom of Dante, who has no hesitation in rejecting the Thomist solution and is therefore taking a personal position, since the essential reason that leads him to deny the use of language to angels and animals does not lie at all within the history of the debate, but – rather – has its key in the core thesis, which is rich in extraordinary applications, according to which language is an exclusive phenomenon, and it is of such nature to set humanity at the centre of creation according to a vision that, as some scholars believe, anticipates Giannozzo Manetti's *De dignitate et eccellentia hominis*.

Having set this out, let us move to the texts. Deploying all his enthusiasm for this 'most excellent delight which suffers no cessation or imperfection, namely true happiness, which is acquired through the contemplation of truth' (*Conv.*, III. ii. 14), Dante removes a doubt that is now familiar to us. Since many things, and above all the divine essence, are bound to remain precluded from our intellect, which – because of its limits – cannot reach a perfection of knowledge that is at least foreseen and wished, would this not mean that the way of knowledge does not lead at all to happiness, but, rather, to the opposite, that is, to unhappiness and frustration which cannot be alleviated as they are rooted in the very constitutive aspiration of human nature? The reply is blunt:

> l'umano desiderio è misurato in questa vita a quella scienza che qui avere si può [...] Onde, con ciò sia cosa che conoscere di Dio, e di certe altre cose, quello che esso è, non sia possibile alla nostra natura, quello da noi naturalmente non è desiderato di sapere. (*Conv.*, III. xv. 9–10)
>
> [Therefore human desire within this life is proportionate to the wisdom which can be acquired here [...] This is why, since it is not within the power of our nature to know what God is (and what certain other things are), we do not by nature desire to have this knowledge.]

---

particulière de langage mental, la locutio angelica, selon Gilles de Rome et ses contemporains', in *Le langage mental du Moyen Âge à l'âge classique* (Louvain: Peeters, 2009), pp. 60–93.

The merit of Porro and Falzone is to have removed Dante's passage from the isolation it had been left in,[24] and to have shown that Dante's solution had already been considered to be potentially viable by earlier thinkers, even though it was finally rejected, as is the case – for instance – in the *Summa* by Henry of Ghent (1276), who ascribes it to the *philosophi*, that is, to the *magistri artium*, and takes it into serious consideration even though he ends up by aligning with Thomas. This is also the case of Giles of Rome and William of Alnwick, whilst Peire d'Alvernhe, Remigio dei Girolami and – in a particular way – Siger of Brabant are doubtless close to Dante.[25] With all this, what is the element that primarily characterizes Dante's passage? It is that he rigorously keeps the discourse anchored in human experience, rejecting – by an implicit, though strong attitude of juxtaposition – the idea of treading Thomas' ground and flattening the knowledge-happiness issue on the basis of a useless attempt to go back to the First Cause and thus entrust the solution of doubt to the happy gratified contemplative condition which the souls of the blessed will certainly enjoy. Once Thomas' scheme is separated from its conclusion, it is obvious that what remains of it can only confirm that – in this world – the way of knowledge does not lead anywhere and generates instead anguish and frustration. There is not much distance from here to the thought that Thomas is Dante's polemical inspiration.

Even more, if we force things a little, it would even seem that Dante considers Thomas' position as some sort of sleight of hand, because, if it is

24 A typical position is the one expressed by Gilson, who does not want Dante's statement to be given too much weight, and who considers it as a sort of occasional witticism without consequences. See Falzone, *Desiderio della scienza e desiderio di* Dio, pp. 210–11. See also Pasquale Porro's essay: 'Tra il *Convivio* e la *Commedia*: Dante e il "forte dubitare" intorno al desiderio naturale di conoscere le sostanze separate', in *1308. Eine Topographie historischer Gleichzeitigkeit*, ed. by A. Speer and D. Wirmer (Berlin: De Gruyter, 2010), pp. 629–60.
25 See Falzone, *Desiderio della scienza*, pp. 180 ff., as related to the close relationship that links Dante's solutions to those already proposed by Siger of Brabant; see pp. 211–30 as related to the examination of the quaestio by Henry of Ghent (1276); pp. 231–3 for Peire d'Alvernhe,: pp. 234–6 for Remigio dei Girolami; pp. 237–8 for Egidio Romano; p. 241 for William of Alnwick. Also see Falzone's conclusion, p. 197.

true that the place of desire is here, and that heaven is not the place of desire and therefore of deprivation, but – rather – of its fulfillment, then it is on this world's terms that the questions raised by desire need to be solved. This is dictated – amongst other things – by the role attributed to Nature, which *nihil facit frustra* [does nothing in vain]: Nature cannot actually be ascribed a responsibility that exceeds its jurisdiction, such as making a promise on earth which will be kept in heaven. If – following the line of argument of Aristotle's *De Caelo* II 11 291b – the unquestionable principle that Nature *nihil facit frustra* is assumed, as everybody does, the only rigorous solution is the one proposed by Dante. As I have indicated, Dante does not reduce the knowledge-happiness issue to the traditional funnel of the First Cause, that is, God, an impossible and therefore undesired knowledge: 'Onde, con ciò sia cosa che conoscere di Dio, e di certe altre cose, quello che esso è, non sia possibile alla nostra natura, quello da noi naturalmente non è desiderato di sapere'. [This is why, since it is not within the power of our nature to know what God is (and what certain other things are), we do not by nature desire to have this knowledge]. Thus, at the heart of the problem, the First Cause plays no role, nor does the backwards chain of causes,[26] and this is absolutely decisive since the process of knowledge had always been meant as a process that could (or could not ...) return every time from the effect to the cause, 'scire per causas'. From the *Preamble* to the comment on Aristotle's *Metaphysics*, for instance: the certainty of science derives from the knowledge 'princeps sive domina' of any of the other universal causes, which only draw things from indeterminateness and can give a 'completa cognitio' (the 'perfect' one in Dante). Or from the *Preamble* to the *Liber de causis*, where we can read that 'the effect is known through the cause', it is necessary that 'the first causes of things are by themselves the highest and noblest objects of intellect, since they are at the highest degree entities and at the highest degree true, because they are cause of the essence and truth of

---

26 The term 'causa' is used only twice in the *Convivio* (at III. xi. 1 and IV. xiv. 16), and not related to our matter, whilst the term used by Dante is 'cagione/cagioni', in the four books, respectively 32, 18, 27 and 31 times (in five cases: III. ii. 4; vi. 5 and 11; vii. 2, and IV. xxi. 9, the *Libro delle Cagioni* is a quote of the *Liber de causis*).

the other things'.[27] Obviously, Thomas clarifies immediately that – in this life – such knowledge is limited and shall be perfect and beatifying only in the after-life, but that is not to say that it ceases to be the powerful spring which is the origin of any act of knowledge and even embodies pathways of each life dedicated to knowledge in the ideal.[28] Now, Dante's resolved gesture breaks such chains according to which that which could never be

27 'effectus per causam cognoscitur [...] Oportet igitur quod simpliciter loquendo primae rerum causae sint secundum se maxima et optima intelligibilia, eo quod sunt maxime entia et maxime vera cum sint aliis essentiae et veritatis causa'.
28 I mention the translation of the Proemio to *Liber de causis* by Cristina D'Ancona Costa, *Tommaso d'Aquino, Commento al Libro delle cause* (Milan: Rusconi, 1986), pp. 167–8, referring to both the rich introduction and to the other studies by the same author, and mainly to her *Recherches sur le 'Liber de causis'* (Paris: Vrin, 1995). As related to Dante's reading of *Liber* through the also very significant comment by Albertus Magnus, see the essential studies by Cesare Vasoli, 'Dante, Alberto Magno e la scienza dei "peripatetici"', in *Dante e la scienza*, ed. by Patrick Boyde and Vittorio Russo (Ravenna: Longo, 1955), pp. 55–70; and most of all by Nardi in 'Le citazioni dantesche del *Liber de Causis*', and 'Raffronti tra alcuni luoghi di Alberto Magno e di Dante', now in his *Saggi di filosofia dantesca* (Florence: La Nuova Italia, 1967); L'origine dell'anima secondo Dante, now in Bruno Nardi, *Studi di filosofia medievale* (Rome: Edizioni di storia e letteratura, 1960); Bruno Nardi, *Dal 'Convivio' alla 'Commedia' (Sei saggi danteschi)* (Rome: Istituto Storico Italiano per il Medio Evo, 1992), pp. 37–150), and E. Massa, 'Alberto Magno' in *Enciclopedia Dantesca*, ed. by U. Bosco *et al.*, 5 vols + appendix (Rome: Istituto della Enciclopedia italiana, 1970–8), I, 100–8. See De Libera, *Penser au Moyen Âge*, pp. 268–72; Vasoli, 'Dante, Alberto Magno', pp. 55–70; M. Gallarino, 'Note sulla dottrina della causazione nel pensiero di Dante Alighieri', *Annali dell'Istituto Italiano per gli Studi Storici*, XX (2003–4), 5–44; Isabelle Battesti, 'La *canzone* Amor che movi tua vertù da cielo', in *Le Rime di Dante*, ed. by P. Grossi (Paris: Istituto Italiano di Cultura, 2008), pp. 123–37; Paolo Falzone, 'La progressione dall'Uno al molteplice nel pensiero di Dante', in *Cosmogonie e cosmologie nel Medioevo*: atti del Convegno della Società italiana per lo studio del pensiero medievale (S.I.S.P.M.): Catania, 22–24 settembre 2006, ed. by C. Martello, C. Militello and A. Vella (Louvain-La-Neuve: FIDEM, 2008), pp. 47–63; Paolo Falzone, '"Sì come dice Alberto in quello libro che fa dello intelletto". La citazione del *De intellectu et intelligibili* di Alberto Magno in *Conv.*, III. vii. 3–4', in *Letteratura e filologia fra Svizzera e Italia. Studi in onore di Guglielmo Gorni*, I, *Dante: la 'Commedia' e altro*, ed. by M. A. Terzoli, A. Asor Rosa and G. Inglese (Rome: Edizioni di storia e letteratura, 2010), pp. 37–56; Alessandro Raffi, 'Dante e

known in this life is nothing but the 'cause' and therefore the content of the truth of what is known.

Allow me a brief parenthetical comment. In a previous essay, I commented that one of the novelties of book IV of the *Convivio* with respect to the previous books lays in the progressive replacement of luminous metaphors by progressively more circumstantial ones relevant to the vegetal world: from the 'seed', to the 'plant' to the 'fruit', and I argued that – versus the lyrics on which he is commenting and which all contain a more canonical repertoire of images of pure visibility, from lights to rays of ennobling effects – the explanation in prose selects a different way, reducing or even overlooking that which is emitted from above and exalting, on the other hand, an image from 'inside' reality which has the strength to grow and produce its own fruits, that is, to live in compliance with its own organic laws of development.[29] In other words, in these last parts of the *Convivio*, Dante moves from the contexts of reception to others which are informed at the expansive moment of the seed. He then passes from an emanationism of Neo-Platonist type to an Aristotelian naturalism.[30] Within this new framework he deals with and defines what we could call the 'place' of knowledge.

---

    il Liber de causis: il problema della creazione nella teologia della *Commedia*', *Campi immaginabili*, 40–41 (2009), 19–45.

29 See Enrico Fenzi, 'L'esperienza di sé come esperienza dell'allegoria (a proposito di Dante, *Conv.*, II. i. 2)', *Studi Danteschi*, LXVII (2002), 161–200.

30 Dronke distinguishes between an active, descending 'Boethian' and an 'Aristotelian' concept, which sees in the motion of things a movement of return to their immovable principle: 'This is the one train of thought, the Boethian one – this love is an active moving power, an outgoing, penetrating force. In the words of Boethius' song, it binds the order of things, rules earth and sea, and dominates heaven. The other train of thought is Aristotelian [...] In this way too the sun and stars are moved by their desire, or love, for the unmoved mover, who, in Aristotle's famous phrase, 'moves by being loved'. The moving power of love, in Aristotelian terms, is not an activating, outgoing thing, diffusing itself in the cosmos like radiance; it is the aspiration of all things towards an immutable' (Peter Dronke, 'L'Amor che move il sole e l'altre stelle', in *The Medieval Poet and His World* (Rome: Edizioni di storia e letteratura, 1965), pp. 439–75 (p. 440).

In the emanationist vision such as that which Dante explores in *Amor che movi [Love, who move]*, we find a strong Dionysian imprint,[31] which is therefore within the notion of creation as 'effect'. The truth of everything does not belong to any such thing: it is elsewhere. From stones to eclipses, to borrow the examples which Thomas himself used, the truth always transcends the object, and immediately flies away towards the 'cause'. The emphasis on the effusion of the grace/light/goodness, which in a different measure informs everything with itself, from the angels to the minerals (see *Conv.*, III. vii. 2–7),[32] actually risks having the 'thing' disappear from your hands, because it will not have the strength to constitute itself as an autonomous object of knowledge, and 'true' knowledge shall consist in taking the thing back to the 'cause', that is, to its essential invariant: the divine light, which differs by quantity, not by quality. It then becomes clear that Dante severs this sort of perennial escape towards a 'cause' that, in this case, he even avoids naming, and he does that in order to return its own object to science. A solid, precise, limited object: exalted in its autonomy by a principle of limitation which becomes the guarantee of its full understandability.

These last considerations indeed risk surpassing the aforementioned text, but they fit the subsequent one (*Convivio* IV. xiii. 1–9) perfectly, which completes it (and that I unfortunately have to discuss outside the rich context that generates it). The question is the one we have already seen, but it is now dealt with by discussing statements in detail which equate the desire of knowledge with that of wealth, and the frustration of the cheapskate to that felt by the man in search of wisdom:

> Che se io desidero di sapere li principi delle cose naturali, incontanente che io so questi, è compiuto e terminato questo desiderio. E se poi io desidero di sapere che cosa e com'è ciascuno di questi principii, questo è un altro desiderio nuovo, né per

---

31   Enrico Fenzi, 'La *canzone* di Dante *Amor che movi tua vertù dal cielo*: una teoria anti-cavalcantiana sulla natura di Amore', in *Grupo Tenzone, Amor che movi tua vertù dal cielo*, ed. by C. López Cortezo (Madrid: Asociación Complutense de Dantología-Dept. de Filologia Italiana (UCM), 2011), pp. 15–59.
32   On this passage, see the significant contribution by Falzone, 'Sì come dice Alberto [...]', mentioned in n. 28.

l'avvenimento di questo mi si toglie la perfezione alla quale mi condusse l'altro; e questo cotale dilatare non è cagione d'imperfezione, ma di perfezione maggiore [...] Sì che, per qualunque modo lo desiderare della scienza si prende, o generalmente o particularmente, a perfezione viene.[33]

[For if I desire to know the principles of natural things, as soon as I know them this desire is fulfilled and brought to an end. If I then desire to know what each of these principles is and how each exists, this is a new and separate desire. Nor by the appearance of this desire am I dispossessed of the perfection to which I was brought by the other; and this growth is not the cause of imperfection but of greater perfection. [...] So that in whatever way the desire for knowledge is understood, whether in general or in particular, it attains to perfection.]

As for the passage of book III, this crucial limitation of the object, which is always different and 'sufficient' as related to the act of knowing, is now more obvious, if possible. It is so sufficient that knowledge is perfect in its every punctual moment. The point is significant, and allows for a shift in the point of view.[34] Yet, it is not only the discourse of the different possible levels of bliss that is important (as Falzone says, the desire to know the divine essence is therefore denied in order to safeguard the bliss of contemplative life, no less than the bliss of active life), rather, what is significant is that Dante's position draws its strength from the strong belief

33   As related to Dante's quotes in these lines, see, in order: *Comm. De Anima* III 4, t. c. 5, 408 and III 7, t.c. 36, 494–5; *Eth*. X 7, 1177b, 31–4: the quote from Simonides is in Thomas, *Exp. In Eth*. X, lect. 11, 2107 and 2109, and *Summa contra Gentiles* I 5; *Eth*. I 1, 1094b, 23–5; Rom. 12. 3.

34   Falzone ends by illustrating the radical opposition that separates Dante and Thomas: 'Che la perfezione della natura sia in sé meno elevata della perfezione comunicata dalla grazia (e che la felicità terrena, di conseguenza, sia meno perfetta della felicità celeste) non significa, infatti, che tale perfezione sia mutila o incompleta. La gerarchia di dignità tra i due ordini non si risolve cioè in un rapporto di subordinazione gerarchica, tale che il primo termine sia sottomesso al secondo e in esso superato, ma ciascun ordine gode di una sua perfezione specifica, conseguibile attraverso modalità altrettanto specifiche di attuazione. La perfezione di grado inferiore, se ne deduce, è autonoma e indipendente dalla perfezione di grado superiore, secondo un criterio logico che, come ha osservato Étienne Gilson, è 'typiquement dantesque', e che consiste nel fondare l'autonomia di un ordine inferiore sulla sua stessa inferiorità' ; *Desiderio della scienza*, pp. 143–4.

that in any statement of truth: no matter how circumscribed, no matter how trivial or scientifically sophisticated it is, there can be no more truth than the one that already exists, and no climbing up the chain of causes can modify it. Echoing Augustine, any true thing is such in the name of that truth, every true thing belongs to and therefore enjoys an unquestionable 'perfect' dignity that founds and legitimates the equally 'perfect' dignity of the act through which it is known.

In short, Dante's discussion dismantles the earlier discourse on knowledge, riveted to the procession of the causes and falling into the funnel of the Prime Cause; it breaks the chain that subordinated the known to the unknowable, and this is a direct demolition of Thomas' construction based on the theological opposition between 'imperfect' and 'perfect' (but also, moving backwards, to the old distinction made by Augustine between *scientia inferior* and *superior*). Dante does not share such a view. Every act of knowledge is always perfect ('comes to perfection') and, as such, is perfectly fulfilling: nothing more could be done to arrange the new conceptual basis on which the building of the full legitimacy and autonomy of sciences and nature could be erected. This applies to the *Convivio*. Further on, the discourse becomes more complicated and widens again, but this is a leap of level that does not imply any actual contradiction.

To conclude, the long passage of book IV, which is dedicated to demonstrate the intrinsic perfection of every specific act of knowledge, leaves a delicate question open: how do different acts articulate one another? Do dialectics leading to others exist, and what are they? This, mainly after Dante excluded (or closed off in parentheses) the solution that was available at that point – this is, putting every single moment into line along the chain of the causes? Well, also in this case, the footprint left by the reflections of the *Convivio*, even though such texts do not touch the matter, is deep and leads us up to the *Paradiso*, where the very voice of Dante in dialogue with Piccarda returns – with substantial precision – in what had already been said:

> Io veggio ben che già mai non si sazia
> nostro intelletto, se 'l ver non lo illustra
> di fuor dal qual nessun vero si spazia.
> Posasi in esso, come fera in lustra,

tosto che giunto l'ha; e giugner puollo;
se non, ciascun disio sarebbe frustra.
Nasce per quello, a guisa di rampollo,
a piè del vero il dubbio; ed è natura
ch'al sommo pinge noi di collo in collo. (*Par.*, IV. 124–32)

[Well I perceive that never sated is
Our intellect unless the Truth illume it,
Beyond which nothing true expands itself.
It rests therein, as wild beast in his lair,
When it attains it; and it can attain it;
If not, then each desire would frustrate be.
Therefore springs up, in fashion of a shoot,
Doubt at the foot of truth; and this is nature,
Which to the top from height to height impels us.]

There are two points I would like to underline briefly. The first is that, in this definition of the internal dialectics of knowledge, Dante – through the beautiful allegory of the beast which hides its prey in the lair – insists on the pleasure of conquering truth and on its becoming a 'possession forever', not threatened by the fact that at the other pole, as the *Convivio* stated, there is the field of the truth that is not yet known, and which is however knowable (infinite other preys ...). Hence the second point, which I consider even more meaningful: it is true that every progressive acquisition of knowledge proceeds from a new doubt that generates a new interrogation, but Dante is careful not to present the passage from one truth to another as a return from the effect to the cause as would have been natural – not to say inevitable – according to some schemes (such as that set out by Thomas). Doubt, on the other hand, is born and positively developed from the 'perfection' achieved by knowledge itself: therefore, not from a condition of pain and frustration but from the state of 'mental happiness' generated by attaining truth. It is not ignorance that generates knowledge, but it is knowledge that generates knowledge and it is 'natura ch'al sommo pinge noi di collo in collo' [nature which from height to height / on to the summit prompts us].

***

A short appendix. If what has been said so far is true, this outlines an answer to a doubt that has been articulated by Pasquale Porro in his book *'Avegna che pochi per male camminare, compiano la giornata'. L'ideale della felicità filosofica e i suoi limiti nel Convivio dantesco*.[35] In the book's opening, Porro refers to Imbach's take on the famous *incipit* of the *Convivio*: 'tutti gli uomini naturalmente desiderano di sapere' [all men by nature desire to know][36] and moves on to wondering why knowledge could be the source of human happiness when it is clear, even to Dante himself (see *Conv.*, I. i. 6) that such ideal, which should correspond to the specific requirements of every man, is precluded from the majority of human beings.[37] Porro continues by investigating the double nature, that is, the *subjective* and *objective*, of what is preventing knowledge, and clearly reiterates that Dante's attempt is to lead mankind as much as possible to the table of the philosophers, opposing the ancient enduring elitism deriving from Aristotle and Averroes, according to whom 'true' men would be the philosophers and all the others would be relegated to an unredeemable condition of half-animal inferiority.[38]

Given his rigorously philosophical field, I cannot pursue here all the following passages of this scholar; thus – hoping I will not be too trivial – I will merely observe that Porro chiefly focuses on the statement in book

35 *Filosofare in lingua volgare. Philosopher en vulgaire. Philosophieren in der Volkssprache*, ed. by Dominik Perler (Freiburg: Sonderdruck der Freiburger Zeitschrift für Philosophie und Theologie, 2012), pp. 389–406.
36 Imbach, *Dante, la philosophie*, p. 189.
37 Porro, *L'ideale della felicità filosofica*, pp. 390–1: 'Si può veramente chiamare "naturale" ciò che spinge, come recitano le prime righe del *Convivio*, verso qualcosa che si rivela poi fin troppo spesso irraggiungibile? È questa la difficoltà che mi sembra emergere dal progetto stesso del *Convivio*'.
38 Porro, *L'ideale della felicità filosofica*, p. 396: 'La vera peculiarità dell'approccio dantesco sta dunque nel fatto che, dopo aver richiamato il desiderio universale di conoscenza, Dante sposta immediatamente l'attenzione sulle condizioni effettive di accesso al sapere filosofico, individuando i limiti interni e soprattutto esterni che impediscono di fatto a tutti gli uomini di poter perseguire tale fine, e ancor più decidendo di contribuire in prima persona alla rimozione di alcuni di questi limiti attraverso l'elaborazione di un trattato di divulgazione filosofica in lingua volgare. La stessa idea di divulgazione si oppone del resto intrinsecamente a ogni forma di elitarismo filosofico'.

III of *Convivio*, according to which, if our nature cannot manage to know 'quello da noi naturalmente non è desiderato di sapere' [we do not by nature desire to have this knowledge]. This leads him to interpret Dante's position as the choice of a 'finite horizon', or 'closed system', according to a principle of self-limitation which guards human knowledge – identified to natural knowledge – against the mainstream way of thinking which could not conceive knowledge except in the boundlessly elitist knowledge of the First Cause. This would however not solve the tension 'between universality and naturalness' that would continue permeating the whole *Convivio*.[39] However, I do not believe that Dante's essential move consists of some sort of instrumentally intended self-limitation or self-censorship, as it would be legitimate to think on the grounds of such statements, since he states in book IV: no act of consciousness is valid *per se*, irrespective of all the rest, and is fulfilling *per se* and therefore a source of happiness.

How could the very project of *Convivio* stand and have any consistency unless Dante acts as a guarantor in front of the *miserable* excluded from the banquet of knowledge, whose hunger would be satiated from the very first mouthfuls falling from the *beata mensa [blessed table]*? How would it have been possible to construct a pathway of knowledge to the multitude of people who were excluded from it without firmly maintaining that the mere fact of taking the first step to the right direction would be a source of happiness: that it would immediately generate extraordinary, insolvable dialectics between tension and fulfillment? And what is so necessarily 'closed' or 'self-limiting' in all this? If it were so, one could not understand the long discourse that – again in book IV – shows the difference between the 'increase' of richness and 'growing' of knowledge, which is always 'successione di picciola cosa in grande cosa' [a progression from small things to great things]. In this perspective, it is unquestionable that few 'complete the journey', but the essential point, I repeat, is that even those who stop late

---

39   Porro, *L'ideale della felicità filosofica*: 'la presa in carico del compito dell'allargamento dell'umanità, ovvero l'opzione pratica verso l'effettiva universalità del sapere, porta Dante a scegliere il volgare per aggirare parzialmente gli impedimenti soggettivi, e a contrarre il desiderio naturale per aggirare parzialmente gli impedimenti oggettivi' (p. 402).

in the morning (Porro) will have had their share of happiness. No doubt there is a great difference between concrete knowledge limited to the exercise of natural knowledge, and the speculations of the philosopher who is dedicated to the procession of cause; it is Dante himself who develops this argument. Not for this, nevertheless, does knowledge even there fail to grant happiness to those who hold and augment it.

At this point, it is clear that another discussion should be opened, concerning what we would call political philosophy, because at the root of Dante's discourse there is not only an intellectual concern, but also a clear-minded diagnosis of the growing disunion between the aged field of knowledge and the new requirements of a rapidly transforming society, calling for updated cultural foundations. From this point of view, the *Convivio* – by its 'progressive' concept of knowledge in book IV – breeds an extraordinary project of social cohesion that gathers the best legacy of Brunetto: a project which – without being afraid of any anachronism – deserves to be defined as 'democratic', or – perhaps better – as 'civil'.[40] That is a matter for another discussion.

---

40 Porro is correct to say: 'Il progetto del *Convivio* è dunque, se mi si consente l'espressione, quello di un "allargamento dell'umanità", nel senso tecnico in cui ne parla oggi ad esempio Martha Nussbaum, e ciò forse spiega il tono messianico che spesso l'opera assume, soprattutto nella chiusa del primo trattato' (*L'ideale della felicità filosofica*, p. 398).

THEODORE J. CACHEY JR

3 'Alcuna cosa di tanto nodo disnodare': Cosmological Questions between the *Convivio* and the *Commedia*

The theme of cosmology was unclaimed at the time I first proposed it for the seminar that has led to this volume. In taking it up I hoped to stimulate discussion about a topic not otherwise addressed in the meeting, as well as to obtain suggestions about how best to proceed with my own research.[1] But I also found myself wondering whether the fact that the original set of proposals did not include any cosmological contributions was not in itself significant. Did the situation reflect a more general attitude of Dante scholarship towards the theme of cosmology in the *Convivio*? Did the topic really matter?

Generally speaking, there has, perhaps, existed a tendency among Dante scholars to take Dante's cosmology for granted, particularly after the convincing and thorough treatments of it in works by Patrick Boyde, Giorgio Stabile, and by Edward Moore before them; and of particular aspects of it, by Alison Cornish and Simon Gilson, among others.[2] Thus

---

1   A project I am currently developing on Dante and cartography naturally involves cosmological questions; for example: Theodore J. Cachey Jr, 'Cartographic Dante: A Note on Dante and the Greek Mediterranean', in *Dante and the Greeks*, ed. by Jan M. Ziolkowski (Washington, DC: Dumbarton Oaks Research Library and Collections, 2015), pp. 197–226.

2   Patrick Boyde, *Dante, Philomythes and Philosopher: Man in the Cosmos* (Cambridge: Cambridge University Press, 1981); Giorgio Stabile, *Dante e la filosofia della natura: percezioni, linguaggi, cosmologie* (Florence: SISMEL Edizioni del Galluzzo, 2007); Edward Moore, *Studies in Dante*, Third series: Miscellaneous essays (Oxford: Clarendon Press, 1968 [1903]); Alison Cornish, *Reading Dante's Stars* (New Haven, CT: Yale University Press, 2000); Simon Gilson, *Medieval Optics and Theories of*

one should not be too surprised to find that Dante scholars spend relatively little interpretive energy on the cosmological aspects of the *Convivio*, and that the recent bibliography does not include many studies dedicated to it.[3] On the other hand, new interpretive questions about Dante's cosmology have been raised in the recent scholarship and remain open, particularly as regards the *Commedia*.[4]

Cosmology is, of course, an anachronistic category when applied to Dante. The earliest uses of the word in the modern sense of a theory or doctrine describing the natural order of the universe date from the early modern period. Given the anachronistic status of cosmology as a category, the tendency of modern scholarship has been to treat under separate headings the various strands that collectively made up Dante's cosmological picture of the universe, which nevertheless leaves the problem unaddressed of their synthesis, that is, of how they ultimately cohered for Dante as a unified picture of the cosmos.[5]

Light in the Works of Dante (Lewiston: Edwin Mellen Press, 2000). For a succinct and insightful review essay about recent studies, see Giuseppe Ledda, 'Poesia, scienza e critica dantesca', *L'Alighieri*, 18 (2001), 99–113.

3   With rare exceptions, cosmology has not been a major theme in interpretative work on the *Convivio*, although the recent edition and commentary by Fioravanti represents a major advance regarding cosmological questions with respect to previous editions: Dante Alighieri, *Opere*, ed. by Marco Santagata; Gianfranco Fioravanti and Claudio Giunta, *Il Convivio* (Milan: Mondadori, 2014), pp. 3–805. All quotations of the *Convivio* are taken from this edition, while the English translation of all Dante's texts are taken from the Princeton Dante Project: <http://etcweb.princeton.edu/dante/index.html> accessed 2 February 2018. See also Sergio Cristaldi, *Verso l'empireo: stazioni lungo la verticale dantesca* (Acireale: Bonanno, 2013).

4   One immediately thinks of Robert Durling and Ronald Martinez's, *Time and the Crystal: Studies in Dante's Rime petrose* (Berkeley: University of California Press, 1990) a study of the 'cosmological poetics' of the *rime petrose*; or of Kay's book about the astrological aspects of the *Paradiso*: Richard Kay, *Dante's Christian Astrology* (Philadelphia: University of Pennsylvania Press, 1994). Several essays contained in the important volume, Patrick Boyde and Vittorio Russo, *Dante e la scienza* (Ravenna: Longo, 1995), suggest new lines of inquiry that intersect with the topic of Dante's cosmology.

5   The entry for 'cosmologia' in the *Enciclopedia dantesca*, accordingly, consists of just a single brief paragraph. Instead of a description of Dante's cosmology, the reader is

Cosmological Questions between the 'Convivio' and the 'Commedia' 57

A handy illustration of this phenomenon is provided by *astrologia*, a word that for Dante could refer to both astronomy and astrology. It was, in fact, during Dante's time that the two increasingly became differentiated.[6] Inevitably, by focusing on the astronomical aspect of *astrologia*, as Dante scholars such as Alison Cornish in her excellent study, *Reading Dante's Stars*, have done, they run the risk of undervaluing the astrological aspect of Dante's *astrologia*. On the other hand, a focus on astrology in Dante such as that of Richard Kay's *Dante's Christian Astrology* tends to diminish the astronomical side of Dante's cosmology. It is perhaps not surprising, given this situation, that after more than three hundred pages dedicated to Dante's use of astrology in the *Paradiso*, Kay concluded that as far as cosmology was concerned, 'just how Dante thought it all worked remains to be determined' (p. 259) and he added,

> If we could construct Dante's cosmological model more precisely, I think we would be in a better position to appreciate the importance he attached to astrology. As it is, we cannot at present be certain how he thought the stars received, exerted, and passed on their powers. In other words, we do not know exactly how astrology is related to cosmology in Dante's thought. (p. 259)[7]

Thus, while we now possess a more or less accurate view of many of the major strands that contributed to Dante's cosmology, we do not have a secure understanding of the way these strands interact, develop and ultimately

---

    referred to distinct articles on a wide array of subjects, ranging from angels to astrology to astronomy, the elements, the Empyrean, the heavens, nature, the planets, and so on. The approach reflects the fragmented state of cosmological knowledge during the late medieval period. See Theodore J. Cachey Jr, 'Dante's Cosmology in Context', in *Dante in Context*, ed. by Zygmunt Barański and Lino Pertile (Cambridge: Cambridge University Press, 2015), pp. 221–40.

6   Alessandro Ghisalberti, 'La cosmologia nel Duecento e Dante', *Letture classensi*, 13 (1984), 33–48.

7   See Robert Durling's judicious review in *Speculum*, 72 (1) (January 1997), 185–7, who sympathizes with Kay's reluctance to address the question of how Dante's astrology fits into his larger cosmography: 'One may sympathize with his reluctance to involve himself in a task whose scope is indeed daunting, though it is one of the most important now confronting Dante studies' (p. 187).

cohere (if, in fact, they do) in the poet's individual works and throughout the œuvre.[8] When it comes to sorting out the respective roles and responsibilities and functions of God, the heavens, the planets, the angelic intelligences, providence, nature, 'universal nature', and fortune to name just a few of the relevant categories, to use a favourite metaphor of Dante's, what we still have is something of a big knot in need of unravelling. Thus, 'with fear and lack of confidence' my modest hope is that by reflecting here on the role and function of cosmology in the *Convivio* one might just 'begin to untie, if not entirely, at least some part of this great knot' (*Conv.*, III. viii. 3: 'temorosamente non sicuro comincio, intend(end)o, e se non a pieno, almeno cosa di tanto nodo disnodare').

But where does one begin? In the first place, it is important to recognize the fact that the critical assessment of Dante's treatment of this theme in his unfinished and abandoned 'quasi- commentary' has been seriously disadvantaged by the fact that as a work of literature, however innovative, the achievement of the *Convivio* pales in comparison to the soaring poetic breakthrough of the *Commedia*. Indeed, Dante radically shifted his approach and point of view in the transition from treatise to poem. Dante himself calls attention to the poem's surpassing of the treatise by including several pointed palinodes or self-corrections of positions taken in the *Convivio*,[9] although the nature of the authorial intentionality one should attribute to these self-corrections remains a question that should be addressed with some care given not only the unfinished but especially the unpublished state of the work. First and foremost there is the turn away

---

8 The question of the extent to which the *Convivio* ultimately coheres as a work of literature, raised by Zygmunt Barański in the conversation in Göttingen (see his chapter in this volume, especially p. 26) can be related to a more general question about the nature of Dante's cosmology. Beneath the surface of its generic hybridity, I would like to suggest that the *Convivio* does indeed display a noteworthy coherence and cohesiveness with regard to its basic cosmological infrastructure.

9 On palinode in Dante, see Rachel Jacoff, 'The Post-Palinodic Smile: *Paradiso* VIII and IX', *Dante Studies*, 98 (1980), 111–22; Daniel J. Ransom, 'Panis Angelorum: A Palinode in the Paradiso', *Dante Studies*, 95 (1977), 81–94; John Freccero, 'Casella's Song (*Purg.*, II. 112)', *Dante Studies*, 91 (1973), 73–80; Robert Hollander, '*Purgatorio* II: Cato's Rebuke and Dante's scoglio', *Italica*, 52 (1975), 348–63.

from Lady Philosophy and the poet's return to Beatrice. But in addition, as if to underscore the heightened epistemological stakes and authority of the poem, Dante revises his position regarding several important cosmological questions, including the cause of the spots on the moon, the respective positions of the Thrones and the Principalities in the order of the angelic hierarchy, and the nature of the Empyrean.

In *Time and the Crystal*, Durling and Martinez went so far as to say that, as regards the relation between *Convivio* and *Commedia*, the *Convivio* did not express Dante's deeper inspiration, and that the *Commedia* represented a return to the principles of cosmological poetics that had governed the *petrose*.[10] In keeping with this attitude critics have generally treated the cosmological parts of the *Convivio* primarily as a quarry or archive of materials useful for the interpretation of parts of the poem or as a support for more or less ambitious readings of the poem. One result of failing to consider the cosmological dimension of the treatise taken on its own terms is the fact that one of the most intriguing interpretative questions, that is, whether there exists any connection between the elaborate analogy of the heavens and the sciences and the angelic hierarchy that Dante develops in *Conv.*, II. xiii–xiv and the structure of the poem, particularly of the *Paradiso*, remains open.[11]

A preliminary reconnaissance of the cosmographical theme aimed at clarifying its importance as well as potential avenues of future inquiry is therefore a first place to begin. For cosmology represents an essential ideological underpinning that is present throughout the *Convivio*, beginning with the proemial first book. In fact, while books II, III, and IV feature cosmology more prominently, its largely implicit presence in the first book foreshadows the capillary ramifications of the theme throughout the work. Indeed, the theme represents an index of the author's pervasive preoccupation with understanding the natural order of the universe as predisposed by God's providence and especially his own place in it. We can already identify in book I more or less implicit strands that are well

---

10   Durling and Martinez, *Time and the Crystal*, p. 2.
11   But see Giuseppe Mazzotta, *Dante's Vision and the Circle of Knowledge* (Princeton, NJ: Princeton University Press, 1993).

worth investigating further alongside the major cosmological interventions of books II, III and IV, and in particular, themes such as 'Providenza' and its instrument Fortune as they relate to Dante's exile, and the cosmically inflected metaphorical interchanges between bread and light. In the end, having more or less exhausted the theme of cosmology according to the predominantly descriptive-didactic orientation of the *Convivio*, did Dante's recognition of the limitations of this approach lead him to undertake a cosmological poem?

The role of providence is, in fact, introduced in the second sentence of the *Convivio*, as a fundamental principle: 'ciascuna cosa, da providenza di prima natura impinta, è inclinabile alla sua propria perfezione' (*Conv.*, I. i. 1) [each thing, impelled by a force provided by its own nature, inclines towards its own perfection].[12] The underlying coherence of Dante's cosmological understanding of the nature of reality here is characteristic, and worth underscoring. This identification of providence with God's establishment of universal order at the beginning of the work is consistent with and foreshadows the culminating cosmological discussion of book IV on the soul's infusion 'by God into the soul that is well placed' (IV. xx. 9), and the discussion of embryology that follows (IV. xxi). Indeed, the evocation of 'Providenza' at the start of the *Convivio* is the same, within Dante's cosmology, as:

> La provedenza, che cotanto assetta,
> del suo lume fa 'l ciel sempre quïeto
> nel qual si volge quel c'ha maggior fretta. (*Par.*, I. 121–3)[13]

---

12   In his commentary to the *Convivio*, p. 94, Fioravanti emphasizes the routine aspect among the Parisian masters of evoking man's natural appetite for the pursuit of knowledge at the beginning of philosophical works. However, it is worth noting that the parallels cited do not feature prominently the role of 'Providenza', as does Dante. See Barański's comments on the 'Christianizing formulations' of the first paragraph of the *Convivio* that 'hint at the religious interests' of the commentary in this volume, p. 20.

13   All quotations from the *Commedia* are taken from Dante Alighieri, *Commedia*, ed. by Anna Maria Chiavacci Leonardi (Milan: Mondadori, 1991, 1994, 1997).

[Providence, which regulates all this,
makes with its light forever calm the heaven
that contains the one that whirls with greatest speed.]

The concept of 'prima natura' ('di prima natura impinta') on the other hand, also introduced in *Convivio* I. i. 1, is to be identified with 'Universal Nature' (a concept unknown to Aristotle). This corresponds to the action of the celestial intelligences who implement God's providential design originating from the divine light of the Empyrean by exercising their influence on the stars and the planets (here Dante follows Avicenna, Albert the Great and St Thomas).[14] Beatrice's elucidation of the cosmological system that enables Dante's providentially willed movement of ascent through the heavens of Paradise in the passage just cited from the start of the *Paradiso*, is thus consistent with and can be traced back to the underlying cosmological framework of the *Convivio*. In this respect Beatrice can be said to confirm the cosmological trajectory of the providentially predisposed return of the exile Dante, a return that was first foreshadowed in the 'quasi-commentary', and ultimately accomplished in *Paradiso* XXXIII.

In fact, God's providence, taking the form of 'Fortuna' is evoked in the proemial first book as the ultimate cause of the author's exile:

> Ahi, piaciuto fosse al *dispensatore dell'universo* che la cagione de la mia scusa mai non fosse stata! ché né altri contra me avria fallato, né io sofferto avria pena ingiustamente, pena, dico, d'essilio e di povertate. (*Conv.*, I. iii. 3)
>
> [Ah, if only it had pleased the Maker of the Universe that the cause of my apology had never existed, for then neither would others have sinned against me, nor would I have suffered punishment unjustly – the punishment, I mean, of exile and poverty.]

And the Stoic and heroic tone of the author's lament for the wound of fortune ('piaga della Fortuna') that his exile has caused him to suffer that

---

14   See the commentary of Fioravanti to Alighieri, *Conv.*, I. vii. 9, p. 143: 'in the peripatetic philosophical tradition the concept of *natura naturalis* as distinct from *natura particularis* (concepts and distinctions not found in Aristotle) can be traced to Avicenna's *Liber de philosophia prima sive de scientia divina*' (my translation).

immediately follows[15] also suggests that the cosmological parameters of the author's situation at the beginning of the *Convivio* are consistent with what we will later find in the *Commedia*, in terms of the equivalence established there between Fortune and providence in *Inferno* VII, and its connection to Dante's courageously embraced biographical experience of exile as represented in the Brunetto Latini and Cacciaguida episodes (*Inf.*, XV. 91–6; *Par.*, XVI. 82–7 and XVII. 106–20). In other words, the most fundamental ideological underpinning of Dante's cosmology appears to have been operative from the very beginning of the *Convivio* and to have already offered the poet a secure framework within which to process his experience of exile and to pursue his project as an author. Explicit in the situation described at the outset is the role of God's providence as a 'dispensator' within this cosmological framework, a role that informs the angelic movers of the heavens, and that Dante will attribute in the *Commedia* to Providence–Fortune in arguably his most original contribution to the cosmological tradition of his time, what C. S. Lewis characterized as Dante's 'brilliant suggestion' that the Earth needed an angelic intelligence assigned to her to guide her and that Fortune fits the purpose:[16]

15 'peregrino, quasi mendicando, sono andato, mostrando contra mia voglia la piaga della fortuna, che suole ingiustamente al piagato molte volte essere imputata' (*Conv.*, I. iii. 4).
16 C. S. Lewis, *The Discarded Image: An Introduction to Medieval and Renaissance Literature* (Cambridge: Cambridge University Press, 1964), p. 139. See Vincenzo Cioffari, *The Conception of Fortune and Fate in the Works of Dante* (Cambridge, MA: Dante Society of Cambridge, Mass., 1940), especially pp. 30–40: 'the possibility of making Fortune a Divine Intelligence was already open to Dante. But the actual representation of Fortune as such does not appear before the *Divine Comedy*' (p. 33). For the originality of Dante's conception of 'Fortuna', see also the entry by Federico Tollemache in the *Enciclopedia dantesca*, ed. by U. Bosco *et al.*, 5 vols + appendix (Rome: Istituto della Enciclopedia italiana, 1970–8), II, 984: 'Dante presents the most elevated synthesis of his doctrine about Fortune in *Inferno* VII. 67–96, and it is a new, very personal synthesis. Fortune is an angelic spirit entrusted by Providence to distribute among individuals as well as peoples the external goods (wealth, honour, beauty, strength, power, glory, etc.) and to transfer them from time to time according to God's impenetrable designs' (my translation).

> Colui lo cui saver tutto trascende,
> fece li cieli e diè lor chi conduce
> sì, ch'ogne parte ad ogne parte splende,
> distribuendo igualmente la luce.
> Similemente a li splendor mondani
> ordinò general ministra e duce
> che permutasse a tempo li ben vani
> di gente in gente e d'uno in altro sangue,
> oltre la difension d'i senni umani [...]. (*Inf.*, VII. 73–81)

> [He whose wisdom transcends all
> made the heavens and gave them guides,
> so that all parts reflect on every part
> in equal distribution of the light. Just so,
> He ordained for worldly splendors
> a general minister and guide
> who shifts those worthless goods, from time to time,
> from race to race, from one blood to another
> beyond the intervention of human wit.]

Dante's 'invention' of a new angelic intelligence in the poem, what Charles Grandgent in his introductory heading to the canto called 'the Angel of Earth',[17] charged with regulating the sublunary realm, reflected the poet's deep need to make sense of his place in God's providential design and for cosmology to reconcile him and the world. The precise details of Dante's cosmology would require working out, and Dante constructed the cosmology of the *Convivio* by means of what has been aptly described as a kind of intellectual bricolage.[18] That the 'dispensator dell'universo' providentially preordained Dante's exile is established in the *Convivio* as a fundamental tenet of that personal cosmology,[19] and this key link would prove to be a

---

17 Dante Alighieri, *La Divina commedia*, ed. by C. H. Grandgent (Boston: D. C. Heath and Co., 1933).
18 Alighieri, *Opere, Convivio*, p. 423.
19 Note that in *Monarchia* II. ix. 8, Fortune is identified directly with Divine Providence: 'Hic Pirrus "Heram" vocabat fortunam, quam causam melius et rectius nos "divinam providentiam" appellamus'. All quotations from the *Monarchia* are taken from Dante Alighieri, *Opere*, ed. by Marco Santagata; II. *Monarchia* (Milan: Mondadori, 2014),

powerful engine for his literary project. It would eventually propel him on the journey of return from exile that took the form of the poetic cosmological journey of the *Commedia*.

Dante was, in fact, deeply and personally invested in questions of cosmology as they impinged upon his own position in the cosmos and his role in God's plan. The *Convivio* reflects a key stage in his coming to awareness of cosmological questions that were evidently vital to him in a way that they were not to other writers of the period. Dante displays a radically more personalized approach to cosmology, if compared, for example, to contemporary cosmological writers.[20] The *Convivio* thus presents not only a fairly comprehensive picture of many of the fundamental elements that

---

pp. 807–1415. A putative contrast between a 'providential' understanding of Fortune and the position Dante takes in *Convivio* IV. xi. 6–8, a question kindly raised in discussion during the Göttingen seminar by Prof. Andreas Kablitz, and noted by some commentators, such as Hollander in his commentary, is more apparent than real. As Tollemache observes, in the *Enciclopedia dantesca*, p. 984: 'Some recent commentators wanted to contrast with this doctrine of Fortune–Providence an important passage of the *Conv.*, IV. xi. 7 about the distribution of material goods in which, according to Dante, 'nulla distributiva giustizia risplende (§ 6): Che se si considerano li modi per li quali esse (le ricchezze) vegnono, tutti si possono in tre maniere ricogliere: ché o vegnono da pura fortuna, sì come quando sanza intenzione o speranza vegnono per invenzione alcuna non pensata; o vegnono da fortuna che è da ragione aiutata, sì come per testamenti o per mutua successione; o vegnono da fortuna aiutatrice di ragione, sì come quando per licito o per illicito procaccio'. Indeed only the perspective shifts, as far as in this passage Fortune, instead of being presented as 'ministra della Provvidenza' [minister of Providence], is considered vis-à-vis the particular agents that concur in the distribution and gain of goods and the game of Fortune really takes place vis-à-vis these agents' (my translation).

20   Claudio Giunta, in *Opere, Convivio*, observes in his commentary on *Voi ch'intendendo il terzo ciel movete*, that: 'the originality of Dante does not reside much in the [cosmological] ideas that he professes, rather in the ability that he alone has, among the writers of his time, to relate this cosmology to the most significant events of his private life, and to interpret these on the background of that private life' (p. 196; my translation). Although it should be noted that by means of his method of intellectual bricolage Dante does arrive at a unique synthesis in the poem that is highly original in certain respects; for example, in Dante's conception of the Empyrean as completely beyond space and time. See Christian Moevs, *The Metaphysics of Dante's*

made up Dante's cosmology but also and no less importantly it expresses their psychological function, that is, the way cosmology assisted Dante in coming to terms with his exiled status (in both the political and Christian existential senses of the term) through an abiding faith in the ultimate coherence of God's providence and, in particular, of God's plan for Dante. The anxiety that colours this fundamental faith in providential design of the cosmic order is expressed in a remarkably consistent manner in both the *Convivio* and the *Commedia*, by repeated imaginings about the disastrous effects for life on earth if the Creator had not perfectly made the universe. For instance, if, on the one hand, the *Primum Mobile* did not in fact move the heavens on their diurnal paths:

> E da vero non sarebbe quaggiù generazione [...] notte non sarebbe né die, né settimana né mese né anno, ma tutto l'universo sarebbe disordinato, e lo movimento delli altri sarebbe indarno. (*Conv.*, II. xiv. 17)
>
> [In truth there would be no generation here below [...] there would be no night or day, or week or month or year, but rather all the universe would be disordered, and the movement of the other heavens would be in vain.]

The same cosmically inflected anxiety is expressed in the poem in a complementary manner at the beginning of *Paradiso* X, where the element of God's providential order of the universe highlighted in the treatise is the point where the diurnal east to west movement of the heavens initiated by the *Primum Mobile* described in the *Convivio* intersects with the west to east motion of the zodiac on the oblique circle of the ecliptic:[21]

'*Comedy*' (New York: Oxford University Press, 2005), pp. 21–5; and Cristaldi, *Verso l'empireo*, pp. 239–92.

21 Fioravanti, in *Opere, Convivio*, p. 336, notes that 'according to Aristotle, the heaven of births and deaths peculiar to the sublunar world is regulated by the movement of the heavens of the diurnal one that guarantees the eternal continuity of it, and by the one which is peculiar to each planet along the ecliptic, and first of all the one of the sun, which explains the alternation of generation and corruption (See *De gen.* II 10)' (my translation).

Leva dunque, lettore, a l'alte rote
meco la vista, dritto a quella parte
dove l'un moto a l'altro si percuote;
e lì comincia a vagheggiar ne l'arte
di quel maestro che dentro a sé l'ama,
tanto che mai da lei l'occhio non parte.
Vedi come da indi si dirama
l'oblico cerchio che i pianeti porta,
per sodisfare al mondo che li chiama.
Che se la strada lor non fosse torta,
molta virtù nel ciel sarebbe in vano,
e quasi ogne potenza qua giù morta;
e se dal dritto più o men lontano
fosse 'l partire, assai sarebbe manco
e giù e sù de l'ordine mondano. (*Par.*, X, 7–21)

[With me, then, reader, raise your eyes
up to the lofty wheels, directly to that part
where the one motion and the other intersect,
and from that point begin to gaze in rapture
at the Master's work. He so loves it in Himself
that never does His eye depart from it.
See how from there the oblique circle
that bears the planets on it branches off
to satisfy the world that calls for them.
And if their pathway were not thus deflected,
many powers in the heavens would be vain
and quite dead almost every potency on earth.
And, if it slanted farther or less far
in the upper sphere or the lower hemisphere,
much would be lacking in the order of the world.]

This signature cosmological sub-theme, however, evokes in both *Convivio* and *Commedia* not only hypothetical negative consequences but also grateful admiration for the perfection of God's creation. This sentiment gets reiterated at the conclusion of the explanation of the sun's orbit around the earth in book II of the *Convivio* in a passage that is directly echoed in the passage cited above from *Paradiso* X:

O ineffabile sapienza che così ordinasti, quanto è povera la nostra mente a te comprendere! E voi a cui utilitade e diletto io scrivo, in quanta cechitade vivete, non levando li occhi suso a queste cose, tenendoli fissi nel fango della vostra stoltezza! (*Conv.*, III. v. 22)

[O ineffable wisdom who has so ordained, how poorly does our mind comprehend you! And you, for whose benefit and delight I am writing, in what blindness do you live, not lifting your eyes up to these things, but rather fixing them in the mire of your foolish ignorance!]

We will return to this passage and the cosmological intersections between *Convivio* and *Commedia* below. For now there is still a third seminal cosmographical theme present in both the *Convivio* and the *Commedia* that merits some attention. It is the connection that is implicitly introduced in the first book between divine celestial light and the 'science' contained in books, including Dante's own vernacular 'quasi-commentary'. This analogy represents an important resonance of the 'pane delli angeli' that 'the few are privileged to feed on', of which Dante proposes to share a few crumbs that have fallen from the table.[22] In addition to the Christological biblical resonances discussed by Fioravanti in his commentary and by others elsewhere in this volume,[23] the expression 'pane delli angeli' (*panem angelorum*) has important cosmological connotations for Dante in so far as it refers to both the active influence of the angelic intelligences that illuminate by the light of the stars all branches of the human sciences, a light which takes the form of writing in books. The connection appears to be a characteristic of Dante's personalized approach to cosmology. In fact, as Fioravanti notes in his commentary, Dante's interpretation of the 'pane delli angeli' as knowledge and learning represents 'un'esegesi abbastanza originale di Dante' (p. 99), possibly inspired according to the commentary of Durling

---

22 'Oh beati quelli pochi che seggiono a quella mensa dove lo pane delli angeli si manuca!' [Blessed are the few who sit at the table where the bread of the angels is eaten] (*Conv.*, I. i. 7).
23 Barański, pp. 20–4.

and Martinez by the analogy Augustine established between the saints and the clergy and heavenly bodies in *Confessiones* XIII. 18.[24]

Be that as it may, by the end of the first book of the *Convivio*, Dante shed his reticence and humility about the status of the bread of his vernacular commentary (and his earlier rather obsequious deference to Latin in favour of the vernacular): 'Questo sarà luce nuova, sole nuovo, lo quale surgerà là dove l'usato tramonterà, e darà lume a coloro che sono in tenebre ed in oscuritade, per lo usato sole che a loro non luce'. (*Conv.*, I. xiii. 12) [This shall be a new light, a new sun which shall rise where the old sun shall set and which shall give light to those who lie in shadows and in darkness because the old sun no longer sheds its light upon them]. And the 'pane delli angeli'-knowledge theme is picked up again and punctually recapitulated in the last chapter of the second book in connection with that book's elaborate cosmological conceit which bundles together the heavens with the arts and sciences and the angelic hierarchy. Dante concludes the second book by emphasizing the influence of the works of Boethius and of Cicero that he had read and that had marked a turning point in his existential pilgrimage:

> Per le ragionate similitudini si può vedere chi sono questi movitori a cu' io parlo. Ché sono di quella movitori, sì come Boezio e Tulio, li quali colla dolcezza di loro sermone inviarono me, come è detto di sopra, nello amore, cioè nello studio, di questa donna gentilissima Filosofia, colli raggi della stella loro, la quale è la scrittura di quella: onde in ciascuna scienza la scrittura è stella piena di luce, la quale quella scienza dimostra. (*Conv.*, II. xv. 1)[25]

---

24 *The Divine Comedy of Dante Alighieri*, ed. by Robert M. Durling, introduction and notes by Ronald L. Martinez and Robert M. Durling; illustrations by Robert Turner (New York: Oxford University Press, 1996), pp. 754–7.

25 The interpretation of the passage has been the focus of some controversy concerning the referent (and therefore the gender) of the demonstrative pronoun in 'Ché sono di quella movitori, sì come Boezio e Tulio [...]'(*Conv.*, II. xv. 1). The first critical edition of the Società Dantesca read 'quello' as referring to the heaven of Venus and therefore to Boethius and Cicero as movers of the heaven while the recent edition/ commentary of Fioravanti reads 'quella', and thus takes the pronoun to refer implicitly to the science of Rhetoric. For a succinct review of the question, see Luca Lombardo, *Boezio in Dante. La Consolatio philosophiae nello scrittoio del poeta* (Venice: Edizioni

[By the resemblances discussed it may be seen who are these movers to whom I speak, who are the movers of this heaven, like Boethius and Tully, who with the sweetness of their discourse guided me, as has been said above, along the path of love – that is, into the pursuit of this most gentle Lady Philosophy, by the rays of their star, which is their writing about her; for in every science the written word is a star filled with light which reveals that science.]

Consistent with this passage from the *Convivio*, the pilgrim's journey through the heaven of the Sun and the heaven of Gemini in the *Paradiso* will feature a return of the poet to his *auctores* which is framed by the same figure according to which, 'the *auctores* – indifferently the texts and their authors – are like the stars because they have poured their power into him, shaping him as the stars help shape sublunar creatures'.[26] With his 'bread as light' commentary of the *Convivio* Dante sought to educate his newly discovered vernacular public with the crumbs of angel's bread that he had recovered from the banquet table of the wise and the holy. Eventually, the providentially 'privileged'[27] and divinely inspired author of the *Commedia* will undertake in the poem to infuse and materially to reshape the world with his poem, as do the angels and the circling heavens, in conformity to the plan of the 'dispensator dell'universo'.

Ca' Foscari, 2013), pp. 177–8: 'the literal interpretation of the whole sentence would be simplified since the reference to Boethius and Tully as 'the movers of this heaven' would be explained as an allusion to Rhetoric, of which the two Latin authors are presented as the champions par excellence'. (My translation). But whether one takes Dante to be speaking of the heaven or the science associated with it, a cosmological-symbolic allusion to the Boethius and Cicero as 'movers' remains; and the cosmological connotation is made explicit in what follows where their writings are compared to the light of the stars ('onde in ciascuna scrittura è stella piena di luce, la quale quella scienza dimostra'). The ultimate cosmological value or significance to attribute to the bread-light-knowledge connection, in particular its relationship to the metaphysics of light that inform Dante's cosmology is a topic worthy of further investigation, but see Joseph Anthony Mazzeo, 'Light Metaphysics, Dante's *Convivio* and the Letter to Can Grande della Scala', *Traditio*, 14 (1958), 191–229.

26 Robert M. Durling, *The Divine Comedy of Dante Alighieri*, p. 242.
27 For the legal resonances of Dante's privilege, see Justin Steinberg, *Dante and the Limits of the Law* (Chicago: The University of Chicago Press, 2013), especially chapter 3, 'Privilegium'.

There are still other cosmological issues that take their point of departure in the first book and that one might eventually pursue in terms of the *Convivio* and of their implications for the *Commedia*: for example, the theme of the author's visceral identification with the place of his birth.[28] But the providential plan of the 'dispensator dell'universo', the role of Fortune as the instrument of Providence, and the mediation of celestial influences through the arts and sciences that take the form of writing each represent fundamental themes that speak to the centrality of cosmology in the development of Dante's project.

Books II, III, and IV of the *Convivio* accordingly feature extended cosmological passages that are central to their respective concerns. Dante took some pains to structure the work and to position these passages according to a discernible numerical order, in an artistic imitation of the providential design of the 1022 starry bodies of the starry heaven and the three numbers that make it up, 2 and 20 and 1000 (*Conv.*, II. xiv. 3).[29] For Dante number regulated the universe and explained all natural things, as it did for the Pythagoreans and as the Bible affirmed: 'omnia mensura et numero et

28 Cf. *Conv.*, I. iii. 4; cf. Albertus Magnus, *Liber de Natura Locorum* (aka *De Natura Loci*), chapter 1: 'There is evidence also in all bodies which are outside the place of their birth for a long time, since they are removed from the source of their preservation and their existence [...] they gradually lose their power'. Cited from Jean Paul Tilmann, *An Appraisal of the Geographical Works of Albertus Magnus and His Contributions to Geographical Thought* (Ann Arbor: Department of Geography, University of Michigan, 1971), p. 27; see, for some interesting implications of this theme for the *Commedia*, David Ruzicka, '"Scegliendo fior da fiore": Exile, Desire and the Fiorentinità of Dante's Matelda', *Le Tre Corone*, 3 (2016), 25–56, for whom 'the exile's *amor patriae*, his yearning to return home, is sublimated and disguised, coded and displaced onto the enigmatic signum of Matelda'.

29 For the relations between nature and art and Dante's imitation of God's art, see Simon A. Gilson, 'Divine and Natural Artistry in Dante's *Commedia*', in *Nature and Art in Dante*, ed. by Daragh O'Connell & Jennifer Petrie (Dublin: Four Courts Press, 2013), pp. 153–86. Cf. *Conv.*, II. xiv. 3 'per lo venti (sì) significa lo movimento dell'alterazione: ché, con ciò sia cosa che dal diece in sù non si vada se non esso diece alterando colli altri nove e con se stesso, e la più bella alterazione che esso riceva sia la sua di se medesimo, e la prima che riceve sia venti, ragionevolmente per questo numero lo detto movimento (sì) significa'.

pondere disposuisti' [thou hast ordered all things in measure, and number, and weight] (Wisdom 11. 21).³⁰ Indeed, E. R. Curtius identified Dante as no less than the culminating exemplar of the medieval practice of what he famously discussed under the heading of 'numerical composition':

> The wonderful harmony of Dante's numerical composition is the end and the acme of a long development. From the enneads of the *Vita nova* Dante proceeded to the elaborate numerical structure of the *Commedia*: 1+33+33+33=100 .... Here number is no longer an outer framework, but a symbol of the cosmic order. (p. 509)³¹

But before there was the *Commedia* and after the *Vita nova* there was the *Convivio*, and in the *Convivio* the number five and its multiples provide the basic structuring pattern. The number of books planned for the complete work would have been fifteen (a proem plus fourteen books), and the subdivision of the chapters of the books repeats the number fifteen: fifteen chapters for book II and fifteen chapters for book III, and two times fifteen, that is, thirty chapters for book IV. Particularly significant is the fact that, as Maria Simonelli was the first to observe, a vertical reading of the fifth chapter of books II, III, and IV reveals that in each case the fifth chapter orients and focuses the cosmographical discussion of that particular book.³²

The fifth chapter of the second book, in fact concludes a triptych of chapters (iii–v), dedicated to the explanation of the angelic hierarchy; chapter five of book III leads off a triptych on the earth and its position within the universe (V–VII); while chapter five in book IV concludes the triptych of chapters dedicated to God's providential plan for the monarchy of Rome (III–V). In light of the doubling of the number of chapters in book IV, chapter twenty of that book, which can be considered the fifth

---

30 Cf. *Conv.*, II. xiii. 18–19; cf. *Par.*, XV. 55–60.
31 Ernst Robert Curtius, 'Excursus XV: Numerical Composition', in *European Literature and the Latin Middle Ages*, trans. by Willard Trask (Princeton, NJ: Princeton University Press, 1953), pp. 501–9: "'Numero disposuit". God's disposition was arithmetical! Must not the writer likewise allow himself to be guided by numbers in his disposition?' (p. 505). See also *Essays in the Numerical Criticism of Medieval Literature*, ed. by Caroline D. Eckhardt (London: Associated University Presses, 1980).
32 In her entry for the *Convivio* in the *Enciclopedia dantesca*, II, 201–3.

chapter of the second series of fifteen, features the culminating definition of human nobility: 'è manifesto che nobilitade umana non sia altro che "seme di felicitade", messo da Dio nell'anima ben posta' (*Conv.*, IV. xx. 9) [human nobility is nothing but 'the seed of happiness', instilled by God within the soul that's properly disposed].

The cosmological characteristics of the number five, which is half of the number ten, which Dante considers the perfect number in *Vita nova* (XXIX. 1) and *Convivio* (II. xiv. 3), merit brief consideration here. Beatrice underscores this principal feature of the number five, that it is half of ten, in her account of the motion of the *Primum Mobile*, and the creation of time and space in *Paradiso* XXVII. 115–20. The motion of the ninth heaven is not measured by any other, she says, 'ma li altri son mensurati da questo, | sì come diece da mezzo da quinto' [but from it all the rest receive their measures, | even as does ten from its half and from its fifth] (*Paradiso* XXVII. 116–17). In a brilliant gloss on this passage and on the associations that two, five and ten could have had for Dante, Christian Moevs notes that to 'measure ten by a half and a fifth is to factor it into (distinguish within it) the prime numbers five and two.'[33] And since prime numbers cannot be measured by any other numbers but by one and themselves they can be said to be the irreducible terms of analysis for an infinity of other numbers. For Martianus Capella, moreover, the pentad is the number assigned to the universe:

> [...] for after the four elements the universe is a body of a different nature (the ether). The number represents natural union, for it is the sum of numbers of each sex for three is considered a male number, and two a female number [...]. Then, too, there are five zones of the earth. In man there are five senses; the same number of classes of creatures inhabit the earth: humans, quadrupeds, reptiles, fish, and birds.[34]

The thematic development of the cosmological theme in the *Convivio* accordingly reveals a universal or comprehensive aspect in the thematic

---

33 Moevs, *The Metaphysics of Dante's 'Comedy'*, pp. 137–40 (p. 137).
34 *Martianus Capella and the Seven Liberal Arts: The Marriage of Philology and Mercury*, trans. by William Harris Stahl and Richard Johnson, with E. L. Budge (New York: Columbia University Press, 1977), viii (Arithmetic), pp. 735, 279–80.

progress of the sequence of chapter fives. From the discussion of the heavens and the sciences and the angelic hierarchy in book II, to the discussion of the earth and the orbit of the sun in book III, to the account of the creation of the human person in book IV, there is an evident movement from macrocosm to microcosm, from the heavens to the earth and to man. The pentad of the *Convivio* appropriately enough informs the structure of a work explicitly dedicated to Lady Philosophy and whose purview encompasses the universe as far as the *Primum Mobile*, just as the Trinitarian number three will later structure the Beatrice-theology inspired *Commedia*. In general cosmological terms then, it might be said that Dante covers everything essential that he will eventually need for the *Commedia* in the first four books of the *Convivio*. This fact may have something to do with why Dante stopped writing the *Convivio*, or at least it might afford the opportunity for some concluding reflections on the limitations of Dante's approach to cosmology in the *Convivio*, and how he radically shifted not so much the contents of his cosmology as his approach to cosmology in the transition to the poem.

In the first place, it should be observed that at the same time that the cosmological parts of the *Convivio* are given prominence within the structure of the work, even to the point of contributing to its numerological infrastructure, the passages themselves, generally speaking, are distinguished, from a rhetorical point of view, by their didactically digressive character. To put it another way, just as Dante did not need to explain the allegory of the theologians in order to explain his own practice according to the allegory of the poets, he really only needed to explicate the heaven of Venus's relation to rhetoric and to the angelic hierarchy of thrones for his immediate rhetorical and interpretive purposes. Instead, he gives a comprehensive account of the structure of the heavens, of the angelic hierarchy and of the arts and sciences. In other words, at the same time that the cosmological theme is structurally vital for the architecture of the treatise, it takes form in a series of digressions from the narrative or argumentative line of the commentary. Digression was, of course, a rhetorical characteristic of the genre of commentary in which Dante was engaged and that distinguishes many parts of the *Convivio*. Nonetheless, I believe this paradoxical aspect of the major cosmological passages that are digressive with respect to the literal and/or allegorical interpretation of the poems in the treatise represents a significant tension at the heart of the work's inspiration. This paradoxical position of cosmology that was both vital to Dante's project yet tangential in another to the aim of the *Convivio* represents a kind of aporia or structural incongruity that threatened to undermine the work's structural integrity. In a similar way, the ostensible goal of the *De vulgari eloquentia* to produce a total rhetorical system down to the individual household (*DVE* I. xix. 3),[35] was ultimately in contrast with Dante's more personal poetic goals for which the purpose of the linguistic treatise was tantamount to the self-justification of the poetic rhetorical direction and the tragic style that characterized his literary project at the time of the *Convivio*. Thus, once the tragic language and style of the illustrious vernacular had been explicated there was no longer any reason to continue the linguistic treatise through to completion.

A passage that illustrates some of these tensions is the one that comes at the end of the discussion of the sun's position in relation to the earth that was highlighted above, at the end of chapter 5 of the third book (*Conv.*, III. v. 22). The discussion of the orbit of the sun around the earth has been straightforward. The author's attitude is analogous to the one Dante will assume in the *Questio de acqua et terra*, where again, he still will be concerned with defending his cultural authority in the cosmological field. Even when he had virtually finished the poem, Dante was still feeling pressure as regards his reputation as 'cosmographos', and his exegetical-poetic methodology in the poem which revealed the natural order of the universe in the poem.

But what is striking about the passage at the end of chapter 5 of the third book of the *Convivio* is Dante's barely concealed frustration with the exercise in which he is engaged, and his impatient attitude toward his public. The point of the demonstration 'may now, by what has been said, be evident to anyone who has a noble mind, of which it is well to demand some little effort' [sì come omai, per quello che detto è, puote vedere chi ha

---

35 'Quibus illuminatis, inferiora vulgaria illuminare curabimus, gradatim descendentes ad illud, quod unius solius familie proprium est'. Quotations from the *De vulgari eloquentia* are taken from The Princeton Dante Project.

nobile ingegno, al quale è bello un poco di fatica lasciare] (*Conv.*, III. v. 20). We are far, I think, from the poetic implementation of the reader response theme Alison Cornish has explicated in her book on Dante and the stars and much closer to the peevish rhetoric of the weary pedagogue.[36] Dante expresses impatience with his public and with the exercise of explaining the cosmological 'facts'. Evidently, a simple recitation of the facts might not be enough to remove those for whose benefit Dante was writing from the 'blindness [...], not lifting your eyes up to these things but rather fixing them in the mire of your foolish ignorance!'.[37]

By the end of the fourth book, having presented most if not all of the basics of a course in cosmology, including most of what would be needed for the *Commedia*, including an account of the heavens and of the angelic hierarchy and of the arts and sciences and of the motions of the sun around the earth and the creation of the noble human soul Dante might well have realized that another approach to cosmology was needed no less than another rhetorical approach to the problem of the 'illustrious vernacular'. Rather than explain how the system worked to others Dante needed to explore it and his role in it by the more direct means that the genre of cosmological poetry afforded him, in the Neoplatonic tradition of the *Timaeus* or the works of Bernard Silvestris and Alain De Lille, which express and participate directly in the cosmos by poetic means rather than describe it from the outside in a scientific mode.[38] To move from the *Convivio* to the *Commedia* was the difference between writing a textbook and doing original research. Writing a textbook on cosmology, or at least the start of

36 Cornish, *Reading Dante's Stars*, pp. 43–61.
37 'E voi a cui utilitade e diletto io scrivo, in quanta cechitade vivete, non levando li occhi suso a queste cose, tenendoli fissi nel fango della vostra stoltezza!' (*Conv.*, III. v. 22).
38 Winthrop Wetherbee's characterization of the cosmological poetry of the twelfth century could be applied to Dante: 'The *Timaeus* is the paradigmatic literary text as well as a *summa* of philosophy, and to the extent that the poets had succeeded in emulating this great model, virtually the embodiment of the natural order itself, their own works attain a similar scope and coherence', Winthrop Wetherbee, 'Philosophy, Cosmology and the Twelfth Century Renaissance', in *A History of Twelfth Century Western Philosophy*, ed. by Peter Dronke (Cambridge: Cambridge University Press, 1992), pp. 21–53 (p. 44).

one, served the purpose of revealing the limitations of philosophy and of the genre of the prose commentary as a vehicle for Dante's project. Indeed, the transformation of society that Dante ultimately sought was beyond the means of philosophical discourse. In order to change the shape of the world Dante had to move beyond describing how the universe worked from the outside. He needed to actualize the providential design of the 'dispensator dell'universo' from within it, which meant spending the last fifteen years of his life writing 'l poema sacro / al quale ha posto mano e cielo e terra'. (*Par.*, XXV. 1-2).[39]

---

[39] Several important studies on Dante and cosmology have appeared since this chapter was written (2013), which I was unable to consider here. These include Maria Luisa Ardizzone, *Reading as the Angels Read: Speculation and Politics in Dante's 'Banquet'* (Toronto: University of Toronto Press, 2016); Bruno Binggeli, '"L'amor che move il sole e l'altre stelle" – Dantes Liebesauffassung aus der Sicht eines Astrophysikers', *Deutsches Dante-Jahrbuch*, LXXXIX (2014), pp. 3–20; Anna Gabriella Chisena, 'L'impurità della "prima stella": la spinosa questione delle macchie lunari', *Lettere Italiane*, 67 (2015), 3, pp. 500–18; Claudia Di Fonzo, 'Cosmological and legal order in Dante's "Convivio"', in Dante Füzetek, *A Magyar Dantisztikai Társaság Folyóirata*, XI (2014), pp. 1–32; Raffaele Giglio, 'Poesia e scienza in Dante. Proposta di rappresentazione del cosmo dantesco', *Critica Letteraria*, 43, CLXVIII–CLXIX (2015), 3-4, pp. 479–508; Christian Moevs, '"Paradiso" II: gateway to Paradise', *Le Tre Corone. Rivista Internazionale di Studi su Dante, Petrarca, Boccaccio*, III (2016), pp. 57–73.

ANNA PEGORETTI

4 'Da questa nobilissima perfezione molti sono privati': Impediments to Knowledge and the Tradition of Commentaries on Boethius' *Consolatio Philosophiae*

The *incipit* of Dante's *Convivio* notoriously quotes that of Aristotle's *Metaphysics*: 'Sì come dice lo Filosofo nel principio della Prima Filosofia, tutti li uomini naturalmente desiderano di sapere' [As the Philosopher says at the beginning of the First Philosophy, all men by nature desire to know] (*Conv.*, I. i. 1). The Aristotelian adage was extensively commented upon by all exegetes, and was almost proverbially quoted in the commendations of philosophy written in the Faculties of Arts.[1] With this choice, Dante immediately attunes his treatise to academic language.[2] Following a

---

1 It is worth noting that Aristotle's sentence is used by Dante commentators as early as by Iacomo della Lana (who certainly did not know the *Convivio*) and Pietro Alighieri (first and third redaction) on *Purg.*, XXI. 1; Iacomo on *Par.*, XX. 58–60; the *Ottimo commento* on *Par.*, X. 22. Dartmouth Dante Project: <https://dante.dartmouth.edu/search.php> accessed 23 June 2016.
2 See the commentary on the *Convivio* by Gianfranco Fioravanti (Claudio Giunta on the *canzoni*) in Dante Alighieri, *Opere*, ed. dir. by Marco Santagata (Milan: Mondadori, 2014), II: *Convivio, Monarchia, Epistole, Ecloghe*, pp. 1–805 (pp. 40–1 and *ad loc.*). Gianfranco Fioravanti, 'Desiderio e limite della conoscenza in Dante', in *Forme e oggetti della conoscenza nel XIV secolo: Studi in ricordo di Maria Elena Reina*, ed. by Luca Bianchi and Chiara Crisciani (Florence: Sismel-Edizioni del Galluzzo, 2014), pp. 7–20. See also Dante Alighieri, *Das Gastmahl*, trans. by Thomas Ricklin, introduction and commentary by Francis Cheneval (Hamburg: Meiner, 1996), I, *ad loc.*. Fine and informative readings of this incipit are provided by Sonia Gentili, *L'uomo aristotelico alle origini della letteratura italiana* (Rome: Carocci–Università degli studi di Roma La Sapienza, 2005), pp. 127–41 (for the presence of the Aristotelian

common development of the problem of the acquisition of knowledge, he confronts straightaway the topic of the obstacles to it, technically known as *impedimenta*. These obstacles limit Aristotle's general statement: despite the fact that all men have a natural desire for knowledge, everyday experience shows that only some of them actually pursue and fulfill it. Boethius of Dacia formulates the problem very clearly (including also idleness among obstacle): 'Cum enim omnes homines naturaliter scire desiderant, paucissimi tamen hominum, de quo dolor est, studio sapientiae vacant inordinata concupiscientia eos a tanto bono impediente' [For all men naturally desire to know. But only the smallest number of men, sad to say, devote themselves to the pursuit of wisdom. Inordinate desire bars the others from such a good].[3] According to Dante, impediments could be either internal (physical disablement and 'malice' of the soul)[4] or external, caused by either unavoidable circumstances ('di necessitade') or by indolence, which

---

quotation in the prologue of the *Novellino*, see pp. 167–80); Paolo Falzone, *Desiderio della scienza e desiderio di Dio nel 'Convivio' di Dante* (Bologna: Il Mulino, 2010), pp. 1–13.

3   Boethius Dacus, '*De summo bono*', in *Boethii Daci Opuscula*, Corpus Philosophorum Danicorum Medii Aevi, VI/2, ed. by N. J. Green-Pedersen (Copenhagen: Gad, 1976), pp. 369–77. [Boethius of Dacia, *On the Supreme Good; On the Eternity of the World; On Dreams*, trans. by John F. Wippel (Toronto: PIMS, 1987), p. 30]. The same problem is formulated in different terms by Siger of Brabant in *Quaestiones in Metaphysicam (Reportatio Parisiensis, quam Godefridus de Fontibus, ut uidetur, retractauit*, ed. by Armand Maurer (Louvain-la-Neuve: Editions de l'Institut Supérieur de Philosophie, 1983), re-ed. in Library of Latin Texts-series B (Turnhout: Brepols, 2010), p. 401: 'Cum ergo dicitur quod naturalia vel semper vel ut frequentius veniunt ad effectum, quia impedimenta rara sunt, sed ad scientiam pauci perveniunt, dicendum quod illud quod est naturale secundum agens, illud contingit semper vel ut in pluribus; sed naturale secundum materiam, cuiusmodi est intellectus ad scientiam, [...] non contingit ut in pluribus'. Anyhow, these are just two formulations of a commonplace.

4   'Veramente da questa nobilissima perfezione molti sono privati per diverse cagioni, che dentro all'uomo e di fuori da esso lui rimovono dall'abito di scienza' (§ 2).

frustrates any attempt to overcome the inconvenience of being born in a place unpropitious to study and education:[5]

> Di fuori dall'uomo possono essere similemente due cagioni intese, l'una delle quali è induttrice di necessitade, l'altra di pigrizia. La prima è la cura familiare e civile, la quale convenevolmente a sé tiene delli uomini lo maggior numero, sì che in ozio di speculazione essere non possono. L'altra è lo difetto del luogo dove la persona è nata e nutrita, che tal ora sarà da ogni studio non solamente privato, ma da gente studiosa lontano. (*Conv.*, I. i. 4)

> [Likewise outside of man two causes may be discerned, one of which subjects him to necessity, the other to indolence. The first consists of domestic and civic responsibilities, which properly engage the greater number of men, so that they are permitted no time for contemplation. The other is the handicap that derives from the place where a person is born and bred, which at times will not only lack a university but be far removed from the company of educated persons.]

Although indolence is deplorable (*Conv.*, I. i. 5), with his *Convivio* Dante aims to overcome it, as well as to mitigate those unavoidable circumstances, which are represented by civic and domestic duties. To this end, he is offering a banquet with the leftovers, which fell from the 'blessed table' of knowledge and wisdom, and which he was able to collect (*Conv.*, I. i. 10–12). This banquet will host those impeded by domestic and civic duties, who will sit around the table, whilst those affected by indolence will sit at their feet (*Conv.*, I. i. 13).[6] With a remarkable development of the metaphorical field of the 'food of knowledge', Dante describes

---

5   This is the safest interpretation of the text, which can anyhow be overinterpreted as 'being far from institutions of higher education'. That is why some scholars print 'Studio' with a capital S: Dante Alighieri, *Il Convivio*, ed. by Maria Simonelli (Bologna: Pàtron, 1966), *ad loc.*; *Convivio*, ed. by Giorgio Inglese (Milan: BUR, 1993), *ad loc.* Lansing's translation further narrows this interpretation, referring to the 'university'. I do not modify it for the mere sake of consistency. However, I must point out that the title of *studium* was not confined to universities, but applied also to religious institutions.
6   On Dante's carefully selected audience, see most recently Luca Bianchi, '"Noli comedere panem philosophorum inutiliter." Dante Alighieri and John of Jandun on Philosophical "Bread"', *Tijdschrift voor Filosofie*, 75 (2013), 335–55 (pp. 340 ff.).

two banquets, both of them with two levels: the first banquet is the elitist one where the 'bread of angels' is offered, and at the feet of which Dante sits; the second banquet is the one offered by himself, in order to share the knowledge he was able to acquire at the feet of the first table with a carefully selected audience. This second banquet aims to partially bridge the gap between the 'happy few' who can acquire knowledge at the highest table, and the large majority of men (and virtually all women), who are doomed to 'eat with the sheep' (*Conv.*, I. i. 7).

The remarkable novelty of Dante's programme of vernacular dissemination has been clearly recognized by scholars. In an unprecedented way, Dante deliberately sets himself the task of overcoming some of the impediments to knowledge. This essay will investigate how the inspiration for what can be identified as a peculiar blend of Scholastic terminology and active commitment could be tentatively traced in the commentary tradition on Boethius' *Consolation of Philosophy*. Before that, it will briefly confront a philological problem, which affects Dante's passage on the impediments to knowledge.

Establishing the Text

In the reference critical edition established by Franca Brambilla Ageno the passage, which introduces the problem of the impediments to knowledge reads as follows: 'Dentro dall'uomo possono essere due difetti e impedi[men]t*i*: l'uno dalla parte del corpo, l'altro dalla parte dell'anima' (*Conv.*, I. i. 3) [Within man there exist two kinds of defects which impede him, one pertaining to the body, the other to the soul]. The word 'impedimenti' is a conjecture already present in the editions provided by Romani, Busnelli-Vandelli, and Vasoli, and accepted by both Cheneval-Ricklin and Fioravanti. It amends an alleged mistake in the archetype text, which reads 'e impedito'.[7] As Sonia Gentili suggested, the archetype text actually makes perfect sense: 'Dentro dall'uomo possono essere due difetti: è impedito l'uno dalla parte del corpo, l'altro dalla parte dell'anima'[8] [Within man there exist two kinds of defects: one is impeded in the body, the other in the soul] (my translation). The philosophical term 'impedi[men]t*i*' would enhance the technical language that Dante seems to be aiming at in the exordium of the *Convivio*. Nonetheless, the unnecessary amendment of a text is rarely the best choice. Moreover, in the overall discussion Dante does not seem particularly interested in the term 'impedimento', and deploys synonyms such as 'cagioni', without any damage to a precise identification of the Scholastic problem of the *impedimenta*.[9] Gentili supports her proposal with a reference to a passage of the *Summa contra gentiles*, in which Aquinas articulates the same topic through a series of 'quidam impediuntur', which closely resemble the 'è impedito' of the archetype text of the *Convivio*:

[7] Variants: 'et è impedito' in mss. L⁶ Mc¹ Mgl Pr; Ott omits and adds 'e impedimenti' in the margins. Dante Alighieri, *Convivio*, ed. by Franca Brambilla Ageno, III: *Testo, ad loc*. See also I: *Introduzione*: 'Ha corretto il capostipite del gruppo degli interpolati Po, Bd R L2 Vg. L'Ott omette la parola e la inserisce poi in margine nella forma esatta; Cap corregge in un secondo momento' (p. 59).

[8] Sonia Gentili, 'Il fondamento aristotelico del programma divulgativo dantesco', in *Le culture di Dante: Studi in onore di Robert Hollander. Atti del quarto Seminario Dantesco Internazionale (Notre Dame–IN, 25–27 settembre 2003)*, ed. by Theodore J. Cachey Jr, Margherita Mesirca and Michelangelo Picone (Florence: Cesati, 2004), pp. 179–98 (p. 184); Gentili, *L'uomo aristotelico*, pp. 141–2. The solution was already suggested by Raffaele Spongano to Maria Simonelli, who actually hypothesized a palaeographic mistake in the tradition, to be corrected with *impedi(rl)o*. This is the passage in her edition: 'Dentro da l'uomo possono essere due difetti, e impedi[rl]o l'uno da la parte del corpo, l'altro da la parte dell'anima'. See also Maria Simonelli, *Materiali per un'edizione critica del 'Convivio' di Dante* (Rome: Edizioni dell'Ateneo, 1970), pp. 65–6.

[9] Falzone, *Desiderio della scienza*, pp. 13 and 21: 'è evidente peraltro che quale che sia la lezione corretta, il significato resta invariato'. On Dante's prologue, see also Paolo Falzone, 'Desiderio naturale, nobiltà dell'anima e grazia divina nel IV trattato del *Convivio*', in *Dante the Lyric and Ethical Poet: Dante Lirico ed Etico*, ed. by Zygmunt G. Barański and Martin McLaughlin (London-Leeds: Legenda, 2010), pp. 24–55 (pp. 27–8).

A fructu enim studiose inquisitionis, qui est inventio veritatis, plurimi impediuntur tribus de causis. Quidam siquidem propter complexionis indispositionem [...] Quidam vero impediuntur necessitate rei familiaris. [...] Quidam autem impediuntur pigritia.

[For there are three reasons why most men are cut off from the fruit of diligent inquiry which is the discovery of truth. Some do not have the physical disposition for such work [...] Others are cut off from pursuing this truth by the necessities imposed upon them by their daily lives. [...] Finally, there are some who are cut off by indolence.][10]

Not surprisingly, this passage is regularly quoted as a prominent antecedent to Dante. However, the theme of the impediments was topical and widespread. What is more, Thomas' threefold partition is too different from Dante's binary subdivisions to be considered a close syntactic and linguistic model. Dante's 'è impedito' seems to stem from a personal linguistic choice. Be that as it may, the archetype text appears to offer a better reading, and does not undermine in any way Dante's engagement with the topic of the *impedimenta*.

10   Sancti Thomae Aquinatis *Summa contra Gentiles [...]*, cura et studio fratrum Praedicatorum, Opera omnia iussu Leonis XIII edita, XIII (Rome: Garroni, 1918), I. 4. Trans.: Saint Thomas Aquinas, *On the Truth of Catholic Faith: Summa contra Gentiles*, ed. by Anton C. Pegis (New York: Hanover House, 1955–7), ed. and updated by Joseph Kenny, O.P. on <http://dhspriory.org/thomas/ContraGentiles.htm> accessed 30 May 2016. The same concept is in the *Sententiae libri Metaphysicae* (Turin: Marietti, 1950), 4, available on <http://corpusthomisticum.org> accessed 30 May 2016: 'licet omnes homines scientiam desiderent, non tamen omnes scientiae studium impendunt, quia ab aliis detinentur, vel a voluptatibus, vel a necessitatibus vitae praesentis, vel etiam propter pigritiam vitant laborem addiscendi'. For the translation, see *Commentary on the Metaphysics of Aristotle*, ed. by John P. Rowan (Chicago: H. Regnery Co., 1961), ed. and updated by Joseph Kenny, O.P. on <http://dhspriory.org/thomas/Metaphysics.htm#02> accessed 30 May 2016.

The Theme of the Impediments

We have already pointed out how the theme of impediments was topical in Scholastic discussions on knowledge and its limits. As Fioravanti states, Dante shares it with the masters of Arts, whilst the quotation from Aquinas' *Contra gentiles* shows its presence also beyond the genre of the commendations of philosophy, as well as beyond proper commentaries or *quaestiones* on Aristotle's *Metaphysics*. For sure, the thirteenth-century Scholastic tradition is the immediate precedent to the prologue of the *Convivio*. However, the theme of the obstacles to the acquisition of knowledge is not strictly Scholastic. Although in my opinion the prologue of Hugh of St Victor to his *Didascalicon*, pointed out by Barański,[11] can hardly be considered as a direct source for Dante's discussion of the impediments, the passage is interesting in its careful differentiation between different categories of men in relation to knowledge:

> Multi sunt quos ipsa adeo natura ingenio destitutos reliquit [...] et horum duo genera mihi esse videntur. Nam sunt quidam, qui, licet suam hebetudinem non ignorent, eo tamen quo valent conamine ad scientiam anhelant, et indesinenter studio insistentes, quod minus habent effectu operis, obtinere merentur effectu voluntatis. Ast alii [...] minima etiam negligunt, et quasi in suo torpore securi quiescentes eo amplius in maximis lumen veritatis perdunt [...] Longe enim aliud est nescire atque aliud nolle scire. Nescire siquidem infirmitatis est, scientiam vero detestari, pravae voluntatis. Est aliud hominum genus quos admodum natura ingenio ditavit et facilem ad veritatem veniendi aditum praestitit, quibus, etsi impar sit valitudo ingenii, non eadem tamen omnibus virtus aut voluntas est per exercitia et doctrinam naturalem sensum excolendi. Nam sunt plerique qui *negotiis huius saeculi et curis* super quam necesse sit impliciti *aut vitiis et voluptatibus corporis* dediti, talentum Dei terra obruunt, et ex eo nec fructum sapientiae, nec usuram boni operis quaerunt, qui profecto valde *detestabiles sunt*. Rursus aliis *rei familiaris inopia* et tenuis census discendi facultatem minuit. Quos tamen plene per hoc excusari minime posse credimus, cum plerosque fame siti nuditate laborantes ad scientiae fructum pertingere videamus.

---

11 Zygmunt G. Barański, 'La vocazione enciclopedica', in *Dante e i segni: Saggi per una storia intellettuale di Dante Alighieri* (Naples: Liguori, 2000), pp. 77–101 (pp. 95 ff.).

[There are many persons whose nature has left them so poor in ability [...] and of these persons I believe there are two kinds. There are those who, while they are not unaware of their own dullness, nonetheless struggle after knowledge with all the effort they can put forth and who, by tirelessly keeping up their pursuit, deserve to obtain as a result of their will power what they by no means possess as a result of their work. Others [...] neglect even the least, and, as it were, carelessly at rest in their own sluggishness, they all the more lose the light of truth [...] Not knowing and not wishing to know are far different things. Not knowing, to be sure, springs from weakness; but contempt of knowledge springs from a wicked will. There is another sort of man whom nature has enriched with the full measure of ability and to whom she shows an easy way to come at truth. Among these, even granting inequality in the strength of their ability, there is nevertheless not the same virtue or will in all for the cultivation of their natural sense through practice and learning. Many of this sort, caught up in the affairs and cares of this world beyond what is needful or given over to the vices and sensual indulgences of the body bury the talent of God in earth, seeking from it neither the fruit of wisdom nor the profit of good work.][12]

According to Hugh, some men are naturally deprived of intellectual abilities (*ingenium*). Nonetheless, whilst some of them try to overcome such shortcoming (*infirmitas*), others completely give up learning, and loose the light of truth. On the other side, those men who are naturally gifted can equally disregard learning for various reasons, none of them excusable. In bodily pleasures we can easily detect the 'viziose delettazioni', which Dante lists as soul's defects, whilst a major specification distinguishes those who are 'caught up in the affairs and cares of this world', described by both Hugh and Dante. Whilst in the *Convivio* domestic and civic responsibilities are one of the 'external' impediments to be addressed and overcome, Hugh attacks those men who care about them 'beyond what is needful', apparently suggesting a further moral shortcoming, an internal fault as detestable as debauchery. In this idealistic reprimand – frankly astonishing when one thinks of living conditions in twelfth-century Europe – knowledge seems

12   Charles H. Buttimer, *Hugonis de Sancto Victore Didascalicon de Studio Legendi, a Critical Text* (Washington: The Catholic University Press, 1939), pp. 1–2. Italics are mine. Translation: Jerome Taylor, ed. and trans., *The Didascalicon of Hugh of St Victor: A Medieval Guide to the Arts* (New York and London: Columbia University Press, 1961), p. 43. A further discussion of the difficulties, which characterize the process of learning, is in V. 5.

to ultimately depend on personal zeal, and even those who live in a state of poverty (*inopia*) are not to be forgiven, not to say relieved.

A reference to *impedimenta* as an obstacle to the pursuit of philosophical knowledge can already be traced in Seneca, in an epistle remarkably reframed in the Scholastic setting of a Faculty of Arts by Matthew of Gubbio. At the end of an introductory sermon to a university course, delivered in Bologna in the first half of the fourteenth century, Matthew inserts the last of a notable series of quotations from Seneca's *Epistles to Lucilius*, which reads as follows:

> Sola autem philosophia excitabit nos. Illi te totum dedica, dignus illa es, illa digna te. Omnibus aliis rebus te nega ferociter, aperte, non est quod precarie philosopheris; et omnia impedimenta dimitte.
>
> [Philosophy is the only power that can stir us up. Devote yourself wholly to philosophy. You are worthy of her; she is worthy of you. Say farewell to all other interests with courage and frankness, do not study philosophy merely during your spare time; throw aside all hindrances.][13]

Interestingly enough, when we go back to Seneca's original text, we find out that, before the final exhortation to get rid of impediments, the philosopher describes them quite precisely as domestic preoccupations and forensic affairs ('curam intermisisses rei familiaris et forensia tibi negotia'). A fourteenth-century Master of Arts, discussing the eminently Scholastic topic of the impediments to knowledge, could therefore find in Seneca a not systematic, but thoughtful consideration of the obstacles to philosophical life.

A further basis for the medieval discussion on the impediments to knowledge is provided by the beginning of Boethius' *Consolation of*

---

13   Gianfranco Fioravanti, '"Sermones" in lode della filosofia e della logica a Bologna nella prima metà del XIV secolo', in *L'insegnamento della logica a Bologna nel XIV secolo*, ed. by Dino Buzzetti, Maurizio Ferriani and Andrea Tabarroni (Bologna: Presso l'Istituto per la storia dell'Università di Bologna, 1992), pp. 165–85 (p. 185). Matthew is quoting from Seneca, *Ep. ad Luc.*, VI. 53, 8–9. Trans. based on Lucius Annaeus Seneca, *Moral Epistles*, trans. by Richard M. Gummere (Cambridge, MA: Harvard University Press, 1917–25), *ad loc.*

Philosophy, a text whose importance in Dante's intellectual formation is declared by the author himself in *Convivio* II. xii. 2, and which is a stable point of reference throughout his entire career.[14] After scorning the Muses, who inspire Boethius' elegiac laments, Lady Philosophy utters the second meter of the *prosimetrum* (which, by the way, starts as a lament itself):

> Heu, quam praecipiti mersa profundo
> mens hebet et propria luce relicta
> tendit in externas ire tenebras
> terrenis quotiens flatibus aucta
> crescit in immensum noxia cura!
> (*Cons. Ph.*, I. m. 2. 1–5)

[Alas, how immersed in a precipitous deep a mind is dull and, forsaking its own light, stretches to go into external darkness, as often as it is enlarged by terrestrial breezes, harmful care arises in immensity!][15]

The thirteenth-century vernacular version provided by master Giandino, as testified by a fourteenth-century manuscript once held in Santa Croce, reads as follows: 'O lasso quanto impegherische [*sic*] la mente afondata nel trabochevole profondo e lassata la propria luce desidera d'andare ne le

---

14   The most extensive survey of the presence of Boethius' *Consolation* in Dante's works is provided by Luca Lombardo, *Boezio in Dante: la 'Consolatio philosophiae' nello scrittoio del poeta* (Venice: Edizioni Ca' Foscari, 2013). For the influential presence of Boethius in both the third cantica of the *Commedia* and the *rime petrose*, see also *The Divine Comedy of Dante Alighieri, 3. Paradiso*, ed. by Robert Durling and Ronald Martinez (Oxford: Oxford University Press, 2011); Durling and Martinez, *Time and the Crystal: Studies in Dante's Rime Petrose* (Berkeley-Oxford: University of California Press, 1990). See also below, n. 20.

15   Anicius Manlius Severinus Boethius, *De Consolatione Philosophiae. Opuscula Theologica*, ed. by Claudio Moreschini, Bibliotheca Scriptorum Graecorum et Romanorum Teubneriana (Munich-Leipzig: De Gruyter–K. G.Saur, 2005). I decided to provide my own, rather literal, translation of passages from the *Consolation*. For this specific passage I kept as a point of reference the translation by Sanderson Beck, available at <http://www.san.beck.org/Boethius1.html> accessed 31 May 2016.

stranie tenebre. Quante volte acresciuta da terreni fiati la nocevole rangola[16] cresce sanza misura' (Laur. Pl. XXIII dext. II, c. 5v).[17] Boethius' situation is very different from that of the unlearned people, who are nonetheless eager to gain knowledge, with whom we had to deal till now, and to which Dante is referring. He is a refined intellectual, whose personal disgrace is causing mental distress. According to Lady Philosophy, Boethius' clouded mind is far from 'light' and is directed towards 'external darkness'. In the glosses by William of Conches on the *Consolation*,[18] which has recently been recognized as a major intermediary source for Dante's appreciation of the Boethian text,[19] 'light' is easily interpreted as discernment (*'intellectus'* and

16   'Rangola' as *cura/sollicitudo* is widely attested in the thirteenth and fourteenth centuries, with both positive and negative meaning: *TLIO–Tesoro della Lingua Italiana delle Origini* <http://tlio.ovi.cnr.it/TLIO>, *sub voce*, accessed 18 June 2016.
17   The marginal Latin glosses at ff. 5v–6r are taken from Trevet's commentary, whilst the interlinear glosses seem to be mainly related to William of Conches' exegesis. This vernacularization, including glosses in books II–IV, has been pointed out by Robert D. Black and Gabriella Pomaro, *La 'Consolazione della Filosofia' nel Medioevo e nel Rinascimento Italiano: Libri di scuola e glosse nei manoscritti fiorentini = Boethius's 'Consolation of Philosophy' in Italian Medieval and Renaissance Education: Schoolbooks and Their Glosses in Florentine Manuscripts* (Florence: Sismel–Edizioni del Galluzzo, 2000), pp. 85–8; Giuseppina Brunetti, 'Guinizzelli, il non più oscuro maestro Giandino e il Boezio di Dante', in *Intorno a Guido Guinizzelli*, Atti della Giornata di studi, Università di Zurigo, 16 giugno 2000, ed. by Luciano Rossi and Sara Alloatti Boller (Alessandria: Edizioni dell'Orso, 2002), pp. 155–91, convincingly identified the author with the Giandino 'master at the *studium*', nominated by Giovanni Villani alongside the Franciscan friar Arlotto da Prato in relation to the death of Charles I of Anjou in January 1285 (1284 in the Florentine tradition).
18   On the commentary tradition of the *Consolation*, see Lodi Nauta, 'The *Consolation*: The Latin Commentary Tradition, 800–1700', in *The Cambridge Companion to Boethius*, ed. by John Marenbon (Cambridge: Cambridge University Press, 2009), pp. 255–78.
19   Lombardo, *Boezio in Dante*, p. 136 and *ad ind*. The circulation and use of William's commentary in late thirteenth-century Florence, and its use by master Giandino in his vernacular glosses on parts of the *Consolation*, has been pointed out by Black and Pomaro, *La 'Consolazione della Filosofia'*, pp. 85–8; see also Brunetti, 'Guinizzelli, il non più oscuro maestro Giandino'. The commentary has been most recently quoted in relation to Dante also by Claudio Giunta, 'Dante: l'amore come destino', in *Dante*

'*ratio*'). Accordingly, darkness represents ignorance, which can be caused by different circumstances:

> MERSA QUAM PRAECIPITI IN PROFUNDO id est ignorantia [...]. TENDIT IRE IN EXTERNAS TENEBRAS id est rerum ignorantias, EXTERNAS id est non naturales. Ignorantia est quaedam per aetatem ut in pueris et in decrepitis; et illa est naturalis, non vitium. Quaedam est per negligentiam, et non naturalis sed externa; et haec mala est. [...] Sed de naturali non est querendum quia non est mala, sed de externa quia vitiosa est. Et ideo dicit Philosophia: RELICTA LUCE TENDIT IN EXTERNAS TENEBRAS. [...] Et hoc contingit QUOTIENS NOXIA CURA CRESCIT IN IMMENSUM. Cura est frequens sollicitudo de aliquo. Et est quaedam noxia, scilicet cura de superfluitate temporalium, quia nocet auferendo curam caelestium. (*Glosae super Boetium*, I. m. 2, ll. 14–38)

> [A MIND IMMERSED IN THE DEEP, i.e. in ignorance [...] STRETCHES TO GO INTO EXTERNAL DARKNESS, i.e. in the ignorance of things, EXTERNAL i.e. unnatural. A type of ignorance can stem from age, like in children and in very old men; that is natural, and it is not a vice. Another type stems from carelessness, and in that case is not natural, but rather external; and this one is bad. [...] But the natural one is not to be investigated, because it is not bad; whilst the external one is to be investigated, because it is vicious. And that is why Lady Philosophy says: FORSAKING ITS OWN LIGHT, STRETCHES TO GO INTO EXTERNAL DARKNESS. [...] Consequently, HARMFUL CARE ARISES IN IMMENSITY. Care is a frequent anxiety about something. And it is harmful, this anxiety about superfluous mundane things, because it causes damage in diverting from thinking about celestial things.][20]

---

the Lyric and Ethical Poet, pp. 119–36, in relation to the overwhelming presence of *Cons. Ph.*, III, m. 9 in *Amor che movi tua vertù dal cielo* (see also Giunta's commentary on this *canzone* in Dante Alighieri, *Opere*, ed. by Santagata, I: *Rime, Vita nova, De vulgari eloquentia*, pp. 384–409); by Paola Nasti, "'Vocabuli d'autore e di scienze e di libri" (*Conv.*, II. xii. 5): percorsi sapienziali di Dante', in *La Bibbia di Dante: esperienza mistica, profezia e teologia biblica in Dante. Atti del convegno internazionale di studi (Ravenna, 7 novembre 2009)* (Ravenna: Centro dantesco dei Frati minori conventuali, 2011), pp. 121–78 (pp. 136–53); and by Bianchi, '"Noli comedere panem philosophorum inutiliter"'.

20 William of Conches, *Glosae super Boetium*, ed. by Lodi Nauta, Corpus Christianorum Continuatio Mediaevalis, 158 (Turnhout: Brepols, 1999). Translations from all Latin commentaries on the *Consolation* are mine.

The reference to 'external darkness' triggers a discussion of different types of ignorance. Whilst some kind of 'natural' ignorance can be caused by age, vicious carelessness draws towards an excessive anxiety about mundane affairs. At the end of a rather tortuous thought, William recognizes that this excessive care for worldly affairs is not just a result, but also a cause of ignorance itself, an impediment to knowledge: 'dum aliquis cura temporalium vel indigentia est oppressus, ad sapientiam tendere non potest' [whilst one is pressured by mundane cares or by poverty, one cannot stretch towards wisdom]. That is why the liberal arts are called as such, 'quia liberum ab omni cura esse oportet qui ad eas accedit' (ll. 67–8, 78–80) [because who approaches them must be free from every preoccupation].

The discussion on the origins of ignorance is further developed in the commentary on the *Consolation* written by the Dominican friar Nicholas Trevet around 1300, one which quickly replaced William's glosses as a reference text for the interpretation of the Boethian work. Despite substantial uncertainties and much debate about the precise date and place of composition of this commentary, the dedicatory letter, which Trevet sent to his fellow-friar Paolo (convincingly identified with the Dominican prior Paolo de' Pilastri) explicitly states that the author was invited by the addressee and by other friars to write it. Trevet dates the origin of this project back to the time when he was moving from the Dominican convent of Pisa to Florence, where he must have spent more or less two years between 1298 and 1300.[21]

---

21 Ruth J. Dean, 'The Dedication of Nicholas Trevet's Commentary on Boethius', *Studies in Philology*, 13 (1966), 593–603. On the chronological problems, which emerge from Trevet's account, see Brian S. Donaghey, 'Nicholas Trevet's Use of King Alfred's Translation of Boethius, and the Dating of His Commentary', in *The Medieval Boethius: Studies in the Vernacular Translations of 'De Consolatione Philosophiae'*, ed. by Alastair J. Minnis (Cambridge–Wolfeboro, NH: D. S. Brewer, 1987), pp. 1–31. Giuseppe Billanovich, *La tradizione del testo di Livio e le origini dell'umanesimo: I. Tradizione e fortuna di Livio tra Medioevo e Umanesimo* (Padua: Antenore, 1981), pp. 34–40, tentatively identified Paolo with Paolo da Perugia. However, the identification with the prominent Dominican friar Paolo de' Pilastri is currently considered as more plausible: see Thomas Kaeppeli, *Scriptores Ordinis Praedicatorum Medii Aevi* (Rome: ad S. Sabinae, 1970), *sub voce*, and Emilio Panella, 'Priori di Santa Maria Novella di Firenze 1221–1325', *Memorie Domenicane*, 17 (1986), 253–84. See also

Since in 1304 Trevet quotes his Boethian commentary in a *Quodlibet*,[22] at least part of it must have been completed by that date. Even though it is not possible to locate the composition of this work entirely in Florence – where, according to his own account, Trevet procrastinated the task, at least for a while, and devoted himself to teaching – it can be safely stated that the commentary dates back to the very first years of the fourteenth century, and that it was conceived in Tuscany. Trevet was urged by the Dominican friars, who had a precise interest in Boethius' *Consolation* as a source of consolation and moral teaching. Interestingly, this is the same approach to the *Consolation*, which emerges from Dante's account in the *Convivio*.[23] Finally, Trevet mentions difficulties in finding a copy of the *Consolation*: scholars tend to straightforwardly refer this shortage to Florence, and to connect it to Dante's statement about the *prosimetrum* being 'not known to many' in *Conv.*, II. xii. 2.[24] That Trevet was referring to Florence certainly

---

Giuseppe Billanovich, 'Il testo di Livio. Da Roma a Padova, a Avignone, a Oxford', *Italia medioevale e umanistica*, 32 (1989), 53–99 (pp. 87–93).

22 Dean, 'The Dedication of Nicholas Trevet's Commentary on Boethius', pp. 598–9.

23 Lombardo, *Boezio in Dante*, states that, for Dante, 'l'approccio sul piano letterario è l'impulso da cui scaturisce anche l'adesione al modello etico-filosofico (e non viceversa)' (p. 530); further on: 'a spingerlo in direzione del libro di Boezio era stata l'urgenza di trovare alla propria ricerca letteraria una risposta che fosse stilisticamente consona alla rappresentazione del dolore e non l'amore per la filosofia' (p. 530, f. 3). My reading of the *Convivio*'s account is quite the opposite: Dante's approach to Boethius and to Cicero's *De amicitia* is urged by a search for a solution to an existential crisis caused by the death of Beatrice. Of course, these personal (in wide terms, 'philosophical') concerns cannot be artificially separated from the development of his own poetics, one which, by the way, is always strongly connected to existential, political, theological issues.

24 For example, most recently, Luca Lombardo, '"Quasi come sognando". Dante e la presunta rarità del "libro di Boezio" (*Convivio* II xii 2–7)', *Mediaeval Sophia. Studi e ricerche sui saperi medievali*, 12 (July–December 2012), 141–52; G. Brunetti, 'Guinizzelli, il non più oscuro maestro Giandino', p. 168. Dante's disputed passage has been fruitfully discussed also by Thomas Ricklin, '"[...] quello non conosciuto da molti libro di Boezio". Hinweise zur "Consolatio Philosophiae" in Norditalien', in *Boethius in the Middle Ages: Latin and Vernacular Traditions of the Consolatio Philosophiae*, ed. by Maarten J. F. M. Hoenen and Lodi Nauta (Leiden: Brill, 1997), pp. 267–86; Robert D. Black, 'Boethius's *Consolation of Philosophy*' in *Italian Renaissance Education*', in

is the most economic hypothesis, but this cannot be incontrovertibly demonstrated. Furthermore, if that was the case, these difficulties must be first of all referred to the Dominican house of Santa Maria Novella, which in those years sold a substantial part of its library to finance a new building for its school.[25] Finally, Trevet certainly searched not for a random copy, but for one with the commentary by William of Conches, which is the basis of his work. Missing data and uncertainties in the interpretation of Trevet's account prevent us from establishing any kind of straightforward connection between Dante and the Dominican friar. However, Trevet's presence in Florence at the end of the 1290s, when Dante was an active member of the Florentine intellectual and civic community, certainly bears some interest.[26] Moreover, Trevet's 'Tuscan' project of commenting the Boethian *prosimetrum* provides further evidence of a widespread interest in the *Consolation* in late Duecento Tuscany, which involved laymen as Dante as well as friars, and saw a proliferation in fourteenth-century production of copies and vernacularizations, and its adoption as a text in grammar schools.[27] Finally, Trevet's profile as a Dominican bachelor,

---

Black and Pomaro, *La 'Consolazione della Filosofia' nel Medioevo e nel Rinascimento Italiano*, pp. 1–50; Nasti, '"Vocabuli d'autore e di scienze e di libri"', pp. 139–43. On the manuscript tradition of this work, see also Paola Nasti, 'Storia materiale di un classico dantesco: la "Consolatio Philosophiae" fra XII e XIV secolo: tradizione manoscritta e rielaborazioni esegetiche', *Dante Studies, with the Annual Report of the Dante Society*, 134 (2016), pp. 142–68.

25 Charles T. Davis, 'Education in Dante's Florence', *Speculum*, 40 (1965), 415–35 (p. 427). For the Dominican library and Trevet's letter, see Anna Pegoretti, 'Lo "studium" e la biblioteca di Santa Maria Novella nel Duecento e nei primi anni del Trecento', in *The Dominicans and the Making of Florentine Cultural Identity: Influences and Interactions between Santa Maria Novella and the Commune of Florence (1293–1313)*, ed. by Elisa Brilli, Johannes Bartuschat, Delphine Faivre-Carron, *Reti Medievali*, forthcoming 2018.

26 Charles T. Davis, 'Ptolemy of Lucca and the Roman Republic', *Proceedings of the American Philosophical Society*, 118 (1974), 30–50, is sceptical about a possible encounter between the two (p. 38).

27 For an excellent overview of the reception of the *Consolation* in Renaissance Italy, see Dario Brancato 'Readers and Interpreters of the "Consolatio" in Italy, 1300–1550', in *A Companion to Boethius in the Middle Ages*, ed. by Noel H. Kaylor and Philip E. Phillips

deeply involved both in his Order's defence of Aquinas' teachings on key theological and philosophical issues, and in the exegesis of a prominent text of the Neoplatonic tradition such as the *Consolation*, is an outstanding example from which to look at the Scholastic reception of the Boethian text, and at the extreme complexity which characterizes the theological and philosophical debate of the time.[28]

This is how Trevet comments the beginning of the second meter of the *Consolation*:

> QUAM PRECIPITI PROFUNDO, id est sollicitudine rerum temporalium qua homo ab altitudine dignitatis precipitatur ad ea que sub se sunt. [...] ET RELICTA LUCE PROPRIA, id est luce intellectus sui que est sapiencia TENDIT IRE IN EXTERNAS TENEBRAS, id est ignorancias. Et dicit signanter EXTERNAS. Quamquam enim in iuvene vel decrepito sint naturales et ideo *interne* quia ex naturali defectu contingunt. Tamen in aliis, in quibus contingunt ex neglicencia eo quod sollicitantur circa alia, dicuntur *externe*, eo quod sunt contra istam naturam de qua dicit Philosophus *in principio Metaphysice*: 'omnes homines natura scire desiderant'. Et quasi respondens antipophore, quia posset aliquis querere unde et quando provenit talis perturbacio, subiungit quod QUOCIENS CURA, id est sollicitudo temporalium; NOXIA quia nocet homini, *impediendo* eum a maiori bono. (*Expositio*, pp. 41-2)[29]

> [IMMERSED IN THE DEEP OF THE RUINED, i.e. in the anxiety about mundane things, that precipitates man from the highness of dignity to those things that are below him. [...] FORSAKING ITS OWN LIGHT, i.e. the light of his discernment that is wisdom STRETCHES TO GO INTO EXTERNAL DARKNESS, i.e. into ignorance. And it expressly says EXTERNAL. Even though in young or very old men they *(tenebrae)* are natural and therefore internal, because they stem from a natural shortcoming, nonetheless in others – in which they stem from carelessness, because men are anxious about other things – they are called external, and that is why they are contrary to that natural disposition about which talks the Philosopher at the beginning of *Metaphysics*: 'all

---

(Leiden: Brill, 2012), pp. 357–411. See also Black and Pomaro, *La 'Consolazione della Filosofia' nel Medioevo e nel Rinascimento Italiano*.

28 See, most notably, Lodi Nauta, 'The Scholastic Context of the Boethius Commentary by Nicholas Trevet', in *Boethius in the Middle Ages*, pp. 41–67.

29 *Nicholas Trevet on Boethius. Expositio Fratris Nicolai Trevethii Anglici Ordinis Praedicatorum super Boecio De Consolacione*, typescript of unfinished ed. by Edmund T. Silk, <http://campuspress.yale.edu/trevet/> accessed 29 May 2016. Italics are mine.

men by nature desire to know'. And – as replying in an anthypophora-like form so that someone could ask from where and when this perturbation comes – it adds AS OFTEN AS CARE, i.e. anxiety about mundane affairs, because it harms man, impeding him from (reaching) a higher good].

In his reading of the 'precipitous deep' in which the mind is immersed, Trevet – going back to Carolingian exegesis[30] – glosses it as mundane anxiety. Age, identified by William as a natural cause, is clearly pointed out as an 'internal' obstacle, whilst carelessness, due to an excessive attention to earthly affairs, is considered as an external cause of the character's distress, an obstacle. What is more, Trevet identifies obstacles as impediments, which undermine the natural inclination described by Aristotle. The discussion on the causes of Boethius' temporary 'ignorance' and anguish is reframed in the Scholastic schema of the *impedimenta*, with a precise reference to the incipit of *Metaphysics*. This is a remarkable passage, which contextualizes the Boethian *Philosophia-Sapientia* in the Aristotelian discourse on the acquisition of knowledge, in a way which is hard to overlook in relation to Dante's project to disseminate wisdom and to overcome some of the limitations to learning.

---

30 *Saeculi noni auctoris in Boetii Consolationem Philosophiae Commentarius*, ed. by Edmund T. Silk (Rome: American Academy in Rome, 1935), pp. 18–19: 'Praecipitem profundum curas et cupiditates huius saeculi vocat, quia demergunt fautores suos in interitum, quia videlicet tantus et tam doctus homo in tantam potuit decidere pertubationem'. Different is the interpretation of 'IRE IN TENEBRAS, id est saeculi perturbationes'.

Removing the Impediments

Whilst the theme of the impediments to knowledge was widespread, the idea of removing them is peculiar to Dante. Actually, this is the striking move, which makes the whole enterprise of the *Convivio* possible.[31] To this end, the author carefully distinguishes between those impediments that can be overcome – the 'external' ones – and those that cannot.[32] The groundbreaking novelty of such an agenda can hardly be overestimated, and a search for precise sources would be pointless. Most notably, Giacomo da Pistoia in his *Quaestio de felicitate* dedicated to Cavalcanti, talks about 'amovere impedimenta quae retrahunt hominem a veritatis speculatione' (l. 219) [removing the impediments, which divert man from the investigation of truth].[33] These impediments, however, very much pertain to one's own body and mind. Even the excessive care for earthly goods is reduced to inordinate feelings, for which the subject himself has to take responsibility, to conclude that 'oportet amovere et detruncare sive regulare in passionibus venereorum, cibi et potus, in passionibus irae et divitiarum affectionibus' (ll. 254–6) [it is necessary to remove from and detach or regulate oneself in love passions, in eating and drinking, in hatred and passion for richness].

Trevet's commentary on Boethius' *Consolation of Philosophy* can perhaps provide an ideological framework and a language within which we can reconsider Dante's ambitious task. At the end of the prose chapter, which

---

31 Francis Cheneval, Introduction to Dante Alighieri, *Das Gastmahl*, I: *Erstes Buch*, pp. li–lii, Francis Cheneval, 'Dante Alighieri, "Convivio"', in *Interpretationen. Hauptwerke der Philosophie. Mittelalter*, ed. by Kurt Flasch (Stuttgart: Reclam, 1998), pp. 352–79 (p. 354). A profound reflection on the Aristotelian premises of Dante's 'ideology of dissemination' is in Gentili, *L'uomo aristotelico*, pp. 127–65.
32 Fioravanti, 'Desiderio e limite', p. 15.
33 Iacobi de Pistorio 'Quaestio de felicitate', in Irene Zavattero, 'La "Quaestio de felicitate" di Giacomo da Pistoia: un tentativo di interpretazione alla luce di una nuova lettura critica del testo', in *Le felicità nel Medioevo. Atti del convegno della Società Italiana per lo Studio del Pensiero Medievale (S.I.S.P.M.), Milano, 12–13 Settembre 2003*, ed. by Maria Bettetini and Francesco D. Paparella (Louvain-la-Neuve: FIDEM, 2005), pp. 355–409 (pp. 395–409).

follows the second meter of the *Consolation*, Lady Philosophy actively removes the gloom that beclouds Boethius' eyes and mind:

> Sui paulisper oblitus est; recordabitur facile, si quidem nos ante cognoverit; quod ut possit, paulisper lumina eius mortalium rerum nube caligantia tergamus. Haec dixit oculosque meos fletibus undantes contracta in rugam veste siccavit. (*Cons. Ph.* I. pr. 2, 6)

> [He has forgotten himself for a while; he will remember easily, if indeed he knew us before; and so that he could, we will for a short time wipe his eyes from the cloudy fogginess of mortal things. She spoke and, with her dress gathered in a fold, she dried my eyes, which were flowing with tears.]

The following meter celebrates the recovering of sight: 'Tunc me discussa liquerunt nocte tenebrae / luminibusque prior rediit vigor' [Then the gloom of night was scattered, / and the prior vigor returned unto my eyes].[34] Lady Philosophy's 'liberation' of Boethius from the mist, which was confusing him, is interpreted by Trevet as follows: 'cum (Philosophia) dicit QUOD UT POSSIT removet impedimentum illius curacionis. Impedimentum autem curacionis fuit ignorancia philosophiae' (*Expositio*, p. 58) [When (Lady Philosophy) says SO THAT HE COULD, she removes the impediment represented by his anxiety. Indeed, the impediment of anxiety was the ignorance of philosophy]. And, on meter 3: 'Postquam Philosophia amovit a Boecio impedimentum cognicionis philosophice, hic docet quomodo eam cognovit' (p. 60) [After having removed the impediment to philosophical knowledge from Boethius, Lady Philosophy teaches him how to recognize her]. The impediment represented by mundane preoccupations, which were previously symbolized by the deep in which the mind had fallen, eventually coincides with the mist that darkens Boethius' eyes. After having painstakingly developed a word-by-word exegesis, Trevet reaches a rather simple conclusion. According to a line of reasoning perfectly consistent with the Boethian text, the mist ultimately is the ignorance of Philosophy, the inability to recognize her, one which leads to (and at the same time

---

34 See the translation by Giandino: 'Allora le tenebre mi lassaro discorsa la notte Et lo primo vigore tornò a' miei lumi' (Laur. Plut. XXIII dex. 11, c. 6r).

is caused by) an excessive care for mundane things: a vicious circle that cannot but foster the character's distress. What is particularly interesting, however, is that Trevet's gloss on Lady Philosophy dissolving the mist provides us with a unique example of an active removal of what is defined as an impediment to philosophical knowledge.

Previous Tuscan texts heavily influenced by the *Consolation* can offer a useful term of comparison, as well as allow a wider survey of the Boethian tradition available to Dante. In the *Elegy* by Henry of Settimello, the intervention of Phronesis in book 3 is very much diluted in a long series of more or less generic exhortations. In his *Libro de vizii e delle virtudi*, Bono Giamboni interestingly concentrates on the second meter exclusively with regards to lines from six onwards. Later on, the mist to be removed by Lady Philosophy is described as a 'sozzura puzzolente di cose terrene, che mi teneano tutto il capo gravato' (III. 1–2) [smelly filth of mundane things, that pushed my head down].[35] A further explanation of these mundane things identifies them in Bono's loose of 'le ricchezze e la gloria del mondo e' beni della Ventura' [richness and mundane glory and goods of fortune]. Richness and goods which Philosophy defines as 'impedimento molto grande di venire al detto fine' (v. 6) [very great impediment to reach the goal]. This occurrence of 'impedimento' is undoubtedly tempting. However, a closer analysis actually reveals the generic quality of Bono's perspective, according to which mundane richness and glory simply are an obstacle to the acquisition of a virtuous, impassible demeanour. Trevet's word-by-word commentary integrates in a more specific way the Scholastic discussion on the impediments that limit Aristotle's statement within the highly symbolic picture of Boethius' distress and Lady Philosophy's intervention. In a conscious way or not, this peculiar mix ends up in the image of the removal of the impediments.

Of course, it is difficult to consider Trevet's exegesis as a direct source for Dante's profound ethical commitment and ideological challenge, not least because what the Dominican friar defines as *sollicitudo* ultimately is an internal condition of the subject. However, it would not

---

35   Bono Giamboni, *Il libro de vizii e delle virtudi e il Trattato di virtù e di vizii*, ed. by Cesare Segre (Turin: Giulio Einaudi, 1968) (my translation).

be too inappropriate to take it as a possible source of inspiration, and, most notably, as a primary example of syncretism, which combines the Scholastic language of the impediments, and the sapiential and allegorical domain of Boethian *Consolation*. The analysis of the impediments as they are described by Dante in the *Convivio* in the light of the reception of the Boethian text in the Middle Ages, reveals an unexpected convergence between the long-lasting theme of the obstacles to knowledge and the Scholastic discussion on the inexorable limitations to the universal desire of knowledge proclaimed by Aristotle's *Metaphysics*. Moreover, it offers a unique image of a removal of the impediments to philosophical cognition. Whilst any contact between Dante and Trevet remains in the domain of the non-demonstrable hypotheses, our discussion has provided a further tessera that can be added to the mosaic of Dante's intellectual milieu, one in which the growing interest for the *Consolation of Philosophy* could react with the technical language of Scholasticism and nourish the debate on the universality of knowledge. Finally, the possible Boethian nature of Dante's discussion of the impediments delimits the supposed Aristotelian character of the opening chapter of the *Convivio*, and points out its profound syncretism, which – as Barański pointed out on the basis of a substantial bibliography – blends different traditions.[36]

---

[36] See the chapter by Zygmunt G. Barański in this volume. On syncretism as a key category to understand Dante's thought, see Barański, 'La vocazione enciclopedica'; Simon A. Gilson, 'Sincretismo e scolastica in Dante', *Studi e problemi di critica testuale*, 90 (2): *Dante. Per Emilio Pasquini* (2015), 317–39.

FRANZISKA MEIER

5 'Questa sarà luce nuova, sole nuovo': Dante and the Vernacular in *Convivio* I

'This shall be a new light, a new sun': the wording taken from the last sentence in Dante's first treatise of the *Convivio* is often quoted as the utmost expression of the poet's appreciation of the vernacular. Yet, strangely enough, those interested in Dante's thought about language are not at ease with what else the poet has to say here. There is a contradiction at the very beginning of Dante's vernacular commentary to his poetry which continues to perplex scholars: while, on the one hand, Dante strongly supports the unchallenged superiority of Latin, on the other hand, he insists that the vernacular possesses outstanding and highly promising qualities. What is more, as the quotation above shows, he does this in words, as well as in deeds, daring to write a philosophical treatise in the vernacular and explicitly referring his reader to his second post-exile work *De vulgari eloquentia*, which overtly celebrates the *volgare*.

In 1965 Cecil Grayson reflected on multiple attempts to make sense of Dante's contradicting views. Having thoroughly analysed Dante's assertions in the two unfinished treatises, he concludes that 'the contradiction lies with *Conv.*, I., which must have been written before he evolved such a theory about language or, having evolved it about human virtue, applied it to language'.[1] With a slightly different take Raffaele Pinto would later come to a similar conclusion: Dante's grappling with 'grammatica' starts from a strong feeling of the existing medieval *diglossia* which, for the

---

1 Cecil Grayson, '"Nobilior est vulgaris". Latin and Vernacular in Dante's Thought', *Centenary Essays on Dante* (Oxford: Members of Oxford Dante Society, 1965), pp. 54–76, esp. p. 76.

vernacular-speakers, went along with a sense of inferiority.[2] From the *Vita nova* to the *Commedia*, according to Pinto, Dante gradually overcomes the inherited dichotomy and ends up praising the vernacular. Pinto places the two treatises in an intermediate phase of this development. Whereas the *Convivio* continues to share the earlier conviction of Latin's uncontroversial nobility, *De vulgari eloquentia* unfolds Dante's uncompromising devotion to the cause of the vernacular. Both Grayson and Pinto are convinced that the *Convivio*, in particular this first part, dates back to a period in which Dante remains doubtful about what to expect of the vernacular.

Since in the first part of the *Convivio* the superiority of Latin is both asserted and implicitly denied, this assessment is rather perplexing.[3] It is strange that it occurred neither to Grayson nor to Pinto to ask whether Dante was or would become aware of what appears to be contradictory, if not self-contradictory within the first treatise; to be more precise: whether in Dante's view the claims scattered across *Convivio* I actually contradict each other at all. Thus, instead of comparing and contrasting the two unfinished treatises once more, this article takes a different approach and concentrates on the *Convivio*'s first part. By engaging in a close reading of the elaborate defence of the mother tongue, it intends to find out more about the strategies which Dante might have had in mind when characterizing and staging his particular relationship with the vernacular and about how that which seems to be inconsistent may have been rooted in his specific expectations and hopes.

Dante's plea underlines a tension: on the one hand a high-pitched emotionality pervades his defence, on the other, the author is keen on displaying strong philosophical argumentation, that is, thoroughly rational

---

2   Raffaele Pinto, 'La Grammatica in Dante', *Quaderns d'Italia*, 18 (2013), 15–44.
3   Within his analysis of Dante's varied strategies of building an authoritative stance the contradictions are of minor interest. According to Albert Russel Ascoli 'What *Convivio* does obliquely, as a defensive digression subordinate to its primary mission of divulgative education and without ever *explicitly* claiming that the vernacular might aspire to the authoritative status of a *grammatica* in its own right, [...] *De vulgari eloquentia* does overtly and as its central concern', *Dante and the Making of a Modern Author* (Cambridge: Cambridge University Press, 2011), p. 133.

reasoning. The tension is best discerned in the twelfth chapter, in which Dante focuses on what he calls a 'perfettissimo amore'. Instead of starting with what makes his love of the vernacular a 'perfettissimo amore', he actually indulges in a somewhat aggressive and perplexing outburst.[4] Who is more deserving of ridicule: the one who asks if smoke issuing from a house indicates a fire within, or the one who answers yes? (*Conv.*, I. xii. 1) By using a *topos* which was very common at that time,[5] Dante may have wanted to make his natural love for the vernacular appear self-evident. However, the emotionality of the digression remains puzzling. Dante seems to be obsessed with describing his love not only as something spontaneous and natural, but also as the effect of a cause. In contrast to Augustine, who in the second book of *De doctrina christiana* uses this very comparison to explain the difference between natural and conventional signs, for Dante only the causal nexus appears to matter: it transforms his natural love into an effect of the vernacular's virtue. The image of the smoke-issued-by-fire conveys an inescapable necessity to the relationship which is conceived of in terms of causality. Hence Dante, while showing off his rational approach and philosophical sophistication, transforms his highly effective and passionate relations to his mother tongue into something rationally evident.

It is generally accepted that Dante describes his relationships following the precepts of classical friendship. According to Emilio Pasquini's entry in the *Enciclopedia dantesca*, the topic of friendship and the ideal of a friend may even be called the hidden Leitmotif of the *Convivio*. Pasquini is convinced that the bits scattered across the four parts of the treatise amount to a small treatise on friendship, though they are, he concedes, always and only used in a metaphorical way. They serve to illustrate the relation

---

4 Maria Corti, conversely, finds the smoke-and-fire metaphor framing Dante's love for the vernacular beautiful and charming: 'La scenetta francamente è deliziosa'. 'Nascita, crescita e morte di un'allegoria', *Scritti su Cavalcanti e Dante* (Turin: Einaudi, 2003), pp. 95–116, esp. p. 95.

5 See concerning the *topos* and Dante's use of it. Zygmunt G. Barański, 'Dante's Signs: An Introduction to Medieval Semiotics and Dante', in *Dante and the Middle Ages: Literary and Historical Essays*, ed. by John C. Barnes (Dublin: Irish Academic Press, 1995), pp. 139–80, esp. p. 139.

between the commentary and the poetry, between Romance languages or the concept of philosophy itself.[6] In other words, the *Convivio* has a stake in friends and friendship, but never for their own sake. Inspired by Dante's own confession of having read Cicero's *Laelius* and Aristotle's *Ethics*, Paolo Falzone, in 2000, underscored the extent to which Dante's representation of friendship in the *Convivio* relies on these two ancient authors. He was the first to highlight that Dante does not only model his love of philosophy along the lines of classical friendship, but also his love of the vernacular. As for Falzone, Dante in the first treatise mainly leaned on Cicero's eclectic notions of the perfect friendship whereas from the second treatise onwards the *Convivio* reveals an increasingly more specified knowledge of book VIII and IX in Aristotle's *Ethics*.[7] It is striking, however, that research on friendship does not usually consider its closeness to love.[8] Among the few researchers who do so is Jerome Mazzaro who sees Dante permanently locked in battle with the issue of 'fin amour'. While primarily concerned with the *Commedia*, he holds that the *Convivio* 'acts as Dante's bridge from *fin amour* in the early lyrics and the *Vita nova* to the "disposition toward a certain mystical mode of feeling" that readers later encounter'.[9] The first post-exile project, for Mazzaro, marks a decisive

---

6   Emilio Pasquini, 'Amico', *Enciclopedia dantesca*, ed. by U. Bosco *et al.*, 5 vols + appendix (Rome: Istituto dell'Enciclopedia Italiana, 1970–8) I, 203–9 (p. 204).
7   According to Paolo Falzone, this may be grasped in Dante's dealing with 'benevolenza' or in the fact that Dante, in the first treatise, does not list the three forms of friendship distinguished by the Greek philosopher. He explores the distinction only in the eleventh chapter of the third treatise. 'Il *Convivio* e l'amicizia secondo i filosofi', *Annali dell'Istituto Italiano per gli Studi Storici*, 17 (2000), 55–101.
8   In a recent article Teodolinda Barolini pointed out the range of meanings which the word 'amico' assumes in Dante's works. In her view the poem *Guido i'vorrei* may already be considered as the 'lyric incarnation of the Aristotelian and Ciceronian ideal of the friend as an other self'. From then on, he takes friendship as 'a subset of love' according to Aristotle's *Ethics*. '*Amicus eius*: Dante and the Semantics of Friendship', *Dante Studies*, 133 (2015), 46–69 (pp. 53–5).
9   See Jerome Mazzaro, 'From *Fin Amour* to Friendship: Dante's Transformation', in *The Old Daunce. Love, Friendship, Sex & Marriage in the Medieval World*, ed. by Robert R. Edwards and Stephen Spector (New York: State University of New York Press, 1991), pp. 121–37 (p. 126). Concerning the *Convivio*, Francesco Ciabattoni takes a

step in Dante's endeavour to rid love of corporeal aspects. Hence, if Dante describes his natural love of the vernacular in terms of friendship, his hope may have been to tame the troubling legacy of his earlier notion of love.

On closer inspection, however, it is far from clear whether Dante really intended to replace his love in the vernacular sense with virtuous friendship in the philosophical sense. Having justified why the vernacular matches the purposes of a commentary to his *canzoni* more appropriately than Latin could, he starts with the specific nature of his love which, in common with all forms of natural love, moves:

> [...] l'amatore a tre cose: l'una si è magnificare l'amato; l'altra è ad esser geloso di quello; l'altra è a defendere lui. (*Conv.*, I. x. 6)
>
> [[...] the lover to do three things: first, to magnify the loved object; second, to be jealous for it; next, to defend it.]

Dante again sticks as much as possible to abstract philosophical terminology. The terms 'amatore' and 'amato' refer to neutral objects. Yet the adjective 'geloso' is reminiscent of vernacular love poetry and hence of Dante's previous ideas about what the vernacular is supposed to convey. As a result, this first definition draws his relationship to his mother tongue nearer to a courtly kind of love between an active idolizer and a passive beloved. In other words, the defence may prove to be interspersed with remnants typical of love poetry passing from the praise of a lady to moments of jealousy and, finally, to standing up in her defence.[10]

That such a reading is not too far-fetched may be deduced from the subsequent polemical representation of the vernacular's enemies. While

---

> similar stand: 'In the *Convivio*, allegorical friendship with Lady Philosophy supplants Dante's love for Beatrice Portinari [...] The *Convivio*, however, was left unfinished', in 'Dante's Rhetoric of Friendship From the *Convivio* to the *Commedia*', in *Friendship and Sociability in Premodern Europe: Contexts, Concepts, and Expressions*, ed. by Amyrose McCue Gill and Sarah Rolfe Prodan (Toronto: Centre for Reformation and Renaissance Studies, 2014), pp. 97–123 (esp. p. 118).

10 The same procedure can be seen in Dante's assertions about how *fama* is born in the mind of a friend who has the proclivity to love and therefore magnify the other's merits (*Conv.*, I. iii. 7–8).

Dante seems to revere the vernacular like a lady whom he loves and defends, his adversaries' use of language is described namely in terms of prostitution and adultery. This applies to their use of Latin as well as of the vernacular. In the ninth chapter he deplores their whoredom of Latin (*Conv.*, I. ix. 5); at the end of the eleventh chapter he bemoans the humiliating effect which their misuse would have on his precious mother tongue. (*Conv.*, I. xi. 21) Thus, as far as metaphors are concerned, Dante's philosophical reasoning on the vernacular remains strongly linked to his former love imagery, while concomitantly being subverted by it.

As soon as Dante starts to explain why his love is to be called a 'perfettissimo amore', his presentation faithfully replicates the ancient philosophers' notion of friendship. Slipping into Cicero's shoes, Dante is eager to distinguish his own from the two lower forms of friendship. Hence, his is not based on mutual utility. He does not even concede that utility might have caused the burgeoning of friendship.[11] On the contrary, the defence is a distinct testimony to his ambition never to treat the *volgare* as a ready-to-use instrument nor as a language to be described or assessed. While articulating his mother tongue, the verb 'usare'[12] is conspicuous by its absence; only its enemies seem to indulge in using and abusing language. Still following Cicero's lead, Dante is at pains to dispel any suspicion that his friendship may have sprung out of a lack.[13] This seems to have been the very reason why he is so keen to emphasize that he is merely unveiling the natural beauty of the vernacular – a statement which resolutely contradicts the subsequent position in this regard (*Conv.*, I. x. 13). Finally, Dante rejects the idea that his friendship may stem from the pleasure of mutual company. While he admits that the pleasure is adjunct since the goodness is, by its own nature, delightful and lovable, there is, in both Dante and Cicero, only one true friendship: that based on the reciprocal appeal of virtue.

---

11 See also Cicero, *Laelius*, 51.
12 Though the vernacular, in contrast to Latin, is said to follow the 'uso', Dante only once yields to the word 'usato' in its regard; and this occurs only when in the service of proving his familiarity with the vernacular. (*Conv.*, I. xiii. 8)
13 This is an important issue in Cicero, *Laelius*, 27.

How then do the two depictions of his relation in chapters X and XI connect? Does the evocation of courtly love only pay tribute to Cicero's statement about the etymological provenience of 'amicitia' from 'amare'?[14] Or is the confusion between love and friendship simply due to the difficulties which Latin translators encountered in attempting to transcribe the Greek word 'philia'? Along with Aristotle's medieval commentators they dither between love, charity and friendship.[15] While in the *Nicomachean Ethics* the notions tend to be interchangeable, they require a clear boundary which neatly distinguishes or specifies 'charity' or 'love of God' once they are adapted to Christian or theological premises. Moreover, the semantic complications could not help increasing under the pressure of emerging vernacular poetry whose crucial medieval concept of love Dante had grown up with yet is a concept which is completely absent in the ancients. It is hard to believe that the poet was not aware of the implications which the notions of love and friendship would set off in his readers' minds. The same kind of confusion, as is well documented, actually lingers around his *canzoni d'amore* in which many readers apparently had failed to grasp the expression of the most perfect form of love in the sense of friendship.

A further complex issue arises. Dante usually speaks of the vernacular as 'la loquela', a feminine noun meaning spoken language. This sits well with his emphasis of the female origins of the vernacular, whereby a child acquires language through the murmuring and singing of nurses and women.[16] In the first definition, however, he starts with a neutral form: 'l'amato', which in Italian is masculine, and, then, goes on to substituting 'la loquela' with the masculine term 'volgare'. Twice in this chapter he writes 'amico'. These masculine forms hardly fit into the frame of a chivalric love

---

14 *Laelius*, 26: 'Amor enim, ex quo amicitia nominata est, princeps est ad benevolentiam coniungendam'. This etymology copied by Isidor of Seville will be widely diffused in the Middle Ages. See the medieval issue with the terms' confusion Anita Guerreau-Jalabert, 'Amour et amitié dans la société médiévale: Jalons pour une analyse lexicale et sémantique', in *Splendor reginae: passions, genre et famille; mélanges en l'honneur de Régine Le Jan*, ed. by Laurent Jégou (Turnhout: Brepols, 2015), pp. 281–9.
15 See Ciabattoni, 'Dante's Rhetoric of Friendship', p. 100.
16 See *De vulgari eloquentia* I. i. 2.

which Dante has evoked. Thus, phrases such as 'geloso di lui' [jealous for it] (*Conv.*, I. x. 10) and the repetitive use of 'amore' sound puzzling. Does switching from the feminine 'loquela' to its masculine alternatives derive from the philosophical jargon in which Dante clothes his explanations? Was it meant to keep the reader's mind away from any implied love imagery? Why then does Dante turn back to feminizing language in addressing the perfect friendship, that is, a form which, notably in Cicero and also in early medieval attempts to adopt the classical notion to Christian ends, is almost exclusively a male domain?[17] Evidently, Dante's gendering of mother tongue articles and pronouns contrast with the respective framework either of love or of friendship.

Can we really imagine that this cross-gendering[18] might fashion the vernacular into a kind of androgynous being? Is it all about pitching the vernacular against a male-dominated Latin? Or could Dante be hinting at something else, that is, at raising the vernacular above its female origins in his prose writing? Such a reading, however, would be at odds with the very specifically gendered examples which Dante gives in the same twelfth chapter when glossing the Aristotelian conception of goodness.[19] In any case, it becomes clear that cross-gendering has not occurred by chance when it makes a fascinating second appearance in the already quoted last sentence of the first treatise: 'luce nuova, sole nuovo'. Here, the nouns – first feminine and then masculine – are bound together, separated by a comma.

---

17 Aristotle actually took into account the relation between man and wife which may grow into a friendship. But this aspect is mostly ignored by Roman philosophers. In subsequent Christian versions forms of spiritual friendship can exist between the sexes but only on the condition that a great physical distance is maintained. See Reginald Hyatte's overview in *The Arts of Friendship: The Idealization of Friendship in Medieval and Early Renaissance Literature* (Leiden: Brill, 1994), pp. 43–86.

18 The aspect of cross-gendering has been studied, most of all in the *Commedia*, by Jeffrey T. Schnapp, 'Dante's Sexual Solecisms: Gender and Genre in the *Commedia*', *Romanic Review*, 79 (1988), 143–63, and Carolynn Lund-Mead, 'Dante and Androgyny', in *Dante. Contemporary Perspectives*, ed. by Amilare A. Iannucci (Toronto: University of Toronto Press, 1997), pp. 195–213.

19 See I. xii. 8: 'sì come ne la maschiezza essere ben barbuto, e nella femminezza essere ben pulita di barba in tutta la faccia'.

Did Dante opt for cross-gendering because he was looking for something irritating and challenging in order to shake the reader off a well-trod path? To put it blatantly: could we understand the cross-gendering as a signal that Dante was not speaking about love or about friendship at all? Could we possibly infer that it reflects his concerns with language in a deeper way?

Dante's way of describing his relations to his mother tongue and to philosophy look almost identical. There is, however, a significant difference, that cannot simply be deduced from his gleaning more from Cicero than from Aristotle.[20] Even if the descriptive terms which Dante chooses tend to make his mother tongue very similar to an animate, if not a human being, he avoids addressing it as a person or fashioning it as a personification. This is a treatment he obviously reserves for philosophy. Hence picturing the vernacular as a friend does not correspond to any classical notion at all. Nonetheless, Dante applies it to his love for a vernacular which is somewhere between the abstract and the material. In the twelfth and thirteenth chapters when he describes how and why he became the vernacular's friend, he states 'io sono fatto a lei amico' – this is a phrase which will reappear, much later, with regard to Philosophy (*Conv.*, IV. i. 3).

Yet Dante must have somehow been conscious of the extent to which his presentation departs from the classical requirement of two animate and rational beings. We garner this from the passage on propinquity, where he immediately passes from the closest relationship, to be the next-of-kin, to the arts which are closest to their respective craftsman, to the land where a man lives, ending with the language which is the first to be embedded in a child's mind. (*Conv.*, I. xii. 4–5) Thus, from the outset, Dante intentionally projects the multiple forms of propinquity, as specified in the classical theory of friendship, onto relations between people and inanimate objects.

---

20   See Falzone's telling expressions: 'L'estensione del medesimo schema argomentativo al sapere filosofico […] riesce operazione meno astratta della precedente, giovandosi dell'invenzione della Donna gentile, la quale, mera allegoria o personaggio storico, fa comunque guadagnare plausibilità ad un discorso che, anche in questo caso, si impegna a dimostrare la natura amicale del sentimento che unisce l'autore ad un oggetto non empirico di dilezione'. In 'Il *Convivio* e l'amicizia secondo i filosofi', pp. 70–1.

The awareness may also be perceived in Dante's being caught in a dilemma once, while still faithful to the classical sources, he calls himself appealed by the vernacular's 'goodness'. In this case 'goodness', he says, consists of conveying concepts which the vernacular shares with all other languages. In Dante's classical precursors' writing on friendship, it is not the individual but goodness which appeals to others. Nonetheless, it is far from evident why Dante is attracted by the vernacular whose beauties are still hidden and which, as far as concepts are concerned, has proved inferior to Latin. No wonder that he conveniently swerves away from the topic and promptly addresses other forms of 'goodness', especially the virtue of justice – which may have been inspired by Brunetto Latini's *Trésor* or by scholastic commentaries on Aristotle's idea placing friendship in the framework of politics.[21]

There are further striking divergences from the classical framework of friendship which often fall by the wayside in modern research.[22] By reassessing them, we may find they have something to say about Dante's expectations of the vernacular. In the thirteenth chapter when it comes down to the 'cagioni d'amore accrescitive' [causes that increase love] (*Conv.*, I. xii. 3), in particular to the benefits which are specific to the best form of friendship, Dante's adaptation of the ancient models takes on an even more daring form. The 'beneficio' which friends should receive from each other is intended to affect the other's life to such an extent that each ends up being the cause of the other's very existence. As for the *beneficii* Dante gets from the *volgare* it goes:

> Onde, con ciò sia cosa che due perfezioni abbia l'uomo, una prima e una seconda (la prima lo fa essere, la seconda lo fa esser buono), se la propria loquela m'è stata cagione e de l'una e de l'altra, grandissimo beneficio da lei ho ricevuto. (*Conv.*, I. xiii. 3)

---

21 Another source may have been medieval commentaries on Aristotle's *Ethics* whose writers, finding themselves at odds with the ancient notion of friendship being based on equality, took refuge in reflections on the analogies between 'amicitia' and justice. See Bénédicte Sère, *Penser l'amitié au Moyen Age* (Brepols: Turnhout, 2007), pp. 101–52.
22 Dante's love for the vernacular does not leave any space for an act of free choice, that is, for the very condition of a perfect friendship. Falzone, on the contrary, claims an 'atto morale libero', p. 56.

[Therefore, since man has two perfections, one primary and one secondary (the first causes him to exist, the second causes him to be good), I have received, if my native tongue has been the cause of both the one and the other, very great benefit from it.]

The *volgare* is celebrated both as the cause of the poet's existence and of his being good, that is, ethically good. Regarding his very being, the *volgare* had produced a sort of fluid that brought his 'generanti' [parents] together and thereby caused them to bring a child into the world. Put into the Latin of Aristotelian terminology, the *volgare* counts as the *causa efficiens*, whereas the parents, if at all, function as a *causa formalis*. In other words, Dante claims – in an astoundingly modern way – to derive almost directly from language.[23] In comparison with Augustine's corresponding description of his coming into existence in the *Confessiones*, it is amazing how arduously in Dante's account the *volgare* assumes the role of God,[24] while procreation is not so much based on the parent's sinful flesh and blood, as Augustine has it, but on putting into practice the driving force of the vernacular and its wish to create a friend for itself.

This extreme form of benefit finds an interesting counterpart in the delight the poet takes in the benefit his friend reaps from him. In the penultimate paragraph of the thirteenth chapter, he places himself beside the vernacular and engages in the 'medesimo studio' [its purpose and mine] (*Conv.*, I. xiii. 7). By doing so, he meets another condition of classical friendship: the concord of will and desire. The word 'studio' first refers to everyone's urge for self-preservation. Since the *volgare* is not able to provide for itself, the friend comes to its rescue. Thus, after having praised the vernacular as a *causa efficiens* of his being, Dante raises himself into the role of an *artifex* who gives shape to a continuously shifting vernacular – a gift that, as has often been noted, overtly contradicts his commitment to uncovering the vernacular's 'goodness'.[25] What is more, it risks stripping

---

23 Aristotle presents this kind of genetic derivation when he compares political constitutions, in this case: monarchy, with parental relations, here: between father and son: *Ethics* VIII. x. 4. and VIII. xi. 1–3.
24 See *Confessiones* I. vii. 12.
25 See I. X. 9: 'E questa grandezza do io a questo amico, in quanto quello [che] elli di bontade avea in podere e occulto, io lo fo avere in atto e palese nella sua pria

the vernacular of its human likeness since it is disgraced into being a merely material state. It is little wonder that Dante, here too, quickly moves on to describing another kind of 'medesimo studio', that is the shared endeavour of learning and studying.

As to the second 'beneficio' lavished upon Dante by the vernacular, being morally good, it stems from the *volgare* pushing him along the right track and making him move towards perfection:

> Questo mio volgare fu introduttore di me ne la via di scienza; che è ultima perfezione, in quanto con esso io entrai ne lo latino e con esso mi fu mostrato; lo quale latino poi mi fu via a più innanzi andare. (*Conv.*, I. xiii. 5)
>
> [This vernacular of mine was what led me into the path of knowledge which is our ultimate perfection, since through it I entered upon Latin and through its agency Latin was taught to me, which then became my path to further progress.]

First, it is puzzling that of all things it is the *volgare* that opens up a road to Latin and to the world of knowledge, which all men by nature desire. This is emphasized by twice using 'con esso'. Obviously, you approach a foreign language from your own. Yet, in the Middle Ages lessons the respective *volgare* was not used in instruction of grammar.[26] Therefore there might be more to it if Dante stresses the *volgare* as the starting point and the constant point of reference.

From Dante's description it becomes clear that learning Latin was not a bold leap into grammar which is roughly the way it was taught in the

---

operazione, che è manifestare concepta sentenza'. In this chapter Dante considers rhymes and numbers as mere ornaments and hence accidental to the substance: 'quando solo sua naturale bellezza si sta con lei, da tutto accidentale adornamento discompagnata' (I. x. 13). In the thirteenth chapter Dante, conversely, uncovers the extent to which 'numbers' and 'rhymes' are necessary to stabilize a natural language.

26 In the early Middle Ages students in the monasteries and, later on, in Cathedral Schools learned Latin by means of 'total immersion'. See Robert Black, *Education and Society in Florentine Tuscany: Teachers, Pupils and Schools, c. 1250–1500* (Leiden: Brill, 2007), p. 47.

early Middle Ages, particularly in the monasteries.[27] Dante, conversely, somehow kept track of, or remained loyal to, his linguistic origins. On the one hand, this depiction may simply testify the change that was well underway in grammar training and would come to its fruition only in the fourteenth century. According to Robert Black, teachers in Italy tried to accelerate the acquisition of Latin language skills by using the vernacular to explain Latin vocabulary or sentence structures.[28] On the other hand, Dante, by stressing the vernacular's company – 'con esso' – may be hinting at a feeling peculiar to him. The last sentence shows him moving forward independently in the world of Latin, but this does not imply that he had by any means dropped his mother tongue. The *volgare* has been and remains an incentive to Dante's studies. Therefore, the formula 'con esso' might uncover the extent to which Dante was conscious of having a mind, so to speak, set by his mother tongue. And the new-fangled teaching methods may have enhanced this innate inclination. Dante was pushed into switching between the two languages and, by doing so, became sensitive to both their particularities.[29]

Shortly afterwards while highlighting his familiarity with the vernacular Dante reminisces about using the *volgare* in 'diliberando, interpetrando e questionando' [deliberating, explaining, and questioning] (*Conv.*, I. xiii. 9). It has already been pointed out that the three gerunds refer to Politics,

27 Augustine's recollection of his first encounter with the foreign language Greek is very telling in this regard. See *Confessiones* I. xiv. 23.
28 The elementary skills of reading and of writing were still exclusively based on Latin texts. The vernacular came into use during grammar lessons. As Robert Black says, even more important was 'the introduction of the vernacular as a tool of Latin teaching in the Trecento', see *Humanism and Education in Medieval and Renaissance Italy: Tradition and Innovation in Latin Schools from the Twelfth to the Fifteenth Century* (Cambridge: Cambridge University Press, 2001), p. 7. Though, as Black later specifies, lists of vocabulary in vernacular may be traced back to the thirteenth century, Black, *Education*, pp. 47–8.
29 Contrary to Boethius of Dacia or Martinus, who focused on Latin as the be all and end all grammatical language and asserted that the same logical-syntactical structure would underlie and affect all other surrounding vernacular languages, Dante in the *Convivio* is committed to the particularities both of the vernaculars and of Latin.

Law and Philosophy. In addition to the political commitment which the verb 'deliberare' evokes, it is worth noting that it implies the analytical use of the vernacular which is considered to be capable of expressing a reflected point of view, or an assessment. The 'interpretare', referring to the commentary in the *Vita nova*, represents a basic medieval practice in learning. The 'questionare', finally, represents a specific form of learning that is genuinely linked to philosophy and theology. Thus, from the pick of verbs it may be gathered that learning things which are written in Latin is continuously referred to the *volgare* and that Dante never ceased thinking and reflecting in his mother tongue. Side by side, Dante and the vernacular are getting to grips with all the facets of philosophy, so to speak. In this, the vernacular proves to be his only true friend.

Beyond this *friendship*, Dante's way of learning Latin nicely mirrors his peculiar way of understanding philosophy and 'teaching' to the many.[30] If learning in the Middle Ages means learning by rote and thereby gaining access to the world of knowledge, Dante takes a different stance by adding a process of linguistic switching to it. By moving back and forth between languages he manages to appropriate the universe of science and incorporate it into his own world. Contrary to Pinto's otherwise fine interpretation of grammar in Dante, the *Convivio* therefore does not so much fall back in line with the poet's earlier inferiority complex, which, except for the vernacular love poetry, is evident in the *Vita nova*; rather Dante is experimenting with other ways of living with and even manipulating the *diglossia*. And, what is more, the *Convivio* itself may be the result, as well as a re-enactment, of what might spring out of language switching.[31] From

---

30   See my article on how Dante does not conceive of education as a passive, somewhat ruminating kind of learning that simply treads in the footsteps of authorities, but tries to transmit philosophy to his audience as an ongoing process of questioning, of making and correcting mistakes. Franziska Meier, 'Educating the Reader', *L'Alighieri*, 45 (2015), 23–33.
31   This, at least, may be gathered from Cesare Segre's stylistic analyses: 'E dunque con Dante che l'imitazione latina diventa nella nostra prosa più meditata, consapevole e proficua: lo scrittore volgare non si trova più in un'abbagliata passività di fronte alla "grammatica", ma assimila alla sintassi romanza l'esperienza costruttiva della prosa

this perspective, Dante's cross-gendering may turn out to be a clue to what he really is about to perform with the vernacular in prose writing.

Finally, by stressing that the vernacular pushed him to become better and that within the Latin world of knowledge he stayed faithful to his roots, Dante might be expressing that, contrary to corrupted Latin, the vernacular is deeply enmeshed with ethics. Therefore it has more potential to fulfill the ambition of making people live up to the highest goals of human species. What is more, in Dante's eyes this quality seems to extend to his Latin-illiterate vernacular-speakers as well, at least those of his audience. Although in his address, Dante does hint that the ancestors of his noble audience must have committed some sort of sin – they had given up on literacy or a Latin education – he does not doubt their 'goodness of mind' in the least. Unless the address was meant as a *captatio benevolentiae*, it makes the *Convivio* look less like a revolutionary act of bringing knowledge to laypeople, as Imbach pointed out, than like an act of restoration, that is, an attempt to return the hand-picked audience to their former, literate condition.[32] This restoration, however, is to be solely carried out in the vernacular. Thereby, what looks from the outside like divulgating Latin philosophy, as far as this passage is concerned, may well turn out to be a collective undertaking which takes the ancient world of knowledge as a starting point but aims at building it anew and on firmer moral ground, that is on a gender-ambiguous vernacular which is informed by a purified Latin and evolves into a new, morally firmer language. Remembering that 'litteratura' is the Latinized version of the Greek word grammar, the

---

latina'; *Lingua, stile e società. Studi sulla storia della prosa italiana* (Milan: Feltrinelli, 1963), p. 249.

32 In *Conv.*, I. ix. 5 Dante both chastises and adulates his audience by saying: 'che la bontà de l'animo, la quale questo servigio (Dante's donation, fm) attende, è in coloro che per malvagia disusanza del mondo hanno lasciata la litteratura a coloro che l'hanno fatta di donna meretrice'. According to Gianfranco Fioravanti's commentary, Dante's illiterate audience in fact used to be Latin literate, but ceased caring about it: Dante Alighieri, *Opere*, ed. by Marco Santagata, vol. II (Milan: Mondadori, 2014), p. 157.

Convivio then might have been meant as a new 'litteratura'. In other words: it may just have been conceived as the very *Moral Art* which the grammar of Latin had failed to be.[33]

33 Dante probably would have given credit to Robert Black according to whom grammar in the Middle Ages was entirely focused on language and philology. In *Humanism and Education*, he says: 'Roman educational theorists such as Cicero and Quintilian had stressed the moral aims of education and yet when actual educational practices of grammarians such as Donatus [...] are examined, one finds only grammar and philology, not morals; indeed, despite emphasizing the moral utility of the classics. The logical consequence of all this is not that actual teaching was in fact moral because the Latin language was assumed to be an ethical subject but the very opposite; because it was taken for granted that Latin was a moral discipline, teachers did not have to inculcate moral lessons in the classroom' (p. 27). The term 'Moral Art', as coined by Paul Gehl with regard to Latin, may however convey what Dante bore in mind while writing 'litteratura' in the *Convivio*.

ALBERT RUSSELL ASCOLI

6 'Ponete mente almeno come io son bella': Prose and Poetry, 'pane' and 'vivanda', Goodness and Beauty, in *Convivio* I

To understand Dante's growth as a poet and the evolution of his poetics between his lyric youth and the massive achievement of the *Commedia*, one has to take a prosaic detour: that is, a detour through his prose,[1] or, rather, through three texts where prose becomes the vehicle for both expanding and reflecting upon the nature and function of Dante's poetry. This is not a particularly astonishing observation, given the prominence that the *Vita nova* and *Convivio*, not to mention *De vulgari eloquentia*, of necessity assume in any account of the run-up to the 'poema sacro'. In the two Italian works, the prose plays both narrative and exegetical roles – although those roles are dramatically reconfigured from work to work. More to my point here, it has an 'apologetic', that is, self-justificatory, function as well. In the *Vita nova* the latter function is largely confined to the chapter formerly known as 25, with explicit focus on the deceptive quality of the figurative language characteristic of poetry, with an implicit justification of the use

---

1   On the nature and importance of Dante's prose, beginning with the *Vita nova*, see, notably, Domenico De Robertis, *Il libro della 'Vita Nuova'* (Florence: Sansoni, 1972), 2nd edn enlarged, ch. 1, this chapter first published 1961; Aldo Vallone, *La prosa della 'Vita nuova'* (Florence: Le Monnier, 1963); Francesco Tateo, '"Aprire per prosa". Le premesse critiche della poetica dantesca', in *Questioni di poetica dantesca* (Bari: Laterza, 1972), pp. 53–75. For the *Convivio* specifically, see De Robertis, 'Il libro della *Vita Nuova* e il libro del *Convivio*', *Studi urbinati di storia, filosofia e letteratura*, 25 (1951), 5–27; Cecil Grayson, 'Dante e la prosa volgare', in *Cinque saggi su Dante* (Bologna: Patron, 1972), pp. 32–60, this essay first published 1963; Vallone, *La prosa del 'Convivio'* (Florence: Le Monnier, 1967).

of prose, namely, to reveal the authorial intentions behind poetic figures.[2] Implicit too is a relation of complementarity between poetry as the site of metaphorical substitutions and the literalizing explanatory power of prose.[3]

In the *Convivio* this apologetic function has taken on a far greater role. Now, instead of apologizing for his apparent mischaracterization of the nature of love as external force rather than as an internal subjective experience, Dante apologizes for confusion that certain of his poems have generated concerning the *object* of his affection: it is not an(other) woman, a *donna gentile*, but rather Wisdom personified *as* a woman, and, in fact, his love for Beatrice remains intact. In both cases the problem is one of figurative substitution in poetry then clarified by literalization in prose, although, in fact, here the clarification moves from the *libello*'s demystification of a personification replacing a human subject (Love for Dante-in-love) in the opposite direction (a female beloved for the abstract personification of Truth).[4]

This aspect of apology, anticipated briefly in book I, chapter i, is actually carried out primarily in the prose commentaries to *Voi che 'ntendendo il terzo cielo movete* and *Amor che nella mente mi ragiona* in books II and III respectively. Book I, rather, is largely dedicated to an apology in prose *for (this) prose* and for Dante's adoption *of prose* as primary vehicle of his philosophical teachings: its use of the first person singular; its occasional lapses into complex argumentation evidently too difficult for his supposed audience; and, of course, its having been written in the vernacular rather than in Latin, the usual language of prose commentary. Here, again, though in some but not all ways more explicitly than *Vita nova*, prose is at once

---

2   Albert Russell Ascoli, *Dante and the Making of a Modern Author* (Cambridge: Cambridge University Press, 2008), esp. pp. 193–201.
3   On Dante's use of metaphor in book I, see Zygmunt Barański, 'Il *Convivio* e la poesia: problemi di definizione', in *Contesti della 'Commedia': Lectura Dantis Fridericiana 2002–2003*, ed. by Francesco Tateo and Daniele Maria Pergorati (Bari: Palomar, 2004), pp. 9–64, and, especially, Laurence Hooper's important essay, 'Dante's *Convivio*, Book 1: Metaphor, Exile, *Epochē*', *MLN* 127 supplement (2012): S86–S104. Neither extends their analysis to consider the issue of figuration in the prose/poetry dialectic.
4   On Dante's 'two loves' generally, see Olivia Holmes, *Dante's Two Beloveds: Ethics and Erotics in the 'Divine Comedy'* (New Haven, CT: Yale University Press, 2008).

contrasted with poetry but also posited as a necessary explanatory supplement to and double of that same poetry.

In what follows, then, I intend to trace the largely oblique and mostly unexamined process by which poetry and prose, Dante's poetry and Dante's prose, are placed in opposition to one another from the outset of the treatise and, at the same time, staged as complementary. What emerges, I believe, is a picture at once complicating and illuminating of Dante's evolving and surprisingly ambivalent attitude toward poetry in general and his own poetry in particular, at this stage in his career, especially as regards the newly defined epistemological and ethical aims that he hopes to realize through it.[5]

As I examine this unfolding process, particularly its dynamic enactment in book I, I will be operating on a series of methodological assumptions, the first and most important of which is that it is a mistake to assume a priori that Dante's representations of the prose/poetry dyad will be internally coherent, or at least resolve themselves into a stable and conclusive meaning. This teleological premise frequently guides and in some cases misleads the interpretation of Dante's texts, whether from the perspective of a traditional philology seeking to specify 'the' primary meaning of key words around and through which his thought is articulated, or from that of the 'history of ideas', pursuing the logically coherent concepts in whose service such words are deployed.[6]

---

5 I first elaborated this understanding of the prose/poetry dialectic in *Dante*, pp. 205–15. Rather late in the process of writing this essay, I discovered Zygmunt Barański's previously cited essay, 'Il *Convivio*,' with which my argument converges on a number of points. Like (and before) me, Barański insists on the point that the first book of the treatise is largely focused on the prose rather than the poetry, while still attempting to elevate the status of the latter. As will become apparent our methods and conclusions do diverge significantly, particularly as regards the anxieties and ambivalence I find in the prose/poetry dialectic.

6 Although his aims and methods are different, Andrea Mazzucchi's demonstration of the stylistic richness and multiplicity of *Convivio*'s language, its effort simultaneously to address multiple rhetorical goals and its indebtedness to several generic discourses appears compatible with my claims concerning the competing discursive elements in the treatise. See Mazzucchi, *Tra 'Convivio' e 'Commedia': sondaggi di filologia e critica dantesca* (Rome: Salerno Editrice, 2004), chs 1–2, building on

Rather, I assert, it is important to recognize that Dante's text is driven by a 'rationalizing' impulse in a double sense: on the one hand, to produce a logical argument or arguments that demonstrate what the nature of the treatise is both as to form and to function; on the other hand, following the logic of a desire rather than of a demonstrable truth, to gloss over contradictions internal to those same arguments that might seem to undermine or subvert them. This procedure is largely intra-textual, and thus, while I acknowledge and make use of, to some extent, the biblical and other intertexts that have been evoked as determining the meaning of the *Convivio*'s self-representation (notably, the 'pane de li angeli', [bread of angels]), my emphasis is on the ways in which those references, and the allusive baggage they bring with them, are subjected to and transformed by the double logic that guides the unfolding diachronic dynamic of Dante's text.

Finally, my own argument proceeds through an examination of the interrelated conceptual and figurative pairings: in the first place, prose/poetry, of course, and, then 'pane'/'vivanda' and 'bontade'/'bellezza'. Yet another key metaphorical pair that is deployed in this context is that of servant and master. That the explanatory, rationalizing prose from the outset makes extensive use of, and is thus deeply implicated in, the figuration that would seem to be proper to the poetry it seeks to elucidate is, in fact, one of the critical complicating factors to be considered.

The difficulty of the question to be confronted can be seen in the clearly contradictory deployment of the metaphorics of bread and nourishment in the very first chapter, which, in glossing the title of the treatise, aims to give a general definition to the purpose of the work and, more specifically,

---

Vittorio Russo, 'Strutture innovative delle opera letterarie di Dante nella prospettiva dei generi letterari,' in *Il romanzo teologico. Sondaggi sulla 'Commedia' di Dante* (Naples: Liguori, 1984, this essay first published 1979), pp. 31–53. Others who have confronted the generic indeterminacy/multiplicity of the treatise are Marianne Shapiro, 'On the Role of Rhetoric in the *Convivio*', *Romance Philology*, 40 (1986), 38–64, and, especially, Hooper, 'Dante's *Convivio*', who, building on Barański, 'Il *Convivio*', argues that Dante 'uses the versatile form of the commentary to syncretize diverse disciplines', S87. One such modality – but not, I am certain, the only one – is satire: see Ambrogio Camozzi Pistoja, 'Il quarto trattato del *Convivio*, o della satira', *Le tre corone*, 1 (2014), 27–53.

to preview the roles of both prose and poetry within that work.[7] Initially 'pane' is used to figure the philosophical content currently available only to an intellectual elite fluent in 'grammatica', that is, Latin:

7   I will enter only marginally into the scholarly investigations that have elucidated the sources upon which Dante has drawn in elaborating his metaphorics of bread and sustenance, confining myself to the problem of the intra-textual articulation of those figures. For these figures in general and for the specific categories of 'pane de li angeli' and 'pane orzato', see Etienne Gilson, *Dante the Philosopher*, trans. David Ward (New York: Sheed & Ward, first published in French 1939), pp. 11–12; Carlo Curto, 'Pane orzato, luce nuova, sole nuovo nel *Convivio* di Dante', in *Giornale storico della letteratura italiana*, 118 (1941), 194–7; Bruno Nardi, '"Lo pane degli angeli" (*Convivio* I. i. 7)', in *Nel mondo di Dante* (Rome: Edizioni di Storia e Letteratura, 1944), pp. 47–53, and 'La *vivanda* e il *pane* nel *Convivio* dantesco', in *Saggi e note di critica dantesca* (Milan-Naples: Ricciardi, 1966, this note first published 1965), pp. 386–90; Gian Roberto Sarolli, *Prolegomena alla 'Divina Commedia'* (Florence: Olschki, 1971), esp. 35–8; Antonietta Buffano, 'Pane', in *Enciclopedia dantesca*, ed. by Umberto Bosco, 5 vols + appendix (Rome: Istituto dell'Enciclopedia Dantesca, 1973), IV, 165; Attilio Mellone, 'Pane degli angeli', in *Enciclopedia dantesca*, IV, 266–7; Daniel J. Ransom, '"Panis Angelorum": A Palinode in the *Paradiso*', *Dante Studies*, 95 (1977), 81–94; William J. O'Brien, '"The Bread of Angels" in *Paradiso* II: A Liturgical Note', *Dante Studies*, 97 (1979), 97–106; Mary Alexandra Watt, 'Take this Bread: Dante's Eucharistic Banquet', *Quaderni d'Italianistica*, 22 (2) (2001), 17–35; Maria Luisa Ardizzone, *Reading as the Angels Read: Speculation and Politics in Dante's 'Banquet'* (Toronto: University of Toronto Press, 2016); esp. pp. 7–21; Hooper, 'Dante's *Convivio*'; Danielle Callegari, 'Dante's Nutritional Vernacular: Food, Hunger and Consumption from *Convivio* to *Commedia*', PhD diss., New York University, 2014, esp. pp. 59–76 (in her dissertation, Callegari supplies a wide ranging survey, with extensive bibliography, both of the metaphorics of food and digestion in Dante and the later Middle Ages, but also the social context of food consumption in which it is embedded). Among earlier scholars, see also Robert M. Durling, 'Deceit and Digestion in the Belly of Hell', in *Allegory and Representation. Selected Papers in the English Institute, 1979–1980*, ed. by Stephen Greenblatt (Baltimore, MD: The Johns Hopkins University Press, 1981), pp. 61–93; notable among recent scholars who have advanced our understanding of the intellectual context for the use of 'pane' as a figure of philosophical knowledge is Luca Bianchi, '"Noli comedere panem philosophorum inutiliter": Dante Alighieri and John of Jandun on Philosophical "Bread"', *Tijdschrift wor Filosofie*, 75 (2013), 335–55, who is careful to note that Dante invariably puts available figures of intellectual nutrition to new and different uses. Few of the above critics have tried

> Oh beati quelli pochi che seggiono *a quella mensa dove lo pane de li angeli si manuca*! e miseri quelli che con le pecore hanno comune cibo! (*Conv.*, I. i. 6–7; emphasis mine)[8]

> [Blessed are the few who sit at the table where the bread of the angels is eaten, and most unfortunate those who share the food of sheep!]

In this initial figuration of philosophical teaching as a banquet, 'pane de li angeli' stands for an essential content, from which a vast majority of people, without access to Latin and/or time for serious study, are excluded.

The banquet metaphor is further elaborated, now to include Dante's subordinate role in the acquisition and subsequent divulgation of philosophical knowledge, and, at first, we apparently remain within the terms of the initial figuration of the intellectual meal:

> E io adunque, che non seggio a *la beata mensa* [where the 'pane de li angeli' is served] ma, fuggito de la *pastura del vulgo* [the food of sheep] a' piedi di coloro che seggiono ricolgo di quello che da loro cade, e conosco la misera vita di quelli che dietro m'ho lasciati, per la *dolcezza* ch'io sento in quello che a poco a poco ricolgo. (*Conv.*, I. i. 10; emphasis mine)

> [Therefore I, who do not sit at the blessed table, but, having fled the pasture of the common herd, gather up a part of what falls to the feet of those who do sit there, and who know the unfortunate life of those I have left behind, for the sweetness that I taste in what I gather up piece by piece.]

---

    to sort out in detail the relationship between the two primary kinds of 'pane', not to mention the various sub-categories (on which, see n. 14). One exception, which has had little echo in the intervening years, is Ransom 'Panis Angelorum', pp. 85–6; more recently, see Hooper, 'Il *Convivio*,' esp. pp. 88–90.

8   Cited from Dante Alighieri, *Opere minori*, vol. 1, part 2, *Convivio*, ed. and comm. by Cesare Vasoli and Domenico De Robertis (Milan and Naples: Ricciardi, 1988). I have also consulted the edition of the *Società dantesca italiana*: Dante Alighieri, *Convivio, Vol. 2, Testo*, ed. by Franca Brambilla Ageno (Florence: Le Lettere, 2015). Translations are taken from Richard Lansing, trans., *Dante's 'Il Convivio' (The Banquet)* (New York and London: Garland, 1990); words in parentheses are my emendations.

As we then learn, not only had Dante provided for his own 'edification', albeit figured as a dog collecting scraps from beneath the table of the great,[9] but he had also made provision for those who have no other access to taste of the 'bread of angels', the 'innumerabili [...] 'mpediti' '[those impeded [...] too numerous to count] (*Conv.*, I. i. 6) who batten like sheep on 'bestiale pastura' (*Conv.*, I. i. 8), as he once did:[10]

> misericordievolmente mosso, non me dimenticando, per li miseri alcuna cosa ho riservata, la quale a li occhi loro, già è più tempo, ho dimostrata; e in ciò li ho fatti maggiormente vogliosi.

9   On the likely biblical provenance of this image, specifically Matthew 15. 26–7, see Watt, 'Dante's Eucharistic Banquet', p. 23.
10 On the question of who Dante's intended readers were and how he constructs them and their interpretive practice, see Richard Lansing, 'Dante's Intended Audience in the *Convivio*', *Dante Studies*, 110 (1992) 17–24; Bianchi, 'Noli comedere panem'; Gianfranco Fioravanti, 'Il *Convivio* e il suo pubblico', *Le forme e la storia* n.s. 7 (2014), 13–21; Mirko Tavoni, *Qualche idea su Dante* (Bologna: Il Mulino, 2015), pp. 77–86; Franziska Meier, 'Educating the Reader: Dante's *Convivio*', *L'Alighieri*, 45 (2015), 21–33; Stanley Levers, 'From Revelation to Dilation in Dante's *Studio*', in *Dante Studies*, 134 (2016), 1–25. There are almost no studies on Dante's actual contemporary readers, for the simple reason that the text did not circulate widely, if at all, during his lifetime. On this, see Lino Pertile, 'Lettera aperta a Robert Hollander sui rapporti tra *Commedia* e *Convivio*', *EBDSA* (<http://www.princeton.edu/~dante/ebdsa/> accessed 2 February 2018), 8 October 1996, as well as Fioravanti, 'Il *Convivio*', p. 13. See also Luca Azzetta, 'La tradizione del *Convivio* negli antichi commenti alla *Commedia*: Andrea Lancia, l' "Ottimo Commento" e Pietro Alighieri', in *Rivista di studi danteschi*, 5 (1) (2005), 3–34, and 'Tra i più antichi lettori del *Convivio*: ser Alberto della Piagentina notaio e cultore di Dante', in *Rivista di studi danteschi*, 9 (1) (2009), 57–91. While it is important not to overlook Dante's interest in educating a growing vernacular middle class (see Imbach and Bianchi, among many others), or to be entering into a specific dialogue with the emperor and/or ruling political class (Lansing; Fioravanti; Tavoni), we cannot overlook the key point that *de facto*, Dante, obsessive exegete and reviser of his texts, was his own primary addressee here as in *De Vulgari*, and that in both works what is *finished* is what prepares him to take the next step down the road to genuine *auctoritas* (see Ascoli, *Dante*, pp. 219–22).

[moved by compassion, though not forgetting myself, I have set aside for those who are unfortunate something that I placed before their eyes some time ago, by which I have increased their desire.]

As we soon learn, the method of that demonstration, here given periphrastically in terms of a hoarding of crumbs from the 'pane de li angeli' he has collected ('alcuna cosa ho riservata'), was the writing of philosophical *canzoni*, which were then circulated to a wider vernacular public.

However, even as the banquet metaphor is elaborated, things quickly become more complicated, not to say confusing. Suddenly, with a jarring shift in figurative referent, 'pane' clearly no longer refers to the 'bread of angels', but rather to something different, and decidedly less exalted:

> Per che ora volendo loro apparecchiare, intendo fare *un generale convivio* di ciò ch'i' ho loro mostrato, e *di quello pane ch'è mestiere a così fatta vivanda*, sanza lo quale da loro non potrebbe esser mangiata. (*Conv.*, I. i. 11; emphasis mine)

> [Wishing now to set their table, I intend to present to all men a banquet of what I have shown them and of the bread which must necessarily accompany such (sustenance), without which it could not be consumed by them.]

Dante, just seen crawling beneath the table of the 'beata mensa', is now himself preparing an apparently figuratively analogous, if derivative and subordinate, banquet, composed of 'that which I have shown them' (previously circulated materials, derived from the greater banquet, which will turn out to be his *canzoni*) and of that bread which is needed for such sustenance. Four paragraphs later there will be an explosion of references to this latter kind of 'pane', culminating in the revelation that it stands for 'la presente disposizione', that is the prose commentary. But for now the referent remains uncertain. As, in fact, does the meaning of 'vivanda', which could either be the 'crumby' content that Dante has collected or, a little more likely, the *canzoni* through which he first translated that content into the vernacular.

And the confusion only grows in the sentence that follows immediately after, a textual crux deriving from the notoriously defective manuscript tradition. What follows are the three principal reconstructions of a hypothetical authorial original in versions offered by the work's most authoritative editors:

> E questo [è quello] convivio, di quello pane degno, con tale vivanda qual io intendo indarno [non] essere ministrata. (*Conv.*, I. i. 11; following Busnelli-Vandelli; adopted by Vasoli)

> [And this is that banquet, worth of that bread (or, of that worthy bread), with such sustenance which I intend shall not be ministered in vain.]

Or:

> E [h]a questo convivio di quello pane degno cotale vivanda qual io intendo indarno essere ministrata. (*Conv.*, I. i. 11; Simonelli)[11]

> [And this banquet, worthy of such bread, has such food as I understood to be ministered in vain [or this banquet has some of that worthy bread together with such sustenance as I understand to be ministered in vain.]

Or:

> Ed ha questo convivio di quello pane degno, co[n] tale vivanda qual io intendo indarno [non] essere ministrata. (Ageno; I. i. 11, 51)

> [This banquet has such worthy bread, together with such sustenance as I intend should not be served in vain.]

Of the numerous interpretative problems posed by the editors in arriving at these conclusions, the one which concerns me here has not been posed by any of them. That problem has to do with which noun is modified by the adjective 'degno'. Does, as the editorial tradition seems to agree, 'degno' modify 'pane', in which case 'pane' and 'vivanda' are again paired as they were in the previous sentence to compose a new 'convivio', alluding to the

---

[11] Maria Picchio Simonelli, *Materiali per un'edizione critica del 'Convivio' di Dante* (Rome: Edizioni dell'Ateneo, 1970), p. 67. The translations of all three versions of the passage are my own.

poems plus commentary that will make up Dante's work?[12] Or, could 'degno' also and perhaps better be understood modify 'convivio' (as is grammatically possible) and does it thus mean that Dante's secondary banquet lives up to, is worthy of, the 'pane de li angeli' from which it derives, that is to the originary meal of the classical philosophers, which it mirrors and doubles? This reading seems to be most in accord with the version of Simonelli, which is also the closest to the 'archetype', although my understanding of the sense of the passage as she reconstructs it is different from hers.[13] It is

12 André Pézard, *La rotta gonna: gloses et corrections aux textes mineurs de Dante. Tome 1: 'Vita nova', 'Rime', 'Convivio'* (Florence: Sansoni, 1967), pp. 125–8, tries to solve the problem by claiming that the sentence here discussed was actually an alternative authorial version of the preceding sentence, where the 'pane' is clearly in subordinate relationship to the 'vivanda'. The strength of his proposal lies in the overlapping lexicon of the two passages, but the hypothesis requires a highly speculative reconstruction of Dante's interactions with a scribal copy of the text (not to say that all of the proposals, including mine, are not speculative!), and, rhetorically speaking, such echoing would be appropriate in the culminating summary of the passage tracing the arc from the 'beata mensa' and the 'pane de li angeli' to Dante's vernacular 'convivio'.
13 One reason for preferring Simonelli's version is that it does not emend, as the others do 'cotale' to 'con tale', making 'vivanda' the direct object of the verb phrase 'questo convivio ha' and thus making it simpler to see 'di quello pane degno' as an adjectival phrase modifying 'convivio' rather than 'un partitivo che costituisce l'oggetto di ha' (Ageno, ed., vol. 2, p. 5, note to I. xi. 51). Just like everyone else, I have no particularly good explanation for the archetype's 'intendo indarno essere ministrata', without the inserted emendation of 'non', though if pressed I might suggest that it could refer back, a bit awkwardly, to the situation of the pre-commentary *canzoni* as 'vivanda' ('I understand that the "vivanda" had previously been served in vain', because no-one understood it/them on their own (see I. i. 10 and 14) but see also n. 27 on the parallel passage in I. xiii. 11 where 'intendere' means 'attend to' rather than 'understand' or 'have the intention of'). But my point is not that I am right and they are wrong, but rather that the text generates confusion by using 'pane' in two different ways without, at least at first, distinguishing clearly between them, and that this confusion shows up in the passage in question. For the debate, see, to start, Vasoli's note (p. 11); Simonelli, *Materiali*, pp. 67–9; Ageno, 'Introduzione', in Dante Alighieri, *Convivio*, vol. 1, pt. 1, p. 60. Ageno, note to I. xi. 51, in vol. 2, p. 5, at least goes to the trouble of explaining why 'degno' should modify 'pane' and not 'convivio', though without noting the interpretative consequences of the latter choice. Fioravanti in his recent edition follows Ageno's reading, but observes 'anche con le correzioni proposte da

Prose and Poetry, 'pane' and 'vivanda', Goodness and Beauty, in Convivio I   125

compatible with the heavily emended reading of Busnelli-Vandelli, while Ageno's version seems to exclude it.

The last passage, as just illustrated, is one of the many defective loci in the textual tradition that have been painfully and uncertainly reconstructed by editors, who have generally been guided by the subsequent pairing of 'pane' and 'vivanda' as the elements of Dante's text, and not by the opening metaphor of the 'pane de li angeli' in deciding which of the two kinds of bread is referred to in this third occurrence of the word. In any event, at this point the reader is still trying to sort out what the relationship between the two banquets and two kinds of breads is, and even if one is persuaded by the never entirely successful editorial attempts to bring clarity and consistency to the passage, a significant degree of contamination and confusion, to a greater or lesser degree sponsored by the author, exists between the 'beata mensa' and the 'convivio' that Dante is offering, between the two kinds of bread, and, indeed, between 'vivanda' as philosophical content and as the poetic vehicle with which Dante intends to deliver it.

Soon thereafter, when we come to the more explicit description of the structure of the bookish banquet Dante has prepared, 'pane' is again and unequivocally used as a figure for the supplementary prose, as it will be from then on, until the very end of book I.[14] But even as one issue is seemingly clarified, another complication arises:

Ageno [...] il testo continua ad essere tutt'altro che chiaro'; Dante Alighieri, *Convivio*, ed. by Gianfranco Fioravanti, in *Opere*, Vol. 2, ed. by Gianfranco Fioravanti, Claudio Giunta, Diego Quaglione, Claudia Villa and Gabriella Albanese (Milan: Mondadori, 2014), p. 103n.

14   The word 'pane' used metaphorically appears 15 times in the *Convivio*, 14 in the first book (6 in the first chapter; 3 in the second), 1 at the beginning of book II, referring back to the meta-discursive apology of book I. Of these uses, 12 clearly refer to the prose commentary, one to the 'pan degli angeli', one ambiguously to either of the previous. One, to be discussed further on, comes at the very end of book I and adds a further wrinkle to the definitional problem. At a certain point, having used the word already 9 times, Dante unceremoniously introduces another distinction, this time between the respective qualities of Latin and Italian prose commentaries, which further muddies the figurative waters. Having qualified his prose 'pane' as 'del mio formento' (i.e. 'frumento'; i.e. wheaten; i.e. of good quality; I. ii. 15),

La vivanda di questo convivio sarà di quattordici maniere ordinata, cioè quattordici canzoni sì d'amor come di vertù materiate, le quali sanza lo *presente pane* aveano d'alcuna oscuritade ombra, sì che a molti loro *bellezza* più che loro *bontade* era in grado. Ma *questo pane*, cioè la presente disposizione, sarà *la luce* la quale ogni colore di loro sentenza farà parvente. (*Conv.*, I. i. 14–15; emphasis mine)

[The (courses) of this banquet will be prepared in fourteen ways: that is, in fourteen canzoni, whose subject is both love as well as virtue. By lacking the present bread they possessed some degree of obscurity, so that to many their beauty was more pleasing than their goodness. But this bread that is, the present explanation, will be the light that renders visible every shade of their meaning.]

Fourteen courses, fourteen canzoni, will be the substance of the banquet, logically equivalent to the 'pane de li angeli'. Once again, however, the place and function of the second type of 'pane', that is, the prose commentary surrounding the poetic feast, becomes confused with another term with which it is paired, in what should be a subordinate and supplementary relationship. The purpose of this 'pane', the 'presente disposizione' of prose commentary, is to remedy the obscurity of the poetry, the (philosophical) 'bontade' of which has previously been overshadowed by its (ornamental) 'bellezza'. In other words, the prose 'pane' is subordinate to poetic 'vivanda'. And yet this prosaic bread immediately mutates into the 'light' ('luce') that

> he then backtracks to address the issue of its being vernacular and not Latin: 'Poi che purgato è questo pane da le macule accidentali, rimane ad escusare lui da una sustanziale, cioè da l'essere vulgare e non latino; che per similitudine dire si può di biado e non di frumento'; (I. v. 1), an opposition he then twice repeats in purging the 'stain' of linguistic inferiority: 'Grande vuole essere la scusa, quando a così nobile convivio per le sue vivande, a così onorevole per li suoi convitati, s'appone pane di biado e non di frumento; e vuole essere evidente ragione che partire faccia l'uomo da quello che per li altri è stato servato lungamente, sì come di comentare con latino' (I. x. 1); 'puotesi vedere questo pane, col quale si deono mangiare le infrascritte canzoni, essere sufficientemente purgato da le macule, e da l'essere di biado' (I. xiii. 11). After which he introduces yet another quality of bread, namely 'pane orzato' (I. xii. 12), of which more below. (I am not entirely convinced by the emendation of Ageno at I. ii. 15 of 'pane del mio formento' to 'pane del mio comento', which sensibly aims to eliminate the apparent contradiction of Dante referring to his 'pane' as both of 'biado' and of 'frumento', but has no solid basis in the manuscript tradition.)

reveals their hidden meaning ('sentenzia'), de facto usurping the role of the poems, thus reversing the hierarchy between them,[15] and, incidentally, to a certain extent closing the gap between the two kinds of bread. It is no accident, as we will see, that the metaphorics of light, once more conflated with that of 'pane', will be picked up at the end of the book (I. xiii. 11–12), although, yet again, with what seems to be a notable slippage in referent.

What I want to suggest, then, is that the shift in the use of the image of 'pane', which refers now to the blessed philosophical content of the *canzoni*, now to the prose supplement that will make the banquet edible, pre-figures a problem that Dante will continue to wrestle with throughout the treatise, and reflects a significant anxiety about the nature of his vernacular poetry in particular and of poetry as a discourse in general. And, further, I will show that this anxiety is especially visible in the tension between (formal, superficial, aesthetic) 'bellezza' and (hidden, substantial, intellectual) 'bontade' first announced in the passage just quoted: an opposition that draws upon available oppositions in the poetic, rhetorical, philosophical and theological fields.[16]

This problem clearly antedates the composition of the *Convivio*, with its addition of prose commentary supplements to previously composed poetic texts, as we can see when we come to the first of the *canzoni* to be commented upon, *Voi che 'ntendendo il terzo ciel movete*, probably written

---

15   This point is anticipated in Barański, 'Il *Convivio*', p. 14.
16   Marianne Shapiro, 'Rhetoric', esp. pp. 56, 59–60, touches upon the importance of the *bellezza/bontà* opposition, especially in book II, linking 'bellezza' to rhetoric rather than poetry, but still in complex relationship to philosophical discourse. Barański, 'Il *Convivio*', pp. 44–53, argues that the pairing of 'bellezza' and 'bontade' in the account of 'Voi che 'ntendendo' given in II. xi is in the service of a dramatically new poetics, one which echoes but reconfigures the Horatian 'dulcis'/ 'utilis' opposition (*Ars Poetica* ll.333–44). He does not note the prior uses of these terms in book I, their use in relation to prose as well as to poetry, or the general applicability of the problematic of the *canzone*'s 'tornata' to the function of the commentary as delineated in I. i. I would suggest, adding to Barański's analysis, that Dante probably also has in view Augustine's opposition of 'uti' and 'frui' in the context of his account of the Bible's mode of signification and the practice of biblical exegesis in *De Doctrina Christiana*, book I, esp. chs 4 and 20 [22].

some ten years before the work into which it has now been inserted was begun. From the very first Dante makes it clear that he addresses the divine ministers who move the heaven of Venus – in virtue of the act of pure and unmediated understanding characteristic of the angelic nature – precisely because they are the only ones he believes capable of understanding him:[17]

> Voi che 'ntendendo il terzo ciel movete,
> udite il ragionar ch'è nel mio core,
> ch'io nol so dire altrui, sì mi par novo.

> [You whose intellect the third sphere moves, now listen to the speech within my heart, for I cannot speak to others, so (strange and new) it seems.]

The obvious corollary is that his human audience is unlikely to see the true meaning of the poem, hence the *congedo*, the final stanza in which the author represents himself to his work:

> Canzone, io credo che saranno radi
> color che *tua ragione* intendan bene,
> tanto la parli faticosa e forte.
> Onde, se per ventura elli addivene
> che tu dinanzi da persone vadi
> che non ti paian d'essa bene accorte,
> allor ti priego che ti riconforte,
> dicendo lor, *diletta* mia novella:
> 'Ponete mente almen *com'io son bella*!' (ll. 53–61, emphasis mine)

[My song, I think they will be few indeed who'll rightly understand your sense, so difficult and complex is your speech. So if by chance it comes to pass that you should

---

[17] The address of the poem to angels as creatures of pure intelligence serves as a belated and partial gloss on the phrase 'pane de li angeli', by reinforcing the point that the sustenance of incorporeal angels consists of the *intelligibilia* which are the object of their incessant activity of understanding. What remains obscure is the object of that understanding, whether the rationally decipherable Truth of the natural world or the revealed and yet mysterious Truth of the Creator. For various interpretations of the latter question, see Nardi, 'Lo pane'; Vasoli, note to I. i. 7, Dante, *Convivio*, 8–9 (see also n. 7).

find yourself with some who do not grasp it well at all, I pray you then, (my new delight), take courage again and say to them: 'Consider at least how (beautiful) I am!']

This inability of Dante's readers to understand the rational content of 'Voi che 'ntendendo' is also responsible for the fundamental misunderstanding that Dante feels obliged to address in *Convivio*, namely that rather than hymns to the Love of Wisdom, that is, to Lady Philosophy, his *canzoni* are symptoms of a disposition to sensual love and hence to an inconstancy that has led him to trade in his dead beloved, Beatrice, for a new 'consolation', a *donna gentile* (see *Conv.*, I. ii. 16–17; also I. i. 16–18; II. ii. 1–6; II. vi. 7).[18] This confusion is certainly not lessened by the fact that the address to the *canzone* doubles the love-relationship described in the poem, by casting 'her' as a beautiful woman with whom the poet is on intimate terms: 'diletta mia novella' and who is invited to declare shamelessly her own beauty in public.[19]

18   The poem's self-staging as susceptible to two different readings might seem to support the long-standing hypothesis that the poem was originally written as an allegory of Dante's 'love of Sophia', as re-articulated in persuasive detail by Enrico Fenzi, 'Boezio e Jean de Meun nelle rime allegoriche', in *Studi di filologia e letteratura, dedicati a Vincenzo Pernicone, vol. II–III* (Genoa: Tilgher, 1975), pp. 9–69. On the other hand, as Teodolinda Barolini has argued (*Dante's Poets: Textuality and Truth in the 'Commedia'* (Princeton, NJ: Princeton University Press, 1984), pp. 36–7 and n. 28; pp. 57–84 passim), it might also be taken to mean that most readers are incapable of appreciating the subtleties of Dante's discourse on the conflict in his mind over thoughts of love for two different (flesh and blood) women. No doubt, however, that once placed in the context of the *Convivio* the poem lends itself to and apparently reinforces the allegorical reading Dante now gives of it. See also n. 24.
19   Thomas Clifford Stillinger, *The Song of Troilus: Lyric Authority in the Medieval Book* (Philadelphia, PA: University of Pennsylvania Press, 1992), ch. 2, esp. pp. 50–1, shows how in the *Vita nova* Dante identifies prose with himself and as gendered male and the poetry with Beatrice and as gendered female. On the gendering of poetry in *Convivio*, see also Ascoli, *Dante*, pp. 212–13. Some interpreters, including Lansing in his translation, take 'novella' to signal a new birth, and the *canzone* then to be figured as Dante's child, not his lover. Still the language is appropriate to a lover, and its novelty is most easily assimilated to the thematics of a new beloved in the body of the poem.

The prose gloss on the 'tornata' of 'Voi che 'ntendendo' in book II, chapter xi. 2–5 rehearses the problem, focusing on the opposition between 'bellezza' e 'bontade', surface ornament and hidden meaning:

> *la bontade e la bellezza* di ciascuno sermone sono intra loro partite e diverse; ché la *bontade* è ne la sentenza, e la *bellezza* è ne l'ornamento de le parole; e l'una e l'altra è con *diletto*, avvegna che la *bontade sia massimamente dilettosa*. Onde con ciò sia cosa che la *bontade* di questa canzone fosse malagevole a sentire per le diverse persone che in essa s'inducono a parlare, dove si richeggiono molte distinzioni, e la *bellezza* fosse agevole a vedere, parvemi mestiero a la canzone che per li altri *si ponesse più mente a la bellezza che a la bontade*. (my emphasis)

> [Therefore I say here that the goodness and the beauty of every discourse are separate and different from one another; for goodness lies in the meaning, and beauty in the adornment of the words; and both the one and the other give pleasure, although goodness is the most pleasing. And so, since the goodness of this canzone was difficult to perceive because of the diversity of persons in it who are presented as speakers, where many distinctions are required, and since its beauty was easy to perceive, it seemed to me necessary for the canzone that others consider its beauty more than its goodness.]

This gloss reinforces what the 'congedo' or 'tornata' of the poem had already told us, namely that the poem is incapable of revealing its own 'bontade' to most readers and thus will require help from without if it is to do so.

The stakes for *Convivio* can be seen most clearly if we turn to a passage later in book I which recalls the initial assertion of a need to add a prose commentary to reveal the 'bontade' beneath the 'bellezza' of the poems, anticipates the exegesis of those terms in II. xi, and insists as well upon the personification of the *canzone* as a beautiful woman that has been and will again be seen in *Voi che 'ntendendo* (to repeat: later in the order of the treatise, though written much earlier):

> Ché per questo comento (i.e. the prose) la gran *bontade* del volgare di sì (si vedrà) [...] (la quale non si potea bene manifestare) ne le cose rimate, per le accidentali *adornezze* che quivi sono connesse, cioè la rima e lo ri[ti]mo e lo numero regolato: sì come non si può bene *manifestare la bellezza* d'una donna, quando li *adornamenti de l'azzimare e de le vestimenta* la fanno più ammirare che essa medesima. Onde chi vuole ben giudicare d'una donna, guardi quella quando solo sua naturale *bellezza* si sta con lei, *da tutto accidentale adornamento discompagnata: sì come sarà questo comento*. (*Conv.*, I. x. 12–13; emphasis mine)

[For by means of this commentary the great goodness of the vernacular of *sì* will be seen, because its virtue will be made evident, namely how it expresses the loftiest and the most unusual conceptions almost as aptly, fully, and gracefully as Latin, something that could not be expressed perfectly in verse, because of the accidental adornments that are tied to it, that is, rhyme and meter, just as the beauty of a woman cannot be perfectly expressed when the adornment of her preparation and apparel do more to make her admired than she does herself. Therefore, if anyone wishes to judge a woman justly, let him look at her when her natural beauty alone attends her, unaccompanied by any accidental adornment; so it will be with this commentary, in which the smoothness of the flow of its syllables, the appropriateness of its constructions, and the sweet discourses that it makes will be seen, which anyone upon careful consideration will find full of the sweetest and most exquisite beauty.]

Particularly striking, given Dante's indisputable vocation as poet, is the apparent dismissal of rhyme and metre as mere 'accidentali adornezze' and, to anticipate, the idea that the prose itself might be said to have a 'naturale bellezza' superior to such ornamentation.

What we have seen in our earlier reading of *Convivio* II. i. 1, then, is, among other things, a *post factum* attempt to articulate and resolve the dilemma already posed by 'Voi che 'ntendendo', with the introduction of the supplemental feature of prose commentary. But, as we have also already begun to see, there is an accompanying risk, namely that the prose will usurp the poetry's function entirely, and reverse the hierarchical structures it is supposedly meant to sustain. This point takes on additional force when we observe that the rest of book I is focused almost entirely on Dante-*prosatore*. The book has sometimes been described as an 'accessus ad auctorem', that is, a kind of scholastic prologue to (poetic) texts about to receive commentary,[20] but is in fact evidently an 'accessus ad commentatorem'[21]:

20   Mario Trovato, 'Il primo trattato del *Convivio* visto alla luce dell'*accessus ad auctores*', *Misure critiche*, 6 (1976), 5–14. See also Shapiro, 'Rhetoric'; Alastair Minnis, *Magister Amoris: The 'Roman de la Rose' and Vernacular Hermeneutics* (Oxford and New York: Oxford University Press, 2001), pp. 273–4; Bianchi, 'Noli comedere panem', pp. 341–2.
21   Alastair Minnis, '*Amor* and *Auctoritas* in the Self-Commentary of Dante and Francesco da Barberino', *Poetica* [Tokyo], 32 (1990), 25–42 (p. 30), anticipates this point when he calls book I a 'veritable commentary on commentary'; Barański, 'Il *Convivio*', pp. 19–26, further highlights the fact that the *accessus* topics concern

the three 'macule' against which Dante defends himself over the course of the book (speaking about oneself; speaking in a way that is too difficult; using the vernacular rather than Latin) are all considered as attributes of the prose (*Conv.*, I. ii. 1–2; I. v. 1). Speaking about oneself is hardly a problem in lyric poetry of which it is a fundamental feature; rather, it is an issue, as the example of Augustine attests (and Boethius too, in fact, despite the *prosimetrum* character of the *Consolatio*),[22] of an intrusive prose 'I' (*Conv.*, I. ii. 3–15). Speaking in a way that is difficult to understand *is*, as we have seen, an apparently insoluble problem endemic to poetry as linguistic mode, but the problem Dante addresses is that the divulgative prose, with which he sets out to give the reader access to hidden poetic *bontade*, itself from time to time takes on the very same difficulty it was intended to overcome: 'Degna di molta riprensione è quella cosa che, ordinata a torre alcuno diffetto, per se medesima quello induce; sí come quelli che fosse mandato a partire una rissa, e prima che partisse quella ne indusse un'altra' (*Conv.*, I. iii. 1) [Deserving of severe censure is that action which, while intended to remove some defect, itself introduces it, like the man who was sent to break up a quarrel, and before breaking it up began another].

Finally, despite the fact that the attribution of profound intellectual content to vernacular poetry would seem to be a key problem to be overcome, the discussion of the use of the vernacular in chapters v–xiii is centred almost entirely on a defence of the use of an Italian prose commentary – most notably, but not exclusively, in the claim that, given the fact that commentary in general is the 'servant' of poetry, it would be inappropriate

---

    Dante-commentator as much as or more than Dante-poet; see also Ascoli, *Dante*, p. 204 n. 60. In any event it is also crucial to note that although book I covers most of the traditional *accessus* topics, it does so in a way unprecedented and virtually unrecognizable in relation to the standard *accessus* format, or even an oddity such as Dante's own, later 'Epistle to Cangrande' (on the relationship between *Convivio* and the *Epistle*, see Ascoli, 'Access to Authority: Dante in the *Epistle to Cangrande*' in *Seminario Dantesco Internazionale / International Dante Seminar I*, ed. by Zygmunt G. Barański (Florence: Le Lettere, 1997), pp. 309–52.

22 As has been observed, in Boethius' *Consolatio* the prose does not serve as a commentary on the poems, rather the reverse (Stillinger, *The Song of Troilus*, pp. 41–2; Ascoli, *Dante*, p. 183).

to use the 'master' language, Latin, to comment on poetry written in a 'servile' tongue:[23]

> conviene questo comento, che è fatto invece di servo a le 'nfrascritte canzoni, esser subietto a quelle in ciascuna sua ordinazione [...]. Le quali disposizioni tutte li mancavano, se latino e non volgare fosse stato, poi che le canzoni sono volgari. Ché, primamente, non era subietto ma sovrano, e per la (sua) nobilità *e per vertù e per bellezza*. Per nobilità, perché lo latino è perpetuo e non corruttibile, e lo volgare è non stabile e corruttibile. [...] Ancora, non era subietto ma sovrano per vertù. Ciascuna cosa è virtuosa in sua natura che fa quello a che ella è ordinata [...]. Così lo sermone, lo quale è ordinato a manifestare lo concetto umano, è virtuoso quando quello fa [...]; onde, con ciò sia cosa che lo latino molte cose manifesta concepute ne la mente che lo volgare far non può [...] [e perciò] più è la vertù sua che quella del volgare. Ancora, non era subietto ma *sovrano per bellezza*. *Quella cosa dice l'uomo essere bella, cui le parti debitamente si rispondono, per che de la loro armonia resulta piacimento*. Onde pare l'uomo essere *bello*, quando le sue membra debitamente si rispondono; e dicemo *bello* lo canto, quando le voci di quello, secondo debito de l'arte, sono intra sé rispondenti. Dunque *quello sermone è più bello, ne lo quale più debitamente si rispondono [le parole]; e più debitamente si rispondono] in latino che in volgare*, però che lo volgare seguita uso, e lo latino arte: *onde concedesi esser più bello, più virtuoso e più nobile*. (*Conv.*, I. v. 6–7. 11–14; emphasis mine)

[(I)t is fitting that this commentary, which is made to play the part of a servant to the canzoni placed below, be subject to them in all of its functions [...]. All of these dispositions would be lacking if it had been in Latin and not in the vernacular, since the canzoni are in the vernacular. For in the first place it would not have been subject but sovereign, because of its nobility, its virtue, and its beauty. Because of its nobility, for Latin is eternal and incorruptible, while the vernacular is unstable and corruptible. [...] Moreover, Latin would not have been subject but sovereign because of its virtue. Everything is virtuous in its nature which fulfills the purpose toward which it is directed; [...] Thus language, which is constituted to express human [conceptions], is virtuous when it does this, [...] therefore, since Latin expresses many things conceived in the mind which the vernacular cannot, [...] its virtue is greater than that of the vernacular. Furthermore, Latin would not have been the subject but the sovereign because of its beauty. One calls a thing beautiful when its parts correspond properly, because pleasure results from their harmony. Thus a man appears beautiful when his limbs correspond properly; and we call a song beautiful when its voices are

23 On this metaphor, see Grayson, 'Dante e la prosa', pp. 41, 43 and 47–51; Stillinger, *The Song of Troilus*, p. 26; Ascoli, *Dante*, esp. pp. 207–9.

harmonized according to the rules of the art. Therefore, that language is the most beautiful in which the words correspond most properly; and they correspond more properly in Latin than in the vernacular, because the vernacular follows custom, while Latin follows art; consequently it is granted that Latin is the more beautiful, the more virtuous, and the more noble.]

My reasons for citing this passage in its entirety, including the superiority of Latin in nobility (i.e. its immutability over time and in space), and in virtue (i.e. its superior ability to express 'concetto umano'), as well as in 'bellezza', will become apparent shortly. At this point, there are two things to highlight. The first, as anticipated, is the affirmation of the two hierarchies, of poetry's superiority to prose and of Latin's to the vernacular, which, however, adds up to giving Dante's vernacular prose the central place in the treatise. The second, less expected, point is that, as against the concept of poetic 'bellezza' as extrinsic adornment put forward in both *Conv.*, II. i. 10 and ii. 11 (not to mention I. i and the congedo to 'Voi che 'ntendendo'), we are presented here with a different kind of beauty, *in bono*, namely, the harmonious blending of parts of speech into an integral whole. *This* beauty is not an extrinsic adornment, but rather a constitutive formal whole, put on a parallel footing with expressive content.

The process of justifying the use of vernacular prose reaches a culmination five chapters later in the following remarkable passage (cited only in part above), in which the hierarchical relationship of prose to poetry is effectively reversed, and in which even the superiority of Latin to vernacular is put into question:

> *nulla fa tanto grande quanto la grandezza de la propia bontade*, la quale è madre e conservatrice de l'altre grandezze. Onde nulla grandezza puote avere l'uomo maggiore che quella de *la virtuosa operazione, che è sua propia bontade* [...] E questa grandezza do io a questo amico [the vernacular], in *quanto quello elli di bontade avea in podere e occulto*, io lo fo avere in atto e palese ne *la sua propria operazione, che è manifestare conceputa sentenza.* [...] *Ché per questo comento la gran bontade del volgare di sì [si vedrà]; però che si vedrà la sua vertù, sì com'è per esso altissimi e novissimi concetti convenevolmente, sufficientemente e acconciamente, quasi come per esso latino, manifestare; [la quale non si potea bene manifestare] ne le cose rimate, per le accidentali adornezze che quivi sono connesse, cioè la rima e lo ri[ti]mo e lo numero regolato: sì come non si può bene manifestare la bellezza d'una donna*, quando li adornamenti de l'azzimare e de le vestimenta la fanno più ammirare che essa medesima. Onde chi vuole ben

giudicare d'una donna, *guardi quella quando solo sua naturale bellezza si sta con lei, da tutto accidentale adornamento discompagnata: sì come sarà questo comento,* nel quale si vedrà l'agevolezza de le sue sillabe, le proprietadi de le sue co[stru]zioni e le soavi orazioni che di lui si fanno; le quali chi bene agguarderà, vedrà essere piene di *dolcissima e d'amabilissima bellezza.* (*Conv.,* I. x. 7–9, 12–13; emphasis mine)

[nothing makes them so great as the greatness of their own goodness, which is the mother and preserver of all other kinds of greatness – for man can have no greatness greater than that of virtuous action, [...] and this greatness I give to this friend, since what it possesses of potential and latent goodness I make it express actively and openly through its own proper activity, which is to make manifest [a conceptualized meaning] conceived. [...] For by means of this commentary the great goodness of the vernacular of *sì* will be seen, because its virtue will be made evident, namely how it expresses the loftiest and the most unusual conceptions almost as aptly, fully, and gracefully as Latin, something that could not be expressed perfectly in verse, because of the accidental adornments that are tied to it, that is, rhyme and meter, just as the beauty of a woman cannot be perfectly expressed when the adornment of her preparation and apparel do more to make her admired than she does herself. Therefore, if anyone wishes to judge a woman justly, let him look at her when her natural beauty alone attends her, unaccompanied by any accidental adornment; so it will be with this commentary, in which the smoothness of the flow of its syllables, the appropriateness of its constructions, and the sweet discourses that it makes will be seen, which anyone upon careful consideration will find full of the sweetest and most exquisite beauty.]

Remarkably, the attribute that set Latin apart from vernacular, namely its 'virtuous' ability to 'make manifest [mentally] conceived ideas', is now the property of that same vernacular. And it is not the property whose *bontade*, if any, remains hidden beneath those 'accidentali adornezze', but rather of the prose which possesses not only expressive *bontade* 'quasi per esso latino' as well as a 'dolcissima e [...] amabilissima bellezza' that clearly echoes the beauty *in bono* that we saw attributed to Latin in the previous quotation.

It should now be quite clear why scholar after scholar has emphasized the importance of the prose in *Convivio*, and why, in fact, with very few exceptions, the poems are not themselves treated as a part of the text to be interpreted when confronting the treatise,[24] given the subtly dismissive way in which Dante himself treats them. A paradox, then: *the* paradox which underpins my argument. Where Dante's poetry is initially presented as the vehicle by which the 'pane de li angeli' will be made into food for the un-learned multitudes, and to which the prose stands as mere servant, in fairly short order it, poetry, becomes effectively mute, in fact, in some sense cedes its 'bontade', even 'bellezza' in the most positive sense, to that same prose. I have, of course, offered elsewhere one explanation of why Dante's focus is so carefully directed away from the poetry and onto the prose: on the one hand, he stresses the worthiness of the poetry to receive commentary, to be treated as an authoritative discourse when everything in Dante's culture says that it should not be so treated; on the other, he simply avoids the problem of justifying that treatment by never actually discussing what it is that makes his poetry worthy of commentary.[25] Yet, while I believe that explanation to be accurate, I do not think it is complete: the relationship of prose and poetry clearly is made problematic in itself, as I believe has now been amply demonstrated.

What I would like to show in closing is that there is also, in book I, a counter-discourse, as it were, by which the essential value and priority of poetry is reaffirmed, albeit at the cost of overtly contradicting the language that had just been used in celebrating the triumph of the prose commentary. After being systematically ignored throughout most of book I, poetry finally is reintroduced into the discourse in support of Dante's choice of using the vernacular, in the thirteenth and final chapter of book I, in the climactic proof of Dante's 'amistade' for his mother-tongue:

> Ciascuna cosa studia naturalmente a la sua conservazione: onde, se lo volgare per sé studiare potesse, studierebbe a quella; e quella sarebbe, acconciare sé a più stabilitade,

---

24 Symptoms of the scholarly inability to treat the poems and prose as part of the same text are the examples of editions in which the annotations to the former are made by a different critic than those to the latter, as in the cases of De Robertis and Vasoli, and of Fioravanti and Giunta, and the fact that by far the majority of attention given to *Voi che 'ntendendo* and *Amor che nella mente* as integral to the treatise comes in work concerned with explaining their later citation in the *Commedia*.
25 Ascoli, *Dante*, esp. pp. 205–18.

> e più stabilitade non potrebbe avere che in legar sé con numero e con rime. E questo medesimo studio è stato mio. (*Conv.*, I. xiii. 6–7)
>
> [Everything by nature pursues its own preservation; thus if the vernacular could by itself pursue anything, it would pursue that; and that would be to secure itself greater stability, and greater stability it could gain only by binding itself with meter and with rhyme. This has been precisely my purpose.]

'Rhythm and rhyme', previously dismissed as external adornments to be stripped away in order to reveal the true conceptualizing beauty and goodness of vernacular prose, are now recuperated as the instruments by which Dante-poet imposes unifying stability on the 'volgare', a stability which echoes both the 'nobility' and the 'bellezza' earlier attributed to Latin, and which will ultimately render it the equivalent of *grammatica* in the 'bene manifestare del concetto'. Poetry, suddenly, returns to the fore, and at least temporarily replaces prose as the vehicle by which the vernacular may aspire to equality with Latin.

Rather than resolving the 'dispute' between poetry and prose, however, this turn of conceptual events complicates our understanding of their relationship still further. Only three paragraphs along, Dante returns simultaneously to the opening and competing metaphors of the 'pane de li angeli' as the telos of the intellectual banquet and of the humble prose 'pane' serving as illuminating supplement to Dante's poetry, the two apparently conflated, as bread made of 'biado' that has been, miraculously, refined into 'pane orzato' (see again note 14):

> Così rivolgendo li occhi a dietro [...] puotesi vedere questo pane, col quale si deono mangiare le infrascritte canzoni, essere sufficientemente purgato da le macule, e da l'essere di biado; per che tempo è d'intendere a ministrare le vivande. Questo sarà quello pane orzato del quale si satolleranno migliaia, e a me ne soperchieranno le sporte piene. Questo sarà luce nuova, sole nuovo, lo quale surgerà là dove l'usato tramonterà, e darà lume a coloro che sono in tenebre e in oscuritade, per lo usato sole che a loro non luce. (*Conv.*, I. xiii. 11–12; emphasis mine)
>
> [So turning our gaze backwards [...] we can see that this bread, with which the canzoni placed below must be eaten, is sufficiently cleansed of its impurities and of being oaten. Therefore it is time to think of serving the (main courses). This commentary shall be that bread made with barley by which thousands shall be satiated,

and my baskets shall be full to overflowing with it. This shall be a new light, a new
sun which shall rise where the old sun shall set and which shall give (illumination)
to those who lie in shadows and in darkness because the old sun no longer sheds its
light upon them.]

We saw earlier how the (meta-)metaphor of illumination ('luce') figuring
the metaphor of bread figuring the prose commentary (*Conv.*, I. i. 14–15)
distantly anticipated a reversal of roles between prose and poetry and, in
the end, triumphantly, between vernacular and Latin.[26] In this passage we
see the 'typological' fulfillment, as it were, of the earlier one. As the phrase
'tempo è d'intendere a ministrare le vivande' specifically reminds us, the
humble 'pane' was initially prepared to be subservient 'minister' to the
'vivanda' of the *canzoni*, themselves a secondary vehicle for the 'divulgation' of the 'pane de li angeli'.[27] Still, it could not be clearer that the prose
comment has now explicitly metamorphosed into something very like,
but not identical to, that 'bread of angels', through an ascending series of
demonstratives: 'Questo pane', 'questo sarà quello pane orzato', 'questo sarà
quella luce nuova'. From merely and doubly (as handmaiden to the *canzoni*
and to poetry) instrumental, the prose 'pane' of Dante's commentary takes
on a higher, quasi-biblical function as redeemer of the previously ignorant
and unlettered.

It is also crucial, however, to recognize that the 'pane di biado' become
'pane orzato', as well as 'luce nuova, sole nuovo' is now not a philosophical
content per se, as the 'pane de li angeli' seemed to be in the first chapter, but
rather a language, capable of expressing 'conceputa sentenza' and thus able
not only to equal but in fact to replace the 'usato sole', that is, Latin.[28] This

---

26 For the catachrestic convergence of light and bread in I. xiii, see again Hooper, 'Il *Convivio*', pp. 98–9.
27 This phrasing explicitly recalls the contested phrasing in I. i. 11 discussed earlier (see n. 13) and anticipates the phrasing in II. i. 2 where the referent of 'vivanda' seems, at least momentarily, to have been displaced from *canzoni* to commentary (see n. 30).
28 One of the basic 'querelles' about the relationship of I. xiii to I. i concerns whether the 'pane orzato' is a metaphor for language only or for epistemological content as well, and, by extension, whether it is simply an evolution of the second, humbler kind of *pane* or in some sense related or even equivalent to the 'pane de li angeli'.

shift was prepared, as we saw, in the earlier passage devoted to the 'bontade' and 'bellezza' of the prose (*Conv.*, I. x. 12–13). And yet despite this – and despite the fact that everything about the syntax of this passage in relation to its immediate context tells us that it is the 'comento', the prose, which is both 'quello pane orzato' and that 'sole nuovo' – we will hardly have forgotten that Dante has just told us that the vernacular's capacity to rival the durability and incorruptibility of Latin, the 'usato sole', is an effect of poetic 'rhythm and rhyme' – indeed of *his own* poetic 'rhythm and rhyme'. Here,

> At least two factors make me propend for the latter, bearing in mind the extremely tortuous and self-contradictory route by which Dante arrives at this point. First is the fact that Dante, in the passages considered above, repeatedly makes the ability to communicate content the basis on which language is to be evaluated. Thus, if the vernacular has become capable of delivering 'conceputa sentenza' to at least the same degree of Latin, it is now not simply capable of relaying knowledge gathered from the 'beata mensa,' but indeed of constituting such a primary intellectual banquet in its own right – a point that will be fully illustrated only with Dante's claim to offer an original definition of true nobility in book IV (see n. 32). Second is the transference of biblical allusivity, which in I. i adhered to the 'pane de li angeli,' with its Old Testament echoes (Psalm 77: 25; cf. Wisdom 16. 20), but not, most commentators would agree, to the 'pane' of the commentary, to this latter and its language through the figure of 'pane orzato', with echoes from the Gospels (esp. John 6. 5–13, as well as 48–52, verses that can easily be read as reinterpreting the OT 'manna' and 'bread of angels' to be Christ as Sapientia [see again Nardi, 'La "vivanda"' and esp. O'Brien, 'Bread of Angels', p. 99]). The movement from Old to New Testament might imply, but only imply, that Dante's *Banquet* supersedes the 'beata mensa' of the classical philosophers from which it initially was said to derive (cf. Ransom, 'Panis Angelorum', who notes the reprise of the banquet image in *Paradiso* 24.1–9, specifically echoing *Conv.*, I. i. 7 and 10). Among those who emphasize 'pane orzato' as a figure of intellectual and/or spiritual substance, see Curto, 'Pane orzato'; Vasoli, note to I. xiii. 12, Dante, *Convivio*, pp. 88–9; Ruedi Imbach, *Dante, la philosophie, et les laïcs* (Freiburg: Éditions Universitaires de Fribourg, 1996), pp. 134–8; For 'pane' as language, see Nardi, 'La "vivanda"'; G. Busnelli and G. Vandelli, 'Note', in *Il Convivio: Ridotto a miglior lezione e commentato*, ed. by Busnelli and Vandelli, 2 vols (Florence: Le Monnier, 1954, 2nd edn), pp. 85–6; Tavoni, *Qualche idea* (by implication). Two critics make the suggestive but perhaps unprovable argument that the metaphorics of bread in book I and especially in chapters i and xiii anticipate the metaliterary reflections on the 'allegory of poets' vs. 'allegory of theologians' in ii. 1: see Sarolli, *Prolegomena*, pp. 35–8; Ransom, 'Panis Angelorum', esp. 85–90.

I submit, the previously mentioned double logic, of rational argumentation and an overriding desire that trumps consistency of argument, is at its most visible. That desire is itself double: to raise Dante's own humble banquet and its 'pane' up to the level of the *beata mensa*, and to overcome the obstacles he faces in valorizing the 'bontade' of his poetry, which has been overshadowed by its 'bellezza'. And one result, as we now see, is, after a gradual, book-long, reversal of the initial prose/poetry, 'pane/vivanda' hierarchy, this turn to an exalted vision of the vernacular which, at least by implication, owes as much to the enduring form that the rhythm and rhyme of poetry bestow as to the clarifying expressivity of prose.

In book I, then, the ambiguous relationship between servant prose and master poetry has not been explicitly resolved – indeed, the final chapter pushes the internally conflicted metaphor of 'pane' to an extreme, with the one clear result that the 'volgare' – whether prose or poetry or both – has now allusively been put on a footing equal, if not superior, to that of Latin. And when the metaphor of 'pane' returns, for the very last time, in the first chapter of the second book, this acquisition is a given, while a certain confusion persists between the standing of the prose and the poetry, notwithstanding the fact that the explicit focus is once again on the role of the prose as interpretive supplement in subordinate relation to the poetry:

> Poi che proemialmente ragionando, me ministro, è lo *mio pane* ne lo precedente trattato con sufficienza preparato, lo tempo chiama e domanda la mia nave uscir di porto; per che, dirizzato l'artimone de la ragione a l'òra del mio desiderio, entro in pelago con isperanza di dolce cammino e di salutevole porto e laudabile ne *la fine de la mia cena*. Ma però che più profittabile sia questo mio cibo, *prima che vegna la prima vivanda voglio mostrare come mangiare si dee*. Dico che, sì come nel primo capitolo è narrato, questa sposizione conviene essere litterale e allegorica. (*Conv.*, II. i. 1–2; emphasis mine)

> [Now that by way of a preface my bread has been sufficiently prepared in the preceding book through my ministrations, time calls and requires my ship to leave port; thus, having set the sail of my reason to the breeze of my desire, I enter upon the open sea with the hope of a smooth voyage and a safe and praiseworthy port at the end of my feast. But so that this food of mine may be more profitable, I wish to show, before it appears, how the first course must be eaten. As I stated in the first chapter, this exposition must be both literal and allegorical.]

In the first place, the language itself is confused, beginning with the drastically mixed culinary and nautical metaphors.[29] In addition, to go by the traditional placement of the *canzoni* before the prose in books II through IV, 'vivanda' could easily be taken to refer to the commentary,[30] rather than, as it has in seven previous references (and as it will be subsequently at *Conv.*, II. xi. 10) to the *canzoni*.[31] And a problem remains even if one simply ignores this referential problem, as well as the difficulty of understanding what *precisely* is meant by 'come mangiare si dee' (what seems to be an instruction for the reader on how to consume the text immediately morphs into a description of what the text itself is doing). This is because, as the last sentence of the quotation states unequivocally, II. i, so often taken

29   Note, incidentally, the way in which Dante's mixture of metaphors, shifting between nautical and nutritional, both calls attention to the figurative quality of the prose and to a certain confusion in the way those figures are being deployed (as, again, in the apparent slippage between kinds of *pane*, as between *pane* and *vivanda*). Gian Roberto Sarolli, *Prolegomena*, p. 35, both calls attention to this conflation of figures and notes that the same juxtaposition recurs in *Paradiso* II.1–18 (the passage where 'pan de li angeli' notoriously reappears for the second and last time in Dante's œuvre (l. 11). On the nautical metaphor particularly applied to Dante himself, see Hooper, 'Il *Convivio*', S94–S96, who also notes the mixing of the two metaphorical strands (S99–S101).
30   In his edition of *Convivio* Giorgio Inglese proposes an innovative solution to this additional inconsistency, that is, that although modern editions generally place the poems before the prose in all three books, the authorial voice speaks of showing how the *vivanda*, previously identified with those poems, should be eaten before the reader encounters it. He does this by placing the *canzoni* after the first chapter in each of books II–IV. Inglese's justification is interpretive and lacks any basis in the manuscript tradition; Inglese, 'Avvertenza', in Dante Alighieri, *Convivio* (Milan: BUR, 1993), pp. 29–30; I am grateful to Beatrice Arduini for confirming that the *canzoni* are present, always placed at the beginning of the book in which they are commented upon, throughout the MS tradition, from the earliest examples forward.
31   I hesitate to add the final use of the word, at the very end of book II, because it has required emendation to make it refer to the *canzoni:* 'E qui si termina lo secondo trattato, [che è ordinato a sponere la canzone] che per prima vivanda è messa innanzi'. Without the emendation (common to Busnelli-Vandelli and to Ageno) the sentence is still coherent, but 'vivanda' now refers to the prose treatise, as it arguably does in II. i. 2 as well.

to reveal Dante's poetics, in fact concerns not the intentions of Dante-*poeta* in writing his *canzoni*, but how his poetry will be 'expounded', literally and allegorically, in and by the prose commentary.[32]

This, of course, is not the end of the story. Whether or not II. i is 'about' the poetry or the prose, the application of a biblical model of signification to Dante's exegetical practices speaks eloquently about his ambitions for the *canzoni*, in despite of the fact that he does not then actually make use of the model he describes). And at the end of the 'literal' exegesis of 'Voi che 'ntendendo', immediately following the apparently dismissive account (cited earlier) of the *canzone*'s inability to make its 'bontade' known without the help of commentary, he partially reverses the thrust of his argument, and in the process goes beyond what could be literally derived from a reading of the *canzoni*:

> Che non voglio in ciò altro dire [...] se non: O uomini, che vedere non potete la sentenza di questa canzone, non la rifiutate però; ma *ponete mente la sua bellezza*, ch'è grande sì per construzione, la quale si pertiene a li gramatici, sì per l'ordine del sermone, che si pertiene a li rettorici, sì per lo numero de le sue parti, che si pertiene a li musici. [...] E questa è tutta la litterale sentenza de la prima canzone, *che è per prima vivanda intesa* innanzi. (*Conv.*, II. xi. 9)

> [For I mean nothing (else) by this [...] save: (O you) who cannot perceive the meaning of this canzone, do not therefore reject (her); rather consider (her) beauty, which is great by virtue of its composition, which is the concern of the grammarians, by virtue of the order of its discourse, which is the concern of the rhetoricians, and by the virtue of the rhythm of its parts, which is the concern of the musicians. [...] This is the complete literal meaning of the first canzone, which, as has been indicated above, constitutes the first course.]

This 'bellezza' – which reflects the full powers of three of the liberal arts – and echoes/anticipates the famous definition of poetry in *De vulgari*

---

32   See 'Tradurre l'allegoria: *Convivio* 2.1', in a special triple issue of *Critica del Testo* entitled 'Dante Oggi', ed. by Piero Boitani and Roberto Antonelli, Fall 2011, vol. 3, 153–75. The point was earlier made by Jean Pépin, *Dante et la tradition de l'allégorie* (Paris: Vrin, 1973) and by John Scott, 'Dante's Allegory of the Theologians', in *The Shared Horizon*, ed. by Tom O'Neill (Dublin: Irish Academic Press, 1990), pp. 27–40.

eloquentia as 'fictio rethorica musicaque poita' (*DVE* II. iv. 2) – is clearly more closely related to the beauty *in bono* earlier attributed to 'grammatica' and to the prose than to the superficial 'ornamento' negatively associated with poetry in book I and, apparently, earlier in the same paragraph.

In book IV poetry will come more fully into its own as the primary vehicle of the vernacular as 'luce nuova, sole nuovo', and this in two ways, one explicit, one implicit.[33] First, there is the third *canzone*, which explicitly departs from the 'dolci rime d'amore' – presumptively *Voi che 'ntendendo* and *Amor che nella mente* – that Dante used to write, and provides without need for any allegorical prose explication a philosophical content.[34] Not only that, but Dante now claims for himself and his poem no mere 'divulgation' of classical philosophical culture but rather genuine originality, namely the redefinition of 'nobility' as an individual trait, rather than as an effect of 'stirpe' and/or of wealth. Second, of course, there is the extraordinary etymological definition of the poetic *autore* from *avieo*, where the binding power of rhythm and rhyme is compared to, in fact, I dare say, implicitly equated with, the vowels that bind together language itself (*Conv.*, IV. vi. 4).[35] In book IV, then, we are offered an account of vernacular poetry able to express its 'bontade', actually its 'nobiltà', without the mediation of prose, and indeed as the agent by which a vernacular is given the permanence and stability that allows it to express 'altissimi e novissimi concetti'. The full fruits of this painstaking process of freeing his poetry from the need for a prosaic supplement, of course, will only be seen after the *Convivio* has been abandoned in favour of a new, poetry-only, project, of far greater ambition: the *Commedia*.

---

33 Ascoli, *Dante*, esp. pp. 115–16, 217–18.
34 The prose commentary is thus entirely literal, serving as an amplification of the poetry, not a revelation of hidden contents. It is nonetheless striking that the explicit change in the status of poetry does not translate into a shorter commentary, quite the reverse, since at thirty the number of chapters in book IV equals that of the two previous books combined. I will not attempt to account for this additional contradiction except to repeat what I have argued at length elsewhere, that the prose of book IV has as an implicit agenda of conferring on Dante personally the authority and nobility which are his explicit topics.
35 Ascoli, *Dante*, esp. pp. 108–21, 129.

MARIA LUISA ARDIZZONE

7 'Ne la selva erronea': Dante's *Quaestio* on Nobility and the Criticism of Materialism

This essay re-reads the third *canzone* of the *Convivio* by focusing on Dante's criticism of riches and material goods as part of his criticism of nobility, conceived as a privilege of ancient possessions and wealth which are assumed to lead naturally to good social manners.

My chapter will consider Dante's new way of writing in this *canzone*, a way of writing based on technicality and syllogism. In fact, *Le dolci rime d'amor ch'io solia* is governed by a syllogistic reasoning that appears to be the *constructio congrua* to the theme discussed. A strong rational tone governs the *canzone*, which is ordered as a medieval *quaestio*, coinciding with the weaving of the text. The *canzone* thus organizes its argument between a *pars destruens*, or refutation, and a *pars construens*. My exploration emphasizes a link between the criticism of riches and the refutation of materialism and materiality. The most important issue is that of the suggested relationship between the criticism of materialism and the doubt about the origin of matter that the prose text of the *Convivio* (I. iv. 8) introduces. I will suggest that this relationship also lies at the heart of Dante's confrontation with the problem of evil and the genesis of his *Inferno*, conceived as determined by the rules of matter and materialism.

The last treatise of *Convivio* was written, like the others, during Dante's exile and perhaps in part while he was living in the north of Italy, between 1304 and 1306. The treatise is conceived as a commentary on the *canzone Le dolci rime d'amor ch'io solia* [The tender rhymes of love I once sought out within my thoughts]. Both the *canzone* and the prose explanation introduce new themes and new interests. Scholars agree that the *canzone* belongs to Dante's Florentine years, and most likely to the early 1290s.[1]

Reading *Le dolci rime d'amor ch'io solia*, we see that the major theme of books II and III of *Convivio* fades away. The model is no longer that of intellectual contemplation. The love-contemplation of the *donna gentile* portrayed as an intellectual goal shared by humans and heavenly intelligences finds no place in the last treatise of the *Convivio*. A new tension arises in which the criticism of nobility, based on ancient privilege and wealth, marks the entrance of a theme of great importance in Dante's age. In fact, the criticism of riches in the *canzone* is part of a larger issue that includes the criticism of materialism and human beings' inclination for it. Dante is dealing with new themes that indirectly work to reshape the ideas that he has previously proposed. A new type of prose takes form, in which two synchronic operations are active. The writing implies both an erasing and a reshaping. Dante tends, in the treatise, to use syllogistic reasoning, clearly aiming at demonstration. He thus signals a break and a new beginning. The *donna gentile* almost disappears and is simply identified with philosophy, the very meaning of which is rethought in the light of this new content.

The Criticism of Material Wealth

The *canzone Le dolci rime d'amor che io solia* opens by signalling a break with what Dante had previously written. It announces a new type of poetry that employs a kind of rhyme that Dante calls 'aspra e sottile' (l. 14) [harsh and subtle]. He presents this as a new mode of writing that is opposed to his previous mode, which he characterizes in the opening of the *canzone* as 'sweet' and centred on love. He informs his readers that in the past he

[1] Maria Corti, in the light of the *canzone*'s organization and syllogistic reasoning, has proposed that its composition should be located close to the years of the writing of the commentary. Maria Corti, *La felicità mentale. Nuove prospettive per Cavalcanti e Dante* (Turin: Einaudi, 1983), pp. 144–5.

has devised this poetry by searching for it in his thoughts ('cercar ne' miei pensieri'; l. 2).[2] The verb *cercar* must be read in relation to *trobar* or *invenire*. It suggests that the poet's 'invention' in the past, in the classical rhetorical meaning of the thing to be found, derived from the mind's inner power of thinking. However, the first of the seven stanzas, together with a *congedo*, that form the scheme of this *canzone*, takes us back in part to Dante's previous mode of writing in order to establish a new way. The announced break with the past is evident, even though the *canzone* includes the attempt to reshape from a new perspective contents already established in the first two *canzoni* on which the *Convivio* has commented. Traditionally, as mentioned above, the date of composition of *Le dolci rime* has been assumed to be that of the Florentine years and close to the composition of the first two *canzoni*, that is, around 1293–4. This date fits with the critique of the theory of nobility that is the focus of Dante's text, in an ideal relationship with the Ordinances of Justice of Giano della Bella of 1293.[3]

The *canzone* is organized as a medieval *quaestio*, which initially puts forth a *thesis* that coincides with a refutation or *pars destruens*, which will be followed by the *pars construens* or *antithesis*. The fact that an eminent jurist, Bartolomeus of Sassoferrato commented on this *canzone* between 1342 and 1355 has drawn attention to the historical theme of nobility.[4] My

2   The opening confirms that the 'dolci rime' of the past were shaped on the authority of the poet's interior language, mostly conceived of in Augustinian terms. I have discussed this issue, relating it to the *ornatus difficilis* of *transumptio* as present in the *Ars poetriae* of Geoffrey of Vinsauf and in a rhetorical treatise of the thirteenth century: the *Rhetorica novissima* by Boncompagno da Signa. See Maria Luisa Ardizzone, *Dante: il paradigma intellettuale. Un'inventio degli anni fiorentini* (Florence: Olschki, 2011), chapters 1 and 2, and Maria Luisa Ardizzone, ' "Verbum valet plurimum": Tracing a Fragment of Dante's Poetics', *Italica*, 90 (3) (2013), 319–42.
3   Giano della Bella was the leader of a 'popular' movement in the 1290s and is known as the promulgator of the *Ordinamenti di Giustizia* (January 1293), the basis of the constitution of the Florentine Ordinances of Justice, drawn up at his instigation, which attacked the privileges of the magnates and gave the minor guilds a share in the government.
4   Paolo Borsa, '*Sub nomine nobilitatis*: Dante e Bartolo di Sassoferrato', in *Studi dedicati a Gennaro Barbarisi*, ed. by Claudia Berra and Michele Mari (Milan: Cuem, 2007), pp. 59–121.

reading here will focus on the first part of the *canzone* and on what the *canzone* refutes: namely, the idea of nobility based on ancient privilege, material wealth, and refined or 'gentle' customs.⁵ The *canzone*, in opposing this traditional idea, introduces a new thought that relates nobility to virtue. This virtue is the result of a gift given by God, a gift named nobility, *bontate*, and also *grazia*. Virtue, here, coincides with the Aristotelian ethical mean (*mezzo*) that allows human beings to shun excess by choosing the medium between two extremes. Excess as something natural to the human being that the gift of *grazia* allows him to control, driving him to the choice of the mean, is a notion that must be highlighted. In the prose section, Dante will explain this notion of the mean, without however mentioning the reason why human beings incline to extremes or excesses. Actually, the theory of the right mean in Aristotle's *Ethics* worked to counteract the natural inclination towards the passions to which human behaviour tends. The Aristotelian moral virtues were shaped on the idea that morality implies control and free will. In *Convivio* IV our inclination to the extremes is recalled in the prose commentary (IV. iv. 17); it is just touched on in the *canzone*. That human nature has a material component on which our passions depend and which is their origin, is a topic that Dante had been tackling since the years in which he was writing the poems which entered the *Vita nova* and the *Vita nova* itself.⁶

Dante will return to this theme later, but this *canzone* shows that he now starts by seeking to create a new referential framework. In this section,

---

5   Borsa, '*Sub nomine nobilitatis*', p. 76. Borsa notes that Dante's discussion seems to be in some ways conservative.
6   Ardizzone discusses the *canzone Donne ch'avete intelletto d'amore*, pointing out the meaning of '*non for misura*' as a clear reference and opposition to Cavalcanti 'oltra misura' (*Donna me prega*, v. 44); *Dante: il paradigma intellettuale*, pp. 48–63. For Cavalcanti's 'oltra misura' as related and derived from the medieval theory of matter, see Maria Luisa Ardizzone, *Guido Cavalcanti, The Other Middle Ages* (London & Toronto: Toronto University Press, 2002), pp. 70–86, 94–102. 'Oltra misura' is related to the idea that matter is in itself an excess, thus the corporeal materiality of the human being is assumed to be responsible for his strong inclinations to passions.

I intend to point out how the criticism of materiality and materialism[7] go together in the *canzone*, and how they preside over the section of the *canzone* that deals with refutation and also with the construction of a new paradigm that parallels and opposes the model of thinking that is refuted. I will consider how, in the first part of the *canzone*, Dante criticizes the concept of nobility summarized above and focuses on a critique of material goods. The link that unifies the two different sections of the *canzone*, which my readings stress, opens up a fresh interpretation of the text and, more importantly, of Dante's future work. I anticipate my reading and the thesis to be proposed as follows. The focus of the *canzone* is socio-political. Its core is the individuation of what creates social discrimination on the one hand and the wrong beliefs that affect society on the other. Dante's analysis offers an answer in which the roots of the problem are located in a unifying principle, that is, in our natural inclination to materiality and materialism. I will also consider that in the initial prose section, Dante will introduce a short but extremely important appeal to the problematic issue of matter and its origin 'se la prima materia de li elementi era da Dio intesa' (*Conv.*, IV. i. 8) [whether the primal matter of the elements was intellected by God], relating this issue to his break with 'philosophy'. My reading attempts to emphasize the existence of a link between this doubt about the ontology of matter and the false values that the *canzone* refutes, and proposes that the prose introducing the doubt indirectly radicalizes and motivates from a philosophical perspective the criticism active in the first section of the *canzone*.

---

[7] *Materialism*, as I use this word, implies the criterion that judges values in a way that is material or assumes as a value something that is material. Thus *materialism* is coincident with the importance given to material things, as the human material component determinates it. In this sense *materialism* and *materiality* are strongly connected and *materiality* is determined by the laws of matter that represent a power that may act to influence human behaviour.

A Philosophical Doubt

At the centre of the above-quoted passage of the prose there is the complex medieval theory of the origin of matter, a debated issue the prose text mentions as a problematic one and that we may understand in its centrality by linking the *canzone* to the meaning that this particular prose passage suggests. I offer as a thesis that at the centre of the *canzone* there is a criticism of materiality and materialism. This continues to be a problematic issue that is confirmed in the first part of the prose text written many years after. It is on this basis that Dante's ontological problem of evil begins to take shape. Actually the discussion about matter can also be fruitfully related to Dante's future work, most especially to the beginning of the *Commedia*.

Going back to the *canzone* now that the sweetness of style is removed, we must evaluate the *aspro* and *sottile* that the *canzone* presents as a new way to write. *Aspro* is opposed to sweet, and *sottile* introduces the *difficilis as operatio ratiocinandi* in a meaning close to the practice of syllogism as given by Aquinas in his commentary on Aristotle's *Posterior Analytics*. Thus the *sottile* seems to coincide with the practice of syllogism.[8] *Aspro*, which De Robertis explains as technical,[9] according to the description given by Dante in the *De vulgari eloquentia*,[10] and is associated with the use of polysyllabic words, seems to return to the vocabulary that is able to introduce the topics at stake. But the fact that the practice of syllogism with a demonstrative cognitive purpose appears in a *canzone* with a sociopolitical nature is an original aspect of Dante's work. In fact demonstration in the *Analytics* is proper to things that are *per se* and eternal.[11] Because of

---

8 Thomas Aquinas, 'In Posteriorum analyticorum, Lectio 4', in *Aristotelis libros peri hermeneias et posteriorum analyticorum, Expositio*, ed. by R. M. Spiazzi (Rome: Marietti, 1955), pp. 158–63.
9 Dante, *Rime*, ed. by Domenico De Robertis (Florence: Edizioni del Galluzzo, 2005).
10 The *De vulgari eloquentia* introduces 'asperitas' at I. xiv. 4–5 and at II. vii. 6, and xiii. 13.
11 'Demonstratio non est de corruptibilis, demonstratio esse de perpetuis'; Aquinas, 'In posteriorum analyticorum', pp. 199–201.

this, Dante's use of syllogism to know things that are in time shows that he applies syllogistic tools to demonstrate things that are part of human earthly life. In addition, Dante seeks to reduce different elements *ad unum*. This works as a kind of subtext that governs the text and aims at creating a unifying principle that is fundamental in both the *pars construens* and the *pars destruens*. This is the critique of materiality. This logical weaving is clearly demonstrated, and the reader must be aware of the socio-political issues and the logical rhetorical apparatus of this.[12] In fact, the *refutatio* is part of both logic and rhetoric.

Since the *Vita nova* (and later in the *canzoni Voi ch'intendendo* [You whose intellect] and *Amor che ne la mente mi ragiona* [Love, that speaks to me within my mind]), Dante had introduced the adjective *gentile* in a way that problematized its meaning. Of course, as he himself writes, he is indebted for this to Guinizzelli's *canzone Al cor gentile* [Love hastens ever to the gentle heart], a treatise in verse on love and *gentilezza*, or nobility, as intellectual.[13] This text had been important to Dante since the time he wrote the poems that would enter the *Vita nova*, as well as the first two *canzoni* of the *Convivio*, in which the *donna gentile* radicalizes in philosophical terms contents of Guinizzelli, mostly utilizing the Neoplatonic and Aristotelian learning which thirteenth-century *philosophantes* were connecting.[14]

---

12 In Ciceronian rhetoric the parts of a speech ('partes orationis') are the 'exordium' or opening, the 'narratio' or statement of facts, the 'divisio' or 'partitio', that is, the statement of the point at issue and exposition of what the orator proposes to prove, the 'confirmatio' or exposition of arguments, the 'confutatio' or refutation of one's opponent's arguments, and finally the 'conclusio' or peroration. This six-fold division is that given in *De Inventione* and *Ad Herennium*, but Cicero tells us that some divided it into four or five or even seven parts, and Quintilian regards 'partitio' as contained in the third part, which he calls 'probatio', proof, and thus is left with a total of five. M. L. Clarke and D. H. Berry, *Rhetoric at Rome: A Historical Survey* (London: Routledge, 1996).
13 Maria Luisa Ardizzone, 'Love and Natural Law in the Manifesto of *Dolce Stil Novo*', in *The Craft and the Fury: Essays in Memory of Glauco Cambon, Italiana*, ed. by J. Francese, 9 (2000), pp. 35–57.
14 Ardizzone, *Il paradigma intellettuale*, pp. 115–16.

In *Voi ch'intendendo*, in fact, the adjective *gentile* attributed to the angel-intelligences (l. 5) connoted nobility as intellectual and suggested a relationship between the minds of the angelic intelligences, the movement of the heavens, and the human mind that conceives the new love for the woman. Later in *Amor che ne la mente mi ragiona*, the new lady is identified as *gentile* confirming the identification between *gentilezza* and the intellect.[15] Now in *Le dolci rime*, *gentilezza* as nobility becomes a category in itself and something to be understood in a different context. The conclusion in the *canzone* will be that nobility is the friend of the lady, identified with philosophy: 'io vo parlando de l'amica vostra' (l. 144) [I speak about a friend of yours] suggesting a tie between the intellectual gift of grace and the activity of thinking.

This *canzone*, which is written in *rima aspra* for its sound and technicality and with subtlety according to the construction of its sentences and use of words, proceeds with arguments and disputations. The announced break with the past way of writing in *Le dolci rime* is said to be derived from something threatening that has appeared in the deeds of the *donna*. These actions have prevented the author from continuing the usual sweet style he had used in his discussion about love. In this context a new word, *valore*, is introduced 'e dirò del valore' (l. 12) [I'll speak about the quality]. It is trisyllabic and technical at once, and points to that value in the light of which one may say that a man is gentle, that is, noble. The reader does not receive any further information about the reason for the lady's threatening aspect, but the prose section will reiterate that something has created a short circuit, which the prose will link to the question about the origin of matter: 'se la prima materia de li elementi era da Dio intesa' (IV. i. 8) [whether the primal matter of the elements was intellected by God]. The reader of the poem is therefore left with a space to be filled in order to get the reason of 'atti disdegnosi e feri | che ne la donna mia | sono appariti' (ll. 5–7) [the proud and scornful manner that my lady bears] the true sense of the change that is announced, and the new poetry the *canzone* is inaugurated.

15 The *Liber de causis* identifies nobility and intellectual. *De causis*, 3. 27, Ardizzone, *Il paradigma intellettuale*, pp. 36–139.

The relationship between true nobility and ethics is at the basis of the texture of the *canzone*. This relationship in turn can be established only if the false idea and judgement regarding *gentilezza* is refuted. After that, the *canzone* will build the new meaning of *gentilezza* and its origin and signs. It is in this second part that the *canzone* will introduce ethics.

Time and Syllogism

We start by considering that the *canzone*, in confronting the notion of *gentilezza*, identified with nobility, organizes a critique of the historical notion of nobility. It apparently eliminates the idea of *gentilezza* as intellectual, which Dante had introduced in *Amor che ne la mente* and whose paradigm is that of separate substances.[16] In book IV, nobility is a divine gift given to the individual and in which the harmony between soul and body emerges as the human being's natural predisposition to grace. Because the adjective *gentile* was qualifying the being of the *donna* as related to the field of *gentilezza* in the *canzone Amor che ne la mente*, it is suggested that the discussion about nobility works also toward redefining nobility and the identity of the Lady. If this is true, then the *canzone* implies a rewriting with the purpose of reshaping certain contents. A reader who is aware of the meanings of the two previous *canzoni* on which the *Convivio* comments is immediately conscious of this enterprise. Not only is *gentilezza* now grounded in a divine gift, but also the notion of virtue as a pure intellectual aim, implicit in the first two *canzoni*, is refuted.[17] Now ethics consists in the moral virtues, and from these virtues the Aristotelian

---

16   Ardizzone, in *Il paradigma intellettuale*, identifies *gentilezza* with the intellect; see in particular chapters 3 and 4.
17   In the *Nicomachean Ethics*, Aristotle distinguishes the intellectual virtues from the moral virtues. *Convivio* II and III deal with the intellectual virtues and intellectual happiness. In *Le dolci rime* happiness is granted by the practice of the right mean. For a discussion about intellectual virtues and intellectual happiness in the *Convivio*, see

theory of the right mean comes in. Teodolinda Barolini has recently written an essay on the Aristotelian mean that is extremely suggestive and scientifically grounded.[18] I refer to this study for my discussion of moral virtue. My reading of the *canzone*, however, will focus on a different issue that can be traced as part of the criticism of the notion of nobility rooted in wealth and materialism.

The first notion that the *canzone* refutes is the false and cowardly judgement of those who think that the criterion for judging *gentilezza* is wealth: 'riprovando 'l giudicio falso e vile | di quei che voglion che di gentilezza | sia principio ricchezza' (ll. 15–17) [By refuting the false and base beliefs | of those who claim that riches | are the source of true nobility]. Here *principio*, 'principle', means criterion of judgement and also source or origin. Dante's method introduces speculation before starting the discussion of nobility at line 18, where he calls as a witness the lord who dwells in the eyes of the lady. The meaning here is that speculation anticipates action, where action is coincident with the content expressed in poetry and poetry itself. Poetry conceived as part of civil discourse, an idea that is active in an influential line of thought in the thirteenth century, is thus part of politics, which is an architectonic art, according to Brunetto, Alfarabi, and Aristotle, and which is a most important science according to the first two.[19]

If the *canzone* was written in the years of Giano della Bella's *ordinamenti di giustizia*, that is in the very years in which Dante enters the political arena (1296), this may be related to the *canzone*. What emerges is a political-social use of speculation that leads to practical activity. The

---

Ardizzone, *Reading as the Angels Read. Politics and Speculation in Dante's 'Convivio'* (Toronto: Toronto University Press, 2016).

18 On this *canzone* see Teodolinda Barolini, 'Aristotle's "mezzo", courtly "misura" and Dante's *canzone* "Le dolci rime": Humanism, Ethics, and Social Anxiety', in *Dante and the Greeks*, ed. by J. M. Ziolkowski (Washington, DC: Dumbarton Oaks Research Library and Collection, 2014), pp. 163–79.

19 I have discussed this issue in relation to Aristotle and Brunetto in *Reading as the Angels Read*, pp. 274–5, 365. For the importance of politics in Alfarabi, see M. Mahdi, 'Science, Philosophy and Religion in Alfarabi's Enumeration of the Sciences', in *The Cultural Context of Medieval Learning*, ed. by J. E. Murdoch and E. D. Sylla (Dordrecht and Boston: Reidel, 1975), pp. 113–47.

logical dialectical discourse shapes poetry, and poetry is written as a call to action: 'Contra-li-erranti mia, tu te n'andrai (l. 141) [My song Against-the-erring-ones, go forth].

Speculation and praxis are related and poetry is part of praxis. This indirectly reiterates what we have read in the *canzone*, *Voi ch'intendendo*, where the angels were able to move the heavens because of their divine speculation. The idea that human beings too are able to speculate permeates the first two *canzoni*. The way in which such speculation takes place is part of the meanings the *canzoni* introduce, and in them a political endeavour must be evaluated, which in light of the third becomes more evident. Here in this third *canzone*, the human ability to speculate is related to the meaning of his love for philosophy. But this speculation, it is suggested, allows human beings to act through poetry. The envoi informs his readers that the *canzone* is written to oppose the *erranti*, that is, those who are responsible for a false idea about nobility. Poetry may influence other human beings: *poiesis* and *praxis* are related. And the link should be operative in the life of the city or politics. Brunetto, in his *Tresor*, while proposing politics as an architectonic science, writes that this science contains both things said and things done, words and actions.[20] Politics as an architectonic science has a command over other sciences, according to the definition Aristotle offers in his *Metaphysics* at A. 2. 982. a. 16–17. Politics has under it technical and linguistic arts. In this way we may trace Dante's awareness of a socio-political goal given to this *canzone*. And what cannot escape is a kind of ideological *militanza* that powerfully contributes to shape the text: 'Contra-gli-erranti mia, tu te n'andrai'.

The second stanza of the *canzone* (ll. 21–40) refutes the error of defining nobility with ancestral possessions and refined customs of life: 'antica possession d'avere | con reggimenti belli' (ll. 23–4) [ancestral wealth | together with fine manners]. In the third stanza this refutation starts to

---

20   Brunetto Latini, *Tresor*, ed. by P. G. Beltrami, P. Squillacioti, P. Torri and S. Zatteroni (Turin: Einaudi, 2007), book 1.5–1.9 establishes politics as the highest science, it presides over the arts and crafts that are useful for the life of human society. Sciences of words include grammar, dialectic and rhetoric. The last in its turn includes the *ars dictandi*, plus law and justice.

run in parallel with a cognitive issue. The parallel is established to show that, in the same way that defining a human being as 'animated wood' is untrue and incomplete ('Chi diffinisce: Omo è legno animato, | prima dice non vero, | e dopo 'l falso parla non intero' (ll. 41–3) [He who claims 'Man is a living tree' | first says what isn't true | and, having said what's false, leaves much unsaid]), when Frederick II defines nobility as long-held possessions, on the one hand says something untrue and on the other argues defectively because wealth cannot either bestow or remove *gentilezza* because the possessions' own nature is base.

Gentilezza and material wealth differ in nature, and the baseness of wealth is manifested because, however vast its accumulation may be, it can give no peace, and the right and true human being does not care to hold or to lose riches. In this discussion, nobility is detached from material value and also from refined manners, insofar as these depend on inherited wealth and are considered formally vitiated by false conventions.

Gentilezza is not a privilege of birth, nor a privilege derived from an inherited tradition, nor a privilege determined by beautiful manners as the result of ancestral riches. Dante announced at line 12 that his goal would be to establish the meaning of *valore* in relation to true *gentilezza*: 'e dirò del valore, | per il quale veramente omo è gentile' (ll. 12–13) [I'll speak about the quality | which makes a person truly noble]. For this reason, the *canzone* is organized in a logical sequence, structured in a para-syllogistic way (via imperfect syllogisms).The goal of such imperfect syllogisms is demonstration.

Here is the first of these, as traditionally formulated and then refuted: *gentilezza* is a value, old riches are a value, *gentilezza* is ancestral riches. But in what follows this is opposed and shaped again as an imperfect syllogism, which opens up a new, problematic territory: *gentilezza* is a value, riches are base, *gentilezza* is not the possession of wealth.

The meaning here is not just that *gentilezza* is not coincident with material wealth, but more importantly and powerfully that value, *valore*, and wealth are opposites. What is material and what is of value are disconnected the one from the other. What takes shape here is also the concept of value as a field of reflection. *Valore* [value] has nothing to do with the material in this *canzone*. The change that is introduced belongs first of all to the area of mental associations that are disconnected, and it is here that the para-syllogistic texture works. The vocabulary utilized is crucially important. *Valore* in Guinizzelli's *Al cor gentil reimpaira sempre amor* meant power as well as energy [Love hastens ever to the gentle heart]. Now the text attempts to open a new relational field for *valore*. The dissimilitude that is established between true nobility and riches works in light of the natural similitude between the image that we create inside our mind when we want to make a *figura* and the fact that this *figura*, before being expressed, must already be in the mind (ll. 52–5). This natural innate link (similitude) cannot be established between *gentilezza* and riches. They are by nature different and cannot have any kind of relation, just as a stream that runs far from a tower cannot be influenced by the distant tower (ll. 54–5). Here distance introduces non-reconciliation, natural dissimilitude.

It is interesting that the devaluation of riches is attributed among other things to the fact that they are rooted in instability ('indiscrezione del loro avvenimento'), that is, in time, change, and the accidental (IV. xi. 6). True nobility, on the contrary, is a divine gift and is thus substantial; that is, it belongs to the category of substance. It is natural and as such part of the individual to whom it is given. The accidental is opposed to what is substantial. Moreover, the roots and phenomenology of materiality are in time. In their structural imperfection, riches can be numerically infinite but do not give peace: 'quantunque collette, | non posson qüieter, ma dan più cura' (ll. 57–8) [for however great they are, | they bring no peace, but rather grief]. Riches are base and imperfect, and the latter adjective is explained in the prose in relation to the fact that they do not give peace (IV. xi). Here Dante announces what *Monarchia* will indicate as *avaritia* and what *Inferno* will identify as the insatiable hunger of the she-wolf. What should be stressed here is the dimension of infinity that penetrates inside time, a time that, according to the Christian tradition starts with creation and has a finite dimension. This infinity, that belongs to the field of materiality and materialism that Dante introduces as part of what is defective, should be understood in relation to the field of materiality itself.

But the basic meaning of the *canzone* lies in the link between the socio-political field of nobility and the ethical field of virtue. Both are confronted in relation to the criticism of materialism and from different perspectives. The vice implicit in materialism is figured as a desire that has no limits and this matches with Aristotle's theory of matter as the principle of infinity, the infinite desire for a potentiality that seeks a form. This vice in the field of ethics is considered an excess peculiar to the human being's materiality. The idea of God as *metron* occurs in the *De divinis nominibus* of the pseudo-Dionysius, who defines 'measure' as a *metron* with which to measure. This may be in relation to the gift of grace that is given by God, which allows us to choose the mean, which is coincident with *misura*. This, as Aristotle explains, is the point of a segment on which a hypothetical rope would fall straight. This is the right (*orthos* in Greek) *medium* or mean between two equidistant points. The field of ethics is shaped on this notion, that implicitly recalls the concept of *misura*, in the field of theology as peculiar to God and to the divine gift shared by those who are able to choose the right mean.

Going back to the text of the *canzone*, in the third stanza time enters as a dimension to be evaluated. Here the positive dimension of time appears to be that of change as development, that includes the educational process. The text organizes an opposition that points out a logical contradiction. Time implies movement and development. In the discussion of nobility, those who do not accept that a low-born person may become *gentile* deny this dimension. Nobility for them is a privilege of birth. It is here that Dante shows how much they fall into a logical contradiction. In fact they accept temporal becoming for what they see as 'antiche ricchezze'. For them, the temporal dimension of ancient riches generates in fact the coming-into-existence of good manners. Because of this, a dimension of value is attributed to riches insofar as they create a tradition of 'reggimenti belli', which are part of high educational standards. The axis of this discussion is the temporal development, which, in the same way that it can create good manners, should allow someone born of a father who is not noble to become *gentile*. From this contradiction a third argument is deduced: if we do not accept the change implicit in becoming, we must hold that we have all been, from the beginning, either all noble or all low-born, because we derive from the same single human being (i.e. Adam), unless we want to argue that there is no first human being, but that there have always been multiple human beings: 'che non fosse ad uom cominciamento' (l. 71) [that mankind had no origin].

Here the logical subject is the becoming of time, to which creation is related. But the issue seems to introduce a bigger topic: that of the eternity of the human race, of course presented as paradoxical, and yet, nonetheless, recalled. Because the eternity of the human race is denied and we are said all to derive from a first man, we are equal in birth. It is therefore wrong to define as 'noble' someone who can say 'I am the son or grandson of someone who is worthy':

> ed è tanto durata
> la così falsa oppinïon tra nui,
> che l'uom chiama colui
> omo gentil, che può dicere: 'Io fui
> nepote' o 'figlio di cotal valente',
> benché sia da nïente. (ll. 32–7)

> [And so ingrained
> Has this false view become among us
> That one calls another noble
> If he can say 'I am the son,
> Or grandson, of such and such
> A famous man', despite his lack of worth.]

The Italian word here is *valente* ('cotal valente'), which is part of the area of value that is criticized in this context. Both *valore* 'e dirò del valore | per lo quale veramente omo è gentile' (ll. 12–13) [I'll speak about the quality which makes a person truly noble] and *valente*, in light of this logical-historical analysis, appear to define a mobile semantic area. The new relations in which these words are utilized, reversing the traditional point of view and reorganizing the meaning of vocabulary through new relationships, powerfully contribute to grounding human excellence.

To better understand how the text organizes a weaving of different threads in order to unify them, let us return to the second stanza. We see that here the text links what is 'false' with incomplete speech, by way of two examples:

> Chi diffinisce 'omo è legno animato',
> prima dice non vero,
> e dopo 'l falso parla non intero;
> ma più forse non vede.
> Similemente fu chi tenne impero
> in diffinire errato
> ché prima puose il falso e d'altro lato
> con difetto procede. (ll. 41–6)

> [He who claims 'Man is a living tree'
> First says what isn't true
> And, having said what's false, leaves much unsaid;
> But possibly he sees no deeper.
> The ruler of the Empire likewise erred
> By making such a claim,
> For first he claims that which is false
> And then proceeds, moreover, defectively.]

In the definition of a human being as 'legno animato', to speak partially means to speak falsely; in defining nobility to proceed with a defect implies making a connection between things which are naturally different. In the definition of a human being, that which is false coincides with that which is 'non intero' or partial, because the above-quoted proposition recalls the vegetative and sensitive functions but does not take into account the third, that is, the intellectual function of the human soul. In this definition, the human being, according to the Aristotelian definition, is reduced to the material dimension of the vegetative and sensitive soul. In the discussion about nobility, what is opposed is the identification of excellence with material things. Both parts of the discussion oppose materialism, but this opposition is the result of two different considerations, which may be complementary. The first is the assumption that the human essence is material; the other assumes that human excellence is related to or dependent on material values. They are the prelude to a third discussion of materialism to be opposed, which is that related to the position of those who deny that 'fosse ad uom cominciamento' (l. 71) [that mankind had [an] origin], that is those who think that the human species is eternal and the world too; but this thread is not unravelled.

While the responsibility given to Frederick II on the material essence of nobility may anticipate the accusation of Epicureanism in *Inferno* X (in *Monarchia*, Dante will correctly attribute this theory of nobility to Aristotle, but *Monarchia* was written after *Inferno* X). It is also true that the assertion 'omo è legno animato' (l. 41) recalls Guido Cavalcanti's discussion of the ontology of love because both the emperor and the poet are together with those, the Epicureans, who celebrated the material essence of the human being and only this.[21] The link indirectly suggested between Frederick and Guido seems thus to anticipate the contents of *Inferno* X. Materialism appears to be by its very nature protean. The fields in which it occurs are different (socio-political, cognitive), but at the root of all that is false and defective is the importance given to materiality or the material as value. What will emerge is that the antidote to materialism should work in both fields: the socio-political and the cognitive. Here, however, an element is felt to be missing; that is, the ontological notion of what materiality is, and on which materialism is based. The doubt about the origin of *materia* seems to be based on the theory of matter, the essence of materiality and materialism.

I mentioned above that it is possible to establish for this *canzone*, as a *post quem* date for its reshaping of the theory of nobility, the period of Giano della Bella's *Ordinamenti di giustizia*, that is, 1293. But the analysis and refutation of materialism cannot be detached from Dante's frequenting the Florentine convents. Franciscan poverty and the preaching and thought of Pietro Giovanni Olivi are either responsible for, or at least influential on, this deep opposition.[22] The discussion of nobility thus goes far beyond

---

21 The philosophy of Epicurus was rooted in materialism. Dante labels as Epicureans those who assume that the soul of human beings dies together with the body. If the human being's soul dies with the body, the ontology of the human beings is material, that is, they are provided as individuals only with the sensitive soul. This is in line with the discussion of Guido Cavalcanti in his *canzone, Donna me prega*. Cavalcanti is in fact recalled in *Inferno* X. For Cavalcanti and the theory of matter see Ardizzone, *Guido Cavalcanti*, pp. 71–102 and *passim*.

22 In Dante's refutation of materialism there are no doubt echoes of his frequenting of the Franciscan convent of Santa Croce in the 1290s. Pietro Giovanni Olivi was a leader of the Spiritual Franciscan movement. His writings on poverty and his radicalism were well known to Dante since Olivi was a lector at the Studium of Santa Croce

the social endeavour in Dante and attempts to introduce a larger issue, in which the theory of nobility and the discussion of the true essence of the human being open up a series of connections that need to be understood. Summarizing, we may see that what is refuted is the result of many tiles in a mosaic organized as an example of imperfect syllogistic reasoning in order to oppose those who in the *canzone* are identified as *errantes*. If *gentilezza* implies antiquity, and antiquity implies time, and time implies mutability, then it follows that the notion of nobility, rooted in time and development, according to the definition attributed to Frederick II, needs to be rethought. It is not just a privilege of birth but it includes also a historical category labelled erroneously as value.

The paradox of this reasoning is the following: If *gentilezza* is created by long-held possessions and ancient customs, its value is built on the temporal dimension, a dimension that is at the same time denied when it is said that it is impossible for a low-born person to become a noble. In fact, time implies becoming and transformation. The fourth stanza shows the false reasoning:

> Né voglion che vil uom gentil divegna,
> né di vil padre scenda nazion che per gentil già mai s'intenda:
> questo è da lor confesso;
> onde lor ragion par che sé offenda
> in tanto [in] quanto assegna
> che tempo a gentilezza si convegna,
> diffinendo con esso. (ll. 61–8)

> [Nor will they grant that one born base may yet
> Be noble, nor that a low-born father's progeny
> Be ever thought to qualify as noble;
> For this is what they claim.
> And so their argument, it seems, negates itself
> Insofar as it asserts
> That time is a prerequisite of nobility,
> Defining it according to this rule.]

---

from 1287 to 1289. On Olivi see D. Burr, *Olivi and Franciscan Poverty* (Philadelphia: University of Pennsylvania Press, 1989).

It is thus the implicit contradiction that shows the fallacy of reasoning and its false nature.

The logic of contraries (Peter Hispanus, *Summulae logicales*, 5. 27: 'contradictio est oppositio cuius secundum se non est medium, inter esse enim et non esse non est medium' [contradiction is an opposition in which, as such, there is no middle ground: there is nothing intermediate between being and not-being]) impels the reader to follow what is constructed here.[23] This way of reasoning touches upon the controversial topic of the debate that questioned the notion of the first man and the Judaeo-Christian theory of Creation – a theory that had come into sharp focus in the thirteenth century thanks to the philosophy of Aristotle and some of his readers, who assumed that the world is eternal.

The complexity that the *canzone* organizes is embodied in a chain of deductions that relate a socio-political issue to problems of a cognitive nature. This is confirmed when it is said that: 'Ancor, segue di ciò che innanzi ho messo | che siàn tutti gentili o ver villani, | o che non fosse ad uom cominciamento' [It further follows from what was said above | That each of us is noble or each base, | Or else that mankind had no origin.]. This would be a position opposed to the Christian faith, which must therefore be refuted 'ma ciò io non consento' (ll. 69–72) [But this I do not grant].

This is the constructed reasoning: if we derive as humans from a first man, and if we deny change and mutability, we are either all low-born or all noble, unless we maintain that the human race is eternal. Of course, at issue here is the notion of time. If this is related to the denial of creation and thus to the eternity of time, then, if the world is eternal, time is eternal too. Creation in Christian culture also marks the beginning of time. The world is created not in time, but with time (Augustine). In this context another question thus takes form in a way that is not explicit: if we do not believe in Creation, then what is the origin of the human race? Are human beings the children of the Sun and of man, as Aristotle says? If this is accepted, a materialistic principle presides over the world and human beings. Dante opposes this point of view. He will organize his answer in

---

23 Petrus Hispanus, *Tractatus* [called afterwards *Summulae logicales*], ed. by L. M. De Rijk (Assen: Van Gorcum, 1972).

the prose text. What is accepted is the notion of the creation of the individual human being's soul in the re-reading of Albert the Great's theory and the mixing of embryology, Aristotle, and theological tenets. But as for what is contained in the *canzone*, the doubt about the creation of the first man is mentioned as a paradox. But in a discussion aimed at refuting materialism, it suggests that the *canzone* is aware that materialism is a pervasive category with many facets in the contemporary philosophical debate. However, when it says that *gentilezza* is a gift given by God, there is an implicit theological reflection. The prose text will introduce, through a question, a key problem that for many reasons is related to the discussion of nobility in its link with the criticism of riches. In this, the problematic issue that suggests that evil is related to materialism seems to penetrate. The doubt expressed in *Convivio* IV. i. 8 about 'Se la prima materia de li elementi era da Dio intesa' [whether the primal matter of the elements was intellected by God] puts forth this question in relation to Lady Philosophy, and her threatening aspect here suggests that it takes shape as result of the material that Dante dealt with in the first two *canzoni* and their commentaries. In the same way continuity can be established between the third *canzone* and its prose commentary.

I summarize in three hypothetical propositions Dante's deductive, imperfect syllogistic reasoning as set out in *Le dolci rime d'amor ch'io solia*:

1) If *gentilezza* is a value and ancient wealth is a value, *gentilezza* is ancient wealth.
2) On the contrary: if *gentilezza* is a value and riches are base, *gentilezza* is not wealth.
3) In addition: if *gentilezza* is ancient wealth with good manners (as erroneously claimed), and antiquity implies time, *gentilezza* implies a becoming.

In the light of this becoming, we should accept that a low-born person can become a noble. Indeed, if there is Creation and thus a first man, if we deny a becoming, we are either all noble or all base because we all derive from the first man. And at line 74 the *canzone*, after having enunciated the refutation 'Per che a 'ntelletti sani | è manifesto i lor diri esser vani; | e io così per falsi li riprovo, | e da lor mi rimovo' (ll. 74–7) [Thus it is clear to every mind that's sound | That what they say lacks sense, | And hence I claim their words are false, | And so dissociate myself from them], introduces the *pars construens* in which its author will say what true *gentilezza* is, from what it derives, and what signs manifest it. The key meaning is that to a materialistic principle there is opposed the main content of ethics: virtue. Within this field Dante reconstructs the principle of value implicitly denying that materiality is a value and that it presides over the origin of the human being.

Earthly Happiness as Right Mean

For Aristotle, ethics presides over the choice and establishment of the rule of self-control. Dante follows the Philosopher when he writes that:

> Dico ch'ogni vertù principalmente
> vien da una radice:
> vertute, dico, che fa l'uom felice
> in sua operazione.
> Questo è, secondo che l'Etica dice,
> un abito eligente
> lo qual dimora in mezzo solamente,
> e tai parole pone. (ll. 81–8)

[I say that every virtue, at its source,
Comes from a single root:
Virtue, I mean, which makes man happy
In his actions.
This is, as stated in the *Ethics*,
A chosen habit
Which occupies the mean alone,
Those are its very words.]

This coincides with the right mean (*mezzo*) and is opposed to the materialism coincident with our inclination to excess that is a part, but only a part, of our human nature. The first line of the fifth stanza introduces the word 'virtue' (l. 81), thereby suggesting a link to value, from which derives the fact that moral virtue is a value. Having erased every connection to the field of materiality, this *habitus* derives from a gift that God has given to us. This gift, because it allows us to make a balanced choice, implies that the rational component of human beings is what defines them.

Here, what makes the human being happy is identified with moral virtue. This will be confirmed in the prose section (IV. xvii–xviii). What is confirmed here too is that nobility and virtue derive from a third element: both are in fact manifestations of the ontology of the human being. This ontology is constructed by opposing materiality and materialism, and establishing the notion of true nobility, its name is *grazia* and its divine origin is clearly asserted because it is a gift from God:

> ché solo Iddio all'anima la dona
> che vede in sua persona
> perfettamente star: sì ch'ad alquanti
> ch'è 'l seme di felicità, si acosta,
> messo da Dio nell'anima ben posta (ll. 116–20)

> [For God alone bestows it on that soul
> Which he perceives dwells perfectly
> Within its person; and so, as some perceive,
> It is the seed of happiness, instilled by God
> Within the soul that's properly disposed.]

The notion that virtue is identical with the practice of the mean, and that the control of passion opposes materiality, must be read in light of the medieval theory of passion and its link with the theory of matter, as traced by Aristotle and his readers. Matter in itself is an excess, since it is absolutely potential as opposed to actual; according to Aristotle, matter is like the womb that has an infinite appetite for being acted upon.[24] So what seems to emerge is that the right mean coincides with the rational choice, which

---

24 Aristotle, *Physics* I. 9. 192a. 12–20. For the theory of matter, see *The Concept of Matter in Greek and Medieval Philosophy*, ed. by E. McMullin (Notre Dame, IN: Notre Dame University Press, 1965).

allows human beings to oppose the inclination to the vice that derives from our material component.

And while the right mean is the way to control our materiality, our inclination to an excess of passion, a comparison or parallel seems to be established in this line of thought between the materiality of possessions and that of the passions. Two forms of materiality are grounded in the physics of matter.[25] The seeds of the problem of evil, as Dante will present them in the *Inferno*, seem to be implanted here. And so, the question that leads to doubt as a method in order to discover the truth – 'se la prima materia de li elementi era da Dio intesa' [whether the primal matter of the elements was intellected by God] – correctly understood means: if matter has been created by God, is its form in the mind of God?[26] If this is true, then matter is subject to God's command and will. But book IV exposes only the doubt about the origin of matter, not the solution. This problem is so difficult and dangerous that Dante tells his readers that because of it he has interrupted his philosophical search.

Materiality and the 'Selva' of Error

The reasons why Dante left the *Convivio* unfinished are suggested here. The strong confrontation with the problem of evil determines what Freccero has seen as the failure, or better 'shipwreck', of Dante's *Banquet*, which he suggests is the result of the arrogance of the philosopher.[27] Dante's philosophical inquiry at this point opens up a new field to be explored. In the poetry of the *Commedia*, Dante starts to give form to the problem of evil and its

---

25 For the medieval theory of matter in its inner link with passion, see Ardizzone, *Guido Cavalcanti*, pp. 71–102.
26 Bruno Nardi, 'Se la prima materia delli elementi era da Dio intesa', in Bruno Nardi, *Dante e la cultura medievale* (Bari: Laterza, 1985), pp. 197–206.
27 John Freccero, *Dante: The Poetics of Conversion* (Cambridge, MA: Harvard University Press, 1986), pp. 1–28.

ontology. The *Inferno*, in its organization, is first of all the dramatization of the problem of evil and its ontological and historical roots. Book IV of the *Convivio* suggests that it originates from a refutation of materialism, whose roots are related to the medieval theory of matter. The last treatise suggests a parallel between the infinite desire for goods as active in *avaritia*, which cannot be satisfied (IV. xii), and the ontology of prime matter as infinite desire, matter being the absolute potentiality that always seeks its actualization or form.

A continuity is established here between the *Convivio* and the *Inferno*, which, in its first canto, indicates in the she-wolf's hunger an appetite that cannot be satisfied (*Inf.*, I. 49–50) and which in *Purgatorio* XX, 10–12 clearly presents the 'lupa' as the *figura* of *avaritia*. This line continues in *Monarchia*. *Convivio* IV. xii establishes that *avarizia* or the endless amassing of goods is dangerous for social life, and the *Monarchia* states that this opposes justice 'iustitiae maxime contrariatur cupiditas' (I. xi. 11) [the thing most contrary to justice is greed].[28] What can be said now is that *Convivio* IV – if one attends to the continuity between the *canzone*'s criticism of material goods and the doubt about the origin and nature of matter – suggests that the roots of *avaritia* or the excessive desire for material goods can be found in the medieval Aristotelian theory of matter, since its infinite potentiality is an excess and this is, according to an ancient-medieval line of thinking, considered as the root of evil. At the beginning of *Inferno*, Dante has lost his way in a dark forest ('Mi ritrovai per una selva oscura'; *Inf.*, I. 1). According to the Platonic and Neoplatonic tradition, this forest could be a way – literal and transumptive at once – of introducing the theme of matter in its relation to evil: *selva* being the Italian translation of the Latin *silva*, wood, of which *hyle* is the original Greek form, whose meaning is 'matter'.[29] *Convivio* IV, beginning with the *canzone*, introduces a refutation

---

28   I will discuss this theme in a forthcoming essay: 'The Dark Forest or the "Selva selvaggia, aspra e forte": an Idea about the Genesis of Inferno'.
29   For matter, *hyle* in Greek and *silva* in its Latin translation, Dante's roots should be in Isidore of Seville, *Etimologiae* XIII. Iii. 1 and in Augustine, *De Natura boni* 8. Augustine discusses matter in *Confessiones* XII, 6. 6.1–2, but here he does not use the word 'silva'. The word is widely used by Chalcidius in his translation of and

Dante's 'Quaestio' on Nobility and the Criticism of Materialism   169

of materiality and materialism, which the prose suggests is related to the problem of the origin of matter. The doubt that Dante formulates includes a question of great importance. God has in his mind the idea of matter. The question then arises: Is matter part of creation, or is it not created? Plato and Aristotle established that matter is uncreated and thus eternal. Like Aristotle, Averroes thought of matter as eternal and uncreated. Plotinus sees in matter the realm of error, obscurity and excess. Augustine, in contrast, regards matter as part of creation. Traditionally, matter and the body were identified. In Dante's age, the issue was discussed by thinkers such as Thomas Aquinas, Pietro Giovanni Olivi, and Bonaventure.

The criticism of materialism is present in *Le dolci rime* and is also active in Dante's last manifesto of courtly ethics *Poscia ch'amor del tutto m'ha lasciato* and again in *Doglia mi reca ne lo cor ardire*.[30] This criticism offers a picture of something more threatening if associated with what Dante writes in the prose section of *Convivio* IV in relation to the doubt about the origin of matter. We may suppose that in the years of exile Dante's criticism of materialism was shifting from the condemnation of wealth to a reflection about the problem of the origin of matter, aligning himself with the contemporary debate. According to *Convivio* IV. i, it was because of what is presented as a doubt that he started to enter the field of ethics in order to detach himself from what he calls philosophy. Philosophy in this context must be understood as the inquiry into the origin of things and thus as 'first philosophy', which, according to Aquinas, is one of the three heads of metaphysics.[31]

In this context ethics offers Dante a way to inquire into the tools human beings can use to moderate their material component. A parallel can be seen here between excess as something proper to matter and the excesses to

---

commentary on Plato's *Timaeus*, who devotes an entire chapter to *silva* as matter. See J. C. M. Van Winden, *Chalcidius on Matter: His Doctrine and Sources* (Leiden: Brill, 1965).

30   *Poscia ch'amor del tutto m'ha lasciato* is the so-called 'canzone della leggiadria'. *Doglia mi reca ne lo cor ardire* is the 'canzone della liberalità' as opposed to *avaritia*. The texts of the *canzoni* are from *Opere Minori* I.i, ed. by D. De Robertis and G. Contini (Milan-Naples: Ricciardi, 1984), pp. 384–9, 463–70.

31   Thomas Aquinas, *In Duodecim libros Metaphysicorum Aristotelis expositio*, 2.

which human beings are inclined if not moderated by the rational choice of the right mean. This parallel recalls the interpretation of *selva* as the region of materiality and error, the latter ('la selva erronea') being introduced by Dante himself in *Convivio* IV.[32] Because matter is associated with the *pathetikos* in Aristotle's *De generatione et corruptione* (324b18), the passivity of matter accounts for why human corporeality is affected by many kinds of desires.[33] *Convivio* IV, together with the ethics of the right mean, shows something different. A general law of inclination toward excess as result of human corporeality can be moderated by the control of the passions and the practice of the right mean.[34] A correlation between the excess of *avaritia* and the excess proper to materiality and error shapes the problem of evil in human history and time and is outlined in *Convivio* IV. What corrects this inclination according to Dante is *grazia*, which is the intellectual power given to us by God.

Dante's discussion in the prose of *Convivio* IV is ruled by ethics, where excess is considered a vice. The moral virtues are the result of a balanced choice. In *Inferno* excess leads to sin. In the *canzone* Dante creates a relational logical structure. The *canzone*, as we have said, is organized as a medieval *quaestio*. Its language is shaped by a syllogistic reasoning, which my chapter has attempted to emphasize. In light of the *De vulgari eloquentia*, we may say that the rhetoric of syllogism is the *constructio congrua* to the theme itself because the aim of syllogism is a demonstration organized through the language of rationality. Rationality rules the *canzone*. Because logic is the expression of human reason, it works as the language appropriate to establishing the right mean; a kind of *mimesis* is established between the ethics of the right mean and the logic of the syllogism. Teodolinda Barolini,

---

32   'È dunque da sapere che, sì come quello che mai non fosse stato in una cittade, non saprebbe tenere le vie senza insegnamento di colui che l'hae usata, così l'adolescente, che entra nella selva erronea di questa vita, non saprebbe tenere lo buon camino, se dalli suoi maggiori non li fosse mostrato. Né lo mostrare varrebbe, se alli loro comandamenti non fosse obbediente' (*Conv.*, IV. xxiv. 12).

33   Dante no doubt is indebted to Guido Cavalcanti for the idea of love as passion ruled by the laws of matter.

34   xxx

in her recent reading of this *canzone*, has stressed that the true heart of the *canzone* is *misura*. She compares the field of ethics with the language of lyric poetry, the Aristotelian *mezzo* with the Provençal *mezura* as it is utilized from the Sicilians to Dante. She discusses at length the Aristotelian weaving of the *canzone* and attends to the details of the Aristotelian theory of moral virtue. Having compared these elements, she allows us to understand something of importance: Dante focuses on measure (*misura*) as the cause and result of the intellectual nobility of the human race, and yet the word itself does not appear in the *canzone*. In this sense, I note, when we evaluate the use of the syllogism, we may understand that the language of rationality is used here as the language of *misura* in opposition to excess. The exercise of rationality leads to *misura*. Because *aspro* includes the calculation of the measure of syllables (*De vulgari*) as mimetic of a language of measure, the *sottile* (*sermo subtilis*) here is not coincident with the *ornatus difficilis* of *transumptio*,[35] but with the *operatio ratiocinium* of logic. Thus, when in the prose section Dante tells his readers that, after having been involved in an intellectual crisis in his philosophical search, he writes *Le dolci rime d'amor*, we may understand that the doubt about the origin of matter, which signalled the crisis itself, is in a dialectical way related to the right mean. The reader should be aware that materiality rooted in excess is counteracted by Dante's attempt to oppose what is beyond measure with that which is ruled by measure and rationality. Thus the 'aspra' and 'sottile' rhyme-scheme coincides with the rhetorical *inventio* of the *canzone*, and the syllogistic rational weaving appears to be the *sermo congruus*, or the natural language of *misura*. It is the link established by Barolini's essay between the philosophical content (*mezzo*) and the poetic tradition (*misura*) that allows us to evaluate the importance of the rhetorical-logical invention of the *canzone*; that is, a not-yet-pronounced identification between the rational *demonstratio* of the syllogism and the rhyme-scheme (*aspra* and *sottile*) linked with *mezzo/misura*. That this invention could preside over a part of Dante's future work is at this time just a hypothesis which requires exploration and verification.

35 See n. 2, above.

ANDREA ALDO ROBIGLIO

8 'Poi che purgato è questo pane': Vindication and Recognition in Dante's *Convivio*

The question of recognition (*reconnaissance, Anerkennung*) is well established and explored in philosophical research. Until recently, however, the pre-modern conceptualizations and uses of it have been overlooked. According to the late Paul Ricœur, the question of recognition first entered the history of philosophy with German Idealism, Hegel's early writings and his *Phenomenology of Spirit* giving birth to a full-fledged discussion of *Anerkennung*. Overlooked by Ricœur, in his seminal monograph *The Course of Recognition* (first published in 2004), is the fact that Axel Honneth, in *The Struggle for Recognition* (1992), had also referred to Machiavelli and Hobbes and discussed their views; the general understanding, however, still privileges the nineteenth- and twentieth-century debates.[1]

1   For a useful and up-to-date synthesis, see Mattias Iser, 'Recognition', *The Stanford Encyclopedia of Philosophy* (Fall 2013 Edition), ed. by Edward N. Zalta: <http://plato.stanford.edu/archives/fall2013/entries/recognition/> accessed 2 February 2018: 'Paul Ricœur has distinguished as much as 23 different usages of the notion "to recognize" grouping under three main categories, namely recognition as identification, recognizing oneself, and mutual recognition. Many authors have challenged Ricœur's view by proposing a distinction between recognition (of oneself as well as of others) and "identification": Whereas we identify an X as an X without necessarily affirming it as (and because of) X, recognition requires a positive evaluation of X. The term "acknowledgment", which some authors use interchangeably with recognition (Appiah), is also contested. Whereas some have argued that we acknowledge the validity of certain insights, values and norms (Ikäheimo/Laitinen), others continue to use the term "acknowledgment" with regard to persons but intend it to denote something less ambitious than the wholesale affirmation of their specific identity (Cavell; Markell). However, it is the meaning of mutual recognition that lies at the heart of the contemporary discussion'. The two classic monographs on the

It is true that intellectual historians have been well aware that Aristotle, in the first book of his *Poetics*, had already defined a notion of recognition, that is, *anagnorisis*.[2] This notwithstanding, Aristotle's notion is credited with implying cognitive and psychological dimensions only, as in the fact of recognizing someone whom we previously knew or, in other words, recognition as identification. The Aristotelian notion would therefore be of use in drama studies and literary theory rather than in philosophy due to the absence of the normative and ethical aspects of the modern notion such as reciprocity and commitment to care, among others.

This may be an oversimplification; however, recent scholarship – apart from isolated exceptions[3] – has reinforced this traditional narrative and limited itself to marginal corrections of the standard picture, such as including early modern thinkers into it, like Jean-Jacques Rousseau[4]

subject remain: Axel Honneth, *The Struggle for Recognition: The Moral Grammar of Social Conflicts*, trans. by J. Anderson (Cambridge: Polity Press, 1995); and Paul Ricœur, *The Course of Recognition*, trans. by D. Pellauer (Cambridge, MA: Harvard University Press, 2005).

2   See Aristotle, *Poetics*, trans. by S. Halliwell (Cambridge, MA: Harvard University Press, 1995), Ch. 11, 1452a30–1452b8, at 1452a29–30: 'Recognition [...] is a change from ignorance to knowledge, leading to friendship or to enmity'. See also Stephen Halliwell, *Between Ecstasy and Truth: Interpretations of Greek Poetics from Homer to Longinus* (Oxford: Oxford University Press, 2011), pp. 208–65 (esp. pp. 223–7).

3   See Risto Saarinen, *Recognition and Religion: A Historical and Systematic Study* (Oxford: Oxford University Press, 2016). Saarinen has been the leader of a research group based at the University of Helsinki and working in the past few years on the pre-modern conceptualizations of recognition: senior members of the team of scholars are Heikki J. Koskinen, Ritva A. Palmen and Maijastina Kahlos.

4   See Robert Shaver, 'Rousseau and Recognition', *Social Theory and Practice*, 15 (1989), 261–83; Frederick Neuhouser, *Rousseau's Theodicy of Self-Love: Evil, Rationality, and the Drive to Recognition* (Oxford: Oxford University Press, 2008); Barbara Carnevali, *Romantisme et reconnaissance. Figures de la conscience chez Rousseau* (Geneva: Droz, 2012).

and Adam Smith,[5] or even Thomas Hobbes[6] and the above-mentioned Machiavelli. 'The Theological Middle Ages',[7] on the other hand, has thus far been neglected. The wind of scholarship is calmly changing and one may safely wager that the pre-modern notions of recognition and the debates underlying them will gain visibility and relevance in the history of ideas. The aim of the current contribution is narrow and yet not unambitious. I would like to draw attention to the struggle for recognition in Dante, focusing on his unfinished philosophical treatise, the *Convivio*. Even though I might be the first who investigates 'recognition' in the *Convivio*, surely I am not the first to analyse Dantean ideas of recognition. Terence Cave devoted a monograph to the fortunes of 'recognition', from Aristotle to Sigmund Freud, touching incidentally upon Dante;[8] moreover, two of Piero

---

5   One of the first to uncover Smith's notion of 'approbativeness' and its rich web of ethical and political implications was Arthur O. Lovejoy, *Reflections on Human Nature* (Baltimore, MD: Johns Hopkins University Press, 1961). See Andreas Kalyvas and Ira Katznelson, 'The Rhetoric of the Market: Adam Smith on Recognition, Speech, and Exchange', *The Review of Politics*, 63 (2001), 549–80; Fonna Forman-Barzilai, *Adam Smith and the Circles of Sympathy: Cosmopolitanism and Moral Theory* (Cambridge: Cambridge University Press, 2010), esp. Ch. 3.

6   See Ludwig Siep, 'The Struggle for Recognition: Hegel's Dispute with Hobbes in the Jena Writings' (trans. by Ch. Dudas), in *Hegel's Dialectic of Desire and Recognition: Texts and Commentary*, ed. by J. O'Neill (Albany, NY: SUNY Press, 1996), pp. 273–88. Leo Strauss, connecting Hobbes' idea of 'glory' with the question of aristocratic virtue, provided useful hints on the role of 'recognition by others'; L. Strauss, *The Political Philosophy of Hobbes: Its Basis and Genesis* (Oxford: Clarendon Press, 1936).

7   This poignant expression dates back to the nineteenth-century history of Western philosophy (e.g. Franz Rosenzweig), when it was used to label medieval Scholastic philosophy and to define it against 'anthropological Modernity', on the one hand, and 'cosmological Antiquity', on the other. It is now a current formula in the scholarly literature, for example, Alessandro Ghisalberti, *Medioevo teologico. Categorie della teologia razionale nel Medioevo* (Bari-Rome: Laterza, 1990).

8   See Terence Cave, *Recognitions: A Study in Poetics* (Oxford: Clarendon Press, 1988), p. 179, n. 103 and *passim*. On this path-breaking publication, see Michel Jeanneret, 'Œdipe aveugle (à propos de Terence Cave, *Recognitions*)', *Littérature*, 77 (1990), 117–24.

Boitani's classic essays are explicitly dedicated to this topic.⁹ As a matter of fact, if philosophers would pay more attention to literary scholarship, they might have long since realized that the struggle for recognition was a main feature of the medieval mind. Michelangelo Picone, for instance, showed the link between Dante's exile in Verona and the quest for recognition as it is represented in the character of Bergamino, in the novella by Giovanni Boccaccio. From Umberto Carpi's investigation into Dante's nobility to Marco Santagata's *Dante: The Story of His Life*, the Poet's endeavour to obtain both social and political recognition has often been scrutinized.¹⁰

The term 'riconoscere' is not frequent in Dante's writings: it denotes the act of recognizing a person whom we have – directly or indirectly, through signs and reputation – known in the past; on top of that, it connotes the awareness of one's guilt that accompanies the willingness to repent.¹¹ The connection with repentance and the state of feeling sorry for incorrect conduct is paramount at the end of *Purgatorio*,¹² in which the Pilgrim completes a laborious process of purification and reaches the top of the mountain. There, in the garden across the river, he can finally recognize Beatrice:

---

9   See Piero Boitani, '"I Know the Signs of the Ancient Flame". Dante's Recognitions', in *The Tragic and the Sublime in Medieval Literature* (Cambridge: Cambridge University Press, 1989), pp. 142–76 and 298–301. See also in the same volume: 'A Spark of Love: Medieval Recognitions'. Boitani, however, concentrated his analysis exclusively on the *Commedia* and did not stress the philosophical implications. In the footprints of Boitani, see also Heather Webb, *Dante's Persons: An Ethics of the Transhuman* (Oxford: Oxford University Press, 2016), esp. Ch. 3.
10 See Michelangelo Picone, 'La maschera di Bergamino (*Decameron* I. 7)', *Letteratura italiana antica*, 6 (2005), 339–52; Umberto Carpi, *La nobiltà di Dante*, 2 vols (Florence: Polistampa, 2004); Marco Santagata, *Dante: The Story of His Life*, trans. by R. Dixon (Cambridge, MA: Harvard University Press, 2016).
11 See Alessandro Niccoli, 'Riconoscere', in *Enciclopedia Dantesca*, available online at: <http://www.treccani.it/enciclopedia/riconoscere_(Enciclopedia-Dantesca)> accessed 2 February 2018.
12 See Lucia Onder, 'Purgare', in *Enciclopedia Dantesca*, available online at: <http://www.treccani.it/enciclopedia/purgare_(Enciclopedia-Dantesca)> accessed 2 February 2018.

> E come la mia faccia si distese,
> posarsi quelle prime creature
> da loro aspersïon l'occhio comprese;
> e le mie luci, ancor poco sicure,
> vider Beatrice volta in su la fiera
> ch'è sola una persona in due nature.
> Sotto 'l suo velo e oltre la rivera
> vincer pariemi più sé stessa antica,
> vincer che l'altre qui, quand'ella c'era.
> Di penter sì mi punse ivi l'ortica,
> che di tutte altre cose qual mi torse
> più nel suo amor, più mi si fé nemica.
> Tanta *riconoscenza* il cor mi morse,
> ch'io caddi vinto; e quale allora femmi,
> salsi colei che la cagion mi porse. (*Purg.*, XXXI. 76–90)
>
> [And when I had raised my head
> my eyes saw that those first-created beings
> had paused in scattering their flowers
> and, my vision blurred and still uncertain,
> saw Beatrice turning toward the beast
> that is one person in two natures.
> Even beneath her veil, even beyond the stream,
> she seemed to surpass her former self in beauty
> more than she had on earth surpassed all others.
> The nettle of remorse so stung me then,
> that whatever else had lured me most to loving
> had now become for me most hateful.
> Such *knowledge* of my fault was gnawing at my heart
> that I was overcome, and what I then became
> she knows who was the reason for my state.][13]

Repentance, contrition and purgation are at the core of the second cantica. Claudia Di Fonzo has paid careful attention to Alberico da Rosciate's *proemium* to the second part of the *Comedia* including reference to the

---

13   Translation by Jean and Robert Hollander (New York: Anchor Books, 2004). On the inchoative recognition of Beatrice from *Purg.*, XXX on (ll. 34–48), see also, besides Boitani (quoted above), Kevin Brownlee, 'Dante and Narcissus (*Purg.*, XXX. 76–99)', *Dante Studies*, 96 (1978), 201–6.

legend of St Patrick's Purgatory and Alberico's explanation of the distinct meanings of 'purgation', as well as the novelty introduced by Dante in the conception of the Purgatory.[14] There are different kinds of purgation, Alberico argues; in law, for instance, there is canonic purgation (*purgatio canonica*) and common purgation (*purgatio vulgaris*).[15] The procedure is different for each, however both share in the same aim: to rid any reputation of guilt and to become clear of suspect shadows. 'Purging is to show one's own innocence' ('purgare est innocentiam suam ostendere') wrote Alberico da Rosciate in his *Dictionary of Civil and Canon Law*,[16] composed in the first half of the fourteenth century. A few folios earlier, the jurist had already established that 'crime brings nobility to nought' ('nobilitas perditur per peccatum').[17] Purification from sin and the claim of innocence

---

[14] Claudia Di Fonzo, 'La leggenda del *Purgatorio di S. Patrizio* fino a Dante e ai suoi commentatori trecenteschi', *Studi Danteschi*, 65 (2000), 177–201. An English translation is available online at: <http://danteide.it/ALLEGORICA/AllegoricaVol26-2009-2010 Galley Di Fonzo.pdf>. 'The revolution which Alighieri brings about – Di Fonzo writes – consists of the definitive removal of Purgatory from underground. He transforms the mountain into a ladder – "que vos guida al som de l'escalina", in Arnaut Daniel's words, *Purg.*, XXVI, 146 –, through which the movement is upwards, in a sort of high tower which is possible to approach only through a door reached by a flight of stairs (*Purg.*, XXI. 48: "scaletta")'.

[15] 'Et ideo scribitur in Iure quod non relacione criminum sed innocencia reus purgatur, ff. de publicis [62] iudiciis [63] lex is qui reus [64] et de requi rei [65] lex ulterius Et ideo preses provincie studere debet suam provinciam purgare malis hominibus ut ff. de officio praesidis [66] lex III et lex congrue. Et inde extra de purgatione vulgari per totum et de purgatione canonica per totum et per Hostiensem et Gotofredum in summa ipsorum titullorum', quoted in Di Fonzo, 'La leggenda'. On the meaning of 'canonic purgation', see Antonia Fiori, *Il giuramento di innocenza nel processo canonico medievale. Storia e disciplina della 'purgatio canonica'* (Frankfurt am Main: Klostermann, 2013). On the meaning of 'common purgation' (or duelling), see Andrea A. Robiglio, 'La nobiltà di spada in Dante: un appunto su *Conv.*, IV. xiv. 1', in *Il 'Convivio' di Dante*, ed. by J. Bartuschat and A. A. Robiglio (Ravenna: Longo, 2015), pp. 191–204.

[16] Albericus de Rosate, *Dictionarium Iuris tam Civilis quam Canonici ...*, ed. by G. F. Deciani (Venice: Guerreri, 1572), Litera P, *ad vocem* 'purgare'.

[17] Albericus de Rosate, *Dictionarium Iuris, ad vocem* 'nobilitas'.

make the link between nobility and purgation structural: this is something we should keep in mind in the following analysis.

The *Enciclopedia Dantesca* explains 'purgation' ('purgazione') as an equivalent for atonement, purification, and refining: it derives from the Latin *purgatio* and means the process through which something or someone becomes pure, flawless, clear, and worthy of good fame. The connection between such a process and the process of ennoblement is almost immediate and can be intuitively discovered by the reader. The juridical element in it, furthermore, refers to some charge and implies a doubt cast upon one's reputation calling for its vindication.[18] It is not surprising that most of the occurrences of the verb 'purgare' are to be found in the second part of the *Commedia*, the very Purgatory 'in which the human soul is cleansed of sin',[19] while the word is absent in the *Inferno* and appears only once in the *Paradiso* (XXVIII, 82), with the figural meaning of 'clearing the scoriae'. In his other writings, Dante uses neither the verb nor the noun 'purgation', apart from in his incomplete philosophical *prosimetrum*, the *Convivio*; here we find many occurrences especially in books I and III.[20] In *Conv.*, II. xv. 5, for instance, the standard analogy between human knowledge and sunlight is employed to convey the idea according to which any truth will manifest itself once the purgation has been accomplished:

> S'elli non teme labore di studio e lite di dubitazioni, le quali dal principio delli sguardi di questa donna multiplicatamente surgono, e poi, continuando la sua luce, caggiono quasi come nebulette matutine alla faccia del sole; e rimane libero e pieno di certezza lo familiare intelletto, sì come l'aere dalli raggi meridiani *purgato* e illustrato. [my italics][21]

18   See Fiori, *Il giuramento di innocenza*, pp. 377–84. On the legal category of 'infamia' and its presence in book I of *Convivio*, see also Justin Steinberg, 'Dante e le leggi dell'infamia', in P. Canettieri and A. Punzi (eds), *Dai pochi ai molti. Studi in onore di Roberto Antonelli*, 2 vols (Rome: Viella, 2014), pp. 1651–9.
19   *Purg.*, I. 5: 'dove l'umano spirito si purga'. See *Purg.*, I. 66; V. 72; VII. 39; IX. 49; XI. 30; XVII. 83; XIX. 116; XXII. 53; XXIV. 23; XXVI. 92; XXVIII. 90.
20   See *Conv.*, I. ii. 1–2 and 15; I. iii. 2; I. v. 1; I. xiii. 11; II. xv. 5; III. i. 14; III. iv. 5 ('argomento di colpa è, non purgamento'); III. ix. 1.
21   For a commentary, see Gianfranco Fioravanti in Dante Alighieri, *Opere*, vol. 2, *Convivio – Monarchia – Ecloge* (Milan: Mondadori, 2014), p. 341.

[Provided that he is not afraid to endure the effort of study and struggling with questions, which spring up and multiply from the moment this lady's looks are first encountered, but which then disappear as her light continues to shine, like small morning clouds before the face of the sun. And once her friend, the intellect remains free and full of certainty, *like the air purged* and made luminous by the noon rays.]

The 'eyes', as Dante explains, stand for the philosophical arguments, which can 'see' (i.e. explain and persuade) under the condition that both they and their medium (i.e. the public sphere, civic life, and language) be purified, become clear.

It might be unexpected that, in the long book IV, entirely devoted to the *quaestio de nobilitate*, the terminology of purification is not explicitly employed. Here I claim that, if the reader understands the author's ordering, the problem of *purgatio* surfaces in book IV of the *Convivio* as well, beyond the terminology used.[22] Book IV constitutes, one could say, the theory of what is 'high' or worthy of recognition and obviously follows the pedagogy and practice of 'elevation', the process of becoming clear announced in book I. Book IV, in other words, follows according to the order of learning, while according to the order of perfection it may precede book I.

In book IV the reader finds herself in the context of a very complex piece of reasoning, considering the nature of social recognition. Recognition of what is truly noble, we shall see, is crucial to avoid the catastrophes both of human society and of civic life, Dante claims. Subsequently, this motive will innervate the entire divine poem. As critics have already noticed, book IV and the second part of the *Commedia* reveal elements of common intertextuality.[23] The question of recognition, however, is more than simply announced in book I. Let us see it in some detail.

---

22 On the possible reference to duelling, or to 'common purgation', in *Conv.*, IV. xiv. 1, see Robiglio, 'La nobiltà di spada in Dante'.
23 It is not possible to elaborate on this problem here; the reader should remark its relevance for the question of the caesura between books I–III and book IV of *Convivio*. See Ulrich Leo, *Sehen und Wirklichkeit bei Dante – mit einem Nachtrag über das Problem der Literaturgeschichte* (Frankfurt am Main: Klostermann, 1957), pp. 71–104; Andrea A. Robiglio, 'La sera del *Convivio*. Per un'ermeneutica del progetto filosofico di Dante: dal *Convivio* alla *Commedia*', in M. Picone and J. Bartuschat (eds), *Le*

The setting is kept in the following two chapters of *Convivio* I: the fifth, in which the author describes the 'nobility' of the Latin language, and the sixth, in which Latin and the vernacular are compared to each other and create a dialectical struggle that seems to play ahead of the Hegelian servant-master relationship.[24]

Let us briefly illustrate how. Since the vernacular can 'serve' the metric sections of the text (the *canzoni*), far better than Latin could do, Dante needs to define the characteristics that one must possess in order to act as an excellent servant. Service requires personal knowledge. The good servant is required to have 'perfect knowledge' of two things (*Conv.*, I. vi. 2). First, the excellent servant must be able to know 'the nature of his master' better than the master himself. In the second place, 'a servant must have close knowledge of his master's friends, for otherwise he can neither honor nor serve them, nor, consequently, can he perfectly serve his master, for friends are like parts forming one whole, for they form a whole in being at one in what they will and do not will' (*Conv.*, I. vi. 5).[25] These friends are those peers who, as Cicero taught while speaking of friendship, make one with him. These friends are gentlemen who are such by birth; this notwithstanding, they could yet fail to be truly noble: some of them are

---

opere minori di Dante nella prospettiva della 'Commedia' (Ravenna: Longo, 2009), pp. 63–82 – and now in Andrea A. Robiglio, *Con Dante. Contributo allo studio della filosofia romanza* (Ravenna: Longo, 2018), Ch. 1.

24 The obvious reference is to Hegel's *Phenomenology of Spirit*, first section of the second part, that is, 'The independence and dependence of self-consciousness: lordship and bondage'; see Georg Wilhelm Friedrich Hegel, *The Phenomenology of Spirit*, trans. by A. V. Miller (Delhi: Motilal Banarsidass Publishers, 1998), pp. 111 ff. My analysis of *Convivio* I limits itself to the elements functional to the understanding of the struggle for recognition; on the internal tensions in book I as well as on the question of the superiority of Latin which is 'both asserted and implicitly denied', see the article by Franziska Meier, '"Questa sarà luce nuova": Dante and the Vernacular in *Convivio* I', in this volume.

25 'L'altra cosa è che si conviene conoscere al servo li amici del suo signore, ché altrimenti non li potrebbe onorare né servire, e così non servirebbe perfettamente lo suo signore; con ciò sia cosa che li amici siano quasi parti d'un tutto, però che 'l tutto loro è uno volere e uno non volere'.

of 'asinine nature',[26] Dante argues. The servant, as Castiglione's courtier will know all too well, must be aware of that and be able to prevent any damage to the reputation of his master. For succeeding in such a subtle task, he should scrutinize the hidden intentions and advise with sweetness, without disclosing disappointment or criticism. Dante's vernacular has an advantage that Latin does not have, because it is the mother tongue and enjoys an intimacy precluded to the language of Virgil. Dante, as is well-known, considers Latin an artificial language, established by some learned scholars of the past to overcome post-Babelic linguistic pluralism and make the common pursuit of knowledge possible: 'però che lo volgare seguita uso, e lo latino arte' [the vernacular is shaped by usage, and Latin by art] (*Conv.*, I. v. 14).[27]

The author recollects that 'it is impossible to know people closely without some personal acquaintance or familiarity'. Latin, Dante continues, 'non ha conversazione con tanti in alcuna lingua con quanti ha lo volgare di quella' [does not have an affiliation with as many people in any language as does the vernacular of that language, to which all are friends] (*Conv.*, I. vi. 10). Imperfect intercourse in social life (expressed by the term 'conversation') is two-fold: in relation to extension and in relation to intention. In the first case, in a determined community or *civitas*, those who know how to communicate in Latin are a small number in comparison with

---

26 On the manifold connotations Dante might have recalled by introducing the reference to the 'ass', see, for example, the sermon 'in dominica ante passionem apud Sanctum Iacobum' by Thomas de Chobham, in *Sermones*, ed. by F. Morenzoni (Turnhout: Brepols, 1993), Sermo 11. See Paolo Falzone, 'Dante e la nozione aristotelica di bestialità', in G. Crimi and L. Marcozzi (eds), *Dante e il mondo animale* (Rome: Carocci, 2013), pp. 62–78.

27 See Bruno Basile and Giorgio Brugnoli, 'Latino', in *Enciclopedia Dantesca*, available online at: <http://www.treccani.it/enciclopedia/latino_(Enciclopedia-Dantesca)> accessed 2 February 2018. For the broader philosophical question behind such a conception, see Irène Rosier-Catach, 'Du vulgaire illustre, le "plus noble du tous", à la noblesse du 4ᵉ livre du *Convivio*', in Bartuschat and Robiglio (eds), *Il 'Convivio' di Dante*, pp. 105–34; Irène Rosier-Catach, 'Babel: le péché originel linguistique?', in I. Rosier-Catach and G. Briguglia (eds), *Adam, la nature humaine avant et après. Épistémologie de la chute* (Paris: Publications de la Sorbonne, 2016), pp. 63–86.

the whole and, at any rate, communication in Latin does not involve the totality of the citizens. In the second case, in the use of Latin one member of a given community does not speak of everything as there are subjects primarily expressed in the vernacular, such as very personal matters, love affairs, and reasoning on 'courtly love'. Dante is not in contradiction with his previous statement, namely, that 'Latin would explain things only to the educated, for the rest would not have understood them' (*Conv.*, I. v. 12), or that 'Latin is more beautiful, more virtuous, and more noble' (I. v. 14); neither does he contradict it when he later affirms that the 'vernacular is closest to a person which is the one most fully united to him' (*Conv.*, I. xii. 5); Dante does not deny any of his claims even when, in *De vulgari eloquentia* (announced in *Conv.*, I. v. 10), he writes that the vernacular is nobler than Latin: 'nobilior est vulgaris' (*DVE* I. i. 4).

As mentioned, a way to dissolve the apparent contrast is by adopting a dynamic and relational perspective, keeping in mind the dialectic model of the struggle for reciprocal recognition and applying it to language, that is, to the relation between two personified languages. The servant, serving, purges himself and is clear to overturn his relationship with his master.[28] This might emerge in the last two chapters of book I. By birth and heritage, in fact, Latin possesses greater dignity than the vernacular (*Conv.*, I. v), but the latter, thanks to its 'virtue', is able to acquire incorruptibility, expressive versatility, and 'beauty' by cleansing all the presumptions raised against his ingenuity. The personified vernacular, who has recognized both his master and his master's network, having trodden the narrow path of purgation and stateliness, surpasses all other vernaculars (*Conv.*, I. x), and, at the end of the day, surpasses even Latin, reaching a higher level of being and 'unity'

---

28 In *Conv.*, I. ii. 15, after having referred to Augustine's *Confessions* (ii. 14), Dante admits that his 'bread' (the vernacular he uses in the prose of the *Convivio*) must pass through several purifications to get rid of all its impurities (*macule*). By careful reading it appears that such imperfections are not imperfections of the vernacular but presumptions of imperfection, or 'infamies'. The verb 'presumere' may also have juridical meaning in Dante's *Convivio*; for example, *Conv.*, IV. v. 16: 'O sacratissimo petto di Catone, chi presummerà di te parlare?'. On the medieval doctrine of *praesumptio probabilis*, cfr. Fiori, *Il giuramento di innocenza*, p. 379 n. 26 and pp. 429–46.

(*Conv.*, I. xii. 5–7). We may now depart from the struggle between Latin and the vernacular and move out of metaphor. Cleansing the linguistic medium mirrors the need for recognition of those who speak it. The banquet to which the author invites the reader is not only an opportunity for disclosure, that is, to open up what is high for those who are base not by nature but by scholarly misrecognition; it is also a true training towards social distinction, overcoming any inferiority complex, and a celebration and an honour for the noble guests.[29] The servant has become lord and invites his friends to the festivities that accompany such a recognition: the purgation has been successful.

Maintaining the philosophical notion of friendship in the background, Dante distinguishes between a basic level of 'love of friendship', characterized by closeness (*prossimitade*) and 'goodness', and an even higher level of friendship, characterized by 'lo beneficio, lo studio e la consuetudine' [benefit, pursuit of a goal, and companionship] (*Conv.*, I. xiii. 3). Only the sophisticated use of both the rational faculties and some of the socially relevant emotions like 'sensitivity to shame' or modesty allows a person to choose and pursue such a natural increase in the union of friendship.[30] A common Scholastic teaching, for that matter, stated that natural relations might receive their perfection by rising to a higher level of union: there is being, and well-being; birth, and good birth, etc. Man has two

29 See Gianfranco Fioravanti, 'La nobiltà spiegata ai nobili. Una nuova funzione della filosofia', in Bartuschat and Robiglio, eds, *Il 'Convivio' di Dante*, pp. 157–63.

30 In book IV, for instance, Dante writes: 'Dico che per vergogna io intendo tre passioni necessarie al fondamento della nostra vita buona: l'una si è *Stupore*; l'altra si è *Pudore*; la terza si è *Verecundia*; avegna che la volgare gente questa distinzione non discerna. E tutte e tre queste sono necessarie a questa etade per questa ragione: a questa etade è necessario d'essere reverente e disideroso di sapere; a questa etade è necessario d'essere rifrenato, sì che non transvada; a questa etade è necessario d'essere *penitente del fallo, sì che non s'ausi a fallare*. E tutte queste cose fanno le passioni sopra dette, che vergogna volgarmente sono chiamate'. (*Conv.*, IV. xxv. 4; my italics). See James T. Chiampi, 'Dante's Education in Debt and Shame', *Italica*, 74 (1997), 1–19 (p. 4). The praise of shame, in book IV of Dante's *Convivio*, might be taken as evidence both for the problem of purgation and for the due conditions to be respected in human society in relation to a fair economy of recognition.

perfections: 'la prima lo fa essere, la seconda lo fa essere buono' [the first conferring being and the second well-being] (*Conv.*, I. xiii. 3). Between the poet and his poetic language grows the mutual recognition, which culminates in full friendship.

The vernacular is not only the mother tongue of Dante, it is also like a second father for him, to whom the poet owes his very being, life, intercourse with other human beings and, finally, the development and refinement of knowledge. One can make out here, in outline, the Neoplatonic triad of Being, Life and Intelligence: the vernacular had ensured that, even before Dante was born, the encounter of Bella with Alighiero was possible. Dante's parents, upon meeting 'speak'[31] to each other and they do so in the vernacular. Lastly, 'questo mio volgare fu introduttore di me nella via di scienza, che è ultima perfezione' [this vernacular of mine set me on the road to knowledge, the highest perfection] (*Conv.*, I. XIII. 5). Being the condition for each additional purchase, the vernacular is the ultimate benefactor of the poet. Let us remember the Latin sentence: 'Idem velle atque idem nolle, ea demum firma amicitia est' [the firmest friendship requires likemindedness, to share in a common will].[32] Dante and his language 'sought the same goal' (*Conv.*, I. xiii. 7) and share in the same desire to acquire 'stable reputation', without which mutual recognition is jeopardized and nobility would be but an unsecured claim.

Not only familiarity and intimacy, then, but 'there has also been a sense of benevolence born of familiarity; for from the beginning of my life I have looked on it with benevolence and been intimate with it, and have used it in deliberating, explaining, and questioning'. (*Conv.*, I. xiii. 8). The last three words of the text, 'diliberando, interpetrando e questionando' should not be translated lightly, since they might indicate the distinct and hierarchically ordered sectors of human activity as seen in its social context:

---

31   An incidental remark: in several Italian dialects, the verb 'to speak' is the equivalent of 'to court', in a romantic sense (see the hint at this in Primo Levi's 1986 essay, 'Bella come una fiore', *La Stampa*, 13 July).

32   Sallust, *De coniuratione Catilinae*, 20. 3, ed. by A. Kurfess (Stuttgart: Teubner, 1957), p. 17. See Fioravanti's comment to *Conv.*, I. v. 5. in Dante Alighieri, *Opere*, vol. 2, pp. 137–8.

political activity in the city ('deliberating'), the knowledge of God's law ('interpreting'), and philosophical and scientific inquiry ('questioning').[33]

In the very first chapter of the proemial book, Dante introduces the reader to the banquet by means of an optical metaphor; language is the food that has been prepared to bring real nourishment, 'But this bread, that is, the present provision, will be the light that will bring out every hue of their meaning' (*Conv.*, I. i. 15). Concluding that proemium, the author retrieves the image and closes the circle: 'This will be a new light, *a new sun* which will rise to take the place of the old sun which is setting, and give light to those now lost in darkness because for them the old sun sheds no light' (*Conv.*, I. xiii. 12; my italics). The vernacular here is the 'new sun', which henceforth will be paired with Latin. The servant of yesterday has become lord today: his brightness is even higher, although its range reaches to illuminate those who otherwise would dwell in darkness. According to Aristotle, human generation has two causes, one immediate (*viz.*, the parents) and one remote (*viz.*, the sun). The language of poetry, for the reasons recalled above, constitutes a kind of generative cause of 'generation'. As the remote parent of all the fathers and mothers who have been speaking it, it may legitimately be called by the poet, 'sun'.

Now, after having re-read book I and noticed the concept of purgation at work in it – mostly applied to language in order to cleanse it from detraction,[34] we can focus on book IV of *Convivio*. Developing the theme of the nobility in the style and method of a scholastic question,[35] Dante addresses the central aspect of his ethical and political conception – an aspect that also remains at the heart of his reflection up to the boundless spheres of Paradise. Establishing what true dignity is, is a fundamental

---

33   See Fioravanti's comment in Dante Alighieri, *Opere*, vol. 2, pp. 184–5.
34   See *Conv.*, I. iii. 2: 'E però che lo mio pane è purgato da una parte, convienlomi purgare dall'altra'. In book I, the notion of 'purgation' has also a hermeneutical ring to it, in relation to the figurative meanings of 'bread'. Cf. L. Bianchi, '"Noli comedere panem philosophorum inutiliter". Dante Alighieri and John of Jandun on Philosophical "Bread"', *Tijdschrift voor Filosofie*, 75 (2013), 335–55.
35   See Fioravanti, 'Introduzione', in Dante Alighieri, *Opere*, vol. 2, pp. 5–79.

question in the eyes of Dante. It is a condition required for men to obtain the perfect clarity of the supreme vision.

I believe that Hegel's *Anerkennung*, and much of what has been gained by contemporary analysis of the concept of recognition, might turn out to be relevant here. The notion, as it seems, is underlying:

> Intra li quali errori uno io massimamente riprendea, lo quale non solamente è dannoso e pericoloso a coloro che in esso stanno, ma eziandio alli altri, che lui riprendano, porta dolore e danno. Questo è l'errore dell'umana bontade in quanto in noi è dalla natura seminata e che 'nobilitade' chiamare si dee; che (per) mala consuetudine e per poco intelletto era tanto fortificato, che (l')oppinione quasi di tutti n'era falsificata; e *della falsa oppinione nascevano li falsi giudicii, e de' falsi giudicii nascevano le non giuste reverenze e vilipensioni*: per che li buoni erano in villano despetto tenuti, e li malvagi onorati ed essaltati. *La qual cosa era pessima confusione del mondo*; sì come vedere puote chi mira quello che di ciò può seguitare, sottilmente. (*Conv.*, IV. i. 6–7; my italics)

> [Among these errors was one that I condemned more than any other, one which is harmful and dangerous not only to those who are caught up in it but also to those who condemn it, to whom it brings pain and suffering. (7) This is the error concerning human goodness insofar as it is sown in us by nature, and which should be called 'nobility', an error that was so entrenched as a result of evil habit and lack of intelligence that the opinion of almost everyone was thereby rendered fallacious. *From this fallacious opinion sprang fallacious judgements, and from fallacious judgements sprang unjust reverence and disdain*, with the result that the good were held in base contempt and the bad were honoured and exalted. *This constituted the worst confusion in the world*, as is apparent to anyone who carefully considers what the consequences of such confusion might be.]

In the acquaintance with Lady Philosophy, mutual recognition coalesces with an attitude of radical obedience to truth in the administration of praise and blame, honour and criticism. Purgation must be the prompt reply to re-establish innocence and maintain the vital friendship with 'the daughter of the Emperor of the Universe'; the latter requires that Dante become free from error. Now, there is a kind of error that we might well call transcendental, as it constitutes the necessary condition of any further misunderstanding, or of any 'fallacious judgement'. Such a transcendental error consists in the confusion between the true and false opinions of persons and, as a consequence, it infects the course of due recognition. Wrong or even inconsistent social approval is here evaluated in its inter-subjective dimension: it is injurious, because it conspires to the 'pain and damage' of the human family as a whole. It blurs the boundaries of the reputation for good conduct and finally corrupts both the mind and the customs of men.

Dante is describing the negative side of the process — the causes which could prevent the realization of recognition. At the same time he shows the positive side: the benefit to the good society of the use of 'purgation'. Another notion is introduced here by Dante: the notion of 'reverence'.[36] Reverence acquires a peculiar importance and becomes one of the hinges in the course of recognition. The sound economy of reverence, as it were, sweeps away 'the worst confusion in the world'.

The reader can immediately feel the emotion that overwhelms the exile and the outrage that urges the thinker to produce a firm and exhaustive response. Determining what true nobility is, is necessary to save society from dissolution; 'discreet minds' must learn to pay tribute to virtuous men, according to justice, to express the recognition they deserve. These are the duties of man, who, to the extent of his accomplishment, imitates the work of God and contributes to the salvation of the world. Moreover, in exercising these 'duties', man assumes the high role of an 'official' of God and acquires the only title of nobility with no shadow, pure and totally clear. One who is truly noble is ultimately one who is recognized by God: the holy and the elect.[37] One may think here of the paradox of Plato's Euthyphro.[38] The

---

36 See Andrea A. Robiglio, 'Per non "mancare l'onore": Dante e le radici razionali della riverenza', *Rassegna europea di letteratura italiana*, 35 (2010), 51–66.
37 On the presence in *Conv.*, IV. xxviii. 19 of the notion of being ill-born (*male natus*), taken in its theological sense, as the equivalent of 'damned', see Andrea A. Robiglio, 'Dante "bene nato". Guido Cavalcanti e Margherita Porete in *Par.*, V. 115', *L'Alighieri*, 46 (2005), 45–62 (now in Robiglio, *Con Dante*, Ch. 2).
38 Criticized by Socrates in Plato's homonymous dialogue, the paradox reveals a difficulty that also enters the medieval theological debate on the relationship between nature and grace: 'Just consider this question – Socrates says – is that which is holy loved by the gods because it is holy, or is it holy because it is loved by the gods?' (Plato, *Euthyphro*, trans. by Harold North Fowler (Cambridge, MA: Harvard University Press, 1977), 10A). See Gennaro Sasso, *Dante, l'Imperatore e Aristotele* (Rome: Istituto Storico Italiano per il Medioevo, 2002), p. 33. On the ecclesiological instantiation

question of what is 'holy' and the theme of election, for medieval writers, might be both the theological climax of the discussion of human nobility and the most complex instance of recognition.

It is an indirect struggle, one might add, since God decides it.[39] However, the way in which each person receives divine grace presupposes the style of the one who receives, a mode that qualifies the meaning of his guilt or remission. As has been claimed by Piero Boitani and a few others, the *Commedia* might be seen as a sophisticated 'peripeteia' calling for perfectly realized recognition. Even if it is grace that operates, it does not do so without assuming a purified nature,[40] as does the light through the clean medium of the air. No one would deny the circular nature of such a process that must be faced: only the true nobleman is able to recognize whom one should deservedly consider noble. On the other hand, only one whose good reputation has been successfully defended deserves to be revered as noble. Once the economy of recognition is re-established, human recognition fairly mirrors divine recognition. The very process of becoming clear, pure and worthy is, in itself, a testimony to the original recognition bestowed upon man by his 'Primo Fattore'. Beyond Dante's *Convivio*, then, the theological mystery of the Incarnation may capture God's full recognition of man, as the Virgin Mary may embody it at the end of Dante's *Paradiso*:

---

of the paradox above, see Risto Saarinen, 'Anerkennungstheorien und ökumenische Theologie', in *Ökumene – überdacht. Reflexionen und Realitäten im Umbruch*, ed. by Th. Bremer and M. Wernsmann (Freiburg: Herder, 2014), pp. 237–61.

39 For example, *Conv.*, IV. xxii. 17: 'Bianchezza è uno colore pieno di luce corporale più che nullo altro; e così la contemplazione è più piena di luce spirituale che altra cosa che qua giù sia. E dice: "Elli precederà"; e non dice: "Elli sarà con voi": a dare ad intendere che *(nel)la nostra contemplazione Dio sempre precede*, né mai lui giugnere potemo qui, lo quale è nostra beatitudine somma' (my italics).

40 See Michelangelo Picone, '"Iacob dilexi". Dante, Cavalcanti e la predestinazione', *L'Alighieri*, 27 (2006), 5–23, which puts to good use, in the background, the insights of Friedrich Ohly, *The Damned and the Elect: Guilt in Western Culture*, trans. by L. Archibald (Cambridge: Cambridge University Press, 1992).

Tu se' colei che l'umana natura
nobilitasti sì, che 'l suo fattore
non disdegnò di farsi sua fattura. (*Par.*, XXXIII, 4–6)

[You are the one who so ennobled human nature
that He, who made it first, did not disdain
to make Himself of its own making.][41]

---

41   At the end of my contribution, I would like to thank Ms Molly De Cleene, who purified my English style.

LORENZO VALTERZA

9 'Però si mosse la Ragione a comandare che ...': Roman Law and Ethics in the *Convivio*

Discussions regarding law among many of the theologians, philosophers, and jurists at the end of the Duecento varied widely from region to region, but all tended to recognize the basic metaphysical contours of the so-called four laws: eternal, natural, divine, and positive. The eternal consisted of those Platonic Ideas, or the ideal forms within the mind of God that gave expression to the various phenomena that we see around us. Divine law, or revelation, offered humanity access to those truths largely beyond the capacity of human ken: for example, baptism, and the Ten Commandments. Natural law accounted for the general course of individual beings' development (that is, their essence, or dispositional properties), while humans themselves created – or posited – the final category of laws (positive) so as to guide their communities in day-to-day living toward ethical comportment. Apart from such essential differences in function, each law had its own particularities or secondary qualities that distinguished it from the others. This chapter examines the latter two as they manifest – or do not – within the *Convivio*.[1]

Grosso modo, we might say that divine law, as revelation, exists especially for the benefit of human life, made accessible to us primarily via Scripture. As such, though specifically for human benefit, its origins are not exclusively of this world. Instead, it comes to humanity from beyond, revealed, as it were, in an act of divine love as the means by which to close the gap between divine truth and the ceiling of human reason. Hence, the

---

1   For a discussion of the four laws in historical context, see Anthony J. Lisska, *Aquinas's Theory of Natural Law: An Analytic Reconstruction* (Oxford: Clarendon Press, 1996), pp. 99–101 and *passim*.

sacraments that, when performed properly (that is, meeting all of the essential criteria), guarantee divine results. Positive law also seeks to guide individuals toward ethical, social comportment in daily life. However, unlike its divine sibling, it originates primarily from our own intellectual efforts. Because it does not come to us from a supernatural source, no matter how sound its initial precepts, positive law depends upon an inexorable tension between logical precept and appreciation of the unique set of circumstances that comprise the case being studied. Born of human reason, positive law demands that this same reason be continually applied to each case anew.

Of course, such a scheme of laws is quite general, and, while such broad contours found wide acknowledgement in philosophical, theological, and even juridical circles of the thirteenth and fourteenth centuries, it nevertheless invites us to seek out and investigate the numerous exceptions articulated alongside it. One such noteworthy example is to be found within the *Convivio*, whose author deftly blurs distinctions between the divine and the positive. Indeed, while Roman law was already widely revered in the Middle Ages – frequently regarded as the pinnacle of human reason (*ratio scripta*) – Dante's quill nevertheless exalts it still further, transforming it from a collection of precepts authored by ancient jurists into something approaching a sacrament existing specifically for humanity's collective benefit. Dante's depiction of these laws is oddly bereft of an account of their human origins, showing the written texts containing the laws as born neither from the hand of emperor nor jurist. In doing so, he significantly blurs the distinction between the divine and positive categories, imparting to the latter the sort of reverence normally accorded to its divine cousin.

Roman Laws in the *Convivio*

The question of the precise extent and nature of Dante's knowledge of Roman law has long remained open. While the poet demonstrates a familiarity with contents of juridical texts in use by contemporary law students and practitioners,[2] this relationship nevertheless appears far more personal than professional. Indeed, one of the few things about which scholars agree is that the poet was almost certainly not trained as a professional jurist. As scholars have noted, Dante's perspectives on legal questions often ring amateurish and idiosyncratic, infrequently reflecting the mainstream thinking of professional lawyers.[3] Still, within the *Convivio*, Dante does cite or make reference to the *Corpus Iuris Civilis* (that is, the collection of texts comprising Roman law) multiple times.[4]

The first actual citation appears early in the *Convivio*, in the tenth chapter of the first book, where Dante addresses his decision to write the philosophical treatise in the vernacular, rather than the more traditional choice of scholastic Latin. He turns to the *Corpus Iuris* with regard to this question of language, referencing a passage from the *Digest* to support his reasoning,

> Però si mosse la Ragione a comandare che l'uomo avesse diligente riguardo ad entrare nel nuovo cammino, dicendo che 'ne lo statuire le nuove cose evidente ragione dee essere quella che partire ne faccia da quello che lungamente è usato'. (*Conv.*, I. x. 3)

---

2 Edward Peters, 'The Frowning Pages: Scythians, Garamantes, Florentines, and the Two Laws', in *The 'Divine Comedy' and the Encyclopedia of Arts and Sciences*, ed. by G. Di Scipio and A. Scaglione (Amsterdam and Philadelphia: John Benjamins Publishing Company, 1988), pp. 285–314.

3 Richard Kay, 'Roman Law in Dante's *Monarchia*', in *Law in Medieval Life and Thought*, ed. by Edward B. King and Susan J. Ridyard (Tennessee: The Press of the University of the South), pp. 259–68. For a full accounting of Roman law's influence in the Dantean œuvre, see Filippo Cancelli, 'Diritto romano', in *Enciclopedia Dantesca*, ed. by U. Bosco *et al.*, 5 vols + appendix (Rome: Istituto della Enciclopedia Italiana, 1970–8), II, 472–9.

4 The exact number of references to Roman law is difficult to ascertain because at several points Dante's language appears to echo that of the legal texts, yet the concepts there discussed could be attributed to other sources. For this reason, I will focus my attention to those places where Dante explicitly refers to the *Corpus Iuris*, or where the language is unmistakably taken from it.

[Therefore Reason[5] was moved to command that a man should pay diligent attention when entering on a new road, saying that 'in establishing new things, there ought to be an evident reason that causes one to depart from that which has long been the custom'.]

Here Dante reproduces a selection from Roman law to validate his decision to depart from the long-standing custom of writing philosophical works in Latin,

> In rebus novis constituendis evidens esse utilitas debet, ut recedatur ab eo iure, quod diu aequum visum est. (*Dig.* 1.4.2)
>
> [In determining matters anew, there ought to be some clear advantage in view, so as to justify departing from a rule of law which has seemed fair since time immemorial.][6]

The *Convivio*'s project of educating a large number of readers lacking in formal education logically requires that it be composed in the more accessible vernacular Italian. Such a point about language appears to be as evident as it is valid, yet Dante shores it up with a single pertinent citation from the *Digest* – one out of many tens of thousands of such statements. While the *Digest* in this instance functions as an *auctoritas*, it does so in a literary/philosophical matter, well beyond its original, legal scope.

While referring specifically to a question of law, *Digest* 1.4.2 enjoyed authoritative renown beyond strictly juridical circles. Even a theologian like Aquinas cites it in his works. The saint cites it in the body of question 97 of the Second part of the First book of the *Summa Theologiae*,

> Unde dicitur a iurisperito quod in rebus novis constituendis, evidens debet esse utilitas, ut recedatur ab eo iure quod diu aequum visum est. (ST. I-II q. 97 a. 2 co)

---

5 Dante used the term Reason, or *ratio scripta* in keeping with the custom of the time, which held that Roman law represented the height of human reasoning. See Walter Ullmann, 'Reflections on Medieval Torture', in *Law and Jurisdiction in the Middle Ages* (London: Variorum Reprints, 1988), p. 123.

6 This translation is taken from Alan Watson, *The Digest of Justinian* (Philadelphia: University of Pennsylvania, 1998), p. 15.

[Wherefore the jurist says that 'In determining matters anew, there ought to be some clear advantage in view, so as to justify departing from a rule of law which has seemed fair since time immemorial.']

Neither Dante nor Aquinas was a professionally trained lawyer, and both use *Digest* 1.4.2 to investigate more broadly philosophical matters. However, comparing the *Summa*'s use of the *Digest* with the *Convivio*'s reveals a telling distinction. While Aquinas cites the legal text within his discussion of the essence of law, Dante instead reproduces it in a context not fundamentally juridical. The saint's citation of the *Digest* appears in a part of the *Summa* that deals specifically with law, which is to say within Questions 90 to 97, a section today commonly referred to as 'The Treatise on Law'. In particular, Question 97 investigates under what circumstances a human law might be changed ('Deinde considerandum est de mutatione legum'), and Article 2 directly addresses whether it should be changed whenever something better is found ('[...] semper lex humana, quando aliquid melius occurrit, sit mutanda'). Aquinas cites the precept within a context similar to the one in which it was originally located; the line appears in both the *Digest* and the *Summa* within specific discussions of a law's elasticity. This keeps with a general tendency; while Aquinas cites Roman law at various places in the *Summa*, he most frequently does so only when treating matters directly related to law or its properties. In fact, the densest collection of such citations – nine, to be precise – appears within *The Treatise on Law*, in the relatively narrow boundaries of I–ii, qq. 90–7.

In contrast, Dante deploys *Digest* 1.4.2 as a means of justifying his own linguistic choices. The translation he produces couches the precept in the more general terms of how one might change long-standing custom 'quello che lungamente è usato', rather than specifically laws (*iura*). Far from simply distorting the original text or inaccurately translating it, Dante recognizes the deeper principle contained therein and applies it to his own unique circumstances. Where Aquinas addresses the general question of whether a law – any law – should be changed whenever something better is found, Dante instead concentrates on a specific case – his own – as delineated by its own unique circumstances. In fact, each of the direct citations of the *Digest* within the *Convivio* functions much like this one. By this, I mean to say that Dante makes use of the *Digest*'s prescriptive force not in service of a universal thesis, but instead in application to a hypothesis delineated by the rhetorical *circumstantiae* of the *Convivio*'s author.[7] It justifies *Dante*'s authorial decisions regarding *this* treatise.

While jurists tended to write for other jurists, the *Convivio* and the *Summa* appeal to broader audiences, and their respective manners of legal citation reflect this. Among legal professionals, the protocol for referring to a legal precept in juridical works had been standardized since the late twelfth century, and it differs from modern methods. While today, one typically cites such passages in numerical sequences of the work, book, section, and lex (e.g. *Dig.* 1.4.1), jurists of the thirteenth and fourteenth centuries employed a numberless system that instead referenced the first lines of the pertinent passages. So, where a modern scholar of Roman law might cite a passage as '*Dig.* 19.2.25.1', a medieval jurist would have written, '*ff.* loc. (l.) *Si merces, Qui fundum*'[8] (jurists after the twelfth century used '*f* to denote a citation from the *Digest*). Dante and Aquinas, however, refer to them in their own ways, and each suggests an assumption about the ultimate locus of a law's agency.

The point here is not so much that Dante and Aquinas did not treat the *Digest* as professional jurists did; that much is evident enough. It is more that while they both recognized it as an authoritative text to be cited in their philosophical discussions, they each did so in very different ways. The saint credits the laws to the jurists that composed them, even doing so by name on occasion. Dante, on the other hand, attributes the laws more impersonally to *Ragione* or *Legge*, or locates them within the three general sections of the *Digest* in which they are found. The *Digest* was divided into

---

7   As Rita Copeland reminds us, in writing the *Convivio*, Dante restores rhetoric's hermeneutical power as the commentary surrounding the original poetry becomes the ultimate locus of meaning for the tractates. See Rita Copeland, *Rhetoric, Hermeneutics and Translation in the Middle Ages: Academic Translations and Vernacular Texts* (Cambridge: Cambridge University Press, 1991), p. 183.

8   H. Dondorp and E. J. H. Schrage, 'The Sources of Medieval Learned Law', in *The Creation of the Ius Commune: From Casus to Regula* (Edinburgh: Edinburgh University Press, 2010), pp. 7–57 (pp. 18–20).

three portions, according to the chronology of its rediscovery: the *Digestum vetus*, containing the first 24 books; the *Digestum infortiatum*, containing books 25–38; and the *Digestum novum*, containing books 39–50. Unlike Dante, however, legal professionals rarely distinguished between them in their citations. Thus, while Aquinas acknowledges the human authorship of laws, Dante, in an especially peculiar variation from his usual practice of citing authors and their texts together, does not. This practice is all the more peculiar, given the *Digest*'s particularly populous composition.

We sometimes forget that the *Digest* is just that – a digest of other works. From the conception to the completion of his masterpiece, Justinian insisted on this point. Issuing the constitution *Deo auctore* on 15 December 530, he commanded the great Tribonian to fashion an extensive compendium of the scholarly writings of classical jurists to accompany his previously assembled *Code*. The resulting text ultimately bore the name *Digest*, or *Pandectae*, and its content offered a compendium of juridical writings of a nature both philosophical and interpretive (which stands in contrast to the *Code* which consisted primarily of actual legislation). The individual components were selected from the works of 38 classical Roman jurists and organized so as to address common questions of law.[9] On Justinian's express command, moreover, within the final product, each of these authors receives due credit, his name attached to the citations of his work.[10] Justinian's *Digest* is thus, at its core, a mosaic fashioned of the works of others, each of whom is carefully cited where appropriate.

---

9   Ulpian's writings make up nearly 60 per cent of those cited, but the *Digest* also includes selections from the works of Paulus, Julian, Papinian, Quintus Mucius Scaevola, Alfenus, Sabinus, Proculus, Labeo, Naratius, Javolenus, Celsus, Pomponius, Valens, Maecian, Tryphoninus, Callistratus, Menander, Marcian, Gallus Aquillius, Modestinus, Tarruntenus Paternus, Macer, Arcadius, Rufinus, [Anthus or] Furius Anthianus, Maximus and Hermogenian.

10 The undertaking was carried out with breathtaking speed; scholars estimate that Tribonian and his committee condensed more than 3 million lines of juridical writing, going back some eleven centuries, into a completed volume of roughly 150,000 lines. The *Digest* was promulgated on 16 December, 533. Federico del Giudice, *Istituzioni di diritto romano e cenni di diritti dell'antichità* (Naples: Simone, 2007), p. 16.

Let us look to Aquinas, once again, who presents *Digest* 1.4.2 by attributing it to the *iurisperitus*, or 'the jurist' ('Unde dicitur a iurisperito quod [...]'). In doing so, he reminds us of Roman law's origins within the works of so many ancient jurists, emperors, and philosophers. Within the *Summa*, the term *iurisperitus* is but one of several that Aquinas employs in conjunction with Roman law, although it is the most common. Elsewhere, he uses the terms *legisperitus*, *legisconsultus*, and, at least once, *imperator*, in reference to Justinian. Beyond this, Aquinas attributes some citations to the actual ancient Roman jurist from whose works they were originally taken, most notably, Celsus (Publius Iuventius Celsus Titus Aufidius Hoenius Severianus, 67–130 CE) and Gaius (*floruit* 130–180 CE). But whatever term or name he elects to use, the fact remains that Aquinas almost invariably acknowledges in his references that the ancient laws originate with the words of men – mostly jurists.

The *Convivio*, in contrast to the *Summa*, portrays Roman law as having no origin in an identifiable human agent. Despite otherwise meticulously associating nearly all *auctores* with their respective works, Dante instead attributes his citations of Roman law to the section of the *Digest* where they are found (i.e. *Infortiatum*, *Vecchio Digesto*), or simply to 'Ragione', or 'reason', that common medieval euphemism for law. While we may regard this as a simple act of poetic licence, it nevertheless sets an important precedent within the treatise, where no citation or reference to Roman law appears in connection with the jurist who wrote it. To provide some perspective, only two other texts that the *Convivio* treats this way are: the *De causis* (erroneously attributed to Aristotle in the Middle Ages) and the Bible.

In fact, we again witness these features when Dante cites the *Digest* in the ninth chapter of book IV:

> è scritto nel principio del *Vecchio Digesto*: 'la ragione scritta è arte di bene e d'equitade'. (*Conv.*, IV. ix. 8)

> [at the beginning of the *Old Digest* it is written, 'written reason (law) is the art of goodness and fairness']

The original quote, taken from Ulpian and Celsus, appears at the start of the *Digest*'s first body of quotations,

Roman Law and Ethics in the 'Convivio'

> Iuri operam daturum prius nosse oportet, unde nomen iuris descendat. est autem a ius-
> titia appellatum: nam, ut eleganter Celsus definit, ius est ars boni et aequi. (*Dig.* 1.1.pr)
>
> [Those who apply themselves to the study of law should know, in the first place, from whence the science is derived. The law obtains its name from justice; for (as Celsus elegantly says) law is the art of knowing what is good and just.]

As the opening line of the *Digest*, this dictum greeted generations of law students as they initiated their study of that text in law school. It appears originally in writings of the celebrated ancient jurist Ulpian who had himself drawn it from the work of another ancient Roman jurist, Celsus. Like *Digest* 1.4.2, it was well known even beyond strictly juridical circles, and also appears in the *Summa Theologiae*. As before, the differences between the manner in which Aquinas used the citation and Dante's own treatment of it establishes Roman law's character in the *Convivio*.

Aquinas presents D.1.1.pr by attributing it to the work of a jurist, much as he did D.1.4.2, only in this case, he does so by name,

> Dicit enim Celsus iurisconsultus quod ius est ars boni et aequi. (*ST* II-II, q. 57, art. 1, obj. 1)
>
> [For the jurist Celsus says that 'right is the art of goodness and equality'.]

These words unmistakably come from Celsus. Aquinas here proves particularly precise, in part because of the citation's complex origins. In this case, the very quote itself contains the name of the classical jurist who had written it. Aquinas thereby leaves out both Ulpian and Justinian, instead attributing the words to Celsus directly.[11]

The *Convivio*, however, associates no historical figures with the quote. It states bluntly only that this line 'is written' (è scritto) in the *Vecchio Digesto*, a peculiarly matter-of-fact sentence structure which bedims the

---

11 In the very first of its many precepts, the *Digest* reminds its readers of its composite nature by quoting an ancient jurist, Ulpian, who quotes the work of another ancient jurist, Celsus: *Dig.* 1.1.1.: '*Ulpianus libro primo institutionum*, pr. Iuri operam daturum prius nosse oportet, unde nomen iuris descendat. est autem a iustitia appellatum: nam, ut eleganter celsus definit, ius est ars boni et aequi'.

historical origins of this idea. The vague phrasing stands out as even more unusual because it is so close to more direct references to authors. In a starkly different fashion, the *Convivio* refers to Solomon by name, indicating his relevant work before quoting it,

> E però *scrive Salomone* nelli Proverbii che quelli che umilemente e obedientemente sostiene [d]al correttore le sue corrett[iv]e riprensioni, 'sarà glorioso'; e dice 'sarà', a dare a intendere che elli parla allo adolescente, che non puote essere nella presente etade. (*Conv.*, IV. xxiv. 16; my italics)

> [Therefore *Solomon writes* in Proverbs that he who humbly and obediently endures his chastener and his just reproofs 'shall be glorified', and he says 'shall be', to indicate that he is speaking to an adolescent, one who in the present age of life cannot be glorified.]

In fact, this paragraph illustrates the far more common way in which the *Convivio* presents the texts cited therein. Dante attributes the words to Solomon, as the presumed author of the Proverb. His identity lends authority to his words. This citation exemplifies all other citations of Roman law; the *Convivio* consistently denies its own version of 'auctoritas' to the jurists whose works it wields. In two other instances, the *Convivio* employs similar citations of Roman legal texts, and in both we find the same sort of treatment.

Dante once again cites the *Digest* in the *Convivio*'s book IV,

> E di questa infertade della mente intende la legge quando lo Inforzato dice: 'In colui che fa testamento, di quel tempo nel quale lo testamento fa, sanitade di mente, non di corpo, è a domandare'. (*Conv.*, IV. xv. 17)

> [It is this infirmity of mind that the law refers to when the *Infortiatum* states 'In anyone who makes a will soundness of mind, not of body, is required at the time when the will is made'.]

The quote, originally composed by the jurist Labeo, appears in the twenty-eighth book of the *Digest*,

> In eo qui testatur eius temporis, quo testamentum facit, integritas mentis, non corporis sanitas exigenda est. (*Dig.* 28.1.2)

> [Soundness of mind is required of a testator at the time that he makes a will, but bodily health is not necessary.]

Here Dante repeats a number of the gestures he previously had made with Ulpian. First, he translates the line from Latin into the vernacular. Second, he appropriates the argument for his own ends, removing it from the original context. In Dante's treatise, the lines appear in support of his assertion that those in control of their mental faculties will undoubtedly recognize the validity of his logic. However, the original context of the statement is far less broad, addressing the narrower question of who may fashion a legitimate last will and testament. Thus, he refrains from introducing the passage as originating from any historical individual, instead attributing it generically to the *Infortiatum*, or the second book of the collected *Digest*.[12]

The final example that we will examine here appears in the context of Dante's discussion of the respect owed by sons to their father. In chapter 24 of book IV, Dante writes,

> dice e comanda la Legge, che a ciò provede, che la persona del padre sempre santa e onesta dee apparere a li suoi figli. (*Conv.*, IV. xxiv. 15)

> [the law that provides for this says and commands that 'the person of the father ought always to appear sacred and honourable to his sons'.]

Once more, the quote, originally composed by the famed ancient jurist Ulpian, appears in the thirty-seventh book of the *Digest*,

> Liberto et filio semper honesta et sancta persona patris et patroni videri debet. (*Dig.* 37.15.9)

> [The persons of a father and a patron should always appear honourable and sacred in the eyes of a freed man and a son.]

---

12 The phrase, like all such precepts from the *Corpus Iuris Civilis*, was drawn from the work of a Roman jurist, in this case Marcus Anistius Labeo (d. 10 CE); it appears in the *Digest* – per Justinian's command – as attributed to him.

Just as before, the citation of Roman law appears here as a separate and autonomous agent; 'the Law' itself tells and commands us, once again presenting the *Corpus Iuris* as a text without author. As he does elsewhere, Dante bypasses every aspect of human authorship of the ancient legal texts, effectively appropriating Roman law out from underneath the authors who produced them.

The Emperor and Law

The *Convivio* foreshadows the *Commedia* in one respect by proposing the idea of an all-powerful emperor armed with Roman laws as a central part of the solution to the chaotic state of Western European politics in general, and of Italy in particular. However, while the *Convivio*'s emperor can certainly make his own laws, these remain a variety distinct from those of ancient Rome:

> E così chi a questo officio è posto è chiamato Imperadore, però che di tutti li comandatori elli è comandatore, e quello che elli dice a tutti è legge, e per tutti dee essere obedito, e ogni altro comandamento da quello di costui prendere vigore e autoritade. (*Conv.*, IV. iv. 7)

> [And thus he who is placed in this office is called the Emperor, since he is the commander of all other commands; and what he says is law for all and ought to be obeyed by all, and every other command gains strength and authority from his.]

The use of the term *legge* here is not in reference to the creation of new written Roman laws. This emperor is a theoretical figure, rather than a historically specific one (Justinian will appear as divine editor of Roman law only later, in the cosmology of the *Commedia*). The *Convivio*'s emperor bears the sole responsibility to 'write, demonstrate, and enforce law' (IV. ix. 9 and IV. ix. 14), yet such tasks focus more on guiding matters related to social stability, than to any individual's ethical comportment,

> [...] ché regole sono in quella che sono pure arti, sì come sono le leggi de' matrimonii, delli servi, delle milizie, delli successori in dignitade, e di queste in tutto siamo allo Imperadore subietti, sanza dubio e sospetto alcuno. (*Conv.*, IV. ix. 14)
>
> [For in the art of imperial rule there are certain spheres of regulation which are pure arts, such as laws pertaining to marriage, slavery, military service, succession in office, in which matters we are entirely subject to the Emperor without any possible doubt or question.]

With perhaps the exception of marriage, all of these matters – slavery, military service, and succession in office – pertain primarily to maintaining social order, to recognizing an individual's status in society, and, from this emperor's infallible judgement, all will be stable and wisely administered (marriage is perhaps less a sacramental concern than it is of matters like transfer of wealth, political alliances, etc.). Dante enumerates these areas under imperial purview immediately before providing examples of those beyond its authority:

> Altre leggi sono che sono quasi seguitatrici di natura, sì com'è constituire l'uomo d'etade sufficiente a ministrare, e di queste non semo in tutto subietti. Altre molte sono, che paiono avere alcuna parentela coll'arte imperiale – e qui fu ingannato ed è chi crede che la sentenza imperiale sia in questa parte autentica –: sì come [diffinire di] giovinezza e gentilezza, sovra le quali nullo imperiale giudicio è da consentire in quanto elli è imperadore: però quello che è di [Cesare sia renduto a Cesare, e quello che è di] Dio sia renduto a Dio. (*Conv.*, IV. ix. 15)
>
> [There are other laws which in a sense follow from the forces of nature, such as determining at what age a man is sufficiently prepared to manage his own affairs, and in these we are not entirely subject. There are many others which seem to be associated with the art of imperial rule, and anyone believing the imperial judgement in such matters to be authoritative was, and still is, deceived. For example, regarding the definitions of maturity and of nobility, the imperial judgement cannot compel assent simply by virtue of the fact that he is Emperor. Therefore let us render unto God that which belongs to God.]

The emperor's power to write laws is thus restricted primarily to ruling the empire and to maintaining social order. His authority does not extend to those matters determined by natural law, nor does it encroach on the authoritative pronouncements of the Philosopher. Likewise, the *Convivio* does not portray him as co-creator of the sort of authoritative texts like the *Digest*, let alone a contributor to *ratio scripta*.

Roman Customs, Roman Laws

While the *Convivio* does not portray any one individual as the ultimate author of Roman laws, it does nevertheless offer us an account of their origins. Its most explicit study of the relationship between laws and individual human behaviour appears in the twenty-sixth chapter of book IV, where Dante addresses the question of how a mature youth should be *leale*:

> Ancora è necessario a questa etade essere leale. Lealtade è seguire e mettere in opera quello che le leggi dicono, e ciò massimamente si conviene allo giovane: però che lo adolescente, come detto è, per minoranza d'etade lievemente merita perdono; lo vecchio per più esperienza dee essere giusto, e non essaminatore di legge, se non in quanto lo suo diritto giudicio e la legge è quasi tutto uno, e quasi senza legge alcuna dee giustamente sé guidare: che non può fare lo giovane, e basti che esso séguiti la legge, e in quella seguitare si diletti. (*Conv.*, IV. xxvi. 14)

> [Moreover, it is necessary in this age of life to be loyal. Loyalty consists of following and putting into practice what the laws decree, and this is especially appropriate in one who is mature; for an adolescent, as has been said, readily deserves to be excused because of tenderness of age; an elder ought to be just by reason of his greater experience, and he ought to conduct himself in a just manner, not as a follower of the law, except insofar as his own right judgement and the law are virtually in conformity, but almost independently of any law, which someone in the age of maturity cannot do. It should suffice for him to follow the law and to take delight in following it.]

Dante is not, of course, talking about generic 'loyalty' in the modern sense of the term, as the passage is often translated into English. Instead, as his subsequent discussion makes clear, he addresses the actual act of internalizing and putting into practice what the laws say.

On the *Convivio*'s account, humans' relationship to the written laws varies, according to maturity; the wiser a person is, the more his or her behaviour will naturally align with the wisdom expressed by the written precepts. Accordingly, *lealtade* is specifically demanded of the inexperienced young rather than of the elders, who, on account of their experience and wisdom, will act well without consulting the laws. Behaving justly in this model means acting in accordance with the principles expressed by the laws, whether consciously or not. The elder will do so out of the justness gained through her experience ('lo vecchio per più esperienza dee essere giusto, e non essaminatore di legge, se non in quanto lo suo diritto giudicio e la legge è quasi tutto uno' [an elder ought to be just by reason of his greater experience, and he ought to conduct himself in a just manner, not as a follower of the law, except insofar as his own right judgement and the law are virtually in conformity], while the youth must recognize, reference, and behave according to the written laws 'e basti che esso séguiti la legge, e in quella seguitare si diletti' [It should suffice for him to follow the law and to take delight in following it].

The *Convivio* employs Aeneas as an example of an individual who demonstrates *lealtade*. In this portrayal, we find an identification of laws with the long-standing customs of the proto-Roman people,

> sì come dice lo predetto poeta, nel predetto quinto libro, che fece Enea, quando fece li giuochi in Cicilia nell'anniversario del padre; che ciò che promise per le vittorie, lealmente diede poi a ciascuno vittorioso, sì come era di loro lunga usanza, che era loro legge. (*Conv.*, IV. xxvi. 14)

> [as the previously cited poet in the above-mentioned fifth book says that Aeneas did when he held the games in Sicily on the anniversary of his father's death, for he loyally awarded to each victor what he had promised for victory, according to their longstanding custom, which was their law.]

Here, Aeneas's actions conform to tradition and are just, but not principally because they consciously adhere to a given written legal dictate. The chain of causality is what instead matters. Aeneas's actions and the laws coincide with one another because both reflect the justness of the traditions from which they emerge. This tradition, we should observe, is happily Greco-Roman and thus fits in with Dante's account of Aeneas's founding of Rome. Had it been a non-Roman in Dante's example, then the custom of *any* people – provided it was ancient – would have been the legitimizing force behind the laws, thereby striking at Roman law's supremacy.

Indeed, when we look back to the quote with which this article began (*Digest* 1.4.2), we can see this conflation of law and custom already at work early in the *Convivio*. Now, for the most part, Dante translates his citations of the Latin of the *Digest* into Italian with a high degree of accuracy. One place where this is notably not the case, however, is *Digest* 1.4.2, where one key word oddly multiplies into five. Whereas the original refers explicitly to when old *laws* (iura) should be changed, Dante instead translates that word in the much more general expression, 'quello che lungamente è usato' [that which has long been the custom]. In doing so, he figuratively and literally removes 'the laws' from the law. Moreover, 'quello che lungamente è usato' is very much how he defines laws in his discussion of Aeneas's act of distributing gifts on his father's birthday, an act which was 'di loro lunga usanza, che era loro legge' [according to their longstanding custom, which was their law]. Here, the conflation of Roman law and ancient Roman custom is complete.

Thus, the *Convivio* establishes a sort of symmetry, between divine law that arrives to humanity from beyond human ken, and Roman law, which arrives to us through collective Roman custom and history. Yet, despite its plainly human origins, the *Convivio* systematically presents Roman law as bearing the mark of no jurist. In doing so, it elevates it from the hands of any professional class, and considerably narrows the distance between it and its divine cousin.

ENRICA ZANIN

10 'Miseri, 'mpediti, affamati': Dante's Implied Reader in the *Convivio*

Dante's implied reader[1] of the *Convivio* is clearly defined at the beginning of the first book. He addresses his work to those with the natural desire to know. However, in the following *canzoni* and commentaries, the reader Dante has in mind is constantly redefined and reshaped. It seems that, in repeatedly addressing an assumed reader, Dante's intention is not only to support and assist in reading this specific text, but to go much further – that is, to test the very possibility that a reader could understand and fully appreciate his work. To be more precise, Dante's political and philosophical enquiries frame the process of reading and understanding the *canzoni*.[2] In other words, the ability of the reader to discern the true meaning of Dante's *canzoni* has a crucial bearing on whether or not he can be taken as achieving the sense of nobility and reaching philosophical knowledge. The process of reading is therefore a central issue in the *Convivio*: it is the vehicle for Dante's epistemological and ethical considerations; furthermore,

1 As a working definition of the implied reader I adopt the one proposed by Iser (*impliziter Leser*). 'The concept of the implied reader is therefore a textual structure anticipating the presence of a recipient without necessarily defining him [...]. Thus the concept of the implied reader designates a network of response-inviting structures, which impel the reader to grasp the text'. Wolfgang Iser, *The Act of Reading: a Theory of Aesthetic Response* (Baltimore, MD: Johns Hopkins University Press, 1978 [1976]), p. 34.
2 For Dante considering the limits and possibilities of philosophical learning in the *Convivio* see Paolo Falzone, *Desiderio della scienza e desiderio di Dio nel 'Convivio' di Dante* (Bologna: Il Mulino, 2005), and for true nobility see Umberto Carpi, *La nobiltà di Dante* (Florence: Polistampa, 2004).

it expresses Dante's own concern and anxiety about the possibility of being correctly understood at the very advent of his exile.

The Readers of the *Convivio*: Those Who Desire to Know

In the first book, Dante expounds the *forma tractatus* and the intention of his work.[3] He states that he addresses 'all', because the desire to know is intrinsically human (*Conv.*, I. i. 1). However, in the *Convivio* he specifically targets those whose desire is hampered by *impedimenti*. Dante asserts that these *impediti* are many, while the learned are few (*Conv.*, I. i. 2). He explicitly aims at making the knowledge that only the few possess available to all. In his first treatise Dante considers his work as a 'volgarizzamento', that is, a simplified and summarized vernacular version of the philosophical knowledge of the time. The biblical references provide a metaphor of the intended audience of Dante's commentary: if the manna nourishes the fortunate seated at the heavenly banquet, the fallen crumbs form the meal that Dante prepares. This meal (*convivio*) does not open the doors of heaven (Luke 14. 15–24), but allows a large audience to taste earthly happiness. This audience is like the Canaanite woman in the Gospel of Matthew: initially she is one of the lost sheep of Israel, but in gathering what is at stake in the crumbs which fall from the table and are eaten by the dogs, her faith is rewarded, her request granted and her daughter instantly healed (Matthew 15. 21–8). These fallen crumbs are enough to feed the multitude of the wretched (*miseri*), because God has the power to multiply – just as He did with the fish and loaves in the miracle of the Feeding of the Five Thousand (Matthew 14. 13–21 or Mark 6. 30–44). By

---

3   See Zygmunt G. Barański, 'Il *Convivio* e la poesia: problemi di definizione', in *Contesti della Commedia*, lectura Dantis Fridericiana, ed. by Francesco Tateo and Daniele Maria Pegorari (Rome: Palomar, 2004), pp. 17–20; and Alastair Minnis et al., *Medieval Literary Theory and Criticism, 1100–1375, The Commentary Tradition* (Oxford: Clarendon Press, 1988), pp. 3–72.

first gathering the crumbs which have fallen from the heavenly banquet, Dante is uniquely able to redistribute the bread of knowledge and thereby make it available to a large public.[4]

Dante does not only define the quantity, but also the quality of his intended audience. His distinction seems to be, at first sight, extremely clear. First he separates the 'learned' (*sapienti*) from those 'deprived of knowledge' (*impediti*). In the *Convivio* he is interested in the latter group, which he divides into four categories: the first two suffer from what is within – whether from infirmity (*infermità*) or malice (*malitia*) – and the second two are deprived by outside factors – being busy with domestic and/or civic responsibilities, or born and bred far away from the company of educated people.[5] Dante then limits his address to the latter two: only those who cannot devote themselves to learning due to either their public engagements or their isolated domicile are permitted to take their place and receive the bread and meat which Dante wishes to supply. Dante not only describes the *impedimenta* which prevent men from attaining knowledge (and are commonly compounded by the scholars of the *studia*), but he also considers that he can and must remove these *impedimenta* in order to allow the multitude to taste the bread of philosophy.[6]

---

4 'Questo sarà quello pane orzato del quale si satolleranno migliaia, e a me ne soverchieranno le sporte piene' (*Conv.*, I. xiii.12).
5 'Dentro dall'uomo possono essere due difetti e impedi[men]ti: l'uno dalla parte del corpo, l'altro dalla parte de l'anima. Dalla parte del corpo è quando le parti sono indebitamente disposte, sì che nulla ricevere può, sì come sono sordi e muti e loro simili. Dalla parte dell'anima è quando la malizia vince in essa, sì che si fa seguitatrice di viziose delettazioni, ne le quali riceve tanto inganno che per quelle ogni cosa tiene a vile. Di fuori dall'uomo possono essere similmente due cagioni intese, l'una delle quali è induttrice di necessitade, l'altra di pigrizia. La prima è la cura familiare e civile, la quale convenevolmente a sè tiene delli uomini lo maggior numero, sì che in ozio di speculazione esser non possono. L'altra è lo difetto del luogo dove la persona è nata e nutrita, che tal ora sarà da ogni studio non solamente privato, ma da gente studiosa lontano' (*Conv.*, I. i. 3–4).
6 Francis Cheneval, 'Dante Alighieri: *Convivio*' in *Interpretationen: Hauptwerke der Philosophie: Mittelalter*, ed. by Kurt Flasch (Stuttgart: Reclam, 1998), pp. 352–80 (p. 354 and passim).

Later in the treatise, Dante outlines a social definition of his intended reader. He addresses his commentary to 'noblemen' – that is, to 'princes, barons, knights and many other noble people, not only men but women'.[7] However, even if Dante has set a social criterion – the requisite of nobility – he does not intend to narrow his audience any further. In a sleight of hand manoeuvre he explains in book IV that nobility is not only granted by 'ancestral wealth and fine manners',[8] but rather that nobility is 'the seed of happiness instilled by God within the soul that's properly disposed'.[9] Therefore, nobility is a divine gift widely granted: one can be born of noble 'seed' or become noble by 'graft'.[10] The noble souls are then many, and many of them are deprived of knowledge.

The audience who is addressed appears, at first glance, very large. While Dante in the first book does not quite aim at supplying knowledge to all, he nonetheless seems to have envisaged a very large cohort group, irrespective of social status or intellectual capacity. Similar to Brunetto Latini in his *Tresor*, Dante's *Convivio* addresses those who do not know Latin and are, due to one of two reasons, impeded from devoting themselves to the acquisition of knowledge. Indeed, the *Convivio* has been thoroughly and convincingly situated in the wider context of *volgarizzamenti*.[11] However,

---

7   'Principi, baroni, cavalieri e molt'altra nobile gente, non solamente maschi ma femmine' (*Conv.*, I. ix. 5).
8   'Antica ricchezza e belli costumi' (*Conv.*, IV. iii. 6).
9   '"Seme di felicitade", messo da Dio nell'anima ben posta' (*Conv.*, IV. xx. 9).
10 'Se da sua naturale radice uomo non ha questa sementa, ben la puote avere per via d'insetazione' (*Conv.*, IV. xxii. 12).
11 Bruno Nardi, *Dal 'Convivio' alla 'Commedia'* (Rome: Istituto storico italiano per il Medio Evo, 1992, [1960]), p. 21 and *passim*; Ruedi Imbach, *Laien in der Philosophie des Mittelalters. Hinweise zu einem vernachlässigten Thema* (Amsterdam: Grüner, 1989); and *Dante, La philosophie et les laïcs* (Paris-Fribourg: Éditions Universitaires Fribourg Suisse/Éditions du Cerf, 1996); Alison Cornish, *Vernacular Translation in Dante's Italy* (Cambridge: Cambridge University Press, 2011), pp. 126–58; Johannes Bartuschat, 'La littérature vernaculaire et la philosophie en toscane dans la deuxième moitié du 13ème siècle', *Tijdschrift voor Filosofie*, 75 (2013), 311–33. Franziska Meier convincingly shows how Dante goes beyond the logic of thirteenth-century vulgarization: Franziska Meier, 'Educating the reader: Dante's *Convivio*', *L'Alighieri*, 45 (2015), 21–33.

Dante's aim seems to exceed the logic of vulgarization. The *Convivio* does not only divulge philosophical knowledge, but it also intends to supply, beyond that knowledge, earthly happiness.

The Readers of the *Convivio*: Those Converting to Knowledge

Dante, in the first book, implies the task of the reader. On the one hand, those deprived of knowledge (*impediti*) need to eat the 'meat' (i.e. Dante's *canzoni*) in order to learn philosophy; on the other hand, those who already know Dante's *canzoni* need the 'bread' (i.e. the commentary) in order to understand their real meaning.[12] Dante addresses both those who desire to know and those who read his poetry, and he sets for them a hermeneutic path which is ultimately intended to lead to philosophy. In other words, instead of concocting a straightforward philosophical compendium, Dante invites the audience to read his *canzoni*, to wonder at their real meaning, and to fathom their philosophical sense from the commentary. In the second book Dante explains that there is a veiled philosophical meaning to his love poetry, and that his readers were not able to perceive that his gentle lady stands for true philosophy (*Conv.*, II. xii. 6). Thus Dante justifies the need for a commentary: without the commentary, the 'unfortunate' readers would not reach philosophy. Fortuitously, the commentary allows Dante to shift from love poetry to philosophical teaching. Dante's use of glosses is not, however, eccentric. The Latin commentary to the Cavalcanti poem,

---

12 'Per li miseri alcuna cosa ho riservata, la quale alli occhi loro, già è più tempo, ho dimostrata; e in ciò li ho fatti maggiormente vogliosi. Per che ora volendo loro apparecchiare, intendo fare un generale convivio di ciò ch'i' ho loro mostrato, e di quello pane ch'è mestiere a così fatta vivanda, sanza lo quale da loro non potrebbe esser mangiata' (*Conv.*, I. i. 10–11).

Donna mi prega, by Dino del Garbo,[13] features a similar scope; that is, to apply a scientific annotation to secular poetry.

The *Convivio* is not intended to merely display philosophical knowledge, but to invite the reader to gradually understand it. Dante insists on how difficult it is to grasp the true meaning of the *canzoni*,[14] and therefore insists on the necessity of the commentary. For him, it is the only way to remove the many obstacles that impede learning. The main hindrance to philosophy is the incapacity to distinguish appearance from truth. In the third and fourth books, Dante dwells upon the danger of appearances, and appeals to the authority of Thomas Aquinas and Albert the Great.[15] Sometimes we see things differently from how they really are because of an eye-disease or some light distortion (*Conv.*, III. ix. 1–10). In the same way, desire may induce us to avoid the help of reason and to judge by appearances, thereby disregarding the truth.[16] The *Convivio* both exposes and tries to undo the danger of desire. The reader, when judging on the basis of the senses, may believe that the love celebrated in the *canzoni* is the love of a man for a woman. Only by dismissing sensual appearances may the reader understand the real meaning of the *canzoni* – that is, the love of wisdom – and thus reach what he or she really desires: philosophical knowledge. Therefore, the commentary leads the reader to change his or her sensual desire into a rational one. The *Convivio* does not only supply knowledge, but it invites the reader to convert to it. Dante states that he

13   See Dino del Garbo, 'Commento latino alla canzone di Guido Cavalcanti *Donna me prega*', in *La canzone d'amore di Guido Cavalcanti e i suoi antichi commenti*, ed. by Enrico Fenzi (Genoa: Il Melangolo, 1999), pp. 86–133.
14   See *Conv.*, I. iii. 2, and compare: 'se difetto fia nelle mie rime, cioè nelle mie parole che a trattare di costei [filosofia] sono ordinate, di ciò è da biasimare la debilitade de lo 'ntelletto e la cortezza del nostro parlare: lo quale [per lo] pensiero è vinto, sì che seguire lui non puote a pieno, massimamente là dove lo pensiero nasce d'amore, perché quivi l'anima profondamente più che altrove s'ingegna' (*Conv.*, III. iv. 4).
15   *Conv.*, II. ix. 13–14, footnote pp. 453–4.
16   'Quanto la cosa desiderata più appropinqua al desiderante, tanto lo desiderio è maggiore, e l'anima, più passionata, più si unisce a la parte concupiscibile e più abbandona la ragione. Si che allora non giudica come uomo la persona, ma quasi come altro animale pur secondo l'apparenza, non discernendo la veritade' (*Conv.*, III. x. 3).

wishes to bring about such a conversion, that is to 'bring back' the reader 'to the right way'.[17] The commentary is meant to erase any 'false reasoning' and to dispose the mind 'toward the truth'.[18]

This conversion is not only possible for those excluded from knowledge because of civic or domestic engagements – as in the first book. Those who reject philosophy because of some 'malice' may also convert to it. Indeed, Dante states in the third book that the beauty of Lady Philosophy is able to remove any vice, that is, according to the Aristotelian partition, not only the habitual vices, but also the innate ones.[19] Therefore, the *Convivio* at this point is even opened up to those affected by malice (*malitia*) who were precluded in the first book. In other words, Dante wishes to allow all the 'unfortunate' people described in *Conv.*, I. i to fulfil their natural desire for knowledge, on the condition that they accept the premise to convert their sensual desire into a philosophical one. In this sense, the commentary in the *Convivio* is close to the tradition of the commentary on the Solomonic books, such as the *Song of the Songs*, in which the love of a woman allegorically signifies the love of knowledge, inviting the reader to convert his secular love into a divine one.[20]

If the commentator has already converted to philosophy, the character staged by the *canzoni* has not. Therefore, the character of Dante serves as a model and a guide for the reader's conversion. Dante claims that philosophy appeared 'proud and disdainful' at first.[21] Later he fell in love with her and

---

17 'Riducer la gente in diritta via'(*Conv.*, IV. i. 9); see also *Conv.*, IV. vii. 4 and *Conv.*, IV. xii. 15.
18 'Di loro false ragioni nulla ruggine rimagna nella mente che alla verità sia disposta' (*Conv.*, IV. xv. 1) and also 'dico che è tempo d'aprire li occhi a la veritade' (*Conv.*, IV. xv. 10).
19 'Dico adunque che queste fiammelle che piovono dalla sua biltade, come detto è, rompono li vizii innati, cioè connaturali, a dare a intendere che la sua bellezza ha podestade in rinnovare natura in coloro che la mirano; ch'è miracolosa cosa' (*Conv.*, III. viii. 20).
20 See Paola Nasti, *Favole d'amore e 'saver profondo', la tradizione salomonica in Dante* (Ravenna: Longo, 2007), pp. 109–11.
21 'Dal principio essa filosofia parea a me, quanto de la parte del suo corpo, cioè la sapienza, fiera, ché non mi ridea, in quanto le sue persuasioni ancora non

became a true philosopher, given that only those who love knowledge can reasonably be called so (*Conv.*, III. xii). Mirroring the *Vita nova*, Dante's character in the *Convivio* concentrates and guides the reader's expectation.

The *Convivio* does not only display philosophical knowledge – such as a *volgarizzamento* – but also aims at reconsidering what philosophy is, and the path that leads to it. Through his commentary, Dante's books I–IV become a propaedeutic to philosophy.[22] Only the reader who can understand the true meaning of the *canzoni* will be able to fulfil his natural desire to know, and therefore to reach earthly happiness. In the same way, the fourth book does not define nobility: it aims at converting the reader to a true understanding of it.

However, if the commentator invites the reader to convert, his appraisal of the outcome is somewhat ambiguous. On the one hand, Dante aims at removing 'malice from the minds' in order to 'instil there the light of truth' (*Conv.*, IV. viii. 4). On the other hand, he states in the same book IV that he will address only 'those intellects who are not sick through infirmity of mind or body' but are 'in the light of truth' (*Conv.*, IV. xv. 17), and furthermore, he 'refutes' the malicious (*Conv.*, IV. xv. 17). Paradoxically, Dante seems to be promoting knowledge for all, while excluding people from it. It appears, thus, that Dante is constantly redefining his public. Rather than explaining what philosophy is and how we can learn to love it, Dante considers the condition that makes knowledge a possibility. In other words, Dante is less interested in leading the way to knowledge, than in examining its limits.

---

intendea; e disdegnosa, ché non mi volgea l'occhio, cioè ch'io non potea vedere le sue dimostrazioni' (*Conv.*, III. xv. 19).

22 See Gianfranco Fioravanti, 'Sermones in lode della filosofia e della logica a Bologna nella prima metà del XIVe secolo', in *L'insegnamento della logica a Bologna nel XIV secolo*, ed. by Dino Buzzetti *et al.* (Bologna: Istituto per la Storia dell'Università, 1992), pp. 165–85. The praise of philosophy (and its allegorical embodiment) is quite common in the *studia*.

The Readers of the *Convivio*: Few Chosen and Many Left Out

Rather than successfully leading to a conversion to knowledge, Dante seems to ponder its difficulties. On the one hand, he suggests that every *misero* can eat the bread of philosophy (*Conv.*, I. xiii. 12), on the other he asserts that only those who 'digest' it (*Conv.*, I. i. 11) can reach knowledge. If Dante writes for the conversion of all, he concedes that many will refuse to convert: his commentary guides the wretched to knowledge but at the same time it bars those who find it too 'hard'. The *canzone Contra-li-erranti* [Against the erring-ones] shows Dante's twofold attitude toward his reader: he writes 'against' (*contra*) the people who err, but simultaneously he is trying to evangelize, in much the same way that Thomas Aquinas wrote both to condemn and to convert the infidels.[23] The ambiguity of Dante's standpoint is underscored by the biblical references. In the first book, Dante refers to the miracle of the Feeding of the Five Thousand, stressing the universal aim of his undertaking. Conversely, in the fourth book Dante compares his task to the work of the Sower (Mark 4. 3–9). Dante disseminates the seeds of knowledge, but expects there to be a very small uptake. The field of 'common opinion' is so 'overgrown' (*trifoglioso*) that 'the spikes of reason' are almost all overtaken by grass, that the 'wheat disappears, and the fruit is finally lost' (*Conv.*, IV. vii. 2–4). In other words, if Dante aims at sowing the seeds of knowledge in every mind, that seed will only take root in very few of them, while the most of them will continue to live like 'brute animals',[24] or like 'sheep'.[25] Dante thus surmises that few

---

23 'Propositum nostrae intentionis est veritatem quam fides Catholica profitetur, pro nostro modulo manifestare, errores eliminado contrarios', Thomas Aquinas, *Summa contra Gentiles*, ed. by Tito Sante Centi (Bologna: Edizioni studio Domenicano, 2000), p. 69.
24 *Conv.*, IV. vii. 4. The distinction between reasonable and 'bestial' often recurs in the *Convivio*. See: *Conv.*, IV. vii. 12; IV. vii. 14; III. ii. 13; III. ii. 18; III. iii. 5; III. vii. 6; III. vii. 13; II. viii. 11.
25 *Conv.*, II. vii. 4; I. i. 7; I. xi. 9.

will convert to knowledge and therefore be able to understand the 'true' meaning of his *canzoni*.

Dante's pondering over the possibilities and limits of knowledge leads to the constant reshaping of the intended addressee of the *Convivio*. As mentioned above, at the beginning of the first book Dante classifies the *impediti* among his potential readers into four categories (those deprived of knowledge because of defects in the body, in the soul, by necessity or by indolence) (*Conv.*, I. i. 2–4). But he revises this in *Convivio* I. ix. 1–9 by listing three groups of readers: foreign scholars, local scholars unable to use the vernacular and noblemen (*Conv.*, I. ix. 1–9), and again recasts them in the fourth book where he divides the readers into those whose intellect is sound, and those whose intellect is debilitated by arrogance, weak-mindedness or capriciousness (*Conv.*, IV. xv. 11). The constant effort of configuring the reader shows that the *Convivio*, rather than focusing on *what* may quench every man's thirst of knowledge, is centred on *who* may be able to drink.

The structure of the *Convivio* conveys Dante's concern for his reader. The simple need for a commentary to the *canzoni* implies that the true meaning of Dante's poetry was previously misunderstood. The commentary reveals that Dante had generally been considered as a lyric poet by his readers (*Conv.*, II. xii. 8), who also shared some fallacious opinions about philosophy and nobility.[26] The commentary aims at rectifying his existing readers' false beliefs.

Notwithstanding his public, the commentary is a self-commentary: its circularity shows the author's anxious desire to control the reading of his poems. Indeed, the commentator is supposed to know the real meaning of the *canzoni*, because he is himself the author of them. The commentary helps to reinforce the author's authority: the commentator tells the 'real' meaning of the *canzoni*, since he is at one with the author of them. But the price of this authorial privilege is to restrict the reader's interpretative freedom. The audience is summoned to share the views of the author and commentator, and the merest sign of dissent is assimilated with a bad

26 *Conv.*, I. ix. 8; III. xi. 10–16.

'digestion' of the bread of knowledge, implying some 'malice', or moral or intellectual deficiency, which radically discredits the dissenter. The enunciated structure of the *Convivio* urges the reader to unconditionally assent to the author's interpretation.[27] In the second book a short example shows how Dante impels the reader to accept his thesis through the triple voice of the commentator, the author, and the character. In this excerpt, the commentator explains why, according to Aristotle, men can think while animals cannot:

> Dirittamente, dico, però che lo pensiero è proprio atto della ragione, per che le bestie non pensano [...]. Dico adunque che vita del mio core, cioè del mio dentro, suole essere un pensiero soave [...] ciò è a dire che io pensando contemplava lo regno de' beati. E dico la finale cagione incontanente per che lassù io saliva pensando, quando dico: *Ove una donna gloriar vedia*. (*Conv.*, II. vii. 4–6)
>
> [Rightly so, I say, because thought is an act peculiar to reason, for beasts do not think [...] I say, then, that the life of my heart (that is, of my inner self) used to be a sweet thought [...] this is to say that I, in thought, contemplated the kingdom of the blessed. And immediately I tell the final cause of my ascending there in thought when I say *Where it would see a lady in glorious light*.]

Here, the pronoun *io* stands concurrently for Dante *agens* ('io pensando contemplava', 'io salia pensando'), for Dante *auctor* ('dico la final cagione [...] quando dico') and for Dante *commentator* ('dirittamente dico [...] dico adunque'). The vehement recurrence of the enunciation act (*io dico*) is reminiscent of the form of the *quaestio*, in which the formula *dixit quod* punctuates the argumentation. However, its repetition is quite uncommon in the commentaries to poetic texts. Besides, the self-commentary to vernacular poetry is quite rare,[28] and generally the commentator differs from the author, which allows for a broader and freer interpretation of the text. Francesco da Barberino fictitiously separates the author from the commentator of his *Documenti d'amore*, a vernacular self-commentary to his poetry.

---

27 Besides, the Platonic tradition of the philosophical symposium is dialogical, while Dante's text is clearly a monologue.
28 See Alastair Minnis: '*Amor* and *Auctoritas* in the Self-Commentary of Dante and Francesco da Barberino', *Poetica*, 32 (1990), 25–42.

The lyrics are sung by many *dominae* inspired by *Amore*, while the poet comments on them as if on the work of others.[29] Conversely, Dante chooses to explicate the perfect fusion of the identities of the author, the commentator and the character of Dante in the *Convivio*. He thus strengthens the authority of the commentary, but at the same time he reduces the task of the reader, who can only agree uncritically with the authority, or reject it thoroughly, and thereby face the allegations of malice levelled against all unruly readers. The conversion of the reader then appears to be fraught with difficulty. The only faithful reader of the *Convivio* is the commentator, who did already convert to philosophy and who rails against any reader who may find Dante's bread too difficult to digest and too 'hard' to stomach.

Progressively the commentary seems to exclude its readers. The many recipients of the *Convivio*, whom Dante carefully defines in the first book, gradually decrease in number. As stated above, Dante first distinguishes between the learned ones, who have seats at the table of knowledge, and those deprived of it (*Conv.*, I. i. 7). Dante claims later that the learned ones are in fact full of malice. They debase literature from a lady to a whore,[30] they are not true philosophers, because they are the friends of wisdom only 'for the sake of utility' or 'to secure financial rewards'.[31] In the same way, Dante criticizes the 'jurists, physicians, and almost all those belonging to religious orders' (that is, university scholars),[32] who do not 'always

---

29 'Somma vertù del nostro sir Amore, / Lo mio intellecto novamente accese, / ché di ciascun paese / chiamasse i servi a la sua maggior roccha. / Io che da lui ò la vita e l'onore / ciò fedelmente ad effecto conduxi. / Poi, tra lor, mi reduxi / da quella parte ch'ai suoi minor' toccha'; Francesco da Barberino, 'Proemio volgare' in *Documenti d'Amore*, ed. by Marco Albertazzi (Lavis: La Finestra, 2008), p. 5. Prologue written between 1305 and 1313.

30 'Hanno lasciata la litteratura a coloro che l'hanno fatta di donna meretrice' (*Conv.*, I. ix. 5).

31 'Né si dee chiamare vero filosofo colui che è amico di sapienza per utilitade, [...] che non per sapere studiano, ma per acquistare moneta o dignitade' (*Conv.*, III. xi. 10).

32 'Li legisti, medici e quasi tutti religiosi' (*Conv.*, III. xi. 10). See Maria Corti, 'La felicità mentale', in *Scritti su Cavalcanti e Dante* (Turin: Einaudi, 2003), p. 100 and *passim*.

give liberally of their great riches to the truly poor,'[33] as a true philosopher should do. If the learned do not supply the bread of knowledge, Dante is the only one able to feed the inner desire of the ignorant multitude. While discrediting the learned, Dante asserts his philosophical authority: he is the only true lover of knowledge, the only one who can supply the bread of wisdom. The learned can neither give nor receive knowledge – as far as mankind's natural desire to know is concerned, they are as useless as the 'viziosi' and the 'infermi' (*Conv.*, I. i. 3–4).

Therefore, only 'noblemen' (*Conv.*, I. xi. 6) who are prevented by 'domestic and civic responsibility' (*Conv.*, I. i. 4) may taste and digest the bread of knowledge and benefit from the commentary.[34] However, in the fourth book, Dante holds that many of them go astray despite their good roots.[35] Indeed, his generation seems to have totally forgotten the way of nobility. Their fathers, notwithstanding many impediments, followed the way of virtue, like those who trace a safe path into the snow. The sons, conversely, saw the footprints but refused to follow the path, and therefore went astray (*Conv.*, IV. vii. 7). They are lost not because of their ignorance, but because of their 'malice', and deserve 'contempt and scorn more than any other ill-bred person'.[36] The only reader who is truly 'noble' and engaged in 'domestic and civic responsibility' seems then to be Dante himself. Dante indeed conspicuously embodies the signs of nobility. True nobility, he says in the fourth book, is revealed by the practice of virtue that changes at every age, and should be, in 'maturity' 'tempered and strong'.[37] Not coincidentally, Dante asserts in the very first book of the *Convivio* that he himself will be 'tempered and powerful'.[38]

33 'Sempre liberalmente coloro che sanno porgono della loro buona ricchezza alli veri poveri' (*Conv.*, I. i. 9).
34 'Questa sentenza [il commento] non possono [non] avere in uso quelli nelli quali vera nobiltà è seminata per lo modo in cui si dirà nel quarto trattato' (*Conv.*, I. ix. 8).
35 'Così fossero tanti quelli di fatto che s'insetassero, quanti sono quelli che dalla buona radice si lasciano disviare!' (*Conv.*, IV. xxii. 12).
36 'Non solamente è vile, ma vilissimo e degno d'ogni despetto e vituperio più che altro villano' (*Conv.*, IV. vii. 9).
37 'Temperata e forte' (*Conv.*, IV. xxiii. 5).
38 'Temperata e virile' (*Conv.*, I. i. 16).

Dante alone is wise and noble. While excluding supposed philosophers and alleged noblemen, Dante cements his own authority.[39] According to the commentary, then, Dante alone can supply knowledge to the desiring multitude. Paradoxically, however, the table of wisdom is deserted; the intended guests refuse to eat bread they cannot digest. Dante's analysis of the possibility of acquiring knowledge and nobility leads him to a pessimistic diagnosis. None of his contemporaries can either convert to knowledge or restore true nobility; no one can read and truly understand his *Convivio*.

The anxious reflectiveness of the self-commentary reveals Dante's search for an audience which might acknowledge his authority, that is to say, an audience which may agree with his notion of wisdom and nobility and therefore recognize Dante as a true noble and ultimately a wise man. In the *Convivio*, rather than an ideal public of philosophers and ancient noblemen, Dante addresses a faithful reader, a supporter, a follower. He looks for a reader as close to him as the commentator. In other words, he seeks a reader who adopts his line of thinking, and may intimately understand the meaning and the 'beauty' of his *canzoni*.

Indeed, the first historical readers of the *Convivio* are mostly Dante's admirers. They do not read the commentary because they desire to learn what true philosophy is, but because they wish to grasp what philosophy is according to Dante. For example, the Ottimo commentator reads the *Convivio* in the service of his work on the *Commedia*, most of all in order to explain Dante's cosmology.[40] The recent study of the sixteenth-century glossed editions of the *Convivio* shows that among the twelve annotated volumes stored in Florentine libraries, only one is considered a consolation, dealing with moral philosophy and aimed at converting to a virtuous life. The volume is bound with other *consolationes* ('consolatorie') and is

---

39   See Albert R. Ascoli, *Dante and the Making of a Modern Author* (Cambridge: Cambridge University Press, 2008), pp. 67–218.
40   *Dante Alighieri, Convivio*, ed. by Franca Brambilla Ageno (Florence: Le Lettere, 1995), p. 969. See also *Censimento dei commenti danteschi, 1. I commenti di tradizione manoscritta, fino al 1480*, ed. by Enrico Malato and Andrea Mazzucchi (Rome: Salerno, 2011). About the transmission of the *Convivio*, see Guglielmo Gorni, 'Appunti sulla tradizione del *Convivio*', *Studi di filologia italiana*, 55 (1997), 5–22.

annotated with short prayers and religious invocations by an unknown reader.[41] The other volumes show different kinds of glosses. Tasso, for example, marks two copies with linguistic corrections, as if he aspires to recreate and reproduce Dante's vernacular. He also points out the *loci paralleli*, and notes many references to the *De vulgari eloquentia* and the *Commedia* in the margins, as if he is seeking to reconstruct the unity of Dante's intentions. Tasso also tries to clarify Dante's commentary, by explaining its doctrinal and astronomical implications.[42] Tasso, then, does not read the *Convivio* because he wishes to convert to wisdom, but because he desires to convert to, or at least to be familiar with Dante's thought and language.

The ideological complexity of the *Convivio*, its controlling enunciation and the pessimistic view it conveys about its possible reception all seem to invite the well-intentioned reader to simply give up. Or maybe it is the apparent exclusion of the reader that actually seduces him. Some readers, at least, were attracted by the seeming hostility of Dante's commentary. Those who actually read the *Convivio* wish to identify with the commentator of the *canzoni*, they aim at producing an additional commentary, which may unravel the true intention of the author. Indeed, the best known readers of the *Convivio*, such as the Ottimo commentator and Tasso, remarked on it, wishing to penetrate Dante's thought rather than converting to his conception of wisdom. Marco Santagata points out how the *Commedia* is not understandable without commentaries,[43] and how its complexity does not prejudice its popularity. In the same way, the *Convivio* seems *a priori* unreadable, but it attracts a select public which desires to redo the commentary in order to unravel the true meaning of Dante's poetry.

---

41 See Dante Alighieri, *Convivio* (Venice: 1531), stored in the Biblioteca Marucelliana, shelf number: 1 00 VIII 19. This book is bound with other *consolatorie di diversi autori nuovamente raccolte e da chi le raccolse; devotamente consecrate al s. Galeoto Picco Conte della Mirandola e Cavallier di S. Michele, in Vinegia, al segno del pozzo, 1550*. See also Natascia Bianchi, *Le Stampe dantesche postillate delle biblioteche fiorentine, 'Commedia' e 'Convivio' (1472–1596)* (Rome: Salerno, 2004).
42 See Natascia Bianchi, 'Le due redazioni delle postille del Tasso al *Convivio*: storia, cronologia e proposte di lettura', *Studi danteschi*, 65 (2000), 223–81.
43 Marco Santagata, *L'Io e il mondo, Un'interpretazione di Dante* (Bologna: Il Mulino, 2011), p. 378.

DONATELLA STOCCHI-PERUCCHIO

11 'Tu l'hai fatto di poco minore che li angeli': Nobility, Imperial Majesty, and the *Optimus Finis* in *Convivio* IV and *Monarchia*

This essay touches a number of interrelated points all subsumed under Dante's belief in the angelic, intellectual nature of the human being. Dante's notion of nobility evolves between *Convivio* IV and *Monarchia* in parallel with his reflection on the finality of human existence and on the empire. The *Liber Augustalis* by Frederick II is a potential catalyser of such reflection. While hereditary nobility, first discounted in *Convivio*, is re-evaluated in *Monarchia*, Dante becomes increasingly inclined to consider nobility as a universal rather than an elitist ethical value. At the same time the nobility of *Convivio*, consisting in the power to make choices according to virtue, gives way in *Monarchia* to *liberum arbitrium* and, *in nuce*, to a theory of love as a petition to the divine which finds its full articulation in the *Commedia* and constitutes the fulcrum of Dante's moral and political vision.

Like with other 'thematic knots' that traverse Dante's corpus, the problem of nobility is one that inevitably elicits questions of continuity and discontinuity, consistency and incongruity or even, as in some recent critical endeavours, of evolution and involution.[1] This is due to the different definitions Dante gives and perspectives he assumes in the various contexts and at the different stages of his career as a thinker and poet. A most conspicuous case is the relation of the *canzone Le dolci rime d'amor ch'i' solia* [The tender rhymes of love I once sought out] with the prose commentary in *Convivio* IV and with *Monarchia*, the two works in which

---

1 Marco Santagata, 'Introduzione', in Dante Alighieri, *Opere*. Vol. I (Milan: Mondadori, 2013), pp. lxxxiv–lxxxv.

Dante's reflection on nobility appears intertwined with the development of his political ideology.

The *canzone* opens announcing a temporary change of style and relative subject matter due to the barrier the writer had encountered in the proud and scornful behaviour ('li atti disdegnosi e feri') of his lady with which *Convivio* III had come to a close. In spite of this acknowledged discontinuity, *Convivio* IV picks up and develops ideas already put forth in *Convivio* III. I refer in particular to *Convivio* III. iii, in which Dante tells us that all things possess in their very nature a force called love that drives them to their proper place (*Conv.*, III. iii. 1). Among them the human mind – which true human nature consists of and which is angelic, that is, rational and most noble – loves truth and virtue (*Conv.*, III. iii. 11–12). In *Convivio* III. xv. 12, approaching the closing of the treatise, Dante speaks of the beauty of his lady and of the flames of fire (right appetite, 'appetito diritto') that 'rain down' from it, from which happiness, defined in Aristotelian terms as 'activity in accordance with virtue in a perfect life',[2] derives. While all these elements enter Dante's discussion of nobility in *Convivio* IV – a discussion that will culminate with the theory of natural appetite – one major novelty of the treatise is indeed the introduction, within this philosophical context, of the idea of the empire. As we shall see, an integration of the two – moral nobility and empire – not yet operative here, is left to *Monarchia* to achieve.

According to Santagata's diachronic analysis of Dante's different positions on the subject of nobility in relation to the various stages of the poet's biographical and intellectual itinerary, *Convivio* IV represents a transition between two uncompromised opposite visions: that of the *canzone* and that of *Monarchia* II. In the poem the 'Florentine Guelph' haughtily takes issue in favour of moral nobility against the opinion of emperor Frederick II who ascribed it to ancestral wealth and fine manners. In *Monarchia*, the political exile endorses the opinion previously rejected and now correctly attributed to Aristotle. Santagata links such a transition to the first nucleus of Dante's thought on empire appearing in *Convivio* IV along with

---

2 In this case the translation is from Christopher Ryan, *The Banquet* (Saratoga, CA: Anma Libri, 1989).

a passage in chapter xxix. 8–11 that he takes to be a small but significant concession to hereditary nobility. Taking Dante's re-evaluation of nobility of blood as a function of his new empire imperial ideology, he interprets Dante's change of heart in *Monarchia* II as an expression of his own frustrated nostalgic aspirations for a political system of the past in which the old nobility served as the necessary pillar of the institution.[3]

Without discounting the validity of this assessment, I find this primarily sociological approach rather partial and in need of being balanced with the overtly philosophical perspective characteristic of both *Convivio* IV and *Monarchia*, book I in particular. The reading I propose here is one in which the inception of the imperial vision in *Convivio* IV remains central to the question of nobility but in the ethical rather than hereditary sense, and mediates a transition not from the former to the latter but from what is still an elitist notion of ethical nobility in *Convivio* to the all-inclusive theory that in *Monarchia* embraces the whole of mankind.

The Legacy of Frederick II

We have no record to attest to the authenticity of the opinion attributed to Frederick II in *Convivio* IV, both *canzone* and prose text, that nobility consisted of 'antica possession d'avere con reggimenti belli' [ancestral wealth together with fine manners] (*Conv.*, IV. v. 23–4). We do know, however, of a *Contentio de nobilitate*, a dispute on nobility, involving two of the major jurists and *dictatores* of the Magna Curia, Piero della Vigna and Taddeo Sessa.[4] We also know that the encomiastic literature that flourished within and about the imperial court invokes nobility in the all-inclusive sense in relation to sovereignty. Two prominent examples are Piero della Vigna's *preconium* and Nicolaus Barensis' *dictamen* to Frederick II. These texts are,

---

3   Santagata, 'Introduzione', pp. lxxxiv–xcvii.
4   Fulvio Delle Donne, 'Una disputa sulla nobiltà alla corte di Federico II di Svevia', in *Medioevo Romanzo*, 23 (1999), 3–20.

in turn, thematically related to Frederick's own ideological pronouncement in the *Proem* of the *Constitutions of Melfi* and, in the case of Piero della Vigna, his *preconium* and Frederick's *Proem* were, in fact, composed by the same hand.⁵

The shift between the *canzone* and the prose text is evident in the fact that Frederick II, initially referred to generically with the words 'tale imperò' [one ruler held], is properly if not reverently introduced in the latter by name and prerogative as 'the last emperor of the Romans' (*Conv.*, IV. iii. 6; trans. Ryan). As soon as the introduction is made, Dante opens what looks like a long digression, preamble, or expansion on imperial majesty and its function: that of leading human society to its end, that is, happiness, by creating the essential condition of peace. The sequence continues on the providentiality of the Roman Empire further sanctioned by the Incarnation and ends on a definition of the imperial art as pertaining to the province of the will. In tune with the voluntarism typical of the Romans, Dante calls the emperor 'lo cavalcatore della umana volontade' [the rider of the human will] (*Conv.*, IV. ix. 10; trans. Ryan). Imperial authority regulates the world of praxis through law, and written law is, as Dante says quoting the *Old Digest*, the art of well-doing and fairness: 'la ragione scritta è arte di bene e d'equitade' (*Conv.*, IV. ix. 8). These factors suggest two considerations from which my line of inquiry branches out. Firstly, it is not so much Frederick's alleged opinion on nobility that catalyses Dante's reflections, but his role as emperor, law-giver, and theorist of sovereignty as it appears first and foremost in his code of laws. Secondly, although maintaining the hierarchy of speculation over action, Dante extends the pre-eminently speculative concern with happiness of the previous treatises to the active sphere.⁶ In

---

5   Of the same opinion is Delle Donne, who says about the *preconium* that 'it appears to have in mind the imperial ideology expressed in the *Proem* of the *Constitutions of Melfi*. I follow Pice in classifying the encomium of Nicolaus as a *dictamen* or epistle rather than a sermon. Nicola Pice, 'Il dictamen di Nicolaus, uno scritto encomiastico dell'età federiciana', in Felice Moretti (ed.), *Cultura e società in Puglia in età sveva e angioina* (Bitonto: Centro Ricerche di Storia e Arte Bitontina, 1989), pp. 283–310 (p. 283).

6   *Convivio* I. i. 1 is emblematic: 'Sì come dice lo Filosofo nel principio della Prima Filosofia, tutti li uomini naturalmente desiderano di sapere'. The reason for this can

doing so, he leaves more room for sources of philosophical inspiration, such as Stoicism, that flourished in the Roman world in response to the needs of its juridical and increasingly universalistic and cosmopolitan culture.

In refuting hereditary nobility in *Convivio* IV. xv. 3–4, Dante has recourse to the argument of the common origin of all human beings from Adam as a way to dismiss any claims of distinction between noble and non-noble progeny.[7] One of the opponents in the *Contentio de nobilitate*, the one who defends hereditary nobility, uses the same argument but draws opposite conclusions. After the Fall, those who wanted to remedy the degeneration caused by the sin of Adam, devoted themselves to great deeds and thus created a distinction from those who struggled, like beasts, for their mere survival.[8] In itself not so interesting, the theory points to the cultural milieu of Frederick II as a field of resonance for certain motifs that enter Dante's work. More importantly, in the *Proem* to the *Liber Augustalis*, while the Augustinian notion of *remedium peccati* serves the different and more traditional purpose of legitimizing sovereignty, the account of Adam's nobility and highest ranking in the order of creation provides a complementary, prelapsarian rationale for such legitimation. To that effect, the author of the *Proem* relies on two scriptural texts, Genesis I. 26, and Psalm 8. 6,

> he, who had foreseen what should be done, looked at what he had done and was satisfied with what he saw. He made man in his own image and likeness, the worthiest creature of the creatures below the globe of the lunar circle. He made him a little less than the angels, and, after deliberate counsel, he decided to put him in charge of the other creatures. He gave life in the spirit to him whom he had taken from earthly

---

> be and is that each thing, impelled by a force provided by its own nature, inclines toward its own perfection. Since knowledge is the ultimate perfection of our soul, in which resides our ultimate happiness, we are all therefore by nature subject to a desire for it'. I follow here the interpretation of Ardizzone in the third chapter of her *Reading as the Angels Read. Speculation and Politics in Dante's 'Convivio'* (Toronto: Toronto University Press, 2016), pp. 170–249.

7 'Dunque se esso Adamo fu nobile, tutti siamo nobili, e se esso fu vile, tutti siamo vili; che non è altro che torre via la distinzione di queste condizioni, e così è torre via quelle'.

8 Delle Donne, 'Una disputa', p. 8.

pollution, and he joined a wife and companion, part of his own body, to him whom he had crowned with a diadem of glory and honor.[9]

So frequently cited as to appear like *topoi*, these verses acquire, in fact, different nuances depending on the contexts in which they are employed. We owe to Kantorowicz the acute observation that the original source of the Psalm is altered here with the insertion of the word *diadem* and the concomitant stress on the fact that, in the Second Letter to the Hebrews, the phrase 'made a little less than the angels' refers to Christ. With this evidence Kantorowicz supports the idea that Frederick claimed not only for his kingly body but perhaps even for his natural one the same perfection, uniqueness, and innocence Adam and Christ had.[10] His intuition is confirmed by the encomiastic texts mentioned above. Piero della Vigna in his *preconium* calls the emperor 'the one whom the supreme author [*opifix*] created man'.[11] Even more emphatically Nicolaus' *dictamen*, which is a veritable monument to the Christomimetic regality of Frederick II, confirms: 'this is the one that the Lord crowned with glory and honour and placed above all His creation'.[12] Aside from the fact that Dante could hardly have overlooked the transgressive character of these identifications as propaganda instruments for the imperial cult of Frederick II, it is true that Dante himself conceives the monarch as a Christomimetic figure.[13] At the beginning of *Monarchia* II, a quotation from Psalm 2. 1–3 – the

9   James M. Powell, *The Liber Augustalis or Constitutions of Melfi Promulgated by the Emperor Frederick II for the Kingdom of Sicily in 1231* (Syracuse, NY: Syracuse University Press, 1971), p. 3.
10 Ernst Kantorowicz, *The King's Two Bodies: A Study in Mediaeval Political Theology* (Princeton, NJ: Princeton University Press, 1957), p. 482ff.; Ernst Kantorowicz, *Federico II, Imperatore* (Milan: Garzanti, 2000), p. 65.
11 Fulvio Delle Donne, *Il Potere e la sua legittimazione. Letteratura encomiastica in onore di Federico II di Svevia* (Arce: Nuovi Segnali, 2005), p. 65.
12 Nicola Pice, 'Il dictamen di Nicolaus', p. 300 (my translation).
13 For an analysis of Nicolaus' *dictamen* in light of Christomimetic regality and in relation to Dante see Donatella Stocchi-Perucchio, 'Federico II e l'ambivalenza del sacro nella *Commedia*', in *Tra Amici: Studies in Honor of Giuseppe Mazzotta. MLN Italian Issue Supplement*, 127.1 (2012), S233–44 (p. S236).

'messianic psalm par excellence'[14] – testifies to what the treatise (and not just the treatise), in fact, argues for: that the providential function of the empire is to continue the work of Redemption.[15] But since the end of Providence coincides in the epilogue of *Monarchia* with the end of nature (to which book I is primarily devoted) it is clear that, for Dante, what is providential is also natural and vice versa. Frederick's *Proem* hints at this duality not only with the emblem of sovereignty bestowed upon Adam in the earthly paradise – the *diadem* – but also by the subsequent narrative of the Fall and its consequences followed by the central legitimizing argument,

> Therefore, by this compelling necessity of things and not less by the inspiration of Divine Providence, princes of nations were created through whom the license of crimes might be corrected.[16]

'The necessity of things' could reveal an early awareness of the socio-political nature of human beings of Aristotelian derivation, a theme on which Dante begins his reflection in *Convivio* IV. iv. 1.[17] However, Dante continues, human aggregations of various sizes will come to conflict because of the desire to increase land possession, and discord and war will create an obstruction to happiness.[18] It is as if the memory of the Fall had surfaced in Dante's narrative in terms that are also reminiscent of the *Liber*:

14 *Monarchia*, in Dante Alighieri, *Opere*, ed. by Diego Quaglioni (Milan: Mondadori, 2014), p. 1052.
15 *Inferno* I. 101 and ff. is a most relevant passage to that effect. See Gentile's reading of the mission of the greyhound-Emperor as the one who 'after Christ had come to redeem man from original sin, rescues him, by submitting his will to the law, from actual sin'. Giovanni Gentile, *Studi su Dante: Raccolti da Vito A. Bellezza* (Florence: Sansoni, 1965), p. 152 (my translation).
16 Powell, *The Liber Augustalis*, p. 3.
17 'Lo fondamento radicale della imperiale maiestade, secondo lo vero, è la necessità della umana civilitade, che a uno fine è ordinata, cioè a vita felice; alla quale nullo per sé è sufficiente a venire sanza l'aiutorio d'alcuno, con ciò sia cosa che l'uomo abisogna di molte cose, alle quali uno solo satisfare non può. E però dice lo Filosofo che l'uomo naturalmente è compagnevole animale'.
18 'Onde, con ciò sia cosa che l'animo umano in terminata possessione di terra non si queti, ma sempre desideri gloria d'acquistare, sì come per esperienza vedemo, discordie

because of the blemish of transgression implanted in them by their parents, they [the progeny of Adam] conceived hatred among themselves for one another. They divided up the common ownership of property by natural law. Thus man, whom God created virtuous and simple, did not hesitate to involve himself in disputes.[19]

In the face of such discord Dante thinks of the monarch as the one who, by virtue of possessing everything, is immune from the desire to possess more, that is, from cupidity.[20] This idea of the ruler who possesses the whole of the land is a medieval juridical concept that could be viewed as bearing the highest possible resemblance to the state of nature in which property was held in common, as declared in the *Proem*, by natural law. In stating that land property unified in the hands of the monarch is propaedeutic to peace, Dante prepares the argument of chapters xii and xiii against the notion of wealth as the foundation of nobility. Interestingly enough, Delle Donne reports that in the final period of the Middle Ages the problem of the essence of nobility 'gets debated with renewed vigour probably in connection with the attempts to give a more precise juridical definition to the concept of land inheritability'.[21] These debates might have been in Dante's mind while developing the idea that law – both Canon and Civil law – is meant to curb cupidity.[22] Within the discussion of wealth that deceptively promises fulfillment while generating more desire, Dante examines the general phenomenon of the dilation of desire itself and establishes that

---

  e guerre conviene surgere intra regno e regno, le quali sono tribulazioni delle cittadi, e per le cittadi delle vicinanze, e per le vicinanze delle case [e per le case] dell'uomo; e così s'impedisce la felicitade' (*Conv.*, IV. iv. 3).

19 Powell, *The Liber Augustalis*, p. 3.

20 'Il perché, a queste guerre e alle loro cagioni tòrre via, conviene di necessitade tutta la terra, e quanto all'umana generazione a possedere è dato, essere Monarchia, cioè uno solo principato, e uno prencipe avere; lo quale, tutto possedendo e più desiderare non possondo, li regi tegna contenti nelli termini delli regni, sì che pace intra loro sia, nella quale si posino le cittadi, e in questa posa le vicinanze s'amino, (e) in questo amore le case prendano ogni loro bisogno, lo qual preso, l'uomo viva felicemente: che è quello per che esso è nato' (*Conv.*, IV. iv. 4).

21 Delle Donne, 'Una disputa', p. 4.

22 'E che altro intende di medicare l'una e l'altra Ragione, Canonica dico e Civile, tanto quanto a riparare alla cupiditade che, raunando ricchezze, cresce?' (*Conv.*, IV. xii. 9).

every thing aspires to return to its principle. In analogy with the *Liber Augustalis*, he starts from the narrative of creation in Genesis 1. 26,

> E la ragione è questa: che lo sommo desiderio di ciascuna cosa, e prima dalla natura dato, è lo ritornare allo suo principio. E però che Dio è principio delle nostre anime e fattore di quelle simili a sé (sì come è scritto: 'Facciamo l'uomo ad imagine e simiglianza nostra'), essa anima massimamente desidera di tornare a quello. (*Conv.*, IV. xii. 14)

> [The reason is this: that the supreme desire of each thing, and the one that is first given to it by nature, is to return to its first cause. Now since God is the cause of our souls and has created them like himself (as it is written, 'Let us make man in our own image and likeness'), the soul desires above all else to return to him.]

Imagining the soul as a pilgrim who, new to the road he is taking, mistakes every house he encounters for his destination, Dante describes the predicament of the soul which mistakes every small good for a big one until it finally realizes that God is the ultimate desirable. What this argument implies is that no wealth or other material possession can confer nobility. God is the only ennobling 'object' of desire. Similitude, since it applies to Adam in his dual body as man and mankind, is an inclusive concept.[23] In further analogy with the *Liber*, Dante complements this reference to Genesis 1 with a quotation from Psalm 8 in chapter xix,

> Di questa nobilitade nostra, che in tanti e tali frutti fruttificava, s'accorse lo Salmista, quando fece quel Salmo che comincia: 'Segnore nostro Dio, quanto è ammirabile lo nome tuo nell'universa terra', là dove commenda l'uomo, quasi maravigliandosi del divino affetto in essa umana creatura, dicendo: 'Che cosa è l'uomo, che tu, Dio, lo visiti? Tu l'hai fatto poco minore che li angeli, di gloria e d'onore l'hai coronato, e posto lui sopra l'opere delle mani tue'. Veramente dunque bella e convenevole comparazione fu del cielo all'umana nobilitade. (*Conv.*, IV. xix. 7)

> [The Psalmist had in mind this nobility of ours, which has produced so many and such various fruits, when he composed that Psalm which begins: 'O Lord our God, how wonderful is your name in all the earth!', where he praises man, as though marvelling at the divine affection for the human creature, saying: 'What is man, that you, God,

---

23   For Adam in the individual and corporate sense, see Aquinas, *Summa Theologica* I^a-II ae q. 81 a. 1 co.

do visit him? You have made him a little lower than the angels, have crowned him with glory and honour, and have set him above the works of your hands'. Therefore the comparison of human nobility with heaven was truly agreeable and fitting.]

The Theory of Appetite and Its Evolution

The citation appears as a way to seal, again inclusively, Dante's central argument on moral nobility. Defined according to Aristotle as *abito eligente*, the habit of choosing the middle among extremes, nobility is the root of every virtue and the seed of happiness, where happiness consists of the exercise of all virtues both moral and intellectual, 'activity in accordance with virtue in a perfect life' (*Conv.*, IV. xvii. 1, 8). This concept of nobility remains, however, in agreement with the *canzone*, an exclusive concept, a gift of God bestowed only upon those who have physical perfection and proper spiritual disposition. It follows that if the seed is exclusive, then happiness, which is its fruit, can only be a prerogative of those who possess the seed. At this point, with chapters xxi and xxii, Dante introduces the other innovative aspect that I isolated as distinctive of the prose text with respect to the *canzone*: the theory of appetite. Dante claims Aristotle and the Peripatetics for his primary authorities but he also mentions Augustine and Cicero (*Conv.*, IV. xxi. 9, 14) while leaving aside the opinion of Epicurus and Zeno (*Conv.*, IV. xxii. 4). In continuity with the botanic metaphors of root, seed, and fruits, he now brings in the concept of *hormé* – a typically Stoic notion – that he calls *rampollo* and *tallo* to signify the noblest shoot of the 'seed of happiness'.[24] He arrives at this concept through the

---

24 For Dante's sources see Cesare Vasoli, 'Note' to *Convivio*, in Dante Alighieri. *Opere minori*, I.ii, ed. by Cesare Vasoli and Domenico De Robertis (Milan: Ricciardi, 1988), pp. 772–3. See also Paolo Falzone: 'Psicologia dell'atto umano in Dante. Problemi di lessico e di dottrina', in *Filosofia in volgare nel medioevo*, ed. by Nadia Bray and Loris Sturlese (Louvain-La-Neuve: Brepols, 2003), pp. 331–66, for an extensive analysis.

explanation of how divine virtue descends on the individual once the soul is ready to be infused with the possible intellect. This infusion affects all human creatures – a significantly different nuance with respect to the *canzone* – although it varies in degree depending on the disposition of the soul to receive it. In the case in which such disposition were optimal, the soul would become almost 'another God incarnated' (*Conv.*, IV. xxi. 10).

In *Convivio* III. iii, in the context of the exegesis of *Amor che ne la mente mi ragiona*, [Love, that speaks to me within my mind], Dante starts from Aristotle's *Physics* and states that every nature, from the simplest to the most complex, has a specific love for, or tension toward, its proper place. The human mind, being the noblest of all natures, loves truth and virtue or, conversely, truth and virtue find their proper place in the mind. When the new element of the *hormé* comes into focus in *Convivio* IV. xxi and xxii, Dante elaborates further on this reflection. After explaining that this shoot must be kept straight and consolidated in its rectitude in order to fructify and result in happiness, he dwells on the definition of 'natural appetite of the mind', and on what it means in terms of love. The Stoic legacy is evident in the fact that *hormé* is presented first as the instinct of self-preservation possessed by human beings and animals alike that induces them to self-love or, as the Stoics would say, to 'self-appropriation'. It then branches out in different directions but the text states that only 'un solo calle' [one single path], leads to our fulfillment: 'alla nostra pace' (*Conv.*, IV. xxii. 6), That is the one pertaining to the mind or the rational part consisting in will and intellect. At this point Dante resumes the question of what constitutes the perfect life already addressed in chapter xvii. In the hierarchy of beatitudes there created, that engendered by the speculative life – what Aristotle talks about in book X of the *Ethics* – was superior to that engendered by the active life – the one which was regulated by the elective habit of the right medium. Now while this hierarchy is confirmed, the speculative use of our mind, the one we love most, is declared inadequate to lead to the supreme beatitude which is not of this world. If we remain within the Stoic conceptual framework that Dante himself suggests, the destination of our rational appetite could be identified with the notion of *oikeiosis*. In the Stoic vocabulary, the term indicates what is 'proper' in the twofold sense of what one owns and what is appropriate, and also the conciliation with what is proper.[25]

Moving from *Convivio* to *Monarchia* it is interesting to see how these concepts rather than disappearing migrate and mutate in the process. In the political treatise, Dante is no longer interested in the possible intellect as an individual prerogative with different degrees of purity, but in the collective participation of all human beings in the actualization of the possible intellect so that the collective effort compensates for individual differences and inadequacies. *Convivio* IV. iv. 1 had already hinted at the same idea (see above). In *Monarchia*, I. iii. 7–8 we read:

> Patet igitur quod ultimum de potentia ipsius humanitatis est potentia sive virtus intellectiva. Et quia potentia ista per unum hominem seu per aliquam particularium comunitatum superius distinctarum tota simul in actum reduci non potest, necesse est multitudinem esse in humano genere, per quam quidem tota potentia hec actuetur. (*Mon.*, I. iii. 7–8)

> [It is thus clear that the highest potentiality of mankind is his intellectual potentiality or faculty. And since that potentiality cannot be fully actualized all at once in any one individual or in any one of the particular social groupings enumerated above, there must needs be a vast number of individual people in the human race, through whom the whole of this potentiality can be actualized.][26]

Here it is the activity of the possible intellect, in its quasi divine character, to become the ennobling factor not for single individuals but for humanity as a whole (*universitas hominum*; *Mon.*, I. iii. 4). The inclusive quality of this new nobility is now consistent with the words of Psalm 8 that Dante quotes again, and prominently so, in the next chapter,

> Satis igitur declaratum est quod proprium opus humani generis totaliter accepti est actuare semper totam potentiam intellectus possibilis, per prius ad speculandum et secundario propter hoc est ad operandum per suam extensionem. Et quia quemadmodum est in parte sic est in toto, et in homine particulari contingit quod sedendo

---

25 Roberto Radice, intro., trans. and notes. *Stoici antichi. Tutti i frammenti* (Milan: Rusconi, 1998), pp. xi–xii, p. 1544.
26 All translations of *Monarchia* are from *Monarchy*, ed. by Prue Shaw (Cambridge: Cambridge University Press, 1996).

et quiescendo prudentia et sapientia ipse perficitur, patet quod genus humanum in quiete sive tranquillitate pacis ad proprium suum opus, quod fere divinum est iuxta 'Minuisti eum paulominus ab angelis', liberrime atque facillime se habet. (*Mon.*, I. iv. 1–2)

[Now it has been sufficiently explained that the activity proper to mankind considered as a whole is constantly to actualize the full intellectual potential of humanity, primarily through thought and secondarily through action (as a function and extension of thought).

And since what holds true for the part is true for the whole, and an individual human being 'grows perfect in judgement and wisdom when he sits at rest', it is apparent that mankind most freely and readily attends to this activity – an activity which is almost divine, as we read in the psalm: 'Thou hast made him a little lower than the angels' – in the calm or tranquillity of peace.]

The return to the Psalm already quoted in *Convivio* in this new context attests to a decisive move in favour of the collective perspective in regard to both moral nobility and happiness. As nobility shifts from a principle of differentiation among human beings to a principle of aggregation, so in the concept of happiness the two strands of *Convivio*, the social-collective and the philosophical-individual, merge in *Monarchia* to become humanity's *optimus finis*, 'best purpose' (*Conv.*, I. iii. 2).[27] In the final part of the treatise the hierarchy of beatitudes created in *Convivio* is supplanted by the dual end of mankind – earthly and eternal – each one perfect in its own right. Also, the meaning of *beatitudo huius vite* [happiness in this life] is not conveyed in the language of the possible intellect as one would expect from the beginning of the treatise, but consists in *operatione proprie virtutis* [the exercise of our own powers] (*Mon.*, III. xvi. 7). This shift in language challenges us readers to redefine the *optimus finis*. If we assimilate the 'proper virtue' to the Aristotelian *theoria* in book X of the *Ethics*, the phrase would seem to confirm the privileged status of the speculative life with respect to the active life that is stated as a premise in book I.iii – 'all of these are subordinate to thinking [speculationi ancillantur] as the best activity for which the Primal Goodness brought mankind into existence'

---

27   Examples of the analogy between the single individual – the individual body – and humanity – the corporate body – are in *Conv.*, I. v. 4 and I. xvi. 8.

(*Mon.*, I. iii. 10). However, we could also read it, as I would like to suggest, in light of Stoic thought, as an appropriation of and reconciliation with what is most intimately proper. Humanity is capable of finding its proper place in the order of things, its end, its beatitude, its *oikeiosis*, in the realization of the principle of its creation: the similitude to God in the cognitive as well as in the volitional sphere or, Aquinas would say, 'per cognitionem et amorem' [through knowledge and love].[28] The rationale for this realization in history through the empire is the subject of *Monarchia*; hence the necessity for Dante to integrate the speculative preoccupation of the first books of *Convivio* with his increased investment, starting with the fourth book, in the world of praxis (see note 6).

The argument of similitude is among the first Dante uses in *Monarchia* I. viii. 2:

> De intentione Dei est ut omne causatum divinam similitudinem representet in quantum propria natura recipere potest. Propter quod dictum est: 'Faciamus hominem ad ymaginem et similitudinem nostram'; quod licet 'ad ymaginem' de rebus inferioribus ab homine dici non possit, 'ad similitudinem' tamen de qualibet dici potest, cum totum universum nichil aliud sit quam vestigium quoddam divine bonitatis. (*Mon.*, I. viii. 2)

> [It is God's intention that every created thing should show forth His likeness in so far as its own nature can receive it. For this reason it is said: 'Let us make man in our image, after our likeness'; for although 'in our image' cannot be said of things lower than man, 'after our likeness' can be said of anything, since the whole universe is simply an imprint of divine goodness.]

While the text of reference is again Genesis 1 as in *Convivio* IV, the objective is different. In *Convivio*, in the context of the necessity of the law to treat the human desire for riches – 'the false traitresses' – the point was to demonstrate that a relation of similitude pulls the human soul to a *redditus* to God as its ultimate end. In *Monarchia* the focus is on the vestige, the

---

28 *Contra Gentiles*, lib. 2 cap. 87 n. 6. For the Stoic correlation between *hormé* and similitude (typosis), see Giorgio Stabile, 'Teoria della visione come teorie della conoscenza', in *Dante e la filosofia della natura. Percezioni, linguaggi, cosmologie* (Florence: Galluzzo, 2007), pp. 9–29 (p. 21).

seal impressed by God on Adam that defines his individual-singular and corporate-collective nature: an inner vestige that corresponds to God's imprint on the whole of creation. This notion of the common vestige implies a natural predisposition of humanity to unity and serves Dante's argument in favour of the universal monarchy as the political system that best reflects the oneness of God and best corresponds to the order of creation.

Dante's process of *reductio ad unum* turns to the cosmos: in the same way that the universe is governed by one motor and one movement or law, so mankind is in a perfect state when it corresponds to the universe with one ruler and one law. The argument, although clearly deriving from Aristotle's *Metaphysics*, is perfectly compatible with the Stoic notion of a law-governed universe whose core principle, the *logos*, is both a rational and an ethical principle. Dante's turn to the ethical plan is immediately evident in the Boethian quotation that seals chapter ix. 3: 'O happy race of men, if only the love by which the heavens are ruled might rule your minds'. A universe governed by law that is a law of love and that applies to human souls alike seems equally compatible with the natural law of the Stoics later appropriated within Christian thought and prior to that within the juridical culture of the Romans.[29] The core of the first book of the *Monarchia* on justice made possible by the unhindered will and unlimited power of the monarch, on charity that makes the monarch pursue the common good, on *liberum arbitrium*, 'free will', as free judgement about the will, and on the concord of the wills as the necessary condition for peace, testifies to Dante's adoption of a typically Roman voluntaristic perspective, a perspective that the emperor 'cavalcatore della umana volontade' [(who) rides in the saddle of the human will] had prefigured in *Convivio* IV. ix. 9.

In discussing the adaptation of the Stoic philosophy from its Greek matrix to the needs of the Roman civilization, Pohlenz makes an observation that further illuminates Dante's transition from *Convivio* IV to *Monarchia*:

---

29 Max Pohlenz, *La Stoa. Storia di un movimento spirituale* (Florence: La Nuova Italia, 1978), pp. 535–75.

The Greek man always takes as his point of departure a clear identification of the end that by itself elicits desire, and therefore does not perceive the will as an autonomous factor next to knowledge, while for the Roman the decisive function belongs to the will.[30]

The decisive function of the will in *Monarchia* determines the transition from a theory of nobility reserved for those whom divine grace endowed with *abito eligente* to a theory of the freedom of the will as the greatest grace – such is the meaning of gift – that God granted to mankind. While the terms *abito eligente* and *hormé* are abandoned in the transition, their conceptual value is incorporated within Dante's notion of the will.

In the definition of *liberum arbitrium* as *liberum de voluntate iudicium* [free judgement in matters of volition] (*Mon.*, I. xii. 2), and in the accompanying explanation of how judgement must intervene between the apprehension and the appetite and guide the appetite, Dante is indebted not only to Boethius, from whom he derives the actual wording, but also to Cicero and Ambrose in their respective versions of *De Officiis* and, above all, to Saint Augustine.[31] Cicero's premise for his doctrine of duty and Ambrose's reliance on Cicero for a thought that can be traced back to a common Stoic matrix are evident from the following clearly related passages,

> Now we find that the essential activity of the spirit is twofold: one force is appetite (that is *hormé* in Greek) which impels a man this way and that; the other is reason, which teaches and explains what should be done and what should be left undone. The result is that reason commands, appetite obeys.[32]

---

30 Pohlenz, *La Stoa*, p. 569 (my translation).
31 On Boethius' definition see Tabarroni and Chiesa: 'free will is the free judgment on the images – *imaginationes* – that stimulate – *irritant* – the will'; Dante Alighieri. *Monarchia*, ed. by Andrea Tabarroni and Paolo Chiesa (Rome: Salerno, 2013), pp. 48–9 (my translation). Boethius' language is reminiscent here of the *phantasia hormetiké* of the Stoics. Radice, *Stoici antichi*, p. 1586.
32 Marcus Tullius Cicero, *De officiis*, trans. by Walter Miller (Cambridge, MA: Harvard University Press, 1975), p. 103. For the influence of Cicero's *De Officiis* on both *Convivio* and *Monarchia*, see Claudia Di Fonzo, 'Dal *Convivio* alla *Monarchia* per il tramite del *De officiis* di Cicerone: l'imprescindibile paradigma ciceroniano', in *Tenzone*, 14 (2013), 71–122.

And Ambrose:

> For there are motions in which there is a kind of passion that breaks forth as it were in a sort of rush. Wherefore in Greek it is called ὁρμή, because it comes out suddenly with some force. In these there lie no slight force of soul or of nature. Its force, however, is twofold: on the one side it rests on passion, on the other on reason, which checks passion, and makes it obedient to itself, and leads it whither it will; and trains it by careful teaching to know what ought to be done, and what ought to be avoided, so as to make it submit to its kind tamer.[33]

As for Augustine, his explicit reference to the *hormé* of the Stoics is to be found in *The City of God* XIX. 4, in the context of a book devoted to the refutation of various philosophers' positions on the supreme good and on the merit of virtue in producing happiness in this life. Here Augustine discounts the claim that sense and intellect are fundamental blessings of the soul by showing their limitations before the diseases of the mind. He advances the same scepticism vis à vis the Stoic reckoning of *hormé* among the gifts of nature ('prota kata fusin'[34]) because it is the same impulse to action that stimulates the motions and the actions of the insane:

> And eagerness, or desire of action, if this is the right meaning to put upon the Greek ὁρμή, is also reckoned among the primary advantages of nature; and yet is it not this which produces those pitiable movements of the insane, and those actions which we shudder to see, when sense is deceived and reason deranged?[35]

Yet, in spite of the doubtful tone of this passage, and in spite of his disenchanted analysis of the cardinal virtues seen as proof of the 'ills of life', Augustine himself is indebted to Stoic philosophy in more than one respect. As Byers has recently shown, in *The City of God* and in other Augustinian texts the Stoic motivation theory of the *hormé* is, in fact, at the basis of

---

33 Saint Ambrose, Bishop of Milan. 'On the Duties of the Clergy', in *New Advent*, ch. 47, p. 237, <http://www.newadvent.org/fathers/34011.htm> accessed 21 June 2015.
34 Radice, *Stoici antichi*, p. 1602.
35 Saint Augustine, *The City of God*, trans. by Marcus Dods (Peabody MA: Hendrickson, 2009), p. 612.

Augustine's theory of the will.[36] Dante, who seems to have followed the same path from *Convivio* to *Monarchia*, approaches the theme of the will in the political treatise in terms that are ascribable to Augustine, but in order to reach opposite conclusions.

In *Convivio* I. xii. 9, while asserting that we love most what is most proper to us, Dante speaks of justice as the most human and therefore most lovable of virtues which resides in the intellectual part of the soul, 'that is in the will'.[37]

Monarchia moves one step further and indicates in love, now called *karitas seu recta dilectio* [charity or rightly ordered love], what sharpens, brightens, and invigorates justice,

> Preterea, quemadmodum cupiditas habitualem iustitiam quodammodo, quantumcunque pauca, obnubilat, sic karitas seu recta dilectio illam acuit atque dilucidat. [...] Quod autem recta dilectio faciat quod dictum est, hinc haberi potest: cupiditas nanque, perseitate hominum spreta, querit alia; karitas vero, spretis aliis omnibus, querit Deum et hominem, et per consequens bonum hominis. Cumque inter alia bona hominis potissimum sit in pace vivere – ut supra dicebatur – et hoc operetur maxime atque potissime iustitia, karitas maxime iustitiam vigorabit et potior potius. (*Mon.*, I. xi. 13–14)

> Moreover, just as greed, however slight, dulls the habit of justice in some way, so charity or rightly ordered love makes it sharper and brighter. [...] That rightly ordered love does what has been stated can be deduced from this: greed, scorning the intrinsic nature of man, seeks other things; whereas love, scorning all other things, seeks God and man, and hence the true good of man. Since among the other goods available to man living in peace is supremely important (as we saw earlier), and justice principally and most effectively brings this about, love most of all will strengthen justice, and the stronger love is the more it will do so.

36 See in particular *Appendix II. 'Will' (Voluntas) as Impulse toward Action (cf. Stoic Hormé) in Augustine*. Sarah Catherine Byers, *Perception, Sensibility and Moral Motivation in Augustine. A Stoic-Platonic Synthesis* (Cambridge and New York: Cambridge University Press, 2013), pp. 227–31.

37 'E quanto ella [bontade] è più propia, tanto ancora è più amabile; onde, avegna che ciascuna vertù sia amabile nell'uomo, quella è più amabile in esso che è più umana, e questa è la giustizia, la quale è solamente nella parte razionale o vero intellettuale, cioè nella volontade' (*Conv.*, I. xii. 9).

Contrary to cupidity – in my reading of the passage – *karitas* pursues what is essential and most proper to man – the *perseitas* consisting in *Deum, hominem, et per consequens bonum hominis*.[38] *Dilectio* is used here as a synonym of *amor*, an interchangeable use whose source is Augustine's *The City of God* XIV. 7. Since in Dante as in Augustine the term *amor* is, by itself, a morally neutral term, Dante qualifies it as *recta dilectio* whereas Augustine translates *bonus amor*, 'good love', with *recta voluntas*, 'rightly ordered will'. As we move into the explanation of *liberum arbitrium* in *Monarchia* I. xii, it is precisely *recta dilectio* in the sense of *recta voluntas* that makes the principle of the freedom of the will instrumental for happiness in this life and the next: 'per ipsum hic felicitamur ut homines, per ipsum alibi felicitamur ut dii' [by virtue of it we become happy here as men, by virtue of it we become happy elsewhere as gods]. It is on this crux, however, that Dante takes his distance from Augustine. Book XIV of *The City of God* comes to an end in chapter 28 on the theme of the two cities. Although Augustine admits at the beginning of the book that those who live according to the spirit can live in peace (XIV. 1), he concludes by stressing that the binomium *amor sui-contemptus Dei* lies at the foundation of the earthly city,

> Fecerunt itaque civitates duas amores duo, terrenam scilicet amor sui usque ad contemptum Dei, caelestem vero amor Dei usque ad contemptum sui.
>
> [Accordingly, two cities have been formed by two loves: the earthly by the love of self, even to the contempt of God; the heavenly by the love of God, even to the contempt of self.][39]

It is possible to perceive in the juxtaposition of *sperno* [spretis aliis] and *quero* [querit Deum, hominem, et per consequens bonum hominis] in

---

38   For a history of the interpretation of *perseitas* and *recta dilectio* in this passage, especially Bruno Nardi's, see Donatella Stocchi-Perucchio, 'The Limits of Heterodoxy in Dante's *Monarchia*', in *Dante and Heterodoxy: The Temptations of Thirteenth-Century Radical Thought*, ed. by M. L. Ardizzone (Cambridge: Cambridge Scholars Publishing, 2014), pp. 197–224 (p. 208). See also Flavio Silvestrini, *Iugum libertatis: Dante e la lettera politica del libero arbitrio* (Rome: Arachne, 2012), pp. 141–228.

39   Augustine. *The City of God*, trans. by Dods, p. 430.

Dante's *Monarchia* I. xi. 14 an echo of the antithesis Augustine creates between the respective objects of *contemptus* and *amor*. But in establishing that charity aims at both God *and* man as a continuum, Dante challenges the either/or Augustinian vision of the two cities. In the *Monarchia*, charity becomes the highest civic virtue. Pursuing the true essence of man, the *perseitas hominum*, amounts for Dante to pursuing the divine vestige in man or, to use the Stoic language again, what is proper to man. While chapter xi states that the consequence of this pursuit is the supreme good of peace, chapter xv elaborates on the idea of the good to arrive at the notion of concord. Similar to what we noticed in chapters ix and x, in which a metaphysical law morphed into a law of love, Dante's reasoning here begins with a metaphysical argument – unity is the root of the good – proceeds to an ethical one – sin is moving toward multiplicity, spurning unity [*ab uno spreta*] – and arrives to a conciliation of physics with ethics – concord is a uniform motion of many wills toward one end, a motion that matches the natural tension of the elements (earth and fire) toward their proper place. *Convivio* III. i had called this tension love, and love, understood as *recta voluntas*, is what we think of when reading that sin spurns the good of man – the only other occurrence of *sperno* after chapter xi. The will of the monarch, the vertex of unity, is necessary, Dante argues, to reduce to unity all others who constitute the base. At the same time we can infer that the base, by virtue of the common divine vestige, is equal in dignity.

Frederick II in his *Proem* to the *Liber* had claimed for himself a distinction that Dante, in *Monarchia*, claims for the whole of humanity. Accordingly, Frederick's objective was to legitimize his power over his subjects, a power of coercion well expressed in the role the *Proem* assigned to rulers. The passage is aptly selected from Seneca's *De clementia* I. 2:

> And these judges of life and death for mankind might decide, as executors in some way of Divine Providence, how each man should have fortune, estate, and status.[40]

Frederick II remains for Dante the great medieval model of the emperor *legis lator* and *legis executor* (*Mon.*, I. xiii. 7) but his political paradigm,

---

40 Powell, *The Liber Augustalis*, p. 4.

although geared to the institution and maintenance of peace and justice, lacks any reference to liberty – a value that in Dante is the mark of human nobility and the pillar of moral and political life. In light of liberty, qualified as *recta dilectio*, *Monarchia* represents, in fact, not only a shift in the concept of nobility from exclusive to inclusive but also an evolution of the theory of nobility into the theory of love whose full articulation finds its way into the central cantos of *Purgatorio* and the first cantos of *Paradiso*.

True liberty means for Dante to be bound to the law (*vinculum humanae societatis* – a definition attributed to Seneca, *Mon.* II. v. 3), but the second book of *Monarchia* makes clear that along with the nobility of Aeneas subsequently inherited by his progeny, the true distinction of the Romans lies in their intention to actualize the end of the law (*finis juris*) – the common good consisting of peace and liberty. The end is the ennobling factor and the character of this nobility is universal since it is based again on the principle of similitude to God. The argumentation of book II opens under the heading of natural love (*naturalis amor*; *Mon.*, II. i. 5) and it includes a profound meditation on nature and its laws. Nature is in the mind of God and it is the instrument of divine goodness via similitude – *similitudo bonitatis ecterne* (*Mon.*, II. ii. 3). Law (*ius*) is a divine idea like nature, and human law (*ius in rebus*) is nothing else but a similitude of the divine will – *similitudo divine voluntatis* (*Mon.*, II. ii. 5). The highest form of liberty is the reconciliation of the will with the law or, as *Epistle* vi. 5 concisely states, the voluntary submission to the law that is the image of natural justice,

> legibus que iustitie naturalis imitantur imaginem, parere vetantem; observantia quarum, si leta, si libera, non tantum non servitus esse probatur, quin imo perspicaciter intuenti liquet ut est ipsa summa libertas. (*Ep.* vi. 5)
>
> [those laws made in the likeness of natural justice, the observance whereof, if it be joyous, if it be free, is not only no servitude, but to him who observes with understanding is manifestly in itself the most perfect liberty.][41]

When he gets to *Purgatorio* XVI, Dante integrates the political with the natural order as he does in *Monarchia*. The additional accomplishment of

41 Dante Alighieri, *Epistolae*, trans. by Paget Toynbee (Oxford: Clarendon Press, 1996).

the *Commedia* is to resume the reflection which originated in *Convivio* on the phenomenon of human motivation, and to absorb the Stoic concept of *hormé* within the theory of love. Following the distinction between natural and mental or elective love, the language of the seed – 'amor sementa in voi d'ogne virtude / e d'ogne operazion che merta pene' [love is the seed in you of every virtue and of all acts deserving punishment] (*Purg.*, XVII. 104–5) – signals in *Purgatorio* XVII the connection with *Convivio* IV, further confirmed by the reference to the instinct of self-preservation which, in Stoic thought, is the primary meaning of *hormé* – 'Or, perché mai non può da la salute / amor del suo subietto volger viso' [Now, since love never turns aside its eyes from the well-being of its subject] (*Purg.*, XVII. 106–7).[42] In *Purgatorio* XVIII Virgil gives an Augustinian account of the cognitive process from perception to desire that seems patterned on the Stoic process of impression and motivation.[43] But the theory of perception is complemented with the presence of an innate, *a priori* 'intelletto de le prime notizie e de primi appetibili l'affetto' [intelligence of primal notions and tending toward desire's primal objects] (*Purg.*, XVIII. 55–7). What is now called natural love is nothing other than the appetite of the rational soul of *Convivio* IV. This natural love corresponds to a hormetic impulse to action – the 'prima voglia' [primal will] – analogous to the one that moves the animal world – 'come studio in ape di far lo mele' [as in bees there is the honey making urge] (*Purg.*, XVIII. 58–9). To this urge all creatures are passively subjected. The active element, the mark of human liberty, comes in the form of an assent preceded by the judgement of reason. This doctrine – also Augustinian-Ciceronian-Stoic in origin[44] – is the same as in *Monarchia* – 'la virtú che consiglia / e de l'assenso dee tener la soglia' [the power that counsels, keeper of the threshold of your assent] (*Purg.*,

---

42 All translations of the *Commedia* are from Dante Alighieri, *Commedia*, trans. by Allen Mandelbaum (Berkeley: University of California Press, 1980).
43 I refer in particular to the theory of perception and image formation in *Purgatorio* XVIII. 22–33 in relation to the Stoic theory of the imprint and representation – typosis and phantasia. Radice, *Stoici antichi*, pp. 1585 and 1619. See also Byers, *Perception, Sensibility and Moral Motivation*, chapters 1–4.
44 Byers, *Perception, Sensibility and Moral Motivation*, pp. 29 and ff.

XVIII. 62–3). The active element of *liberum arbitrium* – accepting the right appetite and rejecting the wrong one – is based on a reconciliation of one's choice to that innate urge which *Convivio* IV and *Purgatorio* XVI call desire to return to one's principle, a reconciliation that *Monarchia* implies with *recta dilectio*. *Paradiso* I identifies the impulse of all creation to return to its principle with the actual word 'instinct' (*Par.*, I. 114) that translates the hormetic urge to self-appropriation. It is left to Beatrice to complete here Virgil's philosophical explanation of natural love given in *Purgatorio* by revealing, in the principle of similitude, the divine vestige that shapes and moves the universe. God is the port in the great sea of being, the *oikos* that all creatures are inclined ('accline'; *Par.*, I. 108) to reach. Looking at the earth but always within the cosmic order, Dante argues in *Monarchia* that the divine historical mandate given by nature and Providence alike to the creatures who have intellect and love, is to reconcile their wills with the hormetic impulse – the rational appetite that distinguishes them from the rest of creation as images of God.[45] Even if he reclaims in *Paradiso* XVI nobility of blood as a value and manifests a measure of nostalgia for past social institutions and mores,[46] he does so by making reference to the other nobility defined by the orientation of the will: imperfect on earth – 'qua giù dove l'affetto nostro langue' [here below, where sentiment is far too weak] – and absolute in Paradise – 'là dove appetito non si torce' [even where desire is not awry] (*Par.*, XVI. 3; 5).[47] In virtue of this absolute standard or *optimus finis* set for humanity in history, the political project unfolding from *Convivio* IV to *Monarchia* testifies to Dante's unshakable faith in human perfectibility.

---

45 G. Stabile, in discussing the 'specific virtue' of the substantial human form in *Purgatorio* XVIII captures its progressive character: 'spetta all'uomo il graduale discoprimento della propria *vertute*'; G. Stabile, 'Volontà', in *Enciclopedia Dantesca*, ed. by U. Bosco *et al.*, 5 vols + appendix (Rome: Istituto della Enciclopedia Italiana, 1970–8), V, 1136.
46 Marco Santagata, 'Introduzione', pp. xcv–xcvii.
47 'O poca nostra nobiltà di sangue, / se gloriar di te la gente fai / qua giù dove l'affetto nostro langue, / mirabil cosa non mi sarà mai: / che là dove appetito non si torce, / dico nel cielo, io me ne gloriai' (*Par.*, XVI. 1–6).

LUCA AZZETTA

12 'Di questo parla l'autore in una chiosa d'una sua canzone': The *Convivio* through the Eyes of Its First Readers*

In an unspecified year in his life, perhaps during his first stay in Verona with the Della Scala family (May 1303–March 1304), Dante found himself embroiled in a *tenzone* with Cecco Angiolieri. The Florentine poet's sonnet has sadly been lost; however, we do have the invective, which appears to be responsive in character and with which the Sienese poet addresses his adversary, *Dante Alleghier, s'i' so' buon begolardo*. In the sonnet, Cecco reminds Alighieri of the miseries of courtly life to which the exile has been subjected: speaking haphazardly, indulging in slander, scrounging meals. This dispute, which must have had a certain circulation, landed in the hands of Ser Guelfo di Collo Taviani, who was a judge, as well as a teacher from Pistoia, friend of Cino da Pistoia, and composer of modest verse. The attacks aimed at Alighieri provoked the scorn of Taviani, who in turn responded with the sonnet *Cecco Angelier, tu mi pari un musardo*.[1]

---

*   Tristan Downs assisted with the English version.
1   'Cecco Angelier, tu mi pari un musardo, / sì tostamente corri, e non vi peni / diliberar, ma incontenente sfreni / come poledro o punto caval sardo. / Or pensa sia dal ferrante al baiardo / ché con Dante di motti tegni meni, / che di filosofia ha tante veni? / Tu mi pari più matto che gagliardo. / Filosofi tesoro disprezzare / dèn per ragione, e loro usanza fue / sol lo 'ngegno in scïenzia assottigliare. / Or queste sono le virtuti sue; / però pensa con cui dèi rampognare: / chi follemente salta tosto rue'. Active until at least 1347, Guelfo Taviani is the author of, as far as is known, three sonnets: two addressed to Cino and one to Cecco. I quote the sonnet addressed to Angiolieri from Dante Alighieri, *Rime*, ed. by Domenico De Robertis (Florence: SISMEL-Edizioni del Galluzzo, 2005), pp. 481–2; see also Guido Zaccagnini, *I rimatori pistoiesi dei secoli XIII e XIV* (Pistoia: Tipografia Sinibuldiana, 1907 [rist. anast.

It is not possible to identify when Guelfo wrote his sonnet; it is possible, however, that he came across Cecco's work in Siena, where in 1307 he was employed as a bread tax official, and rushed to Dante's defence.[2] What is striking in Guelfo's verse is not so much the derisory way in which Angiolieri is likened to an unthinking idler ('musardo'), or an impulsive colt, but rather that Cecco proved himself to be mad in daring to make a comparison with Dante. The latter, according to Guelfo, is an entirely different man from Angiolieri; above all, given that he is a 'filosofo' [philosopher], Dante was right to be careless with money – indeed, his mind should be exclusively reserved for an increasing sophistication of his scientific inquiry.

Guelfo's words constitute the oldest defence that has been made of Dante. They also raise some intriguing questions as to why he acknowledges Dante as a philosopher in the earlier years of his writing career – that is, while he was still writing the *Convivio*, and long before the *Commedia*. On what basis does Taviani construct such an impassioned defence? Why does he consider Dante to be one of the philosophers? Could he have known him to be so, perhaps, as Zaccagnini has suggested in an evocative but indemonstrable way, from having received some information about the philosophical studies that Dante had worked on?[3] Or could he have read the doctrinaire and philosophically more committed work? If readers do not wish to suppose that the sonnet was in fact written many years later, perhaps in the twenties of the fourteenth century, soon after the *Commedia* had been made available, or do not wish to understand the expression 'che di filosofia ha tante veni' (l. 7) as a general tribute that is echoed in the later categorisation of Dante among the 'filosofi' (l. 9), then they are left with no other alternative than to consider the singularity of the tribute

---

Bologna, Forni, 1979]), pp. lxxv-lxxxiv and 103–8; Agostino Zanelli, *Del pubblico insegnamento in Pistoia dal XIV al XVI secolo. Contributo alla storia della cultura in Italia* (Rome: Loescher, 1900), pp. 17 and 117; Claudio Giunta, *Versi a un destinatario. Saggio sulla poesia italiana del Medioevo* (Bologna: Il Mulino, 2002), pp. 276–8.

2 This hypothesis was advanced by Masséra in *I sonetti di Cecco Angiolieri*, ed. by Aldo Francesco Masséra (Bologna: Zanichelli, 1906), pp. 180–1, and has become generally accepted.

3 Zaccagnini, *I rimatori*, p. lxxxiv.

paid by Taviani. After all, in 1307 the exile's celebrity depended solely on the *prosimetro* of the *Vita nova* and the *Rime*.

Guelfo Taviani's testimony remains completely isolated: only many years later and by virtue of the *Commedia* will Dante become a philosopher and theologian in the pages of his commentators and in the epitaphs dedicated to him. In fact, it turns out that during his lifetime Dante never divulged what he had elaborated on in the incomplete *Convivio*. The project of a philosophical work in the vernacular was abandoned after drafting the first four books and remained in that state among his papers; in all probability, a revised and cleanly transcribed copy of the only portion ever written had never been made – in fact, the four books were conserved in a very disorganized clump of papers which were indeed difficult to read. Only after Dante's death, and after being recovered from the poet's papers, did the *Convivio* begin to be spread, albeit very thinly throughout the following decades. The research both on the manuscript tradition and on the first attestations of the circulation of the *Convivio* allows us to identify Florence in the thirties of the fourteenth century as the centre in which the philosophical comment began to be read. In fact, its first readers were all Florentines, who approached it with fairly diverse sensitivities and modes of appropriation: Alberto della Piagentina, the author of the *Ottimo commento*, the 'Amico dell'*Ottimo*', Andrea Lancia, and perhaps Giovanni Villani. Similarly, the testimonies that conserve the text, were all Florentine.[4]

It is not possible to know with certainty how the *Convivio* reached Florence. It is reasonable to suppose that it was taken there by someone who could have pulled it from the deceased poet's papers, namely, by his sons – Jacopo or, more plausibly, Pietro. Their presence in the city is in the first half of the third decade is well documented: Pietro was in Florence in January 1323 and again in January 1324, Jacopo in 1325. The poet's sons represent

---

4   On the tradition of the *Convivio* see Luca Azzetta, 'La tradizione del *Convivio* negli antichi commenti alla *Commedia*: Andrea Lancia, l'"Ottimo commento" e Pietro Alighieri', *Rivista di Studi Danteschi*, 5 (2005), 3–34; Luca Azzetta, 'Tra i più antichi lettori del *Convivio*: ser Alberto della Piagentina notaio e cultore di Dante', *Rivista di Studi Danteschi*, 9 (2009), 57–91, with the bibliography indicated.

the sole credible link – thanks to their family bond – that accounts for the Florentine dissemination of the *Convivio*. Perhaps they had read the text, or at least had known of its existence when living far away from Florence: Jacopo in Ravenna, Pietro in Verona. However, there is no evidence that the manuscripts had circulated in either of these areas. If it were the two sons, or at least one of them, who brought about the circulation of the *Convivio*, we should be aware that even if their output revolved entirely around their father's work, this text was not of primary importance for them.

In the *Chiose all'Inferno* by Jacopo Alighieri, presumably written by April 1322, there is nothing to support the belief that the poet's third-born had had any familiarity with the *Convivio*, nor, incidentally, with any of his father's works beyond the *Commedia*; there is not one explicit citation, thematic repetition or allusion of any kind that points to Jacopo's familiarity with the *Convivio*.[5] Thus it remains speculative to think that the philosophical comment, for the mere reason that it might have been known by Jacopo, could have been a point of reflection or, moreover, an inspiration to write his own glosses in the vernacular, and by the same token, may also have driven Jacopo to give plenty of space to the allegorical interpretation of the poem's verses – this, however, often happens in an incongruous way. In his father's work, the son may well have recognized a literary genre that he intended to adapt to his own purposes, that is, a comment in the vernacular on verses likewise in the vernacular. In this regard Jacopo's individuation

---

[5] Saverio Bellomo, 'Introduzione', in Jacopo Alighieri, *Chiose all'"Inferno"*, ed. by Saverio Bellomo (Padua: Antenore, 1990), pp. 9 and 14–16, states that for his glosses Jacopo used the *Convivio* as a model, including stylistically, and furthermore that he 'seppe fare tesoro' of the *Epistola a Cangrande*; nevertheless the assertion is not substantiated by the facts: Dante's two works do not present any point of proximity to Jacopo's glosses, and in fact, the same editor never has the possibility to call to note its presence (the only case in which he refers to the *Epistola a Cangrande* (p. 86), is in order to signal that Jacopo 'pare ignorare' the indications contained therein). The statement, which should therefore be corrected, has been repeated several times: see for example Saverio Bellomo, *Dizionario dei commentatori danteschi. L'esegesi della 'Commedia' da Iacopo Alighieri a Nidobeato* (Florence: Olschki, 2004), p. 64; *Censimento dei commenti danteschi. I commenti di tradizione manoscritta (fino al 1480)*, ed. by Enrico Malato and Andrea Mazzucchi (Rome: Salerno Editrice, 2011), I, 319.

of his audience is plain – his readers are among 'coloro il cui lume naturale alquanto risplende senza scientifica apprensione' [those whose natural light shines quite a lot without scientific apprehension] (*Proemio*, 6–7), which is an expression that, according to Michele Barbi, could recall *Convivio* IV. vii. 4: 'coloro dirizzare intendo ne' quali alcuno lumetto di ragione per buona loro natura vive ancora' [I intend to set straight those in whom some glimmer of reason still survives by virtue of their good nature].[6] Above all, in addressing a public ignorant of Latin, Jacopo hopes that, thanks to his glosses, 'con più agevolezza si possa gustare' [one might taste more easily] the 'frutto universale novellamente dato al mondo' [universal fruit newly given to the world], that is the *Commedia*. Here, the verb *gustare*, evidently employed metaphorically, is used in the same way as Dante uses it in the first chapter of the *Convivio*, when he calls all those to the table of knowledge who because of domestic or civic duties have remained hungry, so that they can 'la mia vivanda col pane, che la farò loro e *gustare* e patire' [partake

6 Michele Barbi, 'Di un commento al poema mal attribuito a Iacopo Alighieri (1904)', in *Problemi di critica dantesca, Prima serie (1893–1918)* (Florence: Sansoni, 1934), pp. 359–93 (p. 370), but the proximity is more than tenuous; in fact, Jacopo's beginning has been put in parallel with the *incipit* of the *Monarchia*: Dante Alighieri, *Le opere*, IV, *Monarchia* ed. by Paolo Chiesa and Andrea Tabarroni, supported by Diego Ellero (Rome: Salerno Editrice, 2013), p. lxvii. On the other hand it is difficult to sustain that in Jacopo's *Chiose* the 'tensione stilistica tanto forte da indurre a rinunciare sia alla chiarezza espositiva, sia alla densità del pensiero, accettando perfino la tautologia e l'ovvietà pur di raggiungere l'effetto desiderato' could have the *Convivio* as a model, 'snaturato quanto si vuole, ma pur sempre l'unica opera, nel panorama culturale di Jacopo, che potesse spingerlo, con il suo esempio ed esplicitamente, prima di tutto a fare un enorme sforzo per nobilitare e dare dignità artistica alla prosa volgare di un commento, e in secondo luogo a far ciò soprattutto per mezzo della sintassi' (Saverio Bellomo, in Jacopo Alighieri, *Chiose*, p. 16). It is not accidental that in the thorough analysis of the language and the style of the *Chiose* (pp. 52–83), the *Convivio* is never quoted; that is, it never appears as a significant point of reference; nor on the other hand do the handful of references placed in the commentary justify the hypothesis (see Jacopo Alighieri, *Chiose*, pp. 84, 89, 106, 112, 115, 141, 155, 165, 196 and 202). The use of the term 'sorella' in the sonnet *Acciò che le bellezze, Signor mio*, perhaps employed to indicate his *Divisione* (see Alberto Casadei, *Dante oltre la 'Commedia'* (Bologna: Il Mulino, 2013), p. 47), does not strengthen the suggestion that Jacopo has (or has not) read the *Convivio*.

of my meat with bread, for I will have them both taste of it and digest it] (*Conv.*, I. i. 13). There is little more to be garnered from this brief lexical parallel beyond the fact that using the verb *gustare* in this way is very rare in Jacopo's work (besides this example, he only uses the word in its literal sense in the gloss on *Inferno* VI, 1–5), and in Dante's – it is not employed again in the *Convivio*.[7] In any case, even conceding that Jacopo's *gustare* retains a grain of his father, it is a rather poor harvest.

The method by which Dante's older son approaches the *Convivio* is different, and moreover, provable. Pietro, who was a judge by profession as well as the author of some poems in the vernacular and above all of a *Comentum* in Latin of the entire *Commedia*: a work of considerable amplitude, which from its choice of language shows the intention of addressing a learned public and which thus implies a distance, perhaps in part a polemic one, from the younger brother's glosses. Throughout the pages of his *Comentum*, completed in Verona by 1341, he draws on the *Convivio* several times, citing it in a Latin translation but always remaining elusive with regard to both the identity of the work, whose title he never reveals, and the identity of its author. So if we keep the list limited to the secure quotations, the result is still conspicuous: the occurrences can be traced throughout the *Comentum*, with particular abundance in the pages dedicated to the comment on the *Purgatorio*.[8] This inventory shows that Pietro,

---

7   The term is then used exclusively in the *canti* dedicated to the *Paradiso Terrestre*, mostly in the third *cantica*, and on the whole is used figuratively: Andrea Mariani, 'Gustare', in *Enciclopedia Dantesca*, ed. by Umberto Bosco *et al.*, 5 vols + appendix (Rome: Istituto della Enciclopedia Italiana, 1970–8), III, 338.

8   The merit of having pointed out the presence of the *Convivio* in Pietro's commentary belongs to Vincenzo Nannucci, who in 1854, in the appendix to the edition of the *Comentum*, which was edited by him, signalled a large number of repetitions: some certain, others only probable or possible, since *loci* were also matched on the basis of a general consonance between the two texts, often due to using a common source: Petri Allegherii *super Dantis ipsius genitoris 'Comoediam' commentarium, nunc primum in lucem editum consilio et sumtibus G. J. Bar. Vernon*, ed. by Vincenzo Nannucci (Florence: Piatti, 1845), 'Appendice', pp. xlii–cxxxvii: *Inf.*, I (ed. Nannucci, p. 24): *Conv.*, IV. xxiii. 8–10; *Inf.*, I (ed. Nannucci, pp. 35–6): *Conv.*, IV. vii. 14–15; *Inf.*, II (ed. Nannucci, p. 54–5): *Conv.*, IV. x. 3–6; *Inf.*, XIII (ed. Nannucci, p. 157):

as was customary for him, used the *Convivio* mainly as a source of various quotations from other authors, in particular Aristotle, so as to insert them into his critical material, having freed them from their context. It reveals furthermore his predilection for the fourth book of the *Convivio*, which while being by far the most quoted, is nonetheless unevenly spread in his work: it is in fact used at least ten times, although strangely never in the comment on the *Paradiso*; the second book is quoted six times, five of which are found in the comment on the *Paradiso*; the third book a mere twice, once in the comment on the second *cantica* and once in the comment on the third; and he does not quote from the first book at all.

Conv., IV. vii. 10–11; *Purg.*, I (ed. Nannucci, p. 295): *Conv.*, III. v. 7–8; *Purg.*, I (ed. Nannucci, p. 296): *Conv.*, IV. vi. 10; *Purg.*, II (ed. Nannucci, p. 305): *Conv.*, II. i. 7; *Purg.*, V (ed. Nannucci, pp. 322–3): *Conv.*, IV. xix. 9–10; *Purg.*, VI (ed. Nannucci, pp. 331–2): *Conv.*, IV. iv. 1–2; IV. vii. 11–12; *Purg.*, XVI (ed. Nannucci, p. 413): *Conv.*, IV. xii. 14–17; *Purg.*, XVIII (ed. Nannucci, pp. 424–5): *Conv.*, IV. vi. 13, 9–10; *Purg.*, XXXI (ed. Nannucci, p. 518): *Conv.*, IV. xiii. 8; *Par.*, VII (ed. Nannucci, p. 603): *Conv.*, III. vi. 10; *Par.*, VIII (ed. Nannucci, p. 605): *Conv.*, II. iii. 13 and 16; *Par.*, VIII and *Par.*, XIII (ed. Nannucci, pp. 608 and 644): *Conv.*, II. iv. 2–5; *Par.*, XIV (ed. Nannucci, pp. 648–9): *Conv.*, II. xiv. 5–7; *Par.*, XXVII (ed. Nannucci, p. 709): *Conv.*, II. iii. 7–11. For the list of passages in which the two works contain the same quotation of an author, or show a general consonance between them, without significant textual indices for establishing whether Pietro had benefitted directly from the *Convivio* (or whether it had at least been the memory of his father's treatise that had solicited a quotation), or whether he had, on the contrary, autonomously used *auctoritates* whose pieces were also used in Dante's pages, see Luca Azzetta, 'Tra i più antichi lettori', p. 58. Evidently, the question remains open, and at the moment is destined to remain unsolved, as to whether in drafting the *Comentum* Pietro was able to benefit, among the other books available to him, from some volumes in his father's library. The quotations from the *Convivio* disappear in the third draft of the *Comentum*: Pietro Alighieri, *Comentum super poema Comedie Dantis. A Critical Edition of the Third and Final Draft of Pietro Alighieri's Commentary on Dante's 'The Divine Comedy'*, ed. by Massimiliano Chiamenti (Tempe: Arizona Center for Medieval and Renaissance Studies, 2002); Rudy Abardo's review of it, *Rivista di Studi Danteschi*, 3 (2003), 166–76 (pp. 169–70); Luca Azzetta, 'Note sul "Comentum" di Pietro Alighieri (a partire da una recente edizione)', *L'Alighieri*, 45 (2004), 97–118 (p. 104).

Sometimes Pietro was skilful in grasping a significant rapport between the contents of the poem and the philosophical comment. This can be seen, for instance, in the gloss on *Inf.*, II. 10–36, in which the pilgrim has doubts about the legitimacy of his journey since he fears that, in contrast to Aeneas and Saint Paul, grace is not granted to him. Pietro, in arguing the case for the providential nature of the Roman Empire and of Rome, which was of course destined to become the seat of the Church, relies on a series of quotations derived from the *Aeneid* (I. 2–3, 33 and 204–6; IV. 235, 232, 234 and 274; VI. 851–3, 888–92). Then, with a brief connecting phrase, he corroborates them, juxtaposing them with divine goodness, which arranged the birth of Rome itself to be concurrent with the birth of King David. He gleaned this reflection from the prose of the *Convivio*, extracting it from the chapter specifically dedicated to the providential nature of the Roman Empire, which he partly revised and partly translated, to the letter, into Latin. (Appendix 1)

Another passage in which Pietro proves to be an attentive reader, in finding the propinquity between the *Commedia* and the *Convivio*, is his gloss on the speech of Marco Lombardo, which is directed at God's creation of the soul and at natural movement, that is the desire which drives the soul towards the search for an ever greater good (*Purg.*, XVI. 85–93). In fact, Pietro picks up a passage from the *Convivio* in which Dante narrates the story of the soul which is committed to the difficult search for its own happiness. Pietro builds his own exegesis on the passage by placing Dante's pilgrim beside a distinct reference to the 'cammino della nostra vita' [journey of our life] and Dante's pilgrimage to the ultra-mundane realms. (Appendix 2)

If, thus, the *Convivio* was accessible to the sons of the poet, albeit in fairly different ways, it is only in Florence that it enjoyed any fortune (as far as we know) over the course of the fourteenth century. In the city, Dante and his family were in living memory. And it was here, in the works produced by a small, appreciative group that the *Convivio* was read and quoted. The philosophical treatise seems to acquire a particular value in the years immediately following the poet's death. The (re)discovery in fact was a concern of people who had a desire to regain possession of Dante's person, memory, and life's work, as if they wanted to wipe out the shame of the exile inflicted upon Alighieri, an interpretation with which Boccaccio later concurs in the *Trattatello*, paying attention to his 'altissimi meriti' [very high merits] (first edition, Par., 4–6). It is by no means a coincidence that the *Convivio* would be quoted both in the pages of the first Florentine commentators of the *Commedia*, who had a vast and thorough knowledge of Dante's work, and in the translation into the vernacular of Boethius' *De consolatione philosophiae* by Alberto della Piagentina. Piagentina was a Florentine notary who shows, beside his immediate knowledge of the *Convivio*, an assiduous and mature familiarity with Dante's *Rime* and the *Commedia*, to the point that, having assumed Dante's tercet on the grounds of its versatility for rendering Boethius' different metres, he was the first to promote the *Convivio* outside of the small, concise circle of commentators on the poem. Thus in the twenties and then in the thirties, while the cult of Dante flourished in Florence and the distribution of the *Commedia* continued to be unsurpassed in the peninsula, a closed society of connoisseurs and exegetes of the *Commedia* could have had access to the very rare and tormented text of the *Convivio* – and these men knew how to appraise it to their own ends. That the recovery had its starting point among people who were very close to Dante's writing desk is testified by the fact that this entire generation of readers of the *Convivio* who present literary quotations do so with optimal quality, that is, contrary to errors being widespread throughout manuscript tradition at large, there are none here. This indicates that in Florence, however much the *Convivio* presents itself in an incomplete form, it was possible to obtain a better version, which should be placed upstream of the archetype that can be reconstructed today.[9]

Of Alberto della Piagentina we know very little. From a few autographs and a biographical sonnet, which in some testimonies accompanies the translation of the *De consolatione* we learn that Alberto, after having practised as a notary in Florence, dedicated himself to the translation of Boethius into the vernacular and to a commentary (which remained incomplete) while he was in prison in Venice; the sonnet also indicates that he died there in 1332 and that he was buried in the Church of the Eremitani

9   Luca Azzetta, 'La tradizione', pp. 21–34.

(now the Church of Santo Stefano).[10] The personal references inserted into the prologue to the translation make it plausible that he, to an extent, was sharing Boethius' fate. Alberto's knowledge of the *Convivio* is also apparent in the prologue.[11] The prologue is divided into three parts: in the first, Alberto declares the meaning of his work as a translator. After a canonical beginning with the Latin quotation of a biblical *auctoritas* (Alberto claims it to be from the prophet Jeremiah, but actually it corresponds to the apocryphal book of Baruch, 3. 37), and after having declared the insufficiency of our cognitive faculty for discerning the purpose and cause of singular things, Alberto appeals to Seneca's authority and stresses the necessity of seeking a man whose life and whose customs might be an example for us. Alberto knows very well that his search for the unique excellence of a virtuous man and master of life will be hard: as to the places where this man cannot be found, he turns to the dual metaphor of the 'popolesca greggia' [popular flock of sheep] that 'pasce solo cibo terreno' [feeds only on earthen food], that is, to the same dual image that is employed in the opening of the *Convivio*: 'Oh beati quelli pochi che seggiono a quella mensa dove lo pane delli angeli si manuca! e miseri quelli che colle pecore hanno comune cibo!' [Blessed are the few who sit at the table where the bread of the angels is eaten, and most unfortunate those who share the food of sheep!] (I. i. 7). Alighieri is explicitly evoked here by Alberto: the verses of *Par.*, II, 10–12 show that the spiritual guide should be sought among the learned:

> Dove dunque si truova? Chi 'l cerca? Per certo tra que' pochi gloriosi sollerti ed equanimi, i quali la umana spezie, del divino raggio dotata, alzata dalle cose basse

10 Luca Azzetta, 'Tra i più antichi lettori', pp. 65–80; Luca Azzetta, 'Alberto della Piagentina', in *Autografi dei letterati italiani*, I. *Le origini e il Trecento*, ed. by Giuseppina Brunetti, Maurizio Fiorilla and Marco Petoletti (Rome: Salerno Editrice, 2013), pp. 25–31.

11 Gianfranco Folena, 'La tradizione delle opere di Dante Alighieri', in *Atti del Congresso internazionale di studi danteschi* (Florence: Sansoni, 1965), 1–78 (p. 24); Thomas Ricklin, '"[...] Quello non conosciuto da molti libro di Boezio". Hinweise zur *Consolatio philosophiae* in Norditalien', in *Boethius in the Middle Ages. Latin and Vernacular Traditions of the 'Consolatio philosophiae'*, ed. by Maarten J. F. M. Hoenen and Lodi Nauta (Leiden-New York-Cologne: Brill, 1997), pp. 267–86 (pp. 274–6).

conservano, a cui el Poeta Fiorentino nel secondo canto del *Paradiso* parla, quando dice: 'Voialtri pochi, che drizzaste il collo / per tempo al pan de li Angeli, del quale / vivesi qua, ma non si vien satollo'.

[Where, thus, is he? Who searches for him? Certainly among these few industrious and fair glorious ones who keep the human species, which is equipped with divine reason, raised above the base things, to whom the Florentine poet speaks in the second *canto* of the *Paradiso*, when he says: 'Voialtri pochi, che drizzaste il collo / per tempo al pan de li Angeli, del quale / vivesi qua, ma non si vien satollo'. [Ye other few who have the neck uplifted / Betimes to th' bread of Angels upon which / One liveth here and grows not sated by it.]]

Then, Alberto arrives at the most autobiographical part of the preface, in which he evokes the miserable conditions that reminded him of the tribulations of the ancient philosopher and drove him to translate the work into the vernacular:

El quale [book] io naufragato, e *senza legno* che mi levi, percosso *dal secco vento che vapora la dolorosa* ruota che m'ha sommerso, rivolgendo nell'animo, affaticato per le severe e disumane persecuzioni, memoria spessa di tanto famosissimo autore in tribulazione posto e consolarsi, ho redutto di gramatica in volgare, a utolitade de' volgari che sanza lettera hanno intrinseco abito virtuoso. Ficca dunque, lettore, l'occhio dell'intelletto, e cerni; ficca le labbra, e ciba l'approvata dottrina di tanto autore, acciò che dietro a tali orme passeggi.

[Which I, shipwrecked, and *without a raft* that would lift me, beaten *by the dry wind that blows the painful* wheel that has dragged me under, turning in the soul, fatigued by the severe and inhumane persecutions, deep memory of that very famous author placed in tribulations and consoling himself, I have reduced by grammar to the vernacular, for the use of the common people who have intrinsic virtue without being learned. So do fix the eye of the intellect, reader, and sort out; plug your lips, and feed on the approved doctrine of so great an author, so that you may tread in his footsteps.]

This is evidently the decisive passage in Alberto's human story, which relies unequivocally on the very dense metaphor of *Convivio* I. iii. 5:

Veramente io sono stato *legno sanza* vela e sanza governo, portato a diversi porti e foci e liti *dal vento secco che vapora la dolorosa* povertade.

[Truly I have been a *ship without sail* and rudder, driven to different harbours, inlets, and shores *by the dry wind that blows in painful* poverty.]

Alberto must have felt emotionally bound to Dante in terms of a certain biographical contiguity: confined as he was in the Venetian prison, and 'affaticato per le severe e disumane persecuzioni' [tired by the severe and inhumane persecutions], he identified himself above all with the words that Alighieri coined for his exile and poverty – his being cast far from the 'dolce seno' [sweet bosom] of Florence, 'bellissima e famosissima figlia di Roma' [the most beautiful and famous daughter of Rome] (*Conv.*, I. iii. 3–4). Alberto also follows Dante's suit in choosing the vernacular 'a utolitade de' volgari che sanza lettera hanno intrinseco abito virtuoso' [for the use of the common people who have intrinsic virtue without being learned], that is, targeting the same audience as the poet did in the *Convivio* and employing the same metaphor of food (I. i. 7–13 and i. 8–9).

A few years after Alberto della Piagentina, the *Convivio* crops up once more in the context of Dante connoisseurship in Florence. Around 1334, some six or seven years before Pietro Alighieri drafted the *Comentum*, it appears in the anonymous glosses of the *Ottimo commento*.[12] Although its title is never cited, the testimony of the *Ottimo*, which is confirmed by slightly later Florentine commentators, is valuable for it shows that Dante's contemporaries were in no doubt about the literary genre to which the *Convivio* belonged. It is never called a 'treatise'; instead, it is always the form of a comment. Therefore the *Ottimo*, in its references to the *Convivio*, explicitly refers to glosses in explaining *canzoni*: 'qui adducerò una chiosa per l'Autore medesimo circa a questa materia de' Cieli sopra quella sua canzona, che incomincia: *Voi che 'ntendendo il terzo Ciel movete*' [here I will add a gloss by the author himself on this matter of the Heavens in the song

---

12 *L'Ottimo Commento della 'Divina Commedia'. Testo inedito d'un contemporaneo di Dante citato dagli Accademici della Crusca*, ed. by Alessandro Torri (Pisa: Capurro, 1827–9).

which begins: *Voi che 'ntendendo il terzo Ciel movete* [You whose intellect the third sphere moves]] (gloss on *Inf.*, VII. 77).[13]

That the *Convivio* circulated in Florence in the form we know today has been confirmed by multiple sources. The first comes from the comment on the *Commedia* by the 'Amico dell'*Ottimo*'.[14] Ascribable to a Florentine and dating between 1337 and 1341, this comment does not include any of the *Convivio* references which occur in the *Ottimo*. Nevertheless, in the gloss on *Inf.*, I. 1, inserting a quotation in order to define that which is the 'mezzo del camino, cioè il mezo corso della vita humana, nella quale noi come peregrini passiamo' [middle of the road, which means the middle of a human life, in which we pass as pilgrims], it conveniently draws on Dante's work, which too is identified as a comment, a text made of glosses to *canzoni*, and whose title he finally names: 'sì come l'autore medesimo dice capitolo XXII[1] delle sue chiose medesime, scritte in quella sua opera la quale elli chiama *Convivio*, sopra la canzone sua della gentilezza' [as the same author says chapter XXII[1] of his own glosses, written in this work of

---

13 These are the glosses of the *Ottimo* quoted from the *Convivio*: *Inf.*, I. 1: *Conv.*, IV. xxiii. 4, 6–8, 10 and IV. xxiv. 1, 3; *Inf.*, II. 43–54: *Conv.*, II. xv. 4; *Inf.*, II. 104–5: *Conv.*, II.; *Inf.*, VII. 77; *Conv.*, II. iii. 2–10 and 12; II. iv. 2–6, II. v. 4–6, 13, 18; *Inf.*, IX. 91: *Conv.*, II. v. 12; *Par.*, XIII. 4: *Conv.*, II. i. 2–3; *Par.*, XXIII Proemio: *Conv.*, II. iii. 5, 7–8; *Par.*, XXIX. 127: *Conv.*, II. iv. 12. The glosses to *Inferno* I. 1 and II. 104–5 can be found in Giusto Grion, 'Commento volgare ai tre primi canti della *Divina Commedia* del codice di San Daniele del Tagliamento', *Il Propugnatore*, 1 (1868), 332–55 and 435–64 (pp. 334–5 and 453); the gloss to *Inf.*, II. 43–54 in Luigi Rocca, *Di alcuni commenti della 'Divina Commedia' composti nei primi anni dopo la morte di Dante* (Florence: Sansoni, 1891), pp. 293–4.

14 'Amico dell'*Ottimo*' is how the compiler of the comment to the *Commedia* is designated, which for a long time has been indicated as the 'third edition' of the *Ottimo commento*. Since the most recent studies have shown that the so-called 'third edition' is in reality an autonomous and profoundly revised remake of the *Ottimo*, one of them has introduced this formula so as to suggest 'l'originalità di questo progetto ermeneutico, improntato a un peculiare metodo di riappropriazione e rielaborazione di materiale esegetico facente capo principalmente (ma non solo) all'*Ottimo*': see Vittorio Celotto, 'L'Ottimo commento al "Paradiso". Studio della tradizione manoscritta e soluzioni editoriali', *Rivista di Studi Danteschi*, 12 (2012), 63–134 (p. 67).

his, which he calls *Convivio*, on his song of nobility] (New York, Pierpont Morgan Lib., M 676, fols 2ᵛ-3ʳ; *Conv.*, IV. xxiii. 10).[15]

Next to the testimony of the 'Amico dell'*Ottimo*' stands that of Giovanni Villani. In fact, the Florentine chronicler inserts a short biography of Alighieri into his *Cronica* (which today is considered to be the oldest biography of Dante), among whose works he lists: the *Vita nova*, twenty *canzoni*, didactic and of love, written during his exile, the *Monarchia*, three epistles, the *Commedia*, the *De vulgari eloquentia* and, without giving its title, the *Convivio*. Although from the brief mention it is not possible to determine whether Villani directly knew Dante's commentary and if so, the extent to which he was familiar with it – or if he only had heard of it. His hint at the overall structure of the work (for this see *Convivio* I. i. 14) and the definition of it as a 'commento' [commentary] are clear, and agree perfectly with earlier commentators:

> e comincia uno comento sopra XIIII delle sopradette sue canzoni morali volgarmente, il quale per la sopravenuta morte non perfetto si truova se non sopra le tre; la quale, per quello che·ssi vede, alta, bella, sottile e grandissima opera riusciva, però che ornata appare d'alto dittato e di belle ragioni filosofiche e astrologiche.[16]

> [and begins in the vernacular a comment on XIIII of his above mentioned moral songs, which because of his death in the meantime has not been completed except for three of them; he, as far as we can see, achieved an exalted, beautiful, subtle and great work, that shows high dictation and beautiful philosophical and astrological reasoning.]

Finally, it is the Florentine notary Andrea Lancia who confirms with his *Chiose alla Commedia*, written between 1341 and 1343, that when citing the

---

15   Giuseppe Vandelli, 'Una nuova redazione dell'"Ottimo"', *Studi Danteschi*, 14 (1930), 93–174 (pp. 160–9). An allusion to the second book of the *Convivio* is in the gloss on *Par.*, VIII. 34 ('nella sua chiosa di quella sua canzone *Voi che 'ntendendo il terzo cielo movete*' (Amico dell'*Ottimo*, New York: Pierpont Morgan Library, M 676, fol. 99ᵛ)).

16   Giovanni Villani, *Nuova Cronica*, ed. by Giuseppe Porta (Parma: Fondazione Pietro Bembo/Ugo Guanda Editore, 1991), X. 136–48. The passage appears only in what Porta considers the first edition of the *Cronica*; Arrigo Castellani proposes a better interpretation of the available data; see Arrigo Castellani, 'Sulla tradizione della "Nuova Cronica" di Giovanni Villani', *Medioevo e Rinascimento*, 2 (1988), 53–118.

Convivio, readers bore in mind a harmonious work equipped with a distinctive title and structured as a comment to three *canzoni*. Thus, it is accepted as a work which contains in prose the author's gloss on three poems, with the 'ragionamento proemiale' (*Conv.*, II. i. 1) or 'prologo' [prologue] (Lancia, gloss to *Purg.*, II. 76–8), which today is commonly referred to as the first book of the work.[17] In fact, in the gloss on *Inf.*, XIV. 1–3, Lancia identifies the structure and the title of the *Convivio* impeccably: 'Nota che l'amore de la patria molto strigne, sì come pruova l'autore medesimo nelle chiose sopra le sue tre canzoni morali, libro detto *Convivio*' [Note that the love of home holds strongly, as the same author proves in his glosses on his three moral songs, [in a] book called *Convivio*]. On other occasions he prevalently uses the expression 'nella [sua] chiosa sopra di quella [sua] canzone' [in [his] gloss on this [his] song], with wordings similar to those used by the *Ottimo* and Villani. These testimonies, far from attesting a circulation of the text in a 'gaseous' state, perhaps in the form of note-cards – as some have suggested[18] – show how deeply they are indebted to what Dante himself had done in two works in the vernacular, where he speaks of his prose as glosses on poetry.[19]

17   Andrea Lancia, *Chiose alla 'Commedia'*, ed. by Luca Azzetta (Rome: Salerno Editrice, 2012).
18   Guglielmo Gorni, 'Appunti sulla tradizione del *Convivio* (a proposito dell'archetipo e dell'originale dell'opera)', *Studi di filologia italiana*, 55 (1997), 5–22 (pp. 10–11), further in Guglielmo Gorni, *Dante prima della 'Commedia'* (Florence: Cadmo, 2001), pp. 239–51; on the distribution of the *Convivio* see also the observations of André Pézard, *Le 'Convivio' de Dante. Sa lettre, son esprit* (Paris: Les Belles Lettres, 1940), pp. 121–9.
19   'E avvegna che forse piacerebbe a presente trattare alquanto de la sua partita da noi, non è lo mio intendimento di trattarne qui per tre ragioni. [...] La terza si è che [...] non è convenevole a me trattare di ciò, per quello che, trattando, converrebbe essere me laudatore di me medesimo, la quale cosa è al postutto biasimevole a chi lo fae; e però lascio cotale trattato ad *altro chiosatore*' (*VN*, XXVIII. 2); 'Lo dono veramente di questo *comento* è la sentenza delle canzoni alle quali fatto è, la qual massimamente intende inducere li uomini a scienza e a vertù. [...] Ancora: darà lo volgare dono non dimandato, che non l'averebbe dato lo latino: però che darà sé medesimo per *comento*, che mai non fu domandato da persona; e questo non si può dire dello latino, che per *comento* e per *chiose* a molte scritture è già stato domandato' (*Conv.*, I. ix. 7 and

Lancia's *Chiose*, which mark the last of the Florentine commentaries before Boccaccio, are central for the *Convivio* not only because of an explicit and thorough use, that is, using all four books, but moreover for the extraordinary ability and for the acuteness shown in revealing passages from the philosophical prose which match specific verses in the *Commedia*.[20] Despite his faithfulness to Dante's words, Lancia, even in quoting the *Convivio*, is not at all a passive reader. On the contrary, he shows a considerable expertise in endowing glosses by merging concordant passages taken from very different sections in the philosophical comment in order to illuminate how Dante's thought pervades the two works. Elsewhere, Lancia turns to the prose of the *Convivio* to pick out episodes of the poet's biography. This is, for example, the case when Beatrice reappears on top of the Mountain of Purgatory and puts the poet's former conduct on trial. Nevertheless, Lancia's interpretative freedom finds a sympathetic textual basis in the concept of the *donna gentile* in the *Vita nova* (XXXV–XXXVIII), a work that Lancia knew: in fact, Dante explicitly identifies her as Philosophy in the *Convivio* (II. xii. 6). Lancia skilfully selects paragraphs from Dante's prose so as to introduce the notion of a historically real young girl, whose 'flesh and blood'-existence he is convinced of, and whom he evidently considers to correspond to the *donna gentile* (*Purg.*, XXX. 121–32).[21] (Appendix 3)

---

10); 'E se l'avversario pertinacemente si difendesse, [...] degno è che la *chiosa* a ciò risponda' (*Conv.*, IV. xiv. 6).

20   These are those among Lancia's glosses that quote from the *Convivio*: *Inf.*, XIV. 1: *Conv.*, general allusion; *Purg.*, II. 76–8: *Conv.*, I. vii. 15, I. xii. 3 and II. i. 4; *Purg.*, III. 79–84: *Conv.*, I. xi. 1, 8–10; *Purg.*, VI. 76–8: *Conv.*, IV. ix. 10; *Purg.*, XVIII. 19–39: *Conv.*, III. ii. 3 and III. iii. 2–5; *Purg.*, XIX. 70–3: *Le dolci rime*, ll. 49–51, 56–8, *Conv.*, IV. xii. 1, 4, 6–7 and IV. xiii. 10–14; *Purg.*, XXVI. 97–102: *Conv.*, IV. xx. 7; *Purg.*, XXIX. 37–45: *Conv.*, III. ix. 15; *Purg.*, XXX. 121–32: *Conv.*, II. ii. 1 and II. xii. 1–3, 5, 7; *Purg.*, XXXI. 49–60: *Amor che ne la mente mi ragiona*, ll. 19–22, 37–8; *Par.*, III. 1–9: *Conv.*, general allusion; *Par.*, VII. 49–51: *Conv.*, IV. iv. 1; *Par.*, VIII. 13–15: *Conv.*, II, general allusion; *Par.*, IX. 103–8: *Conv.*, II. v.14 and II. xiii. 13–14; *Par.*, XI. 67–69: *Conv.*, IV. xiii. 12; *Par.*, XVI. 1–6: *Le dolci rime*, ll. 79–82, 101; *Par.*, XXVII. 97–99: *Conv.*, II. iii. 7.

21   For the identification of the *donna gentile* with the young girl (*pargoletta*): Kenelm Foster and Patrick Boyde, *Dante's Lyric Poetry*, II. *Commentary* (Oxford: Clarendon

Lancia's penchant for historicizing Dante's references also surfaces when quoting the song *Amor che ne la mente mi ragiona*. Having reached the shore of Purgatory, Dante encounters his friend Casella, who, having just arrived, chooses, at the poet's request, to perform the song, resuming a custom that the two had enjoyed during their lifetimes (*Purg.*, II. 106–14). Knowing that this is one of the *canzoni* dedicated to Philosophy (the *donna gentile*) and commented on by Dante in the *Convivio*, we first of all have to take into account that neither he nor any of the following exegetes refer to the philosophical work when commenting on the episode of Casella (the first to do so will be Cristoforo Landino). It is striking that Lancia introduces precise and significant references to other passages of the *Convivio*, showing himself to have understood that the encounter with the friend Casella is an episode laden with affection, evocative of Dante's poetic experience in the vernacular and intertwined with the other Florentine friendships of his youth which were later expunged by the hard experience of exile. Thus, when he explains the rapport between Dante and Casella he bestows a more lively style on the very intense gloss by interspersing it with reminiscences of the *Convivio*, his work of exile, in which Dante elucidated his love of home, as well as friendship, of the resonance between poetry and music and, as far as the historical references to the jubilee are concerned, a calibrated application of Giovanni Villani's *Cronica* (Appendix 4).

When Lancia, however, quotes *Amor che ne la mente mi ragiona* in the gloss on *Purg.*, XXXI. 49–60, where Beatrice reproaches the poet and recalls her youthful beauty, he separates Dante's verses from the allegorical interpretation of the third treatise of the *Convivio* and attributes their origin to the poet's love for Beatrice (Appendix 5).[22]

Press, 1967), pp. 186–7; Giorgio Petrocchi, 'donna gentile', in *Enciclopedia Dantesca*, II, 574–7.

22 Lancia, *Chiose alla 'Commedia'*, II, 828. The stylistic feature of the *falso amante* employed by Lancia is also found in Guittone's sonnet *Consiglioti che parti; e se 'l podere*, in which the woman ironically provokes her lover, exhorting him to go away to one more beautiful than her and equal to him: Guittone D'Arezzo, *Canzoniere. I sonetti d'amore del codice Laurenziano*, ed. by Lino Leonardi (Turin: Einaudi, 1994), p. 132.

This interpretation, for us both evocative and surprising, is not at all unique in the older tradition. It can be found in the glosses on *Purg.*, II. 112, both by the 'Amico dell'*Ottimo*' and, later, quite independently of the two predecessors, by Benvenuto da Imola.[23] While this is neither the time nor the place for delving into the origins of Dante's *canzone*, which in contrast to the philosophical commentary did have a wide circulation in the fourteenth century, it is interesting to keep in mind the extent to which the reading of the encounter between Dante and Casella was altered by a widespread ignorance of the *Convivio*. If a large part of the criticism today is inclined to believe that the episode of *Purgatorio* II represents a sort of recantation, of retraction or at least of overcoming the *Convivio* (and the philosophy it professed), or of the allegorical-doctrinal song in particular, earlier commentators tried to understand Cato's reprimand as caused by encumbering penitence, which the sweetness of a sort of *stilnovo* love song amounts to. This implies a very different evaluation of the episode.[24] It is evidently a complex case which raises important questions about what Dante's intentions were, both as a man and a poet, and about the extent

23 'Questo è uno cominciamento d'una canzone le cui parole disse Dante per mona Beatrice e 'l Casella la intonòe' (Amico dell'*Ottimo*, New York, Pierpont Morgan Library, M 676, fol. 51ʳ); 'Casella *cominciò a dir*, scilicet cantando: *Amor che nella mente mi ragiona*. Hic nota quod Dantes fecit istam cantationem de virtutibus et pulcritudine Beatricis. Ipse enim nimium delectatus ab ipsa iuventute sonis et cantibus musicis fuit amicus omnibus optimis musicis et citharedis sui temporis, et presertim Caselle, qui intonavit multos sonos eius; et praedictam cantilenam de amore Beatricis intonavit cum summa delectatione ipsius Dantis' (Benevenuti de Rambaldis de Imola, *Comentum super Dantis Aldigherij 'Comoediam'*, ed. by J. P. Lacaita, 5 vols (Florence: Barbèra, 1887), IV, 75–6); Matteo Chiromono then drew on Benvenuto's gloss: Matteo Chiromono, *Chiose alla 'Commedia'*, ed. by Andrea Mazzucchi (Rome: Salerno Editrice, 2004), gloss to *Purg.*, II. 112.
24 On the origin of *Amor che ne la mente mi ragiona* and its relationship with Beatrice and with the *donna gentile* see Maurizio Fiorilla, '*Amor che nella mente mi ragiona* tra ricezione antica e interpretazione moderna', *Rivista di Studi Danteschi*, 5 (2005), 141–54; on the importance of the performative and musical element in the episode of Casella see Paolo De Ventura, 'Dante e Casella, allusione e performanza', *Dante*, 9 (2012), 43–56.

to which he wanted his readers to understand the episode, in itself and within the context of the second *cantica*.

A further significant example of how Lancia profoundly assimilated the lesson of the *Convivio* is offered in the gloss on *Paradiso* XI. 67–9. Dante, narrating via the mouth of Thomas Aquinas on how poverty had long remained 'dispetta e scura' (scorned, obscure) until the times of Francis of Assisi, recalls the episode of Amyclas, as narrated by Lucan (*Pharsalia* V. 507–31): a fisherman, because of his extreme poverty, remained tranquil and unperturbed when he was woken one night by the sound of Cesar's voice, 'ch'a tutto il mondo fé paura' [He who struck terror into all the world]. None of the older commentators hesitated in identifying the source of the episode; in particular, the two commentaries principally perused by Lancia for the third *cantica*, the *Ottimo* and the *Comentum* by Pietro Alighieri, conform to their respective modalities: Pietro briefly summarizing the episode and quoting the Latin verses of the classical poet *ad litteram* (*Pharsalia* V. 519–23, 526–31); and the *Ottimo*, after having declared the source 'Lucano [...] libro quinto, capitolo decimo ottavo', narrating the episode in a rather roundabout way while translating lines 527–31 faithfully:[25]

> O vitae tuta facultas / pauperis angustique lares! O munera nondum / intellecta deum! Quibus hoc contingere templis / aut potuit muris nullo trepidare tumultu / Caesarea pulsante manu? (Lucan, *Pharsalia* V. 527–31)
>
> Oh sicura facultà della povera vita! Oh stretti focolari! Oh doni delli Dii non ancora conosciuti! A quali templi, o a quali cittadi poté questo addivenire, che per neuno romore avesse paura, picchiando la mano di Cesare? (*Ottimo*, gloss to *Par.*, XI. 67)
>
> [O secure ease of the poor man's life! O constricted dwellings and furnishings! Oh not yet understood riches of the Gods! In what temples, within what walls could this ever happen without their shaking with fear when the hand of Caesar knocks?]

Lancia had both the comments of Pietro and the *Ottimo* to hand as well as the Latin text by Lucan, which he quoted several times. However, after

---

25 Petri Allegherii *super Dantis ipsius genitoris 'Comoediam' commentarium*, pp. 627–8; *L'Ottimo*, III, 272–3.

summarizing the episode, which the *Ottimo* translates, Lancia nevertheless relied unreservedly on the version given by Dante in the *Convivio* (Appendix 6).

Besides the readers who – except for Pietro Alighieri – could be traced among the earliest Florentine commentators and admirers of the *Commedia* and are very often notaries, or at least people close to the notary world, a privileged role in the first reception of Dante's self-comment is played by the copyists of the two oldest manuscripts: perhaps the only ones from the first half of the fourteenth century among the forty-six testimonies, all Florentine, and documenting how the *Convivio* only became widespread literature at the beginning of the second half of the fifteenth century. In fact, at this later time, too, the *Convivio* is a Florentine concern, whose graphical education in the manuscript tradition can be partly put down to the professional and cultural horizons of the notaries and, partly (and the more surprisingly), to those of the merchants. The ms. Vaticano, Barb. Lat. 4086 (Vb), a composite artefact comprised of two distinct parts (fols 1–112 and 113–30), is in its original and oldest core a paper codex, produced in Florence and dating from the third or fourth decade of the fourteenth century. Particularly homogenous and coherent are the fols 1–110, which were written by one single mercantile hand and which gave life to an anthology of texts in vernacular prose, several of which are *unica*: a fragment of a translation into the vernacular of Livy's *First Decade* in a version not otherwise attested (fols 1^r-6^v); the *Convivio* (fols 7^r-49^r); a translation into the vernacular of Andrea Cappellano's *De Amore* in a version different to the conventional one (fols 52^r-86^v); the translation into the vernacular of the *Aeneid* attributed to Andrea Lancia (fols 88^r-110^v); then, in the final pages which are left white, a chancery hand added Hannibal's address to Scipio, taken from the translation into the vernacular of Livy's *Third Decade* (fols 111^v-12^v).[26] As codicological and palaeographical considerations induce us to presume, the copyist also ordered the codex. Therefore, it is important to profile the personality, who, in the choice of the texts conserved in the

---

26   Luca Azzetta, 'Un'antologia esemplare per la prosa trecentesca e una ignorata traduzione da Tito Livio: il Vaticano Barb. lat. 4086', *Italia medioevale e umanistica*, 35 (1992), 31–85.

fols 1–110, seems to reveal the intention of assembling a collection of texts related to different typologies of vernacular prose. In consequence, he draws on very rare works (only the translation of the *Aeneid* into the vernacular enjoyed a noteworthy manuscript circulation), which in turn raises questions both about the identity of this patron and about the people he knew, as well as the places he frequented which allowed him the chance to get his hands on texts which were otherwise inaccessible.

The story of the second fourteenth-century codex of the *Convivio*, Firenze, Bibl. Naz., II III 47 (F), is also articulate and complex. It consists of two different manuscripts bound together in the nineteenth century, the first containing miscellaneous works copied in the fifteenth century occupies fols 1^r-116^v, while the second, which contains Dante's self-comment makes up fols 118^r-184^v. What is surprising is the fact that the *Convivio*, in a copy made probably between 1335 and 1340, was written in Florence by at least nine different hands, alternating and interweaving with each other, sometimes from one quire to another, sometimes from one page to another, and sometimes within a few lines, bringing about a manuscript that was realized in an authentic mercantile *bureau*, that is, probably inside one or other of the Companies, the only places, as far as is known, in which merchants and notaries could meet and work together.[27] The well-organized copyists who collaborated on this copy of the *Convivio* reveal fairly different graphical backgrounds, and all show great skill: while four appear to have been notaries or were in any case close to the notary environment and graphical culture, the other five employ a clearly mercantile script. Since whoever coordinated the copying work annotated the name of the respective copyists in the margin of the first sheet of the quire or of the group of

---

27 The dating of the codex and the hypothesis of the mercantile *bureau*, with its important implications, were proposed by Teresa De Robertis: Irene Ceccherini and Teresa De Robertis, 'Scriptoria e cancellerie nella Firenze del XIV secolo', in *Scriptorium. Wesen, Funktion, Eigenheiten*, Comité international de paléographie latine, XVIII. Kolloquium, St Gallen, 11–14 September 2013, ed. by A. Nievergelt, R. Gamper, M. Bernasconi Reusser, B. Ebersperger, E. Tramp (Munich: Bayerische Akademie der Wissenschaften, 2015), pp. 151–4; see also Beatrice Arduini, 'Alcune precisazioni su un manoscritto trecentesco del Convivio: BNCF II. III. 47', *Medioevo e Rinascimento*, 20, n.s. 17 (2006), 383–91.

sheets assigned to each of them, it is possible to reconstruct a glimpse of the identities of five of the cohorts: Brunello, Zanobi, Manovelloro, Ser Giovanni, Paolo. As the analysis of the codex reveals, the coordinator of the enterprise must have been Ser Giovanni, who certainly was a practising notary: it was his task to assign the papers to write up, and to watch over the work of each one.[28] Furthermore, a recent discovery confirms that at least one of the people involved in the enterprise was not new to this kind of undertaking; in fact, Zanobi is credited with the copy of ms. Firenze, Bibl. Laurenziana, 76.80: an elegant membranous manuscript of 174 papers which conserves the translation into the vernacular of Seneca's *Epistole a Lucilio*.[29] So, as it had already been with the Vaticano, Barb. Lat. 4086, we find Dante's *Convivio* bundled together with Latin classics, which were translated into the vernacular by the wish of a copyist who employs mercantile chirography.

The first, albeit limited, fame to be enjoyed by *Convivio* is thus due to Florentine personalities, still mostly anonymous, united by their interest in Dante and his work, and by the contemporaneous rediscovery of antiquity, which they promoted through the production and copying of translations of Latin classics into the vernacular. Today, it is no surprise to us that a learned and passionate circle of notaries played a leading role in this project. What is unexpected, though, is the role played by merchants who we would not usually expect to find bent over lecterns. But they did actually collaborate with those notaries, keen to skilfully and competently copy the difficult pages of Dante's vernacular prose.[30]

28 Teresa De Robertis, 'Scriptoria e cancellerie', pp. 152–3.
29 Teresa De Robertis, 'Scriptoria e cancellerie', p. 154.
30 A significant case of collaboration between a copyist who uses a mercantile script and who shows perfect familiarity with the books, and Andrea Lancia, a notary and enthusiast of Dante's work and also active as a translator into the vernacular of classics, is given in the ms. Florence, Bibl. Naz., II I 39; see Luca Azzetta, in Andrea Lancia, *Chiose alla 'Commedia'*, pp. 88–93; Irene Ceccherini, 'La cultura grafica di Andrea Lancia', *Rivista di Studi Danteschi*, 10 (2010), 351–67 (p. 359). For an analysis of a strictly palaeographical nature on the relationship between mercantile script and notarial script, see Irene Ceccherini, 'Le scritture dei notai e dei mercanti a Firenze

After Lancia's death, the *Convivio* was read only occasionally for several decades.[31] Yet Dante's self-comment is absent from Boccaccio's work. Having re-entered Florence in the winter of 1340-1, at the end of his Neapolitan period, Boccaccio knew the set of people who were tightly knit around the poet's memory, of whose inheritance he would be the beneficiary. In the city, among other things, he engaged in an enthusiastic and serious research that drove him to approach people that had known (or claimed to have known) the poet. However, the only hint that the Certaldese makes at the philosophical commentary is in the first edition of the *Trattatello in laude di Dante*, in which he defines it as 'uno commento in prosa in fiorentino volgare sopra tre delle sue canzoni distese' [a commentary in prose in Florentine vernacular on three of his extended songs] and suggests in a dubitative way that it had been interrupted 'o per mutamento di proposito o per mancamento di tempo' [either because of a change in purpose or because of a lack of time] (first edition, Par., 199; the double hypothesis is omitted in the second edition, Par., 137). These are rather general observations which are congruent with Boccaccio's absence from the history of the tradition of the *Convivio*: this is striking indeed because he played a fundamental role, as copyist as well as editor, in the developing tradition of many of Dante's other works, both in the vernacular (*Vita nova, Rime, Commedia*) and in Latin (*Epistole, Egloghe*). It is very likely that Boccaccio never bent over the pages of the philosophical text, of which, however, he may well have had an inkling: perhaps via Villani, or

tra Duecento e Trecento: unità, varietà, stile', *Medioevo e Rinascimento*, 24, n.s. 21 (2010), 29-68.

31 Among the commentators of the *Commedia* in the second half of the fourteenth century, the *Convivio* remains extraneous to the exegesis of Boccaccio, Guglielmo Maramauro, Benvenuto da Imola, Francesco da Buti and Anonimo Fiorentino, who knew its prose only via Lancia; there are perhaps some possible citations in the *Expositiones* by Filippo Villani; for other authors or texts where a knowledge of the *Convivio* has to be excluded see Luca Azzetta, 'Tra i più antichi lettori', pp. 82-90. For a single quotation that appears in two works by Galvano Fiamma, the *Chronicon maius* and the *Politia novella*, who, however, could not have had access to a ms. of the *Convivio*, see Paolo Chiesa, 'Una citazione precoce del *Convivio* nelle cronache di Galvano Fiamma', *Filologia italiana*, 11 (2014), 111-17.

thanks to Lancia, with whom he collaborated as a tax official in Florence from August 1352 until February 1353, in the years close to his drafting the first edition of the *Trattatello*.[32] Similarly, the prose of the *Convivio* seems to remain unknown to Boccaccio's friend, the Florentine Agnolo Torini, who in his *Brieve collezzione della miseria della umana condizione*, written between 1363 and 1374, explicitly quoted lines 57–8 of the song *Le dolci rime d'amor ch'i' solia*: 'd'esse (i.e. riches) bene disse il nostro poeta Dante che "quantunque collette, non posson quïetar, ma dan più cura"' (XIV. 9–13) [of these says well our poet Dante that 'quantunque collette, non posson quïetar, ma dan più cura' [for however great they are, They bring no peace, but rather grief]].[33] Since the quotation is located within a thorough reflection on the perversion intrinsic to riches, the absence of any indication whatsoever of the *Convivio*, in which such verses are commented on, and which would have been beneficial to the argumentation, makes it probable that Torini, a reader of the *Commedia*, knew Dante's song through a miscellany of rhymes and not as part of the philosophical self-comment (see *Conv.*, IV. iv. 11–13).

Beyond those already mentioned, the sole author whose knowledge of the *Convivio* is unequivocal is Coluccio Salutati, further demonstrating how the rarity of circulation of the *Convivio* is limited to the Florentine area. In fact, the Chancellor of the Republic of Florence, in a letter dated 11 November 1403 and addressed to Domenico Bandini, discusses Dante's concept of nobility, according to which 'è gentilezza dovunqu'è virtute, / ma non vertute ov'ella' [Nobility resides wherever virtue is, But virtue not wherever there's nobility], and, after having quoted lines 101–4 of the song *Le dolci rime d'amor ch'i' solia*, makes an explicit reference to Dante's exposition of his own song, that is to the fourth book of the *Convivio*.[34]

---

32 Luca Azzetta, 'Introduzione', in *Ordinamenti, provvisioni e riformagioni del Comune di Firenze volgarizzati da Andrea Lancia (1355–1357)*, ed. by Luca Azzetta (Venice: Memorie dell'Istituto Veneto, Classe di scienze, lettere ed arti, 2001), 9–49 (pp. 34–5).
33 Irene Hijmans-Tromp, *Vita e opere di Agnolo Torini* (Leiden: Universitaire Pers Leiden, 1957), p. 253.
34 'Vult ergo Dantes nobilitatem esse optimam dispositionem a natura datam nobis ad omnes virtutes et laudabiles passiones, sicut licet ex cantico suo videre et

Only later, in the sixties of the fifteenth century, did the *Convivio* experience a certain degree of fame in the wider sense, becoming the object of intense philological rediscovery and textual investigation. But this is another story, the fruit of new ways of reading, elaborated by men, scholars and readers, now far removed from the handful of audacious Florentines who were the first readers of the *Convivio*.

---

expositione propria, quam super illud composuit' ; Coluccio Salutati, *Epistolario*, ed. by Francesco Novati (Rome: Forzani and C. Tipografi del Senato, 1896), III, 646; Thomas Ricklin, 'Das missglückte Gastmahl. Philosophiehistorische Hinweise zum späten Publikumserfolg des *Convivio*' in *'Ad ingenii acuitionem'. Studies in honour of Alfonso Maierù*, ed. by Stefano Caroti, Ruedi Imbach, Zénon Kaluza, Giorgio Stabile, Loris Sturlese (Louvain-La-Neuve: Fédération Internationale des Instituts d'Études Médiévales, 2006), pp. 353–76 (pp. 360–1); Simon A. Gilson, 'Reading the *Convivio* from Trecento Florence to Dante's Cinquecento Commentators', *Italian Studies*, 64 (2009), 266–95 (p. 273).

Appendix 1

Pietro, *Inf.*, II (ed. Nannucci, pp. 54-5)	*Conv.*, IV. v. 3-6
Ad evidentiorem intellectum circa hoc attende. Deus *volens* mittere filium ad *concordiam* et redemptionem humani generis, *coelum et terra debuerunt esse in optima sua dispositione: sed terra tunc optime disposita est, quando sub monarcha est et unico principe*, ut per descendentes gradatim Aeneae fuit; et incoepit in persona Iulii Caesaris in Roma, in cuius Romae creatione eodem tempore *ordinatum fuit* virginale hospitium de Beata Maria descendente de stirpe David, et uno tempore natus est David, et creata est Roma. *Ad quod ait Isaias: nascetur virga de radice Iesse, qui Iesse fuit pater David. Et dixit de eo tempore, quo natus est David, et etiam Roma, subaudi sic fieri, scilicet, quod quando Aeneas venit in Italiam*, tunc natus est David; *et sic apparet quod divina electio fuit romani Imperii et Ecclesiae*.	*Volendo* la 'nmensurabile bontà divina l'umana creatura a sé riconformare, [...] eletto fu in quello altissimo e congiuntissimo consistorio della Trinitade che 'l Figliuolo di Dio in terra discendesse a fare questa *concordia*. E però che nella sua venuta lo mondo, non solamente *lo cielo ma la terra, convenia essere in ottima disposizione; e la ottima disposizione della terra sia quando ella è monarchia, cioè tutta ad uno principe*, come detto è di sopra; ordinato fu per lo divino provedimento quello popolo e quella cittade che ciò dovea compiere, cioè la gloriosa Roma. E però [che] anche l'albergo dove 'l celestiale rege intrare dovea, convenia essere mondissimo e purissimo, *ordinata fu* una progenie santissima, della quale dopo molti meriti nascesse una femmina ottima di tutte l'altre, la quale fosse camera del Figliuolo di Dio: e questa progenie fu quella di David, del qual [di]scese la baldezza e l'onore dell'umana generazione, cioè Maria. *E però è scritto in Isaia:*

	'Nascerà virga della radice di Iesse, e fiore de la sua radice salirà'; *e Iesse fu padre del* sopra detto *David. E tutto questo fu in uno temporale, che David nacque e nacque Roma, cioè che Enea venne* di Troia *in Italia,* che fu origine della cittade romana, sì come testimoniano le scritture. *Per che assai è manifesto la divina elezione del romano imperio,* per lo nascimento della santa cittade che fu contemporaneo a la radice de la progenie di Maria.

Appendix 2

Pietro, *Purg.*, XVI (ed. Nannucci, p. 413) Circa quod advertendum, quod *summum desiderium cuiuslibet rei a natura primo datum est redire ad suum principium et factorem* animarum nostrarum, et ideo naturaliter *anima desiderat ad eum redire. Et sic* est quod ingreditur primo anima caminum nostrae vitae, de quo etiam dixi Capitulo primo in Inferno, ut peregrinus, qui redit, et *dirigit oculos* ad ipsum Deum, ut *ad summum bonum.*	*Conv.*, IV. xii. 14–17 *Lo sommo desiderio di ciascuna cosa, e prima dalla natura dato, è lo ritornare allo suo principio.* E però che Dio è principio delle nostre anime *e fattore* di quelle simili a sé [...], essa anima massimamente *desidera di tornare a quello. E sì come peregrino* che va per una via per la quale mai non fue, che ogni casa che da lungi vede crede che sia l'albergo, e non trovando ciò essere, dirizza la credenza all'altra, e così di casa in casa, tanto che all'albergo

Ideoque quicumque qui videt habere aliquem bonum, putat esse illud. Et quia in principio inexperta est, omnia parva bona videntur sibi magna. Quod patet in puero, qui primo ad pomum, deinde ad nummum, inde ad vestitum, et sic consequenter ulterius plus *desiderat, eo quod non invenit quod quaerit, et putando ulterius invenire, et sic unum desiderabile praecedit alterum per modum pyramidalem,* quod *ultimum* punctum *desiderabile* est, *ut Deus* qui obiectum est voluntatis.	viene; così l'anima nostra, incontanente che nel nuovo e mai non fatto cammino di questa vita entra, *dirizza li occhi al* termine del suo *sommo bene, e però, qualunque cosa vede che paia in sé avere alcuno bene, crede che sia esso. E perché la sua conoscenza prima è imperfetta,* per non essere esperta né dottrinata, *piccioli beni le paiono grandi,* e però da quelli comincia prima a desiderare. *Onde vedemo li parvuli* desiderare massimamente *un pomo; e poi,* più procedendo, desiderare uno augellino; *e poi, più oltre,* desiderare bel *vestimento*; e poi lo cavallo; e poi una donna; e poi ricchezza non grande, e poi grande, e poi più. *E questo incontra perché in nulla di queste cose truova quella che va cercando, e credela trovare più oltre.* Per che vedere si può che *l'uno desiderabile sta dinanzi a l'altro* alli occhi della nostra anima *per modo quasi piramidale*, che 'l minimo li cuopre prima tutti, ed è quasi punta dell'*ultimo desiderabile, che è Dio*, quasi base di tutti.

Appendix 3

Lancia, chiosa a *Purg.*, XXX. 115-20 Qui commemora come Dante, quando elli \<era\> nella sua pueritia, allora ch'elli scrisse quello libello chiamato la *Vita nova*, fue habituato ad ogni altissima scientia. E sogiugne: come quando la terra ferace non coltivata e non sterpata e gittatovi mal seme come ne fa molto e reo, onde è scritto: 'qui serere vult agrum' etc. [Boezio, *Cons. Ph.*, III *carm.* 1].	
Lancia, chiosa a *Purg.*, XXX. 121-32 L'autore medesimo sopra quella sua *canzone* 'Voi che 'ntendendo' dice: *due volte rivolta era la stella di Venere in quello suo cerchio che la fa parere serotina e matutina apresso il trapassamento di quella Beatrice beata che vive in cielo con li angeli e in terra nella mia* mente, *quando* inamoròe in quella ch'elli chiamòe *Pargoletta*. E dice che per lo trapassamento di Beatrice *rimase in soma trestitia* tutto quello mezo tempo, e per trovare alcuna consolatione si diede allo studio e *non sanza divino imperio* pervenne a studio di *filosofia* andando *nelle scuole de' religiosi e alle disputationi de' filosofanti*.	*Conv.*, II. ii. 1 Cominciando adunque, dico che *la stella di Venere due fiate rivolta era in quello suo cerchio che la fa parere serotina e matutina* secondo diversi tempi, *apresso lo trapassamento di quella Beatrice beata che vive in cielo colli angeli e in terra colla mia* anima, *quando* quella *gentile donna* (di) cui feci menzione nella fine della *Vita nova*, parve primamente, acompagnata d'Amore, alli occhi miei e prese luogo alcuno nella mia mente. *Conv.*, II. xii. 1-3, 5, 7 Dico che, come per me fu perduto lo primo diletto della mia anima, dello quale fatta è menzione di sopra, io *rimasi di tanta tristizia*

punto, che conforto non mi valeva alcuno. Tuttavia, dopo alquanto tempo, la mia mente, che si argomentava di sanare, provide, poi che né 'l mio né l'altrui consolare valea, ritornare al modo che alcuno sconsolato avea tenuto a consolarsi. [...] E sì come essere suole che l'uomo va cercando argento e fuori della 'ntenzione truova oro, lo quale occulta cagione presenta; *non forse sanza divino imperio*, io, che cercava di consolar me, trovai non solamente alle mie lagrime rimedio, ma vocabuli d'autori e di scienze e di libri: li quali considerando, giudicava bene che la *filosofia*, che era donna di questi autori, di queste scienze e di questi libri, fosse somma cosa. [...] E da questo imaginare cominciai ad andare là dov'ella si dimostrava veracemente, cioè *nelle scuole delli religiosi e alle disputazioni delli filosofanti*.

Appendix 4

Lancia, chiosa a *Purg.*, II. 76–8 Qui introduce l'autore in figura uno suo noto, huomo di corte e maestro di canto mondano. Fue fiorentino, ebbe nome Casella e diede le note a canzoni che l'autore fece, e spetialmente a quella che comincia 'Amor che nella mente mi ragiona' etc. Et qui fa l'autore IIII cose. Prima pone come l'amore della patria e quello de l'amicitia lega li huomini virtuosi; poi tocca alcuna cosa della purgatione del peccato in questo mortale mondo; poi della vertude della indulgentia papale; poi della vertù del canto ordinato per legge di musica. [...] Alla prima scrive l'autore in suo prologo sopra quella *canzone* che comincia 'Voi che 'ntendendo il terzo cielo movete', dove mostra le cagioni di sua benivolentia verso il suo volgare parlare e così per conseguente possiamo dire verso la patria, che la proximità e la bontade sono cagioni generative d'amore et lo beneficio e lo studio e la consuetudine sono cagione d'amore accrescitive. Le quali v cagioni si può dire che congiugnessoro l'amore col Casella: proximani furono sì per natione di luogo come per studio di scientia musica; beneficii si conferiro	*Conv.*, I. xii. 3 (but cf. *Conv.*, I. xii. 3 – xiii. 10) La prossimitade e la bontade sono cagioni d'amore generative; lo beneficio, lo studio e la consuetudine sono cagioni d'amore accrescitive.

mutuamente l'uno in dare materia di trovare nuove modulationi di canto, l'altro di bandire la fama de l'autore; lo studio colui in trovare canzoni forti per sententie e dolci per ornato, costui studiòe in melodico canto trovare. Insieme usaro quanto e quando si convenne. Alla seconda parte. Questo Casella morìe anzi l'anno di Cristo MCCCI et l'autore fa questo suo entramento in purgatorio nel MCCC circa mezo marzo. Papa Bonfatio VIII fece generale perdono chiamandolo l'anno del Iubileo. E ordinòe che qualunque cristiano nel detto anno visitasse le chiese de' beati apostoli Piero e Paolo di Roma, per XXX continui dì li Romani e ciascuno altro per XV dì, fosse absoluto de' suoi peccati da colpa e da pena. Dicesi che visibilmente vi furo vedute andare innumerabile quantitade d'anime a questo perdono per Roma visitando le dette chiese. E questo pare qui toccare l'autore, dove dice: veramente Idio da tre mesi egl'ha tolto chi ha voluto entrar con tutta pace. Dove mostra che l'anima del Casella fosse una di quelle, con ciò sia cosa che 'l detto perdono cominciasse il kalendi di genaio e 'l presential tempo fosse di marzo e 'l Casella morìe anzi il detto kalendi di gennaio per più tempi e pur ora venia	Villani, *Cronica*, IX 36 1–14

al purgatorio. Così è mia oppinione, se vera o no altri la cerchi. Alla III per quello che è detto mostra la vertù della indulgentia. Alla IIII, come scrive l'autore medesimo sopra la canzone toccata, *Voi che 'ntendendo* etc., che li versi del *Saltero* perderono la dolceza di musica e d'armonia, perché furono traslatati d'ebreo in greco e di greco in latino, e nella prima traslatione tutta loro dolceza venne meno. Ed è scritto che fue tanta l'eficatia del canto e del suono che lo spirito maligno che turbava Saul al suono del *Saltero* di Davit e al suo canto cessava di molestarlo. Et l'autore toccando la favola d'Orfeo ***.	*Conv.*, I. vii. 15 (62–5) E questa è la cagione per che i versi del Salterio sono sanza dolcezza di musica e d'armonia; ché essi furono transmutati d'ebreo in greco e di greco in latino, e nella prima transmutazione tutta quella dolcezza venne meno. *Conv.*, II. i. 4 (17–8) Orfeo facea colla cetera mansuete le fiere, e li arbori e le pietre a sé muovere.

Appendix 5

Lancia, chiosa a *Purg.*, XXXI. 49–60	*Amor che ne la mente mi ragiona*, ll. 19–22, 37–8
A lettera sponendo, tu non vedesti mai sì bella cosa naturale o artificiale quanto fu' io Beatrice, se tu parlasti il vero, altrimenti eri falso amante, che tu dicesti di me: 'Non vede il sole, che tutto 'l mondo gira, / cosa tanto gentil, quanto 'n quel'hora / che luce nella parte ove dimora / la donna di cui dir Amor mi face' etc.; e ne l'altra stanza: 'in lei discende la vertù divina, / sì come face in angelo che 'l vede' etc.	Non vede il sol, che tutto 'l mondo gira, / cosa tanto gentil, quanto in quell'ora / che luce nella parte ove dimora / la donna di cui dire Amor mi face. [...] In lei discende la vertù divina, / sì come face in angelo che 'l vede.

Appendix 6

Lancia, chiosa a *Par.*, XI. 67–9 Qui tocca la storia della guerra cittadina che fu tra Cesare, *ch'a tutto 'l mondo fé paura*, e Pompeo Magno. In quella parte che scrive Lucano, libro v, Cesare essendo in Tesaglia e aspettando Antonio ch'era ancora in Italia, attendendo Cesare di combattere con Pompeo e anoiandoli lo tardamento d'Antonio, elli medesimo celatamente partito del suo campo per venire a Brandizio venne al mare di nottetempo e quivi trovòe una scafa d'uno pescatore, nome Amiclas, possessore di questa unica scafa, il quale dormia sotto una sua casetta di frasche a llato alla ripa del mare. Cesare picchiòe l'uscio della casetta, levossi Amiclas e domandollo ch'elli volea. Scrive Lucano, come dice l'autore, che Amiclas povero non ebbe paura di Cesare, il quale mettea paura a tutto il mondo: 'Oh sicura facultade della povera vita! Oh stretti abitacoli e masseritie! Oh ricchezze delli dii ancora non intese! A quali templi o a quali muri potée questo avenire, cioè non temere la mano di Cesare?'.	*Conv.*, IV. xiii. 12 Oh sicura facultà della povera vita! Oh stretti abitaculi e masserizie! Oh non ancora intese ricchezze delli Dei! A quali tempî o a quali muri poteo questo avenire, cioè non temere con alcuno tumulto, bussando la mano di Cesare?

Index

Index of Names and Themes

Albert the Great 15, 23, 24, 45, 61, 70, 164, 212
Alberto della Piagentina (Ottimo) 121, 220–1, 249, 255–8, 261, 264–6
Alderotti, Taddeo 20
Alfarabi 154
Alighieri, Jacopo 250–2
Alighieri, Pietro 249, 252–4, 258, 265
allegory 50, 73, 139
angelic intelligence 58, 61–3, 67, 128, 146, 152
Angiolieri, Cecco 247–8
Ardizzone, Maria Luisa 148, 227
Aristotle 13, 16–7, 31–4, 36, 41, 44, 46, 51, 77–8, 83, 93, 96, 102, 105–8, 148, 150, 153–5, 158, 161, 163–5, 169, 174, 186, 217, 224, 232–3, 237, 253
Ascoli, Albert R. 3, 19, 100
astrology 57
auctoritas 19, 25, 34, 42, 121, 194, 200, 253, 256
Augustinus 21, 28, 49, 68, 101, 109, 111, 127, 132, 163, 168–9, 183, 227, 232, 238–42
Averroes 34, 41, 51, 169
Avicenna 61

Barański, Zygmunt 83, 97, 117–8, 127, 131
Barbi, Michele 251

Barolini, Theolinda 102, 129, 154, 171
Bartolomeus of Sassoferrato 147
Beatrice 4, 59, 61, 72–3, 116, 129, 176, 245, 262–3, 275, 279
Benvenuto da Imola 264
Bible 11, 13, 16, 21, 22, 24–5, 27–9, 32, 34, 70, 127, 198, 200, 213, 227–9, 231, 234–5, 256
Black, Robert 87, 110–1, 114
Boccaccio, Giovanni 176, 254, 262, 269
Boethius 46, 68–9, 77, 80, 85–7, 89–90, 93–5, 238, 255–6
Boethius of Dacia 78
Bonaventure 13, 29–31, 169
bread (*pane e vivanda*; *pane degli angeli*) 17, 21–4, 27–8, 60, 67–9, 80, 115, 118–20, 121–8, 125–7, 136–9, 173, 252, 256

Capella, Martianus 72
Castiglione, Baldassare 182
Cavalcanti, Guido 35, 94, 161, 170, 211–2
Cecco d'Ascoli 247–8
Cicero (Tulio) 31, 68, 90, 102, 104–7, 151, 181, 232, 238
Cino da Pistoia 247
commentary 1, 7, 9, 10–2, 15–9, 26, 58, 73, 76, 80, 124, 126–7, 130–2, 136, 138, 141–3, 164, 211–4, 216, 220, 260
Contini, Gianfranco 11
Cornish, Alison 3, 55, 57, 75
cosmology 12, 55–8, 60, 62–5, 70, 73–5, 202, 220

court, courtly life 2–3, 5–6, 103, 105, 169, 183, 225, 247

De Lille, Alain 75
De Robertis, Domenico 2, 150
Digest 193–9, 200–1, 206, 226
diglossia 99, 112
digression 15, 73, 101, 226
donna gentile 107, 116, 129, 146, 151, 262–3

encyclopedia 2, 11, 13, 26
Epicureanism 161, 262
exile 1, 3, 6–7, 60, 61–2, 63, 65, 169, 188, 254, 258

Fioravanti, Gianfranco 5, 56, 60, 65, 67, 68, 83, 124–5
Fortune (*Fortuna*) 61–2
Freccero, John 167
Frederick II 156, 161–2, 223–9, 242
friendship 101–8, 181, 184–5, 187

genre 2, 10–1, 15, 17, 19, 73, 75, 76, 83, 250, 258
gentilezza 151–4, 156–8, 164–5, 259, 270
Gentili, Sonia 20, 81
Giacomo da Pistoia 34–5, 94
Giamboni, Bono 95
Giano dalla Bella 147, 154, 161
Giunta, Claudio 64
goodness (*bontade*) 47, 104, 106, 108, 110, 113, 118, 126–7, 130–4, 137, 142–3, 184, 187, 235, 243, 254, 270, 277
grazia 148, 166, 179, 188
Guinizzelli, Guido 151, 157

happiness (*felicità*) 20, 34, 36–43, 50–3, 72, 153, 165, 208, 210–1, 224, 226–7, 229, 232, 235, 239, 241, 254

Hegel, Georg Wilhelm Friedrich 173, 181, 187
Henry of Settimello 95
Hugh of St Victor 20, 83–4

Imbach, Ruedi 2, 6, 17, 40, 51, 113
impediments (*impedimenti*) 52, 80–1

Kantorowicz, Ernst 228

Lady Philosophy 59, 69, 73, 86–8, 94–6, 107, 116, 129, 146, 151, 164, 187, 213, 262–3
Lancia, Andrea 249, 260–6, 268, 270, 275–6, 279
Landino, Cristoforo 263
Latin (*grammatica*) 12, 68, 99–101, 103–4, 106, 108, 110–2, 114, 119, 137, 143, 181–4, 186
Latini, Brunetto 62, 108, 155, 210
Livy 266

Machiavelli 173, 175
Maierù, Alfonso 25
Martinez, Ronald 59, 68
Matthew of Gubbio 85
misura 87, 148, 154, 158, 171

Nardi, Bruno 1, 12
Nasti, Paola 12, 24, 26
Neoplatonism 75, 91, 151, 168, 185
nobility (*nobilitas*) 72, 100, 134, 137, 143, 145–9, 151–8, 161–2, 164, 166, 171, 176, 178–81, 183, 185–9

Olivi, Pietro Giovanni 161, 169

Peraldus, William 13
Peter Hispanus 163
Piero della Vigna 225, 226, 228
Plato 169, 188, 191, 217

poetry (*poiesis*) 2, 7, 12, 115–8, 127, 129, 132, 134–8, 140, 142–3, 155, 186
politics 21, 108, 112, 154–5
Primum Mobile 65
prosimetrum 10–2, 14, 16–7, 19–21, 24, 26, 86, 90, 91, 132, 179, 249
Providence (*Providenza*) 60, 61, 63, 65, 69, 70, 71, 226, 229, 254
pseudo-Dionysius 158
purgation 117, 178–80, 183–4, 186–8, 276

recognition 173–6, 180, 183–5, 187–9
rhetoric 68–9, 73–4, 151, 171
Ricklin, Thomas 2, 80

Salutati, Coluccio 270
Santagata, Marco 176, 221, 224
Scholasticism 10, 15, 80, 81, 83–5, 92, 96–7, 108, 131, 184, 186
science (*scientia*) 12, 13, 16, 21, 24, 29, 31, 36, 37, 40, 44, 47, 49, 59, 67, 73, 112, 154, 155
Seneca 85, 242, 243, 256, 268
Silvestris, Bernhard 75
Simonelli, Maria 71, 81
Stabile, Giorgio 55, 245
Stoicism 227, 232–3, 236–7, 238, 239, 244

Taviani, Guelfo 247–9
Thomas Aquinas 36–41, 81, 83, 91, 150, 169, 194–9, 212, 215, 236, 265
Torini, Agnolo 270
transumptio 147, 171
Trevet, Nicholas 87, 89–96

Varzy, Jean de 31, 34
Venus, heaven of 73, 128
vernacular (*vernaculare illustre*) 12, 74, 75, 99, 101–12, 216, 221
Villani, Giovanni 87, 249, 260, 261, 263, 269, 276

virtue (*virtù*) 11, 95, 99, 101, 108, 133–5, 148, 153–4, 157, 165, 166, 170–1, 183, 219, 223–4, 232–3, 239–40, 242

William of Conches 87, 91

Zaccagnini, Guido 248

Index of Works by Dante

Commedia 1–2, 56, 62, 66–7, 69, 73, 75–6, 167–8, 179–80, 189, 202, 220–1, 223, 244, 249, 252, 254–5, 259, 262
  Inferno 62, 145, 157, 161, 167–8, 170, 179, 252
  Paradiso 49, 57, 59, 61, 65–7, 69, 72, 179, 186, 189–90, 243, 245, 253, 265
  Purgatorio 168, 176, 178–9, 243–5, 252, 263, 264
Convivio
  book I 1 3, 4, 15, 17–8, 22, 41, 59–62, 67–8, 70, 77–80, 99–114, 115–143, 138, 181–6, 193–4, 207–9, 231, 235, 240, 256
  book II 13–14, 16, 20, 59, 65–6, 68–70, 90, 127, 130–1, 140–2, 179–80, 211, 216–7, 261, 262
    Voi ch'intendendo 64, 116, 127–31, 151–2, 155, 258–9, 275, 277, 278
  book III 41–2, 47–8, 52, 56, 67, 74–5, 96, 116, 212, 214, 233, 242
    Amor che ne la mente 151, 152, 153, 233, 263, 279

book IV 10, 47–8, 60, 64, 143, 145–71, 180, 186, 198, 200–1, 202–6, 210, 214–5, 223–46, 251, 270
Le dolci rime d'amor 26, 145, 146, 147, 152, 153, 164, 169, 171, 223, 270
De vulgari eloquentia 4, 41, 74, 99–100, 150, 170, 183, 221, 260

Epistole 243, 250
Monarchia 157, 161, 168, 223–5, 228–9, 234–8, 240–51, 260
Questio de acqua et terra 74
Rime 56, 249, 255
Vita nova 1, 6, 25, 71, 72, 102, 112, 115, 116, 129, 148, 151, 214, 249, 262

Leeds Studies on Dante

Series Editors
Claire E. Honess, University of Leeds
Matthew Treherne, University of Leeds

International Advisory Board
Zygmunt G. Barański, University of Notre Dame
Lucia Battaglia Ricci, University of Pisa
Simon Gilson, University of Warwick
Ronald Martinez, Brown University

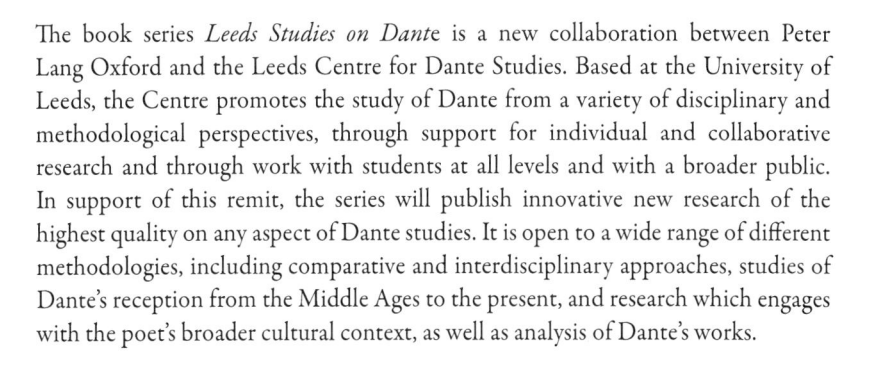

The book series *Leeds Studies on Dante* is a new collaboration between Peter Lang Oxford and the Leeds Centre for Dante Studies. Based at the University of Leeds, the Centre promotes the study of Dante from a variety of disciplinary and methodological perspectives, through support for individual and collaborative research and through work with students at all levels and with a broader public. In support of this remit, the series will publish innovative new research of the highest quality on any aspect of Dante studies. It is open to a wide range of different methodologies, including comparative and interdisciplinary approaches, studies of Dante's reception from the Middle Ages to the present, and research which engages with the poet's broader cultural context, as well as analysis of Dante's works.

Proposals are welcomed for monographs or collections of essays in either English or Italian. Editions, commentaries and translations of exceptional scholarly value will also be considered. Potential contributors should send a detailed outline of their proposed volume, including a statement of the aims and remit of the volume and the critical methodology adopted, a chapter breakdown, and a sample chapter. In the case of edited volumes, editors are asked to send a paragraph outlining the cohesiveness of the volume and the rationale for the collection of essays. Complete manuscripts should not be sent unless invited.

For further information, please contact the series editors, Claire E. Honess (c.e.honess@leeds.ac.uk) or Matthew Treherne (m.treherne@leeds.ac.uk).

Published volumes

Claire E. Honess and Matthew Treherne (eds)
Reviewing Dante's Theology: Volume 1
2013. ISBN 978-3-0343-0924-0

Claire E. Honess and Matthew Treherne (eds)
Reviewing Dante's Theology: Volume 2
2013. ISBN 978-3-0343-1757-3

Franziska Meier (ed.)
Dante's *Convivio*: Or How to Restart a Career in Exile
2018. ISBN 978-3-0343-1835-8